Inclusive Rule-Making by International Organisations

LEUVEN GLOBAL GOVERNANCE

Series Editor: Jan Wouters, *KU Leuven, Belgium*

The Leuven Global Governance series comprises high-quality monographs and edited volumes dedicated to innovative research on global governance. The series covers a wide range of themes, from the EU and global multilateral governance to trade, sustainable development, peace and security, human rights, democracy and rule of law, private standards, and global commons. In full recognition of the complex issues involved, the series favours studies approaching global governance from a multidisciplinary, multi-level and multi-actor perspective.

For a full list of Edward Elgar published titles, including the titles in this series, visit our website at www.e-elgar.com.

Inclusive Rule-Making by International Organisations

Innovations and Challenges

Edited by

Rita Guerreiro Teixeira

Assistant Professor of Public International Law, Utrecht University, the Netherlands

Marianna Karttunen

Acting Deputy Head of the Open, Innovative and Digital Government Division, OECD Public Governance Directorate, France

Axel Marx

Deputy Director, Leuven Centre for Global Governance Studies, KU Leuven, Belgium

Jan Wouters

Full Professor of International Law and International Organizations, Jean Monnet Chair ad personam EU and Global Governance, and Director of the Institute for International Law and Leuven Centre for Global Governance Studies, KU Leuven, Belgium

LEUVEN GLOBAL GOVERNANCE

EE Edward Elgar PUBLISHING

Cheltenham, UK • Northampton, MA, USA

Published by
Edward Elgar Publishing Limited
The Lypiatts
15 Lansdown Road
Cheltenham
Glos GL50 2JA
UK

Edward Elgar Publishing, Inc.
William Pratt House
9 Dewey Court
Northampton
Massachusetts 01060
USA

A catalogue record for this book
is available from the British Library

Library of Congress Control Number: 2025935553

This book is available electronically in the **Elgar**online
Law subject collection
https://doi.org/10.4337/9781035355860

MIX
Paper | Supporting responsible forestry
FSC® C013604

ISBN 978 1 0353 5585 3 (cased)
ISBN 978 1 0353 5586 0 (eBook)
ISBN 978 1 0353 7079 5 (ePub)

Printed and bound by CPI Group (UK) Ltd, Croydon, CR0 4YY

Contents

Figures

Tables

Contributors

Hasan Akintug, Doctoral Researcher, University of Helsinki, Centre for Nordic Studies, Finland

Femi Amao, Professor, School of Law, University College Cork, Ireland

Emma Bertipaglia, UNFCCC sectoral engagement consultant under the Communication and Engagement division

Xuechen Chen, Assistant Professor in Politics & International Relations, Northeastern University London, United Kingdom

Melissa J. Durkee, William G. Hammond Professor of Law, Washington University School of Law, United States

Jan Karol Farfal, Deputy Editor-in-Chief, *Res Publica* magazine, Poland

Florence Felsheim, Doctoral student, University of St Andrews, United Kingdom

Xavier Fernández-i-Marín, Ramón y Cajal Fellow, Universitat de Barcelona, Spain

Xinchuchu Gao, Lecturer in International Relations, University of Lincoln, United Kingdom

Juan N. García-Nieto, Research Assistant, ESADEGeo, GLIGP, Spain

Carolina Gerli, Doctoral student, University of Bologna, Italy

Rita Guerreiro Teixeira, Assistant Professor of Public International Law, Utrecht University, the Netherlands

Marianna Karttunen, Acting Deputy Head of Open, Innovative and Digital Government Division at the OECD Public Governance Directorate, France

Nathalie Koubayova, Doctoral student, Charles University, Czechia

Cyprian Liske, Lawyer and Sworn Translator, Jagiellonian University in Kraków, Poland

Konstantinos D. Magliveras, of the Athens Bar Association; Professor of the Law of International Organisations, University of the Aegean, Greece

Antonio Marcacci, Financial Compliance Expert and a Lecturer (Lehrbeauftragter) at the University of Passau and at the University of Leipzig, Germany

Axel Marx, Deputy Director, Leuven Centre for Global Governance Studies, KU Leuven, Belgium

Claudia Negri Ribalta, MSCA COFUDN Postdoctoral Fellow, Institute of Advance Studies and Research Associate, IRiSC , University of Luxembourg, Luxembourg

Michèle Olivier, Research Fellow, Department of Mercantile Law, University of Stellenbosch, South Africa

Keith Prushankin, Non-resident fellow, NATO Defense College, Italy

Aïda Rahmouni, Junior Policy Analyst, OECD, France

María Rodríguez Alcázar, PhD Student at Ghent University and the United Nations Institute on Comparative Regional Integration Studies, Belgium

Ángel Saz-Carranza, Full Professor, Esade Business School, Spain

Diane Schumann, Doctoral Researcher, Peace Research Institute Frankfurt, Germany

Kseniia Soloveva, PhD Candidate, Grotius Centre for International Legal Studies, Leiden Law School, Leiden University, the Netherlands

Hayley Walker, Assistant Professor in International Negotiation at IÉSEG School of Management in Lille, France

Jan Wouters, Full Professor of International Law and International Organisations, Jean Monnet Chair ad personam and Global Governance, Director of the Institute for International Law and Leuven Centre for Global Governance Studies, KU Leuven, Belgium

Kaho Yu, Chief Research Officer, Asia Carbon Institute, Singapore

1. *Inclusive rule-making by international organisations*: setting the scene

Rita Guerreiro Teixeira, Marianna Karttunen, Aïda Rahmouni, Axel Marx and Jan Wouters

1 INTRODUCTION

International organisations (IOs) play a central role in global governance today. They increasingly engage in international rule-making in a wide range of areas, from the environment to taxation, postal services, and health. Taken in its broadest meaning, international rule-making encompasses the design, development, implementation, and enforcement by international organisations of legal, policy, or technical instruments aimed at shaping conduct, regardless of their legal effects or attributes and of the nature of the organisation (OECD, 2021). Hence, the international organisations that have been collaborating in the Partnership of International Organizations for Effective International Rule-Making (IO Partnership) – a voluntary platform hosted by the OECD that brings together secretariats from some 50 IOs and a broad range of stakeholders, including governments, the private sector, civil society, and academics, to foster cooperation in international rule-making[1] – estimate to have produced together some 70,000 international instruments of varying denominations, nature, and legal effects (OECD, 2019). These range from treaties to legally binding decisions, (non-legally binding) recommendations, model treaties or laws, declarations, international technical standards, statements of intent, and any other guidance.

As scholars and practitioners have turned their focus to IOs, their functioning and decision-making processes, one of the most pressing issues on the agenda has been a call for greater representation and inclusiveness in their rule-making practices. Representation of all stakeholders in negotiations, including marginalised groups, can increase the legitimacy of international rules; it impacts upon their reception and implementation by states, private

1 See section 3 infra.

actors, and the general public; and it ultimately leads to better and more effective rules, which consider the different interests involved. Simultaneously, as certain private actors (particularly multinational enterprises and non-governmental organisations (NGOs) with a global reach) have conquered a significant role in global governance, IOs often have to engage or coordinate with them in order for any rules to be meaningful. Inclusiveness, however, is not without its challenges. Involving more actors in rule-making processes frequently results in slow and more shallow cooperation, making it more difficult to address some of the more urgent and divisive issues in which coordinated international action is required. In addition, it is not always clear who the relevant stakeholders for each negotiation are, nor who can represent them. Finally, even when actors are invited to sit at the table, they often must overcome yet another set of challenges – for example they may have limited financial means and may not be familiar with the type of international rule-making processes that they are being asked to intervene in.

The present edited volume contributes to the discussion on international rule-making by IOs. It builds upon some of the general trends observed in the IO Partnership and explores telling examples of how international rule-making processes can be more inclusive at all levels, from setting the agenda, shaping the content of new instruments, and decision-making, to implementation, follow-up, and evaluation; and importantly, how this can be reconciled with improving the effectiveness and legitimacy of such rule-making. In selecting the examples analysed in the volume, a wide definition of IO was used, encompassing not only IOs in the traditional sense – that is, intergovernmental organisations with primarily states as members –, but also informal organisations (such as the G20), institutional structures of international agreements (such as the UN Framework Convention on Climate Change), and transnational networks of regulators (such as the International Organization of Securities Commissions (IOSCO)). Our objective is to portray the variety of international actors supporting governments in addressing global challenges. All these organisations contribute to international rule-making in one way or another, and they all have decision-making processes where delegates from different countries participate. In all these cases, therefore, questions of stakeholder engagement and representation emerge.

This volume is the result of a collaboration between the IO Partnership and the Leuven Centre for Global Governance Studies, which aims to improve the dialogue between IOs and academia on topics of common concern. It testifies to how much discussions within IOs on improving inclusiveness overlap with, and can benefit from, debates in academic research on the same topic.

2 INCLUSIVENESS OF IO RULE-MAKING – STATE OF PLAY

2.1 Why inclusiveness matters

As IOs increasingly develop international rules that affect not only their member states but also individuals and companies, attention has increasingly been paid to the inclusiveness and democratic accountability of their rule-making processes. The classical argument that the consent of states was sufficient to guarantee the legitimacy of actions and legal instruments adopted by IOs is no longer satisfying, and commentators have called for a wider application of principles of accountability, deliberative democracy, and rule of law directly to IO processes (Kingsbury, Krisch, and Stewart, 2005; von Bogdandy et al., 2010; Pauwelyn, Wessel, and Wouters, 2012).

As a result, many IOs have developed mechanisms to include stakeholders in their decision-making and operational processes (Tallberg et al., 2013; Grigorescu, 2021), taking steps to make these processes and global governance more inclusive. Some authors, like Dryzek et al. (2019), plead for deliberative global governance, which fully engages stakeholders and the public in decision-making on global rules. They identify different mechanisms through which multilateral negotiations, IOs, and global governance networks can be made more deliberative and democratic. These include citizens' assemblies, nested forums, transnational mini-publics, and crowdsourcing. Similarly, Stewart (2014) provides an extensive discussion on the importance of including all types of stakeholders in the decision-making process of global regulatory bodies. He discusses the 'disregard' of stakeholders in global governance institutions, which is defined as both procedural and substantive neglect of certain key stakeholders in decision-making. He observes that many IOs and global governance institutions have mechanisms for participation and consultation, but these mechanisms are highly uneven in terms of stakeholder participation and create unequal patterns of participation. He also proposes several ways to address skewed participation in global decision-making, including by granting decisional authority to the disregarded through deliberative and inclusive stakeholder decision-making.

Hence, one can find several references in academic scholarship to the importance of inclusiveness and inclusive global policy-making. However, few explicit definitions of inclusiveness exist. In our view, inclusiveness involves identifying and mapping all relevant stakeholders, reaching out even to stakeholders who do not participate on their own initiative, and using mechanisms for stakeholder participation which are open and non-exclusive. This can be operationalised through many different mechanisms and procedures, some of which are further described and analysed in this volume.

The inclusion of stakeholders serves many objectives. First, such inclusion can *inform and educate affected stakeholders* about existing international rules, guidelines, and standards. This can contribute to awareness-raising as well as to a better understanding of existing international regulatory initiatives. Inclusion also allows these stakeholders to contribute to the implementation of such international rules, guidelines and standards, and may even empower them to better foster compliance. For example, the inclusion of stakeholders in international environmental rule-making might help them to identify violations and non-compliance (Beierle & Cayford, 2002).

Second, the involvement of stakeholders may enable the integration of *different sets of preferences* in rule-making processes (Beierle & Cayford, 2002). This might add more complexity to decision-making but could also provide an opportunity to reduce conflicts among stakeholders through a deliberative process geared towards finding consensus. The inclusion of more diverse sets of preferences may lead to decisions that have a broader acceptance, which might in turn impact their legitimacy and effectiveness.

Third, stakeholders can hold specific *information and knowledge* on issues that are relevant from the perspective of effective and legitimate rule-making. The inclusion of this knowledge and information in the rule-making process can enhance the substantive quality of the decision-making process. Stakeholders could identify factual mistakes, bring in new facts, or propose alternative courses of action. Abbott et al. (2017) argue that stakeholders are sometimes involved as regulatory 'intermediaries' in transnational regulatory processes because of their specialised knowledge. This can include knowledge on local conditions in which rules need to be implemented, as well as on the possibilities and limitations of proposed policy actions.

Fourth, several authors (Dryzek et al., 2019; Dingwerth, 2007) point to the importance of gaining and maintaining *legitimacy and trust* in institutions as a key goal for including stakeholders. A key mechanism to enhance legitimacy and foster trust is empowering and involving stakeholders or the public at large in decision-making. This is often referred to as strengthening input legitimacy (Scharpf, 1999). Input legitimacy focuses on the process of rule-making or decision-making and is assessed by examining whether decisions are developed according to a set of procedural requirements, such as representation of relevant stakeholders, inclusiveness, transparency and deliberativeness (Auld and Gulbrandsen, 2010). If the latter is the case, the legitimacy of organisations and decision-making processes increases. Furthermore, involving stakeholders in the rule-making process can strengthen the sense of ownership towards the adopted instruments and improves the likelihood of implementation (OECD, 2021).

Fifth, including stakeholders is seen as a means to strengthen *accountability*, that is, the mechanisms through which actors explain and justify their conduct to a 'forum' (Bovens, 2007, p. 450). Grant and Keohane (2005) identify different accountability mechanisms in IOs, which can be classified into two broad theoretical models of accountability: the participation model and the delegation model. In the delegation model, the performance by IOs is accounted for by those entrusting them with power (often member states). In the participation model, the performance of decision-makers is evaluated by those who are affected by their actions and is highly dependent on the effective inclusion of affected stakeholders. Strengthening accountability through a participation model is especially relevant in IOs which have relatively high de facto autonomy in terms of policy development and execution (Lall, 2023).

Sixth, stakeholders might bring in specific *operational capacity*. IOs often turn to stakeholders or private actors to carry out concrete activities in the field for which they lack capacity, which would be too expensive to carry out on their own, or for which IOs lack 'access' to the field. Operational capacities of stakeholders can include financial support, the ability to deliver goods and services, providing monitoring which is crucial for evaluation, and providing technical support for implementation (Abbott et al., 2017). The latter function of stakeholder involvement is becoming increasingly important in a context of growing reliance on public-private partnerships (Marx, 2019; Pattberg et al., 2012). While it holds a danger of creating conflicts of interest problems with inclusive stakeholder participation ('stakeholder capture'), it might also enhance the effectiveness of IOs in delivering on commitments.

2.2 Current efforts and challenges in improving inclusiveness

Given the importance of inclusive stakeholder participation, the different objectives which can be reached through thisparticipation, and the persistent calls for rethinking internationalrule-making processes, most IOs now provide opportunities for participation by non-state actors (NSAs), in addition to IOs and non-member states, in their internal processes. Increasingly, private sector and business groups, academia and scientific institutions, philanthropic foundations, civil society, and, in some cases, even citizens,[2] can participate in different stages of IO rule-making (Tallberg, 2014).

Stakeholder participation has been largely mainstreamed at the developing stage of new rules. Stakeholders often participate in consultations during the negotiations and drafting of an instrument, having the opportunity to provide information and comment on working drafts. They can have standing

[2] See chapter 10 in this volume.

participation in the meetings of governing organs of IOs, often being admitted as observers to plenary organs or as experts in advisory or technical organs. For instance, the World Health Organization (WHO) admits the participation of representatives of non-member states, other IOs, NGOs, international business associations, and philanthropic foundations as observers in the meetings of the World Health Assembly. In some cases, they can submit memoranda to the Director-General or even make oral statements (WHO, 2008, Rules 3, 44–46). In addition, the WHO brings together individual experts in advisory panels and committees, who provide scientific and technical support to rule and policymaking in their fields of expertise.

Stakeholders can also be called upon to participate in the dissemination and implementation stages of international standards, although engagement at this level remains less widespread (OECD, 2019). For example, the United Nations (UN) has established numerous multi-stakeholder partnerships for the implementation of the Sustainable Development Goals (SDGs), including with member states, other IOs, private corporations, and NGOs.[3] It has further developed resources to support similar partnerships being established by other IOs, states, and private actors.[4]

Finally, in certain cases, stakeholders participate in the monitoring and evaluation of international instruments. For instance, the Food and Agriculture Organization (FAO) invites stakeholders such as other IOs, regional fisheries organisations, and NGOs, in addition to its member states, to reply to a biannual questionnaire on the implementation of its code of conduct and guidelines on responsible fisheries (FAO, 2021; Guggisberg, 2019). It includes questions on the level of implementation of responsible fisheries practices and on persisting challenges, and the results of the questionnaire are presented to the Committee on Fisheries, the main organ in charge of FAO's fisheries policy.

Despite these developments, many challenges persist in broadening the number and variety of stakeholders that participate in international rule-making by IOs and incorporating their contributions in a meaningful manner in the development, evaluation, and implementation of new international instruments. Three of these challenges are picked up in the various contributions to this volume.

---

[3] Several of these initiatives have been registered in the 'SDG Actions Platform', a UN-administered public registry of partnerships and initiatives by a broad range of stakeholders for the implementation of the SDGs, available at 'Partnerships Registry | Sustainable Development' https://sdgs.un.org/partnerships/browse.

[4] Different UN offices have jointly developed a 'Partnership Accelerator', an initiative aimed at accelerating the establishment of effective multi-stakeholder partnerships and engagement in support of the Sustainable Development Goals.

First, the identification and selection of the relevant stakeholders that IOs should invite and/or admit into their rule-making processes is not a straightforward task. There is often a balance to be struck between enlarging the circle of stakeholders called upon to participate, ensuring meaningful opportunities for their engagement and participation, and maintaining the effectiveness of decision-making. Admitting an excessively large circle of participants in negotiations comes with the risk that effective decision-making is moved to smaller, more manageable meetings, often behind closed doors. Simultaneously, selecting a limited pool of stakeholders to engage with requires ensuring the representativeness and completeness of that group.[5] In addition, inclusive rule-making often requires searching and engaging with 'silent' stakeholders, that is, stakeholders that do not actively seek to intervene in rule-making processes even when they are directly or indirectly affected by the ensuing rules, and with 'unwilling' stakeholders, who actively resist participation.[6] Overcoming these difficulties requires IOs to increase the allocation of human and financial resources to their efforts of identification and selection of relevant actors, which are not always easily available. It further requires them to reach decisions on what criteria should be used to identify relevant stakeholders, how to reach out to them, and how these functions are to be divided between the IOs and member states.

Second, the meaningful inclusion of stakeholders in international rule-making often requires the redesign of decision-making processes to include opportunities for effective participation of various actors at various stages. This might require opening the meetings of the governing organs of IOs to the participation of observers, establishing bodies or processes specifically targeted at improving engagement with stakeholders,[7] the inclusion of goals of improving stakeholder engagement in the strategic plans of the IOs,[8] or the adoption of specific guidelines for stakeholder participation.[9]

---

5 See chapter 5 in this volume.

6 See the discussion of these difficulties in chapter 3 in this volume.

7 An example is the establishment by UNEP of a Civil Society Unit that organises Global Major Groups and Stakeholders Fora, which provide a platform for policy dialogues ahead of its Assembly meetings.

8 For example, the Strategic Plan for Biodiversity 2011–2020, adopted by the Conference of the Parties to the Convention on Biological Diversity, sets out as one of its goals to 'enable participation at all levels to foster the full and effective contributions of women, indigenous and local communities, civil-society organisations, the private sector and stakeholders from all other sectors' in the implementation of the Convention (Biodiversity Convention, 2010).

9 Such as the adoption by the WHO of a Framework for Engagement with Non-State Actors (WHO, 2016) or the adoption by the FAO of a Strategy for

Important requirements in this respect are the establishment of clear rules of procedure and transparency in decision-making. These, however, tend to conflict with recent developments towards flexibility and informality in rule-making and with the growing preference for decision-making by consensus. While the so-called informalisation of international rule-making has created opportunities for more actors to intervene in the development of international rules (Pauwelyn, Wessel, and Wouters, 2012), it simultaneously has made it more difficult to know who is effectively participating in discussions and driving decisions. Rule-making procedures have often been developed in the practice of IOs rather than being based on written rules of procedure. Reports of negotiations and meetings of IO organs typically provide only topical information and do not attribute particular views to specific actors. With a few notable exceptions,[10] meetings are not broadcast, nor are detailed minutes produced. Documents related to rule-making processes are not always made available by IOs and, even when document databases exist, they are not always easy to use. This makes it difficult for stakeholders and the public to follow discussions and, consequently, to effectively participate in them – particularly when stakeholders have limited resources and need to rationalise their use.

Third, even when a variety of actors are admitted into decision-making rooms, it would be nothing more than fiction to consider that they have equal opportunities for participation. In the real world, power and resources are unequally distributed among stakeholders, and this determines their ability to meaningfully participate in consultations and debates. Rule-making processes that do not take into account these factual differences run the risk of being captured by the most powerful actors in the field – developed states, big multinational corporations, or special interests – and reproducing existing patterns of inequality and marginalization (Berman, 2021). Certain IOs have tried to address these challenges by developing capacity-building and financial aid programmes targeted at under-represented groups or by making resources available for all stakeholders,[11] but the playing field is still far from balanced. In addition, recent reports of unrestrained influence of corporate actors in

---

Partnerships with the Private Sector (FAO, 2021).

10 The plenary meetings of several UN organs are broadcast online, including meetings of the General Assembly, the Human Rights Council, and the International Law Commission.

11 For instance, the COP-UNFCCC has been engaged in improving capacity-building in developing countries, having established the Paris Committee on Capacity-building in 2015 to develop strategies for stakeholder engagement, outreach, and communication (UNFCCC, 2015). Simultaneously, the UNFCCC Secretariat has developed online resources addressed to all stakeholders that gain observer status, explaining their role in decision-making within the UNFCCC

rule-making in certain arenas, where representatives of national corporations have similar access and participation opportunities as member state officials, have raised concerns and highlighted the need for IOs to develop encompassing policies and strategies for stakeholder engagement (Wouters, 2023). To date, only a few IOs have developed whole-of-organisation instruments that reflect on the aims of stakeholder engagement and how to mitigate associated risks (OECD, 2021).

The present volume contributes to this debate and provides insights into how these three sets of challenges can be approached in the rule-making practices of IOs.

3 EXPERIENCES IN THE PARTNERSHIP FOR EFFECTIVE INTERNATIONAL RULE-MAKING

The IO Partnership has explored the avenues for increasing the quality and effectiveness of international rule-making since 2014, and it has identified stakeholder engagement as one of the low-hanging fruits and priority areas to improve the quality and effectiveness of international rule-making (OECD, 2016). Discussions in this forum revealed that, while all IOs are striving to increase their inclusiveness via stakeholder engagement, thereby adapting to changing dynamics in the global governance system, this engagement takes place to varying degrees and towards different actors (OECD, 2016; OECD, 2019; OECD, 2021). A significant challenge in this respect is the lack of an international agreement on the concept of 'stakeholders', which varies significantly depending on the IO, its governance system, and constituency.[12] This has led to very different types of engagement, with two main trends emerging.

On the one hand, a number of IOs have sought to diversify the actors involved in rule-making by offering 'decisional' participation to non-member stakeholders. Accordingly, several IOs now provide alternative forms of participation, such as partial membership (which generally remains a status for states), observer status, or stakeholder engagement. This trend goes in parallel with the shift from multilateral governance to 'multistakeholder governance', observed in particular within transnational networks of regulators and private standard-setting bodies (OECD, 2021; Abbott, Kauffmann, and Lee, 2018). On the other hand, IOs set up specific mechanisms to collect inputs from external, 'non-decisional' stakeholders in their rule-making activities. In this sense, most IOs have set up specific standing bodies or processes to engage

system - https://unfccc.int/process-and-meetings/parties-non-party-stakeholders/non-party-stakeholders/overview/observer-organizations.

[12] See chapter 2 in this volume.

stakeholders at key points in the development of their instruments. Stakeholder engagement practices mainly take place in substantive committees and working groups, and much less in governing bodies (OECD, 2021).

And yet, in practice, many IOs continue to face significant challenges in engaging with relevant stakeholders in a meaningful and inclusive manner. The main challenges observed across IOs involve managing existing or potential conflicts of interest, avoiding undue or improper influence on the organisation's work, reaching out to unaware or under-represented stakeholders, and engaging effectively with marginalised stakeholders (OECD, 2021).

To support IOs in increasing the inclusiveness of international rule-making through more efficient stakeholder engagement, in 2021, the IO Partnership published a report identifying IO experiences and laying down best practices, the Compendium of International Organisations' Practices (Compendium). The Compendium identifies five key principles for engagement, drawing from good practices at the domestic level (OECD, 2021).

First, for successful stakeholder engagement to take place, IOs can benefit from a strategic and comprehensive approach. This will allow IOs to plan and act strategically, while at the same time providing stakeholders with enough information to participate in a transparent, uniformly applied, and accountable process.

Second, the Compendium encourages IOs to identify, keep track of, and reach out to relevant stakeholders depending on their nature, purpose, and mandate as well as the relevant type of engagement. This entails, on the one hand, a mapping of stakeholders according to type, mandate, function, expertise, interests, and responsibilities; and on the other hand, the establishment of clear and objective criteria informing the selection of stakeholders.

Third, the Compendium specifies that transparent and robust stakeholder engagement procedures are an important prerequisite for truly transparent and inclusive international rule-making. To ensure well-established and consistent stakeholder engagement, IOs may define the methods, tools, and structure of the engagement process. These can be aligned with the general objectives, principles, and standards included in the organisation-wide strategy. Digital tools can be helpful for IOs to facilitate the participation of stakeholders at a global level, ensuring broader participation while requiring limited resources logistically and for those participating. Finally, IOs may provide feedback regarding the receipt and handling of the contributions received, including consideration of the input in the final instrument.

Fourth, the Compendium emphasises that the timing of stakeholder consultations is essential in ensuring their effectiveness. In particular, the consultations may need to adapt to the IO rule-making process and its flexibility for modifications, and need to provide the necessary time for stakeholders to react.

Fifth, whatever the purpose of the engagement, whichever the modalities followed, whoever the stakeholders consulted, the Compendium highlights that clear, effective, and detailed communications about each individual consultation with stakeholders are key for an effective two-way process.

The chapters in this volume engage with these core ideas across regional and international organisations. They confirm the underlying overall trend towards more diverse, inclusive, and transparent international governance, while identifying many remaining opportunities for improvement to reach a new level of truly inclusive international rule-making.

4 CONTRIBUTIONS TO THIS VOLUME

4.1 Why and how to engage with stakeholders

The contributions to this volume are presented under three overarching themes. The first part deals with the broader question of why IOs ought to engage with stakeholders, how they can benefit from the participation of a variety of actors in their decision-making processes, and what challenges they face when seeking to improve the inclusiveness of their rule-making.

The chapter by *Ángel Saz-Carranza, Xavier Fernández-i-Marín, Marianna Karttunen and Juan N. García-Nieto* explores the most recent trends across a range of IOs in stakeholder engagement, with the specific objective of identifying the effects such engagement has on the legitimacy of IOs. Running an in-depth empirical study using a GDELT large-n database, and analysing it with a sentiment dictionary, and comparing this with stakeholder engagement practices across IOs allow the authors to suggest that perception about IOs in the media correlates with the intensity of stakeholder engagement and the type of rule-making activities conducted by the IOs. On the one hand, the authors find that IOs with more far-reaching stakeholder engagement mechanisms tend to have a more positive perception in the media than other organisations. On the other hand, the authors suggest that rule-making activities of a more 'coercive' nature, that is, including binding law, adjudication, enforcement, and sanctioning, are generally associated with less positive perception in the media.

The chapter by *Emma Bertipaglia and Hayley Walker* discusses the challenges faced by a variety of non-state actors in meaningfully engaging in the rule-making processes of IOs, focusing on participation in the annual Conferences of the Parties (COP) of the UN Framework Convention on Climate Change (UNFCCC). While these COP meetings have gathered an unprecedented level of public interest and have successively broken records for the highest number of observers participating in a meeting of a body of an IO (COP28 in 2023 gathered 25,360 participants from observer organisations), they have also faced consistent criticism for being exclusive, with many observers reporting that they feel excluded from key negotiations and unable to meaningfully engage with the UNFCCC system. In response, the UNFCCC launched a review process to strengthen observer engagement in 2022, in which the authors of this chapter were engaged as consultants. In their contribution, Bertipaglia and Walker outline the different phases of the review process and its guiding principles, before delving into the identified obstacles faced by various groups seeking engagement. They find that certain actors risk systemic exclusion from consultative and decision-making processes on account of structural and resource inequalities. Burn-out, lack of time and capacity, translation, and technological constraints are some of the barriers identified throughout the review process. To be genuinely inclusive, these IO processes must provide opportunities for under-resourced actors to overcome the practical barriers they face in engaging. Until that is globally achieved, IOs should consider focusing their resources on tailoring a smaller quantity of engagement opportunities and avoiding multiplying processes. The authors' conclusions offer valuable insights and advice for other IOs wishing to embark on a similar consultative process to enhance representation and inclusion.

Femi Amao, Michèle Olivier, and Konstantinos Magliveras discuss rule-making in the African Union (AU), identifying the variety of international and external stakeholders that intervene and how their participation impacts the functioning of the organisation. They map out rule-making processes in the AU and its predecessor, the Organization of African Unity, and examine the challenges faced by these organisations in their specific regional context. They note that a lack of transparency continues to be one of the main difficulties in understanding which stakeholders influence the rule-making process and that this is jeopardising the ability of the organisation to set its own agenda and achieve its goals of promoting security, economic development, democracy, and human rights on the African continent. The authors write with concern about the role that several external stakeholders (namely, third states and other organisations) play in shaping political, economic, and security policies within the AU, through financing the organisation's activities, offering their expertise and skills, and providing assistance in implementation.

4.2 Challenges of engaging with private actors

Part II of this volume considers the specific challenges faced by IOs in engaging with private actors. The chapter by *Melissa J. Durkee* introduces the topic by discussing the arguments for including for-profit entities in international rule-making, as well as the unique risks that their participation presents. She argues that, in regulating the participation of these actors, IOs should acknowledge that for-profit stakeholders can use a variety of channels to communicate their input, including individual business entities, trade and industry associations, other non-governmental groups, academics and think tanks, and domestic officials. This makes it unlikely that approaches attempting to distinguish between for-profit and other actors are effective over time. Instead, the chapter suggests that two basic governance models are most likely to succeed, separately or in combination: a roundtable model, that includes only a small set of actors through an invitation or application process but invites deep substantive engagement by those stakeholders; or a public comment model, that allows participation by all interested parties but at an arm's-length level of engagement.

Kaho Yu, Xinchuchu Gao, and Xuechen Chen turn to global climate and energy governance and investigate how IOs can improve private actors' participation in this field, as they are critical contributors in addressing global environmental problems and often the de-facto implementers of climate standards. They propose three sets of actions to be undertaken by IOs: (i) demonstrating the business relevance of IO activities to motivate private sector partnerships; (ii) enhancing their partnerships with private actors in setting agendas and establishing standards, which can empower private actors to better understand and adhere to these standards and promote long-term compliance; (iii) institutionalising their stakeholder engagement with private actors through membership networks, policy formulation processes, and structured training programs. The authors acknowledge that further collaboration between IOs and private actors faces certain challenges, particularly concerning the legitimacy and accountability of these stakeholders and communication barriers that lead to a lack of trust. They argue that these can be overcome by establishing clear incentives for private actor participation, fostering open and efficient communication channels, and simplifying sustainability standards in order to make them more accessible to a wider range of companies.

Antonio Marcacci looks at the participation of private actors in the standard-setting processes of IOSCO, the only IO that brings together public securities regulators from around the world. His chapter sheds light on IOSCO's efforts to collect private actors' input and obtain specific information and knowledge that, on the one hand, can make its standards more effective and, on the other hand, brings specific insights regarding the implementation of those standards by the industry. On the basis of three case studies, Marcacci finds that IOSCO's approach represents a successful practice in terms of stakeholders' qualitative and quantitative inclusion in a very technical field. This is illustrated by the amount and sophistication of input that industry organisations provide in consultation processes and how they manage to influence the policy propositions coming from regulatory authorities and propose alternative solutions. Furthermore, IOSCO relies on different means to receive feedback from the private sector, namely round tables and fact-finding exercises. The author concludes that, despite IOSCO's successful engagement with industry, significant challenges persist and that there is room for improvement regarding the participation of civil society representatives.

4.3 Participation of civil society and citizens

The contributions in Part III focus on civil society and citizens' participation in international rule-making. The chapter by *María Rodríguez Alcázar* provides an overview of the mechanisms for citizen participation in 70 regional organisations (ROs). The author finds that the first RO to include provisions related to citizen participation in their founding treaties did so in the 1950s and that only in the 1990s such provisions became a trend. In addition, her analysis reveals important differences between ROs in different continents: ROs in the Americas are more likely to have developed mechanisms for civil participation and delivered on their treaty commitments, whereas such mechanisms are most commonly absent in ROs in Asia. Notably, however, the large majority of founding treaties analysed do not include any mention of civil participation nor mechanisms to promote citizen engagement. Finally, the author examines the practice of ROs in relation to two mechanisms of participation: access to information about meetings and deliberations, and direct elections for parliamentary organs. The analysis of direct parliamentary elections illustrates the difficulties in implementing region-wide elections, as a result of the different national regulations and traditions, but also due to the different level of understanding of ROs in different member states.

Diane Schumann, in turn, considers stakeholder engagement within informal governance institutions, namely the G7 and G20. The chapter discusses the design and practice of Engagement Groups, self-organised networks where different sets of stakeholders meet and discuss policy recommendations, and their relation to the G7 and the G20, focusing on the civil society groups Civil7 and Civil20. The author asks how conditions of informality influence formalised non-state actor engagement. Based on the analysis of G7 and G20 communiqués, expert interviews, and extensive participative observation, she finds that the practices of the G-Engagement Group are primarily influenced by two factors: their degree of formalisation and the institutionalization into the respective G-process, which can be influenced by the presiding country's form of government. Formalisation impacts a group's capacities for organisational learning, cohesion, and impact. Civil society groups have greater difficulties impacting negotiation because they require more internal organisational efforts while also having fewer (financial) resources. Institutionalisation of outreach processes is a double-edged sword, as it can lead to increased support and opportunities to participate in negotiations but can also be used to control criticism and interfere with the Engagement Group process, particularly as certain states might misuse Engagement Groups as marketing tools to promote a positive image.

Finally, *Kseniia Soloveva, Keith Prushankin, Hasan Akintug, Florence Felsheim, Carolina Gerli, Nathalie Koubayova, Cyprian Liske, Claudia Negri Ribalta, and Jan Karol Farfal* conduct an in-depth examination and evaluation of the 'Have Your Say!' Platform (HYS), a platform for digital public consultations in the European Union (EU). The chapter discusses HYS from the perspective of three key components for inclusive public participation: accessibility, outreach, and transparency, and finds that it faces several challenges in relation to each of these elements. The authors propose several improvements to increase the effectiveness of public consultation platforms and promote broader civic participation in the EU. These relate to simplifying HYS's structure, language, and features in order to make it more accessible to a broader range of users; providing clear and straightforward user guidelines; introducing AI content moderation; presenting a centralised dedicated dashboard to eliminate user confusion and achieve increased transparency; and enhancing awareness among different groups of users by targeting various age, economic, and gender categories to foster greater engagement. Finally, the chapter extrapolates the lessons from HYS to other digital tools designed by IOs in order to ensure the increasing involvement of citizens in participatory processes.

In the concluding chapter, the editors come to cross-cutting findings based on the different contributions to this volume and reflect on the three major challenges to improving inclusive rule-making by IOs identified earlier in this introduction: (i) identification and selection of stakeholders; (ii) effective participation; and (iii) unequal power and resources among stakeholders and civil society participation.

BIBLIOGRAPHY

Abbott, K.W., D. Levi-Faur & D. Snidal (2017) Theorizing Regulatory Intermediaries: The RIT Model. *The Annals of the American Academy of Political and Social Science,* 670(1), pp. 14–35.

Abbott, K.W., Kauffmann, C., Lee, J-R. (2018) The contribution of trans-governmental networks of regulators to international regulatory co-operation, *OECD Regulatory Policy Working Papers 10*, OECD Publishing, https://www.oecd.org/en/publications/the-contribution-of-trans-governmental-networks-of-regulators-to-international-regulatory-co-operation_538ff99b-en.html (accessed 7 October 2024).

Auld, G. & L. Gulbrandsen (2010) Transparency in Non-state Certification: Consequences for Accountability and Legitimacy. *Global Environmental Politics,* 10(3), pp. 97–119.

Berman, A. (2021) Between Participation and Capture in International Rule-Making: The WHO Framework of Engagement with Non-State Actors'. *European Journal of International Law,* 32(1), pp. 227–254.

Beierle, T. & J. Cayford (2002) *Democracy in Practice: Public Participation in Environmental Decisions.* Washington: Resources for the Future Press.

Biodiversity Convention (2010) COP Decision X/2 – The Strategic Plan for Biodiversity 2011–2020 and the Aichi Biodiversity Targets.

Bovens, M. (2007) Analysing and Assessing Accountability: A Conceptual Framework. *European Law Journal*, 13(4), pp. 447–68.

Dingwerth, K (2007) *The New Transnationalism: Transnational Governance and Democratic Legitimacy.* Basingstoke: Palgrave MacMillan.

Dryzek, J. et al. (2019) *Deliberative Global Governance.* Cambridge: Cambridge University Press.

FAO (2021) 'Progress in the Implementation of the Code of Conduct for Responsible Fisheries and Related Instruments', COFI/2020/Inf.7, https://www.fao.org/3/ne627en/ne627en.pdf.

FAO (2021) FAO Strategy for Private Sector Engagement 2021–2025.

Grant, R.W. and R. Keohane (2005) Accountability and Abuses of Power in World Politics. *American Political Science Review,* 99(1), pp. 29–43.

Grigorescu, A. (2021) *The Ebb and Flow of Global Governance. Intergovernmentalism versus Nongovernmentalism in World Politics.* Cambridge: Cambridge University Press.

Guggisberg, S. (2019) The Roles of Nongovernmental Actors in Improving Compliance with Fisheri es Regulations Special Issue Articles: New Frontiers in Ocean Environmental Governance. *Review of European, Comparative & International Environmental Law*, 28(3), pp. 314–372.

Kingsbury, B., N. Krisch and R. Stewart (2005) The Emergence of Global Administrative Law. *Law and Contemporary Problems*, 68, pp. 15–61.

Lall, R. (2023) *Making International Institutions Work.* Cambridge: Cambridge University Press.

Marx, A. (2019) Public-Private Partnerships for Sustainable Development: Exploring Their Design and Its Impact on Effectiveness. *Sustainability*, 11(12), pp. 1–9.

OECD (2021) *Compendium of International Organisations' Practices: Working Towards More Effective International Instruments*, OECD Publishing, Paris, https://doi.org/10.1787/846a5fa0-en.

OECD (2019) *The Contribution of International Organizations to a Rule-Based International System: Key Results from the Partnership of International Organizations for Effective Rulemaking*, OECD Publishing, Paris, https://www.oecd.org/gov/regulatory-policy/IO-Rule-Based%20System.pdf.

OECD (2016) *International Regulatory Co-operation: The Role of International Organisations in Fostering Better Rules of Globalisation*, OECD Publishing, Paris, https://doi.org/10.1787/9789264244047-en.

Pattberg, P. et al. (2012) *Public-Private Partnerships for Sustainable Development: Emergence, Influence and Legitimacy.* Cheltenham: Edward Elgar Publishing.

Pauwelyn, J., R. Wessel and J. Wouters (eds) (2012) *Informal International Lawmaking.* Oxford: Oxford University Press.

Scharpf, F.W. (1999) *Governing in Europe: Effective and Democratic?* Oxford: Oxford University Press.

Stewart, R. (2014) Remedying Disregard in Global Regulatory Governance: Accountability, Participation and Responsiveness. *The American Journal of International Law*, 108(2), pp. 211–70.

Tallberg, J. et al. (2014) Explaining the Transnational Design of International Organizations. *International Organization,* 68(4), pp. 741–774.

Tallberg, J. et al. (2013) *The Opening Up of International Organizations*. Cambridge: Cambridge University Press.

UNFCCC (2015), Decision 1/CP.21 - Adoption of the Paris Agreement.

von Bogdandy, A. et al. (eds) (2010) *The Exercise of Public Authority by International Institutions*. Berlin Heidelberg: Springer.

WHO (2016) Framework of Engagement with Non-State Actors, adopted by Resolution WHA69.10, Sixty-ninth session of the World Health Assembly.

WHO (2008) , Rules of Procedure of the World Health Assembly, adopted by Resolutions WHA8.26 and WHA8.27, Eighth session World Health Assembly, and last amended by Resolution WHA61.11, Sixty-first World Health Assembly, https://apps.who.int/gb/bd/pdf/bd47/en/rules-of-procedure-en.pdf (accessed 2 October 2024).

Wouters, J. (2023) Corporations and the Making of Public Standards in International Law: The Case of China in the ITU. In P. Delimatsis, S. Bijlmakers and K. Borowicz (eds), *The Evolution of Transnational Rule-Makers Through Crises*. Cambridge: Cambridge University Press, pp. 66–82.

PART I

Stakeholder engagement: opportunities and challenges for international organisations

2. Stakeholder engagement and media perception among international organisations

Ángel Saz-Carranza, Xavier Fernández-i-Marín, Marianna Karttunen and Juan N. García-Nieto

1 INTRODUCTION

International organisations (IOs) play a key role in shaping international norms in a myriad of sectors and policy issues, from climate action to global health. The current system of global governance necessitates strong, effective, and inclusive IOs to tackle the several risks plaguing an increasingly fragmented world. This is applicable to other types of global governance bodies (GGBs) beyond the traditional understanding of an IO.[1]

While global cooperation has been growing in several areas, ours remains a world of states. Therefore, IOs need to be seen as legitimate actors in order to be able to pursue their policies and to persuade other actors to implement them (Daugirdas 2015). This is why the perception of IOs, as held by external observers, is central to understanding their effectiveness and their legitimacy. For IOs, a positive perception can be instrumental in making their policies a reality. At a time when several countries are increasingly challenging some of the pillars of the current global governance architecture and adopting a zero-sum approach to international relations, IOs emerge as an instrumental tool to boost cooperation and collaboration – which explains the need for IOs to

[1] In this respect, we adopt the understanding of a global governance body from Pauwelyn et al. (2022, p. 1): transnational or global bodies and networks which 'at a minimum, provide a forum and a set of procedures for drawing up rules, setting standards, articulating principles, developing policies, and making decisions' on a certain area or part of the global sphere. In any case, since this chapter has 22 IOs as its main object of study, it will usually use the term IO instead of GGB.

be viewed in a positive light. As the world grows in complexity, more actors are becoming involved in the making of international rules and policies. In the domestic realm, the adoption of inclusive approaches towards stakeholder engagement, such as consultations, has been documented over the last decades (OECD Regulatory Policy Outlook 2021). Similarly, the literature has been cognisant of the gradual turn from a multilateral to a multi-stakeholder global governance (Berman et al. 2022, p. 30). However, there is still a dearth of empirical analysis on the intricacies of stakeholder engagement in IOs, especially in relation to its implications for an IO's perception by external observers.

This chapter looks at the link between these two factors (stakeholder engagement and IO perception), which are undoubtedly an important feature of today's global governance, but which have seldom been studied together. The research question which this chapter seeks to ascertain is the following: Does stakeholder engagement affect IO perception, and if so, how?

This chapter focuses on the 22 IOs that participated in the 2022 Partnership of International Organisations for Effective International Rulemaking (IO Partnership), conducted by the Organisation for Economic Co-operation and Development (OECD). The survey aimed to complement the 2021 Compendium of IO Practices and support the effectiveness, efficiency, transparency, and trust of international instruments and global governance.

The chapter focuses on two sets of variables. The independent variable, 'Stakeholder Engagement', stems from the answers given by the 22 IOs to the IO Partnership Survey. The dependent variable, 'IO Perception', is a score given to each of the 22 IOs according to the sentiment analysis of a vast number of n-grams,[2] which were extracted from news pieces from the GDELT database.[3]

The surveyed IOs are later divided into four clusters according to what we label 'approaches' towards stakeholder engagement: essentially, with which stakeholders do the IOs engage. This includes both the *quantity* and the *type* of stakeholders with which IOs engage – revealing whether IOs are selective or wide-reaching in their approach, and whether they target a particular typology

[2] An n-gram is a string of words surrounding a particular term in a text. In this chapter, we looked for n-grams surrounding the acronyms for each of the surveyed IOs (the text before and after the IO's acronym).

[3] GDELT (Global Database of Events, Language, and Tones) is a network and database which monitors news from all around the world since 1979 and updated every 15 minutes. Its massive, multilingual dataset makes GDELT one of the most important open-research networks. GDELT contained 8.14 trillion datapoints as of 2021.

of stakeholders.[4] Last, the chapter concludes with a comparison of the average perception scores among the four clusters.

This chapter demonstrates one main empirical finding. When comparing IO clusters according to their stakeholder engagement approaches, encompassing IOs (understood as those with more far-reaching stakeholder engagement approaches than the other three clusters) are positively correlated with higher IO perception scores than the other clusters.

2 THEORETICAL FRAMING

2.1 IO perception

For the purposes of this chapter, the concept of perception refers to the evaluation of a subject, entity or actor as observed by a stakeholder. Several stakeholders will harbour a different perception of a given actor or agency, depending on a variety of factors and variables, including the observer's own interests and priorities when evaluating said actor or agency (Maor 2016; Raithel & Schwaiger 2014).

Perceptions of IOs can refer to two major concepts: effectiveness and appropriateness. Moreover, the field of public administration has conceptualised perceptions along four dimensions (Carpenter 2010; Verhoest et al. 2021):[5] two closely related to effectiveness (Performative and Technical-Professional dimensions) and two with appropriateness (Moral and Procedural dimensions). The latter is closely related to what Bitektine (2011) calls social acceptance (or sociopolitical legitimacy) and to Dellmuth et al.'s (2022) idea that governing IOs should be perceived to have the right to rule and to exercise that right appropriately. Daugirdas (2019) adds a fifth dimension specific to IOs in global governance: perceptions of the 'IO's independence from, or responsiveness to and cooperation with, its member states' (Daugirdas 2019, p. 228). This reflects the importance of the relationship between IOs and its member states. This fifth dimension will be examined later in the light of stakeholder engagement and its interplay with an IO's perception.

Perceptions are externally-oriented, involving comparisons with 'others' (Bitektine 2011) in the same ecosystem. Perception is thus about what sets one act apart from others, focusing on differences compared to other organisations (Bitektine 2011, pp. 160–162). Furthermore, perceptions can relate to the past,

---

[4] For example, many IOs prefer to engage mainly or exclusively with stakeholders of a political nature.

[5] Carpenter (2001) lays out these dimensions in his Bureaucratic Reputation Theory (BRT), upon which much of the literature builds its conceptualisation of perception.

informing evaluators' expectations about the organisation's future conduct based on its past actions (Bitektine 2011, p. 160).

Perceptions can be quantified and, in our study, we scale an IO's media perception relative to other IOs. As a quantifiable score or value, perception can be measured by comparison to other organisations precisely due to its externally-oriented nature.

In addition, each given observer can have a different perception of an IO. As a result, there are multiple perceptions of each IO, each by a different set of stakeholders or observers. The literature agrees that perception itself is multi-faceted, given that an organisation is usually evaluated and assessed by a plurality of observers and stakeholders, both within and outside the organisation. In other words, organisations are exposed to several audiences which have different ways of perceiving reality, and each perceive different threats and opportunities based on divergent information. Each external audience selects the dimensions that will receive priority in assessing the organisation (Maor 2016).

Raithel & Schwaiger (2014) point out that the general public is widely accepted as a relevant stakeholder group whose perceptions are to be considered (Raithel & Schwaiger 2014, pp. 945–947). However, conceptualising the general public as an audience is hard, and the media can usually act as an intermediary between the organisations and its evaluators in the general public: 'The media, therefore, have an active influence on public opinions, including their judgment' (Verhoest et al. 2021, p. 20). Similarly, Bertelli & Sinclair (2015, p. 856), stress that media attention has been used as a proxy for the public's perceptions of issue salience. Thus, media perception is an aggregation of several individualised perceptions held by each stakeholder (Helm 2007, pp. 239–241).

Accordingly, while we can speak about organisations having an aggregation of many perceptions (plural) as assessed by many stakeholders, this article will put the limelight on media perception (singular).

2.1.1 Antecedents and effects of IO perception

Perception is undeniably important for IOs, as it is for other agencies and organisations. Perceptions of organisations involve two different mental processes (Verhoest et al. 2021, pp. 6–9; also Maor 2016, pp. 82–84): cognitive assessment, which is based on the observability of task behaviour and the attributability of results associated with those tasks; and affective assessment, which involves emotions. The literature finds that domestic agencies are more likely to face perception threats if their tasks are associated with a degree of authoritativeness and coerciveness, which are processed through an affective assessment due to these values' association with negative emotions (Verhoest et al. 2021, pp. 13–14). Negative perception of an agency can lead to public distrust, especially if the media voices perception threats (Verhoest et al. 2021).

When it comes to IOs in particular, perception is even more crucial because, unlike states, which have a high coercive capacity and material resources, their effectiveness depends on their capacity to persuade, and a negative perception can threaten their collapse or dissolution (Daugirdas 2015; 2019). IOs with a negative perception will be less effective and garner less support and cooperation from member states than IOs perceived positively. Relatedly, improved perception enhances the chance of survival, performance, effectiveness, and access to resources, and reduces transaction costs (Daugirdas 2015).

Verhoest et al.'s study (2021) concludes that agencies involved in various policy areas tend to be less threatened in their reputational perception.[6] While this chapter does not focus on reputation, the section above explained that media perception itself is one of the several perceptions which can make up an organisation's overall aggregated reputation, as conceptualised by Verhoest et al. (2021) and other authors (Pauwelyn et al. 2022; Carpenter 2010; Helm 2007).

Moreover, operating with a variety of policies and performing multiple tasks does not lead to a lower reputation as perceived by stakeholders, and in fact, policy multiplicity can even be an antecedent of good perception. Bertelli & Sinclair highlight that media coverage can be an antecedent of the public perception (be it negative or positive) of domestic agencies and even their likelihood of termination (Bertelli & Sinclair 2015, p. 863).

Bitektine et al. (2020) identify the following antecedents:

- Media coverage and size have positive effects on perception.
- The organisation's alliances with reputable partners, history of past performances, and certifications and endorsements are specific antecedents of positive perception.

Some of these antecedents are mirrored in this study, where coordination with partners, including other IOs, and media coverage are central elements.

In conclusion, the main consequences of perception for IOs (as well as other GGBs) are:

- Improved (or harmed) chance of survival.
- Enhanced (or weakened) public trust.

[6] According to the authors, reputation threats are "*negative judgments that are voiced towards agencies*' (in our case, by the media) (Verhoest et al. 2021, pp. 3–4).

- Effectiveness (understood as the capacity of the IOs' to persuade states and to foster their cooperation and participation).

2.2 Stakeholder engagement

Stakeholder engagement is a mechanism for IOs 'to appeal to a wider range of constituencies than the traditional membership' which constitute them – meaning, states (OECD 2021, p. 80). Stakeholder engagement ensures that international instruments have a strengthened ownership by reaching out to any stakeholder concerned by their normative activity.

Stakeholder engagement has long been a topic of discussion for scholars from a variety of fields, including organisational studies, international relations, public policy, economics, political science and even psychology. However, the study of stakeholder engagement has traditionally been ascribed to domestic scenarios, often through a comparative analysis (Verhoest et al. 2021). When the scope has been enlarged to the global field, the GGBs selected as case studies have been few and limited to a rather narrow understanding of the concept of IO (Agné et al. 2015).

While the concept of stakeholder engagement has been studied and analysed in length in the scholarly literature, some challenges remain.

The first and most difficult challenge to overcome both in literature and in practice is identifying who to engage with, i.e. defining a 'stakeholder'. There is no international agreement on the concept of stakeholder, which is broadly conceived and highly IO-specific (OECD 2021_1). IOs use quite different definitions of stakeholders, resulting in very different outreach approaches. Similarly, different authors use diverse taxonomies to distinguish among stakeholders within IOs.

In essence, a stakeholder is, at a minimum, an actor affected by the activities of an organisation, but they may also have an influence on that organisation and participate directly or indirectly in its procedures, such as through a stakeholder committee or information-sharing processes. The literature offers several definitions of stakeholder.

Stakeholders, according to general stakeholder theory, are individuals who believe they both affect and are affected by the actions of a particular firm (Álvarez and Sachs 2023, p. 187; Freeman 1984). Therefore, stakeholders not only include those impacted by an organisation's decisions, policies, and actions but also those who perceive themselves as influencing the organisation (Álvarez and Sachs 2023).

At the global governance level, Berman et al. (2022) define stakeholders as all those affected by and having a stake in the rules and decisions of a particular GGB (Berman et al. 2022, p. 4). Meanwhile, Agné et al. (2015) add the requirement that stakeholders are individuals or groups with significantly affected interests who may participate directly in political procedures or be indirectly represented through NGOs, philanthropic foundations, business associations, labour unions, and private companies (Agné et al. 2015, p. 469).

Pauwelyn (ed.) et al. (2022) differentiate between two types of stakeholders, based on the dichotomy between states and non-state actors. Within states, they specifically highlight the distinction between traditionally marginalised states from the Global South and states from the West, emphasising the exclusion of governmental actors from the Global South in GGBs.

Agné et al. (2015, p. 466), on the other hand, focus on non-state actors and identify several stakeholders, including self-organising non-state actors such as civil-society groups, advocacy organisations, and self-appointed representatives, as well as IOs, non-governmental organisations (NGOs), companies, and expert networks. These organisations' advocacy aims to promote increased stakeholder engagement, often referred to as 'stakeholder democracy'.

Additionally, Hanegraaff et al. (2020) use a core-periphery distinction among non-state actors based on levels of participation. Core players are persistent and central actors in the policymaking process, while peripheral players quickly exit the transnational domain after initial mobilisation. Their study finds that non-state actors from developing countries face higher constraints than those from developed countries in developing long-lasting patterns of advocacy, echoing Pauwelyn (ed.) et al.'s (2022) claims about marginalised state stakeholders.

To characterise the types of stakeholders that exist, this chapter draws from the typology and related data facilitated by the OECD and its IO Partnership, which has been active in supporting and promoting more efficient and inclusive governance in IOs.

In the context of the Partnership's work comparing IO practices, the Compendium of International Organisations' Practices: Working Towards More Effective International Instruments (OECD 2021) finds that the concept of stakeholder varies largely according to the IO at stake. It thus proposes a multi-layered classification system, grouping stakeholders into three broad categories: governmental actors, commercial actors, and non-commercial actors, with room for hybrid actors that do not fit neatly into one category.

Sharing experiences across IOs has shown that the concept and approaches to stakeholder engagement varies depending on the nature and rulemaking processes of the IO. IOs mainly engaged in purely soft activities[7] – such as

---

[7] As defined in Saz-Carranza et al (2023), soft regulation tasks are those which '*develop[...] or promulgate[...] guidelines, principles, best practices, suggestions, or nonbinding rules*' (Saz-Carranza et al 2023, p. 14). Soft rule-making activities can more broadly be equated with non-binding activities (Saz-Carranza et al 2023, p. 25).

the production of consensual frameworks and exchange of information – tend to use fewer stakeholder engagement mechanisms than the total sample. By contrast, IOs mainly engaged in accreditation services, in the production of technical standards and in development of legally binding tools use these mechanisms more systematically. This is confirmed by an analysis by nature of IOs: secretariats of convention, which tend to have more legally binding tools, also tend to engage stakeholders more systematically (OECD 2016). The list below provides a detailed breakdown on the OECD's typology of stakeholders as regarded by IOs.

OECD's typology of stakeholders (OECD 2019):

- International nongovernmental organisations
- International business organisations
- Government representatives for member countries
- National regulatory agencies
- Parliamentarians and political parties
- Individual experts
- Private sector entities
- Government representatives from non-member countries
- Academic institutions
- Other entities/organs at the domestic level
- Philanthropic foundations
- Consumers
- Academic unions
- Labour or trade unions
- Other

2.2.1 Purpose of stakeholder engagement

The engagement of stakeholders by IOs serves two central purposes: inclusiveness and effectiveness of international rulemaking (OECD 2021).

Firstly, stakeholder engagement seeks the inclusiveness of international rulemaking, considered a core element of good governance (OECD 2021, p. 80). This normative approach advocates that everyone affected by a decision should have a voice in its making, thereby strengthening the democratic legitimacy of IOs in the eyes of stakeholders (Agné et al. 2015, pp. 466-468).

Additionally, Coni-Zimmer et al. (2023) found that IOs establish dialogue fora to bolster their legitimacy through institutional legitimation strategies, responding to increasing audience demands from within civil society for a space for deliberation. The authors cite the Civil 20 (C20) and the Civil Society

Policy Forum (CSPF) as an example of legitimation strategies.[8] Coni-Zimmer et al claim that these fora allow international institutions to strategically address stakeholder criticisms without proactively manipulating their agenda or priorities. Thus, these fora carry the risk of becoming a way for global governance institutions to channel the several interests of their stakeholders without enacting meaningful changes to their structure or their agenda, in what Coni-Zimmer et al call the 'path of least resistance' (Coni-Zimmer et al. 2023, pp. 960–961). Previous research, like that by Hannah et al. (2017), similarly looked at the traditional models of stakeholder engagement in IOs and political contestation.

Secondly, stakeholder engagement is rooted in pragmatism, as it enhances the quality of decision-making, responsiveness, and overall effectiveness of IOs (OECD 2021; Pauwelyn (ed.) et al. 2022). By strengthening ownership of those affected by international instruments, stakeholder engagement can be used a practical vehicle to better progress toward the objectives of international instruments, fostering trust, implementation, and compliance (OECD 2021, p. 80).

Conversely, stakeholders engage with IOs to influence their decision-making and ensure that their voices are heard in the process (Berman et al. 2022). It is essential to note that engagement alone does not grant stakeholders decision-making capacity, which solely resides with full members. Similarly, willingness to engage does not guarantee the capacity to engage effectively, as this necessitates an array of resources and capabilities often not readily available for some stakeholders. Therefore, there is often a gap between the opportunities facilitated by IOs and stakeholders' ability to seize them due to their scant material, analytical and political resources (DeMenno & Büthe 2022, pp. 45–53).

Despite increasing efforts to provide stakeholders an opportunity to participate, IOs still face constraints in setting up reforms for 'good participation' that entail removal of barriers to involvement and managing risks such as conflict of interest and undue influence. Challenges of stakeholder engagement around national rulemaking may be amplified at the international level (OECD 2021_1). In this sense, Alemanno (2015) notes that, to seize engagement opportunities effectively, several other obstacles must be overcome: among others,

---

[8] The C20 is an official engagement group set up by the G20 and it comprises civil society organisations and NGOs. The C20 meets annually in a summit hosted by the country holding the G20's rotating presidency. The CSPF is an event held twice a year during the World Bank Group-International Monetary Fund (IMF) spring and annual meetings and works as a platform of civil society organisations which aim to have a say in development issues and to engage with the World Bank Group or the IMF.

lack of awareness of opportunities to engage; low participation literacy and know-how; and information overload can all hinder well-intentioned stakeholder engagement mechanisms (Alemanno in OECD 2015, p. 117). This harks back to the importance of bridging the gap between the opportunities available to stakeholders and their capability to take advantage of them (DeMenno & Buthe 2022, pp. 45–53).

2.2.2 Modes of engagement

Stakeholder engagement can manifest itself through various participation modes, or 'engagement modalities' (OECD 2021). The IO Partnership identifies a list of procedures by which stakeholders can engage in the decision-making process, which mirrors the survey answered by the IOs involved in the OECD's IO Partnership
(OECD 2021):

1. Opportunity to be consulted on proposed instruments
2. Invitations to participate in instruments development (OECD)
3. Invitations to participate in the dissemination and implementation of instruments
4. Invitations to participate in the monitoring of use and implementation of instruments
5. Official status enabling regular inputs from stakeholder groups
6. Invitations to participate in governing body meetings
7. Specific processes allowing engagement of wide audiences, opening to the general public
8. Expert processes facilitating technical inputs from stakeholders, such as expert groups or technical committees.

DeMenno & Büthe (2022, pp. 39–43) build on these procedures by mentioning other 'participation modes', which can be grouped under three categories: notice and comment procedures, hearings and public meetings, and advisory committees.

Across these different procedures, stakeholders have different levels of contribution to the IO activities: some are entitled to participate as fully-fledged members, either as a result of explicit recognition or IO membership, with what Richard Stewart calls 'decisional' power (Stewart 2014, p. 214; Berman et al. 2022, p. 19). In contrast, others are only allowed 'non-decisional' participation. Decisional power in IOs entails having the right to have a say in the established policy-making process of an IO through voting. It follows that stakeholders with non-decisional power in an IO are those which are present in the policy-making process (or a part of it) but cannot vote, and hence their engagement carries no direct influence in the outcome of the process. DeMenno & Büthe (2022) conclude that having decisional (voting) power is what sets aside stakeholders with *influence* from those who merely have *voice* (DeMenno & Büthe 2022, pp. 69–70). Indeed, in this paper, full members are deemed to be those which have voting power in the surveyed IOs (and often called as such by the IOs themselves).

To summarise, stakeholder engagement plays a critical role in enhancing the inclusiveness, effectiveness, and legitimacy of IOs. Stakeholders seek to influence decision-making processes, and engagement enables them to offer insights and positions. For engagement to be effective, stakeholders must be aware of opportunities, find the issues relevant to them, and possess the necessary resources. Engagement occurs through various modalities, allowing stakeholders to contribute their perspectives and influence IO policies and decisions.

2.3 The gap between stakeholder engagement and IO perception

Studying the typologies and the depth of stakeholder engagement in IOs is important to understand whether the trend towards better inclusiveness and diversity in stakeholder engagement observed at the domestic level is reflected in the global governance arena. Studying the media coverage of IOs in parallel with stakeholder engagement mechanisms allows to explore, whether any efforts towards increased inclusiveness and transparency translate to better perception in the public opinion. While it is a truism to state that the most pressing issues facing today's world require inclusive global cooperation as enabled (amongst others) by IOs, stakeholder engagement can be an effective tool to amplify the opportunities for participation of diverse actors in pre-established governance frameworks with an interest on the issue. Global governance is idiosyncratically more cumbersome and complex than domestic governance, with a vastly more varied slate of stakeholders. Stakeholder engagement at the international level thus comes with its challenges. Identifying, let alone reaching out to the affected stakeholders at a global scale, without giving undue prominence to specific actors, requires proactive efforts, incentives and safeguards which exist to varying degrees across IOs (OECD 2021). Therefore, equipping IOs with a variety of stakeholder engagement mechanisms can help to bolster their effectiveness.

As aforementioned, Bureaucratic Reputation Theory has laid out four different dimensions by which entities may be perceived and evaluated: performative, technical-professional, moral, and procedural (Carpenter 2010; Maor

2016).[9] However, only Daugirdas' fifth dimension is specific to IOs in global governance. This dimension is the perception of the 'IO's independence from, or responsiveness to and cooperation with, its member states' (Daugirdas 2019, p. 228). It reflects the importance of the relationship between IOs and its member states. Indeed, this fifth dimension is crucial for this chapter, as it introduces the relationship between an IO's perception and the way it engages with its stakeholders.

While not using the term 'stakeholder engagement' itself, the importance assigned to this dimension, which emphasises cooperation between the IO and its members, is certainly similar to the conceptualisation of stakeholder engagement laid out in earlier sections of this chapter. Therefore, the relationship between stakeholder engagement and IO perception has certainly been conceptualised. However, we find that a gap remains in the literature when it comes to finding empirical evidence between these two variables.

Several authors (Pauwelyn (ed.) et al. 2022, Verhoest et al. 2021, Coni-Zimmer et al. 2023) refer to the increasing trend towards stakeholder governance; similarly, the literature has documented the gradual adoption of stakeholder engagement mechanisms and strategies by several IOs and other GGBs. This turn towards better inclusiveness and widening of stakeholder engagement has also been welcomed by the OECD in its Compendium (2021).

However, few authors have examined how this trend relates to the way in which IOs are evaluated by external observers. Agné et al. (2015) did not find evidence that improved stakeholder engagement improved democratic legitimacy in IOs as perceived by stakeholders themselves. Nonetheless, their study assessed only four IOs, and focused on internal stakeholders (meaning those which were involved to some extent with the IOs).[10] Verhoest et al. (2021) compared 40 domestic public agencies in two countries (Denmark and the Netherlands) and analysed their evaluations by the media. However, their study mainly centred on the tasks pursued by these agencies. While they did find that task matters for the agencies' reputational perception in the media, stakeholder engagement was outside of the purview of the study. Bertelli & Sinclair (2015) similarly looked at media attention and evaluation of agencies, but again in a domestic-only context.

Concisely, there is ample evidence that global governance (as well as domestic governance) has been incorporating stakeholder engagement mechanisms, and much of the literature examining the ways in which IOs or domestic agencies are evaluated by either their own stakeholders or external observes such

---

[9] See note 4 supra.

[10] Besides, Agné et al. (2015) look at democratic legitimacy, as opposed to IO perception, which is the object of study in this chapter.

as the media. However, there remains an empirical gap when it comes to the interplay between stakeholder engagement and the perception of IOs. If, like Daugirdas mentions, one of the dimensions by which observers perceive an IO is '*independence from, or responsiveness to and cooperation with*' its stakeholders, it is paramount to analyse how does stakeholder engagement affect IO perception. This is precisely what this chapter sets out to do.

3 METHODS

This study's variables are derived from three main sources, making up two 'sets'. The first set, 'Stakeholder engagement variables', is collected from the OECD IO Partnership Surveys. These surveys were distributed in 2022 by the OECD among the international organisations which make up the IO Partnership and aim to collect data on the inclusiveness of international rule-making (which, crucially, includes stakeholder engagement). The 22 IOs which answered the survey are the ones studied in this chapter. The surveys aimed to complement the 2021 Compendium of IO Practices and support the effectiveness, efficiency, transparency, and trust of international instruments and global governance. For the purpose of this chapter, these surveys allow us to know the extent to which each IO conducts its stakeholder engagement strategies.

The second set of variables (the dependent variable) is 'Media Perception of IOs', derived from the GDELT database, using n-grams surrounding each organisation's acronym to calculate sentiment values. A sentiment dictionary (SenticNet) provides an average sentiment value, resulting in the perception score.[11]

Once the perception score is retrieved via the sentiment dictionary, the next step is to carry out a linear regression analysis to understand the interplay between the two main sets of variables: stakeholder engagement and IO perception. However, this study makes an important addition. The 22 IOs are grouped into four clusters, each containing several IOs whose stakeholder engagement processes are similar in nature,[12] in accordance with the answers given in the survey. These four clusters also have an average perception score.

Table 2.1 below provides an overview of each set of variables.

---

[11] A sentiment dictionary provides a value for the emotions or sentiment expressed in a text – in our case, in the n-grams analysed for each of the surveyed IOs. The sentiment dictionary chosen for this chapter is SenticNet, which gives each n-gram a score from -1 (most extreme negative sentiment) to +1 (most extreme positive sentiment).

[12] For our purposes, the 'nature' of stakeholder engagement mainly refers to the variety of stakeholders (or lack thereof) with which the surveyed IOs engage – addressed in Question 1.1 of the IO Partnership of the OECD.

Table 2.1 Summary of the sets of variables

Set of variables	Source
Stakeholder engagement (independent variable)	IO Partnership Survey, in particular, questions 1.1 and 1.2
IO Perception (dependent variable)	GDELT database to extract the media pieces mentioning the IO's acronyms Sentiment analysis of the text by reference to a sentiment dictionary (SenticNet).

3.1 Sampling

This study focuses on 22 IOs that participated in the 2022 IO Partnership Survey conducted by the OECD. While there are no specific criteria for admitting organisations into the IO Partnership, guidelines state that participating organisations should have a secretariat, international membership, and generally aim to have a standard-setting role in global governance, whether narrow or broad in scope.

The following IOs took part in the survey:

- American Society for Testing and Materials International (ASTM International)
- Bureau International des Poids et Mesures/International Bureau for Weights and Measures (BIPM)
- International Accreditation Forum (IAF)
- International Electrotechnical Commission (IEC)
- International Federation of Accountants (IFAC)
- International Laboratory Accreditation Cooperation (ILAC)
- International Labour Organization (ILO)
- International Organization for Standardization (ISO)
- International Telecommunications Union (ITU)
- Organisation Internationale de Métrologie Légale/International Organisation of Legal Metrology (OIML)
- Organisation Internationale de la Vigne et du Vin/International Organisation of Vine and Wine (OIV)
- Organisation Intergouvernementale pour les Transports Internationaux Ferroviaires (OTIF)
- Pharmaceutical Inspection Cooperation Scheme (PIC/S)
- Sistema de Integración Económica Centroamericana/Central American Economic Integration System (SIECA)
- United Nations Commission on International Trade Law (UNCITRAL)

- United Nations Framework Convention on Climate Change (UNFCCC)
- United Nations Industrial Development Organization (UNIDO)
- World Anti-Doping Agency (WADA)
- World Customs Organization (WCO)
- World Intellectual Property Organization (WIPO)
- World Organisation for Animal Health (WOAH) – called OIE (Office Internationale des Epizooties) until May 2022
- World Trade Organization (WTO).

All the IOs provided responses to the survey questions. This study focuses on the first bloc of questions in the survey (questions 1.1. and 1.2), which primarily address three aspects first introduced in the theoretical framework:

1. The typologies of stakeholders with whom the IOs engage.
2. The rulemaking stages in which they pursue stakeholder engagement.
3. The extent to which the IOs pursue stakeholder engagement mechanisms.

3.2 Variables and data collection

3.2.1 IO perceptions variable

The 'Media Perception' variable is derived from the GDELT database, using n-grams surrounding each organisation's acronym to calculate sentiment values. The sentiment dictionaries provide an average sentiment value, resulting in the raw perception score.

To determine the perception score for each IO, the study utilised the GDELT database. It analysed all articles mentioning the IOs considered within the natural year 2022, from 1 January to 31 December . The study focused on n-grams surrounding the IO's acronym from these articles. Specifically, only entries with the IO's acronyms were considered, resulting in a total of 276,673 entries, with a total size of 55 MB. On average, each article contained 3.197 n-grams.

To ensure the relevance of these entries, they underwent a filtering process using an algorithm. This step aimed to verify that the entries and surrounding n-grams were indeed related to the specific IO in question. After filtering, 30,004 documents (about 34.7% of the initial entries) were retained for further analysis.

The next step involved calculating the perception score for each article based on its sentiment. Four sentiment dictionaries (NRC, Sentic-Net, Sentiword, and SO-CAL Google) were used to gauge the overall sentiment of each IO. Among these dictionaries, Sentic-Net was chosen to compute the final 'Perception' variable.

It is worth noting that the number of appearances of IOs in the media varied considerably, ranging from 84 mentions for SIECA to 88,318 mentions for ISO.

3.2.2 Stakeholder engagement variables

The Stakeholder Engagement Survey collects data from the IO Partnership Survey 2022. The survey consists of five variables, each derived from the five responses provided to the questions laid out above. Note, however, that only the first two questions refer to stakeholder engagement. Therefore, the focus of this chapter is put on the first two questions, from which the clusters emerge.

The survey variables are as follows.

1. 'Type of Stakeholder': This variable aims to categorise stakeholders based on the diverse actors that are affected by, and potentially influence, the decisions and outcomes of IOs. The source of this data is Question 1.1. of the IO Partnership Survey, which asks the IOs to identify the types of actors they consider as stakeholders. It highlights significant variations in how the term 'stakeholder' is perceived among the surveyed IOs. Out of 26 options, international governmental organisations, international NGOs, international business associations and organisations, and government representatives of member countries were the most popular stakeholders with whom the surveyed IOs engage, with an overwhelming majority of the IOs selecting them. Conversely, some of the options were not selected by most surveyed IOs: advocacy groups, investors, and parliamentarians and political parties were selected as stakeholders by less than a quarter of the surveyed IOs.
2. 'Participation in Policy Stages': This variable examines the extent to which stakeholders participate in various stages of international rulemaking by IOs. Question 1.2. of the IO Partnership Survey 2022 is the source for this data. IOs are asked to specify which stakeholders participate in each of the rulemaking stages.

Government representatives of member states are actively involved in all stages, while national regulatory agencies also play a role, albeit to a lesser extent. IGOs are more engaged in early policy stages than in later ones (during and after adoption).

3.2.3 Clustering

Four main clusters of IOs were identified, based on their stakeholder engagement approaches and the nature of stakeholders with whom they interact . The clusters stem from the responses to the 22 OECD IO Partnership Surveys, from which the set of variables labelled 'IO stakeholder engagement variables' were collected. Thus, clusters are an effective way of categorising IOs according to the way in which they approach stakeholder engagement, and the extent to which they practise it.

The methodological approach to find out the four clusters has been to implement a dendrogram[13] to group the IOs into the four categories according to the different approaches to stakeholder engagement pursued by the 22 IOs, as stated by the IOs themselves in their responses to the OECD IO Partnership Survey. A dendrogram is a visual representation of the classification of a specific set of observations. In our study, observations are represented by the IOs. The dendrogram in this chapter shows how close IOs are between them and how far away they are from the rest when comparing their stakeholder engagement approaches.

4 RESULTS

This section is divided into two main parts. The first part introduces the four clusters and explains and explains how they are formed. These clusters categorise the 22 IOs in the study based on the nature of their stakeholder engagement mechanisms – using the set of 'IO Stakeholder Engagement variables' as a source. These clusters aim to classify the surveyed IOs according to their stakeholder engagement practices, including how they engage stakeholders, the extent of their engagement, and the stages of the policy-making process in which they involve stakeholders, as indicated in their responses to the IO Partnership Survey 2022.

The second part consists of a comparative analysis which estimates the relationship between stakeholder engagement and IO perception when grouping the 22 IOs among clusters.

4.1 Stakeholder engagement clusters

The clustering of the surveyed IOs, which groups together IOs with a similar approach to stakeholder engagement, results in a dendrogram with four clusters, as shown below in Figure 2.1.

[13] The main function of a dendrogram is to visually show the similarities between a number of objects. A dendrogram has the shape of an inverted tree with several branches, one for each object analysed – in this case, the surveyed IOs each constitute a branch. Dendrograms are useful because they allow us to quickly understand how patterns of stakeholder engagement approaches differ across the 22 surveyed IOs. While no IOs have identical stakeholder engagement approaches, the dendrogram shows that they can be grouped according to the relative similarity of their approaches looking at the nodes under which several clusters stem.

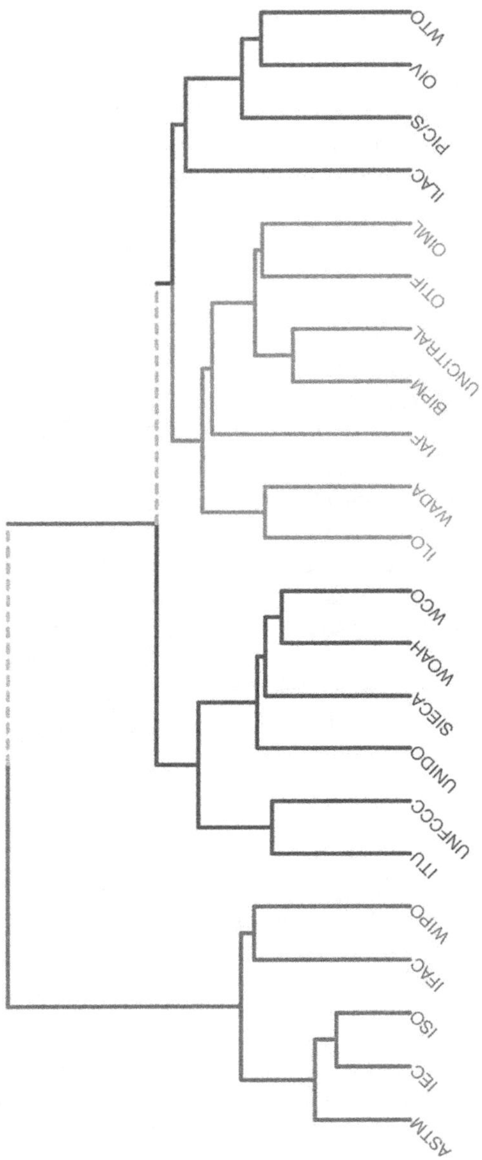

Figure 2.1 Stakeholder engagement clusters' dendrogram

The dendrogram can be interpreted as follows: each organisation falls from a branch that links it with another organisation. Thus, the smaller the vertical distance of the branch, the more the IOs' stakeholder engagement approach resemble each other. And conversely, the longer the vertical distance of the branches, the difference between the groups. Similarly, the closer the nodes (the point where the branches meet), the more similar the cluster of IOs under the nodes. The lower the node , the more similar the branches emerging from that node are.

This is represented by the group of 5 IOs in the left-hand side (ASTM, IEC, ISO, IFAC and WIPO), that fall from a single, long vertical branch. This means that these five IOs are quite different (in their stakeholder engagement approaches) to the other large group, but that they are quite similar among themselves. At the same time, two IOs in this group (IEC and ISO) are linked by a branch with low vertical distance, which signals a great similarity between them.

The dendrogram shows four main clusters of IOs according to their stakeholder engagement approaches. This step allows us to assess what are the features that determine the similarities between IOs within each cluster, and therefore, the differences between clusters.

The next logical step is to assign a label to each of the four clusters, according to the nature of their stakeholder engagement approaches. A detailed study of the dendrogram shows that the four clusters can be labelled as follows:

1. Encompassing Cluster (far left): Consisting of five IOs, this cluster actively engages with a diverse range of stakeholders at various rulemaking stages, demonstrating a widespread and inclusive stakeholder engagement strategy. The organisations in this cluster are ISO, IEC, ASTM, WIPO, and IFAC.
2. Societal Cluster (far right): Comprising four IOs, this cluster primarily engages with social actors based on their tasks and the sector they operate in. Social actors include scientific and academic communities, private companies, experts, consumers, and associations such as women, youth, and Indigenous groups. The organisations in this cluster are ILAC, PIC/S, WTO, and OIV.
3. Political Cluster (centre left): With six IOs, this cluster engages primarily with political stakeholders, including member states and representatives, domestic regulatory agencies, NGOs, other IOs, political parties, and MPs. The organisations in this cluster are WCO, ITU, SIECA, UNFCCC, WOAH, and UNIDO.
4. IO-Specific Cluster (centre right): Comprising seven IOs, this cluster operates in narrow sectors or specific settings, with a targeted mandate and

scope. These organisations engage with specific actors not included among the OECD's options in the Partnership Survey, indicating a focused stakeholder community. The organisations in this cluster are BIPM, WADA, ILO, UNCITRAL, OTIF, OIML, and IAF.

It is worth mentioning that these clusters echo the argument posed by Coni-Zimmer et al. IOs, the authors argue, tend to replicate the stakeholder engagement mechanisms and strategies used by like-minded organisations (what the authors label 'isomorphism'), as it becomes harder for IOs 'to deviate from the established practice' (Coni-Zimmer et al. 2023, p. 943). This holds especially for the encompassing cluster, as the findings show that the five IOs within this group have remarkably similar patterns of stakeholder engagement, as revealed by the proximity of their nodes.

4.2 Stakeholder engagement and IO perception

Figure 2.2 shows the relationship between the perception scores, as evaluated through a sentiment dictionary from the news pieces extracted from the GDELT database and its relationship with stakeholder engagement clusters. The regression analysis compares the average perception scores of the four clusters which emerged from grouping IOs according to their similarities in their stakeholder engagement approaches.

The perception scores of all IOs ranged from a minimum of 1.34 and a maximum of 11.84, with the average standing at 6.88.

The regression analysis shows that encompassing IOs have the highest perception values, with an average of 9.524. Political IOs have an average perception score of 6.379, while societal IOs have an average perception of 6.293. IO-specific organisations have the lowest average perception at 5.747. Four of the eight IOs with the highest perception are in the encompassing cluster, whereas none of the ten IOs with the lowest perception scores are .

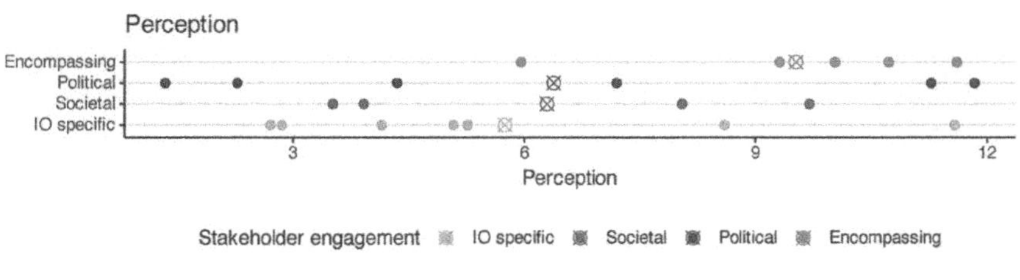

Figure 2.2 Perception by cluster

These findings are relevant, as they suggest that having far-reaching stakeholder engagement approaches (which the encompassing IOs do) has positive implications for the perception of an IO.

Statistically, encompassing IOs have a higher perception score than IO-specific ones, though less so when compared with the political and with societal clusters, as shown in Table 2.2.

Table 2.2 Probability of having a higher perception, compared among clusters

Comparison	Prob. (SE of Encompassing > SE of Comparison)
Stakeholder engagement: IO specific	0.77
Stakeholder engagement: Political	0.58
Stakeholder engagement; Societal	0.59

5 CONCLUSION

This chapter seeks to make two additions to existing literature. First, it aims to contribute to studies on global governance by recognising the importance of stakeholder engagement in the international sphere. This chapter has shed light on how IOs' stakeholder engagement approaches contrast with each other by carrying out a comparative analysis of 22 IOs, building on the knowledge of surveys and reports conducted in the context of IO Partnership (OECD 2016; OECD 2019).

Second, it aims to contribute to the emerging literature on stakeholder engagement in global governance by examining the interplay between stakeholder engagement approaches employed by surveyed IOs and the perception of said IOs. While other scholars have looked at several antecedents and effects of stakeholder engagement in global governance, the relationship which stakeholder engagement may have with an IO's perception has remained a largely understudied gap in this area – a gap which this chapter has addressed.

This chapter makes an important contribution to the empirical study of IOs' perception. When comparing IO clusters according to their approaches towards stakeholder engagement, the encompassing IOs (classified as those with more far-reaching stakeholder engagement approaches than the other three clusters) are positively correlated with higher Perception scores (and by extension, with a more positive perception by the media) than the other clusters.

Besides, methodologically, the results of this study suggest that using a large-n database such as GDELT, and running an analysis with a sentiment dictionary, can prove effective in measuring perceptions by an audience, in this case, English language media.

ACKNOWLEDGEMENTS

The authors acknowledge that this research has received funding from the Agencia Estatal de Investigación, grant award PID2021-129002NB-I00.

REFERENCES

Agné, H. ; Dellmuth, L., & Tallberg, J. (2015). Does Stakeholder Involvement Foster Democratic Legitimacy in International Organisations? An Empirical Assessment of a Normative Theory. *Review of International Organisations 10*(4): 465–488. doi:10.1007/s11558-014-9212-6.

Alemanno, A. (2015). Stakeholder engagement in regulatory policy. In *Regulatory Policy in Perspective: A Reader's Companion to the OECD Regulatory Policy Outlook 2015* (OECD, 2015). http://dx.doi.org/10.1787/9789264241800-en.

Álvarez, S. & Sachs, S. (2023). Where do stakeholders come from? *Academy of Management Review, 48*(2), 187–202. https://doi.org/10.5465/amr.2019.0077.

Berman, A., Büthe, T., Maggetti, M., & Pauwelyn, J. (2022) Introduction: Rethinking Stakeholder Participation in Global Governance. In Pauwelyn, J. et al (Eds), *Rethinking Participation in Global Governance: Voice and Influence after Stakeholder Reforms in Global Finance and Health.* Oxford: OUP.

Bertelli, A.M., & Sinclair, J.A. (2015). Mass Administrative Reorganisation, Media Attention, and the Paradox of Information. *Public Administration Review, 75*(6), 855–866. https://doi.org/10.1111/puar.12396.

Bitektine, A. (2011). Toward a Theory of Social Judgment of Organisations: The Case of Legitimacy, Reputation, and Status. *Academy of Management Review, 36*(1), 151–179. https://doi.org/10.5465/amr.2009.0382.

Bitektine, A., Hill, K., Song, F., & Vanderberghe, C. (2020). Organisational Legitimacy, Reputation and Status: Insights from Micro-Level Measurement. *Academy of Management Discoveries, 6*(1), 107–136. https://doi.org/10.5465/amd.2017.0007.

Carpenter, D. (2001). *The Forging of Bureaucratic Autonomy: Reputations, Networks, and Policy Innovation in Executive Agencies 1862–1928.* Princeton: Princeton University Press.

Carpenter, D. (2010). *Reputation and Power: Organisational Image and Pharmaceutical Regulation at the FDA.* Princeton: Princeton University Press.

Coni-Zimmer, M., Deitelhoff, N., & Schumann, D. (2023). The Path of Least Resistance: Why International Institutions Maintain Dialogue Forums. *International Affairs 99*(3), 941–961. https://doi.org/10.1093/ia/iiad032.

Daugirdas, K. (2015). Reputation and the Responsibility of International Organisations. *European Journal of International Law 25*(4), 991–1018. doi:10.1093/ejil/chu087.

Daugirdas, K. (2019). Reputation as a Disciplinarian of International Organisations. *American Journal of International Law, 113*(2), 221–271. doi:10.1017/ajil.2018.122.

Dellmuth, L., Scholte, J.A., Tallberg, J., & Verhaegen, S. (2022). *Citizens, Elites, and the Legitimacy of Global Governance.* Oxford: OUP.

DeMenno, M.B. & Büthe, T. (2022). Voice and Influence in Global Governance: An Analytical Framework. In Pauwelyn, J. et al (Eds), *Rethinking Participation*

in Global Governance: Voice and Influence after Stakeholder Reforms in Global Finance and Health. Oxford: OUP.
Freeman, R.E. (1984). *Strategic Management: A Stakeholder Approach*. Boston: Pitman.
Hanegraaff, M., Vergauwen, J., & Beyers, J. (2020). Should I Stay or Should I Go? Explaining Variation in Nonstate Actor Advocacy over Time in Global Governance. *Governance, 33,* 287–304.
Hannah, E., Scott, J., & Wilkinson, R. (2017). Reforming WTO-Civil Society Engagement. *World Trade Review*, *16*(3), 427–448. https://doi.org/10.1017/S1474745616000446.
Helm, S. (2007). One Reputation or Many? Comparing Stakeholders' Perceptions of Corporate Reputation. *Corporate Communications: An International Journal*, *12*(3), 238–254. https://doi.org/10.1108/13563280710776842.
Maor, M. (2016). Missing Areas in the Bureaucratic Reputation Framework. *Politics and Governance, 4*(2), 80-90 . http://doi.org/10.17645/pag.v4i2.570.
OECD (2016). *International Regulatory Co-operation: The Role of International Organisations in Fostering Better Rules of Globalisation*, OECD Publishing, Paris. http://dx.doi.org/10.1787/9789264244047-en.
OECD (2019). *The Contribution of International Organisations to a Rule-Based International System*, OECD Publishing, Paris. https://www.oecd.org/gov/regulatory-policy/IO-Rule-Based%20System.pdf.
OECD (2021). *Compendium of International Relations' Practices: Working Towards More Effective International Instruments 2021*. OECD Publishing, Paris, 82–83. https://doi.org/10.1787/846a5fa0-en.
OECD (2021_1). *OECD Regulatory Policy Outlook 2021*, OECD Publishing, Paris, https://doi.org/10.1787/38b0fdb1-en.
Pauwelyn, J., Maggetti, M., Büthe, T., & Berman, A. (Eds) (2022). *Rethinking Stakeholder Participation in Global Governance*. Oxford: OUP.
Raithel, S. & Schwaiger, M. (2014). The Effects of Corporate Reputation Perceptions of the General Public on Shareholder Value. *Strategic Management Journal*, *36*: 945–956. https://doi.org/10.1002/smj.2248.
Saz-Carranza, A., Maggetti, M., Yesilkagit, K. and Coen, D. (2023) Mapping and Unpacking Global Governance Bodies: A Cross Sectional And Cross Organizational Analysis. *International Studies Quarterly*, 67(3), sqad040 https://doi.org/10.1093/isq/sqad040.
Stewart, R. (2014). Remedying Disregard in Global Regulatory Governance: Accountability, Participation, and Responsiveness. *The American Journal of International Law*, *108*(2), 211–270. https://doi.org/10.5305/amerjintelaw.108.2.0211.
Verhoest, K., Boon, J., Boye, S., & Salomonsen, H.H. (2021). How Does Organisational Task Matter for the Reputation of Public Agencies? *Regulation and Governance, 17(1),* pp. 158–176. https://doi.org/10.1111/rego.12441.

APPENDIX

Table A2.1a Number of IOs by stakeholder engagement cluster

Stakeholder engagement	1 (N=7)	2 (N=5)	3 (N=4)	4 (N=6)	Total (N=22)
IO specific	7 (100.0%)	0 (0.0%)	0 (0.0%)	0 (0.0%)	7 (31.8%)
Societal	0 (0.0%)	0 (0.0%)	4 (100.0%)	0 (0.0%)	4 (18.2%)
Political	0 (0.0%)	0 (0.0%)	0 (0.0%)	6 (100.0%)	6 (27.3%)
Encompassing	0 (0.0%)	5 (100.0%)	0 (0.0%)	0 (0.0%)	5 (22.7%)

Note: p-value: < 0.001

Table A2.1b Stakeholder engagement clusters by age

Age	IO-specific (N=7)	Encompassing (N=5)	Societal (N=4)	Political (N=6)	Total (N=22)
Mean (SD)	67.000 (44.889)	84.000 (35.574)	31.500 (14.248)	74.500 (48.161)	66.455 (41.505)
Range	24.000–148.000	46.000– 125.000	19.000–52.000	31.000–158.000	19.000–158.000

Note: p-value: 0.277

Table A2.1c Stakeholder engagement clusters by budget

Budget (log)	IO-specific (N=7)	Encompassing (N=5)	Societal (N=4)	Political (N=6)	Total (N=22)
N-Miss	0	0	1	0	1
Mean (SD)	6.975 (0.951)	8.019 (0.599)	6.779 (1.367)	7.563 (0.651)	7.364 (0.927)
Range	5.740– 8.638	7.531– 8.709	5.820–8.344	6.420–8.217	5.740–8.709

Note: p-value: 0.154

Table A2.1d *Stakeholder engagement clusters by annual memories*

Annual memory public and online	IO-specific (N=7)	Encompassing (N=5)	Societal (N=4)	Political (N=6)	Total (N=22)
Mean (SD)	0.714 (0.488)	1.000 (0.000)	1.000 (0.000)	0.667 (0.516)	0.818 (0.395)
Range	0.000– 1.000	1.000– 1.000	1.000– 1.000	0.000– 1.000	0.000– 1.000

Note: p-value: 0.371

Table A2.1e *Stakeholder engagement clusters by regular press releases*

Regular press releases	IO-specific (N=7)	Encompassing (N=5)	Societal (N=4)	Political (N=6)	Total (N=22)
Mean (SD)	0.857 (0.378)	0.800 (0.447)	1.000 (0.000)	1.000 (0.000)	0.909 (0.294)
Range	0.000– 1.000	0.000– 1.000	1.000– 1.000	1.000– 1.000	0.000– 1.000

Note: p-value: 0.634

Table A2.1f *Stakeholder engagement clusters by proportion of Global South countries*

Global South	IO-specific (N=7)	Encompassing (N=5)	Societal (N=4)	Political (N=6)	Total (N=22)
Mean (SD)	0.487 (0.247)	0.518 (0.314)	0.522 (0.192)	0.823 (0.041)	0.592 (0.251)
Range	0.000– 0.800	0.000– 0.800	0.300– 0.770	0.790– 0.880	0.000– 0.880

Note: p-value: 0.056

Table A2.1g *Stakeholder engagement clusters by territorial scope: regional*

Territorial scope: Regional	IO-specific (N=7)	Encompassing (N=5)	Societal (N=4)	Political (N=6)	Total (N=22)
Mean (SD)	0.143 (0.378)	0.000 (0.000)	0.000 (0.000)	0.167 (0.408)	0.091 (0.294)
Range	0.000– 1.000	0.000– 0.000	0.000– 0.000	0.000– 1.000	0.000–1.000

Note: p-value: 0.718

Table A2.1h *Stakeholder engagement clusters by membership*

Membership	IO-specific (N=7)	Encompassing (N=5)	Societal (N=4)	Political (N=6)	Total (N=22)
Broad/Open	5 (71.4%)	1 (20.0%)	1 (25.0%)	5 (83.3%)	12 (54.5%)
Specialised/Closed	2 (28.6%)	4 (80.0%)	3 (75.0%)	1 (16.7%)	10 (45.5%)

Note: p-value: 0.085

Table A2.1i *Stakeholder engagement clusters by sector*

Sector	IO-specific (N=7)	Encompassing (N=5)	Societal (N=4)	Political (N=6)	Total (N=22)
Measure/ Standards	3 (42.9%)	2 (40.0%)	0 (0.0%)	0 (0.0%)	5 (22.7%)
Climate	0 (0.0%)	0 (0.0%)	0 (0.0%)	1 (16.7%)	1 (4.5%)
Finance	0 (0.0%)	1 (20.0%)	0 (0.0%)	0 (0.0%)	1 (4.5%)
Health	1 (14.3%)	0 (0.0%)	3 (75.0%)	1 (16.7%)	5 (22.7%)
Infrastructure	1 (14.3%)	0 (0.0%)	0 (0.0%)	1 (16.7%)	2 (9.1%)
Technological	0 (0.0%)	1 (20.0%)	0 (0.0%)	1 (16.7%)	2 (9.1%)
Trade	2 (28.6%)	1 (20.0%)	1 (25.0%)	2 (33.3%)	6 (27.3%)

Note: p-value: 0.325

Table A2.1j *Stakeholder engagement clusters by perception*

Perception	IO-specific (N=7)	Encompassing (N=5)	Societal (N=4)	Political (N=6)	Total (N=22)
Mean (SD)	5.747 (3.240)	9.524 (2.168)	6.293 (3.056)	6.379 (4.491)	6.877 (3.502)
Range	2.706– 11.581	5.957– 11.606	3.515– 9.695	1.340– 11.838	1.340– 11.838

Note: p-value: 0.294

Stakeholder Engagement Variables

Questions from the IO Partnership Survey:

1.1. Which of the following actors are regarded as 'stakeholders' by your organisation?
   * Tick all boxes that apply, add rows if necessary.

1.2. Which of the stakeholders identified in question 1.1 participate in one or more of the following stages of international rulemaking?

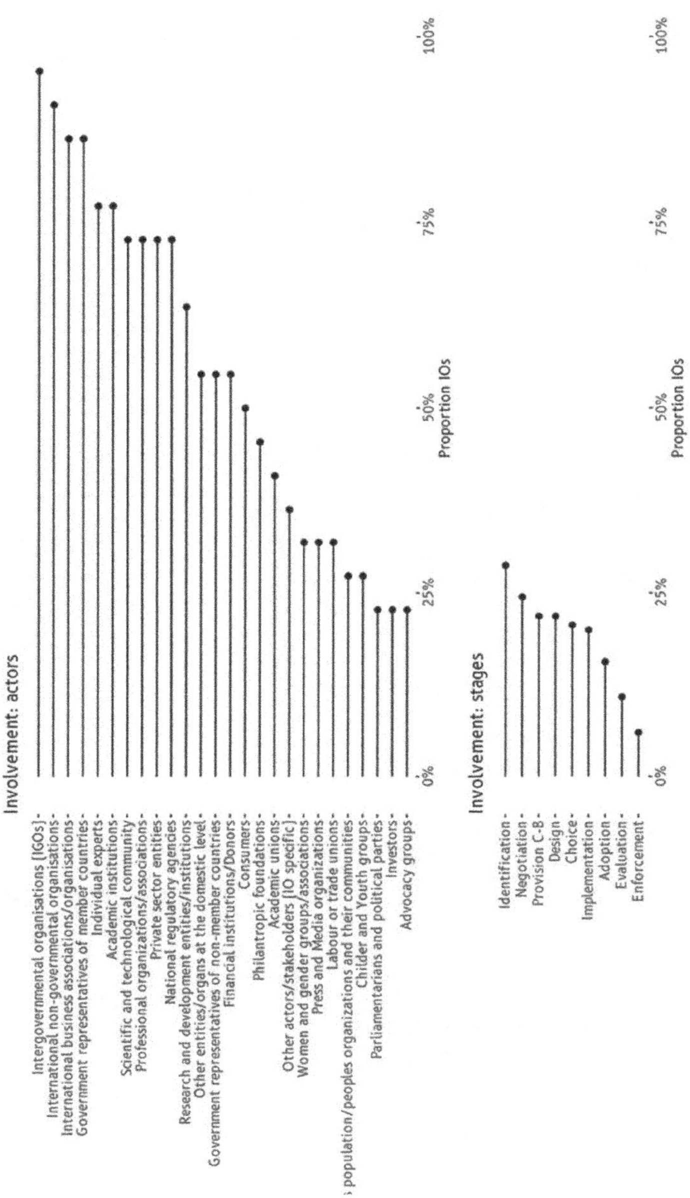

Figure A2.1 *Proportion of different actors involved in rule-making processes and distribution of involvement across stages of rule-making*

'Stakeholder Engagement' Variables by Cluster

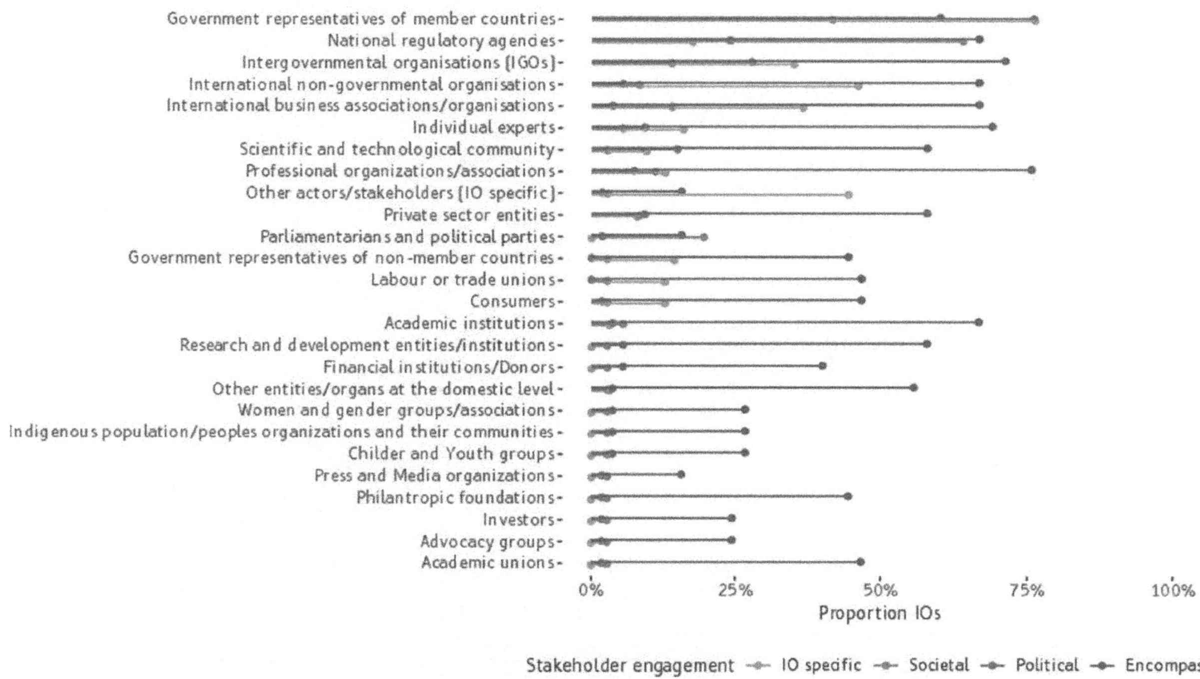

Figure A2.2 *Proportion of actors involved in rule-making by cluster*

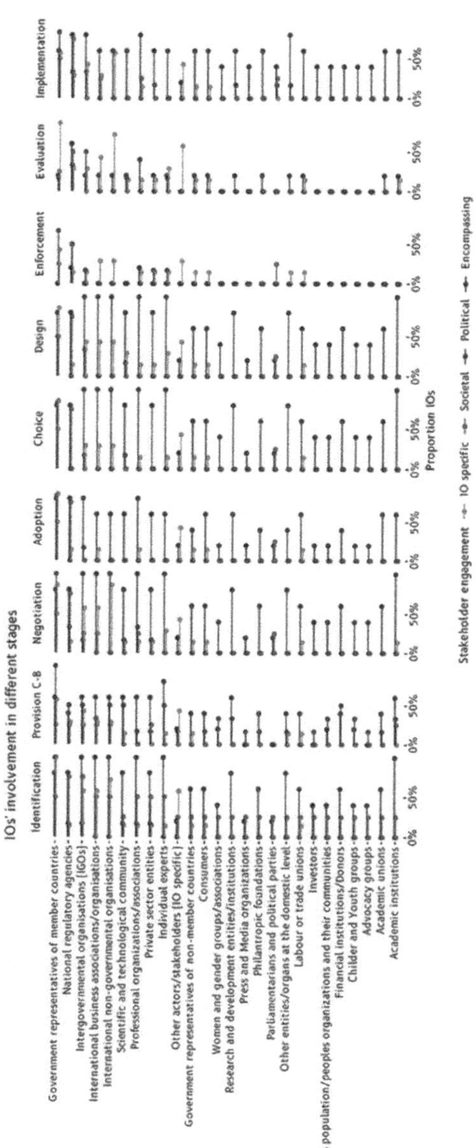

Figure A2.3 Proportion of different actors involved in rule-making processes by cluster across stages of rule-making

3. Beyond participation: meaningful engagement of non-state actors in international organisations – lessons learnt from the process to strengthen observer engagement in the UNFCCC

Emma Bertipaglia and Hayley Walker

1 INTRODUCTION

As the threat of climate change becomes increasingly stark, the United Nations Framework Convention on Climate Change (UNFCCC) has taken on an unprecedented level of public and political interest. The annual Conference of the Parties (COP) is frequently the largest gathering of heads of state outside the United Nations General Assembly (UNGA) and attracts tens of thousands of participants. COP 27, held in Sharm-el-Sheikh in November 2022, opened its doors to 33,449[1] delegates, of which 13,981 were representatives of non-state actors ("observers'), and COP 28 in Dubai counted 97,372 registered participants, including 25,360 participants from observer organisations (UNFCCC, 2023).

While the UNFCCC welcomes more observers than any other UN process, COPs have often been criticised for being exclusive, with many observers reporting feeling shut out and unable to meaningfully engage with the UNFCCC system. When considering the engagement of non-state actors in international organisations (IOs), there is an evident need to move beyond mere participation. As the UNFCCC transitions from a primary focus on intergovernmental negotiations to a new chapter focused on implementing the landmark Paris Agreement and on raising ambition, the need for effective stakeholder engagement has never been greater (Bäckstrand et al., 2017; Hale, 2016; Kuyper et al.,

[1] This is a conservative number as the list of participants does not cover all categories.

2018). To address this, the UNFCCC launched a review process to strengthen observer engagement. The authors of this chapter were engaged as consultants by the UNFCCC to design and deliver the review process.[2]

Findings suggest that certain actors risk systemic exclusion from consultative and decision-making processes on account of structural and resource inequalities, even when these are designed with inclusivity and fair representation as guiding principles. Burnout, lack of time and capacity, translation, and technological constraints are only some of the barriers identified throughout the review process. When aiming to be genuinely inclusive, organisers should make specific provisions that allow under-resourced groups to contribute to the process by overcoming the very practical barriers they face. The chapter shares some best practices and lessons learnt from the review process and observer consultations, aiming not only to advance the state-of-the-art on stakeholder engagement at the UNFCCC, but also to offer valuable insights and advice for other IOs wishing to embark on a similar consultative process to enhance representation and inclusion.

The contribution of this chapter is twofold. Firstly, after providing a brief description of the review process's structure, including the principles, phases, and issues addressed, and presenting the participation data, it will summarise the key challenges faced by non-state actors wishing to engage with one of the world's largest and most politicised IOs and some possible solutions. The chapter will distinguish between actions that can be taken by the UNFCCC secretariat and actions that fall beyond the limits of the secretariat's mandate or capacity, or which would require the consent of the 198 governments that collectively constitute 'the Parties'.

Secondly, the authors will reflect upon their experiences in implementing the process. The chapter will highlight logistical and technical aspects that proved beneficial and enriched the experience and will draw attention to the challenges and barriers faced in ensuring fair and inclusive participation of stakeholders. While the co-creative and flexible characteristics of the review

[2] As practitioners and researchers, we are speaking in our individual capacities, and our views do not reflect the opinions or positions of any singular organisation or group. Having actively participated in the delivery of the review process, we bring our own set of experiences, skills, and knowledge to the table. Our positionality informs our approach to this project, and we recognise this may influence the perception of the actions taken within the project and their effectiveness. To mitigate this, we seek to be transparent about biases and limitations, actively seek feedback from colleagues and the stakeholders we worked with, and continually reflect on our own positionality. This study brings together the authors' and CFPs' views on the review process and does not include the views of the wider group of participants, as these were not available at the time of writing.

process were generally appreciated by the participants, overall participation was considerably lower than the total number of admitted observer organisations that could have potentially taken part. Though carried out remotely in its entirety, the distribution of participants based on their UN groupings did not drastically deviate from the constituency distribution during in-person engagements such as COPs. Most strikingly, although many participation and access barriers were removed, under-resourced groups, such as indigenous peoples' and youth organisations, did not benefit from increased involvement and even reported difficulties in catering to an additional workstream on top of an increasingly complex intergovernmental mechanism.

2 CONTEXTUAL OVERVIEW

The UNFCCC entered into force on 21 March 1994, with the objective to 'stabilise greenhouse gas concentrations in the atmosphere at a level that would prevent dangerous anthropogenic interference with the climate system' (UNFCCC, 1992, article 2). The COP is the supreme decision-making body of the Convention and is the meeting that garners the most media attention every year.

It is important to note that UNFCCC conferences are not open to the public. The admission of non-state actors as observers is provided for in Article 7, paragraph 6 of the Convention. Non-state actors do not have decision-making power and must be registered to an admitted observer organisation belonging to one of the following three categories:

- The United Nations System and its Specialised Agencies;
- Intergovernmental organisations (IGOs);
- Non-governmental organisations (NGOs).

Of the three observer categories in the UNFCCC process, NGOs represent the largest group, and many of them are organised within a 'constituency' system of loose groups with diverse but broadly clustered interests or perspectives. Each NGO constituency is represented and organised by a constituency focal point (CFP). CFPs are individuals selected from among the member organisations. As each constituency has its own governance structure, the process for selecting CFPs varies by constituency, as well as the duration of the mandate and the number of CFPs. CFPs provide a conduit for the exchange of official information between their constituents and the UNFCCC secretariat and assume the role on a voluntary basis, in addition to their regular workload. The constituencies mirror the nine Major Groups (see the list below), established in Agenda 21 and re-confirmed in the outcomes of the Rio+20 summit (A/

RES/66/288 – The future we want). Notably, not all admitted observer organisations are affiliated with a constituency, and of those that are affiliated, not all are active members.

NGO observer constituency groups

- Business and Industry NGOs (BINGO)
- Indigenous peoples' organisations (IPO)
- Trade Union NGOs (TUNGO)
- Environmental NGOs (ENGO)
- Local government and municipal authorities (LGMA)
- Women and gender constituency (WGC)
- Farmers
- Research and Independent NGOs (RINGO)
- Children and Youth constituency (YOUNGO)

2.1 Origin of the observer review process

Ensuring meaningful, inclusive, fair and transparent engagement of all stakeholders in the UNFCCC has become increasingly challenging due to the linear growth in observer[3] participation (Figure 3.1) and the diversified engagement channels in the UNFCCC sessions. At COP 26 in 2021, observers faced logistical difficulties and limited access to engagement opportunities. Some were due to COVID-related restrictions and technical problems, such as issues with the launch of the COP 26 virtual platform, but others were inherent to the process, such as the large number of observer participants and limited engagement opportunities. In response, the UNFCCC secretariat decided to initiate a holistic '*Process to strengthen observer engagement in the UNFCCC*' (hereafter 'the review process').

The review process had two objectives: first, to collectively find concrete and implementable **action points** to address inherent challenges that the secretariat and observer organisations face in ensuring meaningful, inclusive, fair and transparent observer engagement in the UNFCCC process within their respective responsibilities and mandates. Secondly, to provide both the observers and the UNFCCC secretariat with a **shared understanding** of the constraints, opportunities, and evolving contexts within which they each operate. The process convened consultations on a broad range of issues; it was

---

[3] From now on, when referring to the category of 'observers', both NGOs and IGO-admitted organisations are to be considered included. As they constitute the largest group, NGOs will be mentioned more frequently, but the review process was open to both.

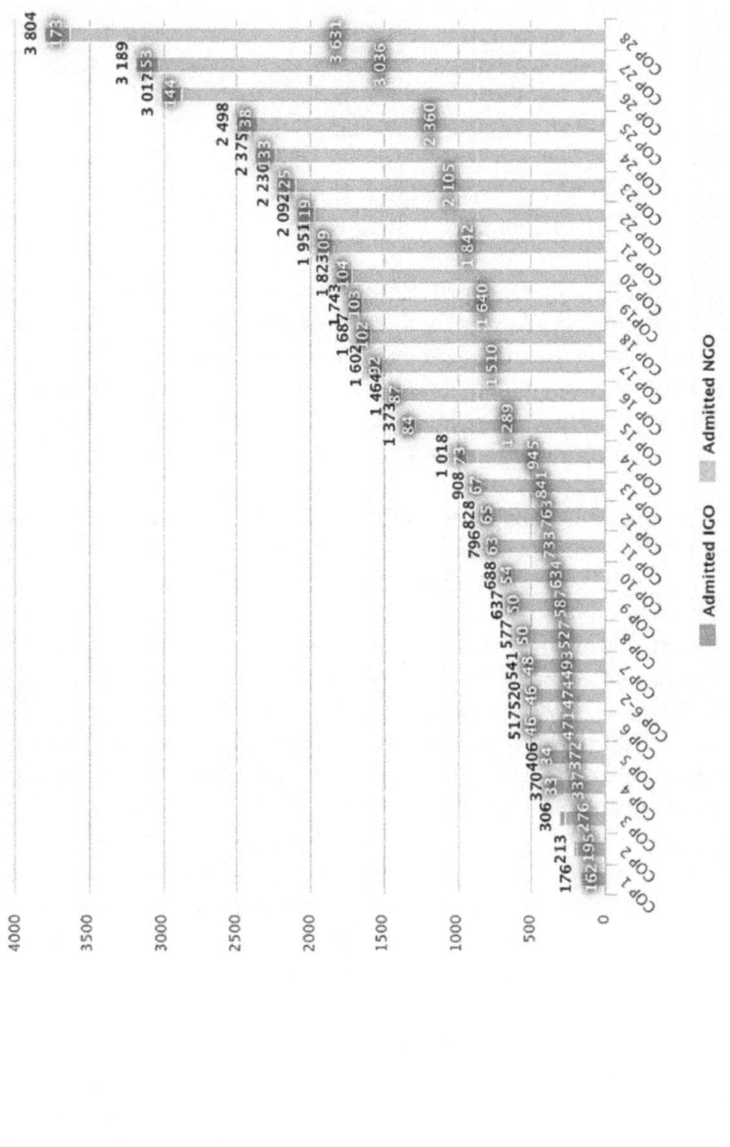

Source: UNFCCC (n.d.), 'Statistics on admission webpage'

Figure 3.1 *Cumulative number of admitted observers 1995–2023*

co-creative, collaborative, and solutions-focused in nature and fully remote in its implementation.

2.2 Phases of the review process

The process was open to the approximately 3,050 observer organisations admitted to the UNFCCC and took place throughout 2022 and early 2023. It was broadly divided into three parts. During *Phase one*, the issues relating to observer engagement under the purview of the secretariat and observer organisations were collaboratively identified with focal points of NGO constituencies and interested IGOs as follows:

- Agenda item 1 was dedicated to identifying the highly diverse roles, responsibilities, and goals of the various observer organisations, in order to facilitate more effective engagement during the sessions.
- Agenda item 2 delved into the issues of representation and equitable access, including representational deficits such as the scarce numbers of observers from developing countries, and discussions around potential conflicts of interest.
- Agenda item 3 considered proposals to improve the existing admission and accreditation systems, including a differentiated badging system linked to the purpose of observer participation and related activities.
- Agenda item 4 assessed the extent to which existing modes of observer engagement allowed for meaningful engagement and highlighted a number of lesser-known channels for observers to get involved in the work of the UNFCCC throughout the year, not just during the COP.
- Agenda item 5 offered an opportunity for participants to share their views and experiences and align their expectations around the most effective way for observers to engage with the constituted bodies,[4] considering the technical nature and specific mandates of these groups.
- Agenda item 6 explored the measures that can be taken by the organisers of UNFCCC sessions to improve the operational arrangements in and around the COPs, including venue logistics and virtual participation, and the financial barriers that are faced by many observers.

[4] The COPs and the meetings of the Subsidiary Bodies (SBs) are the most high-profile and well-attended UNFCCC sessions. However, there are over a dozen 'constituted bodies' that meet throughout the year to work on specific topics and that offer engagement opportunities for observers.

In order to assess the level of interest and engagement in the process, two surveys were conducted.

- Expression of interest survey
- Registration to focus groups.

The first survey was sent out to all admitted organisations (both NGOs and IGOs) – 3,047 – and the total number of respondents amounted to 304. The second survey was subsequently sent to the respondents of the first survey, and the final number of registrants amounted to 283.

Phase two consisted of a series of focus groups with observers in the form of virtual meetings, and the submission of written inputs. To make the involvement flexible, participants could use either format or both.

A total of 20 focus group meetings were held between July and September 2022 (see Table 3.1), with the participation of 157 representatives from admitted organisations in total – some took part in only one meeting, while others participated in a number of focus groups, according to their specific interests. A total of 71 written submissions were received. The constituency and regional distribution for both the focus groups and written submissions are available in Figure 3.2a, Figure 3.2b, Figure 3.3a, and Figure 3.3b, to be compared with

Table 3.1 Summary of focus group meetings and written submissions

Agenda item	Number of meetings	Timeline of focus group meetings	Total number of focus group participants	Total written submissions
Observer organisations	5	August	46	13
Representation and equitable access	5	September	48	8
Admission and registration	4	August	40	10
Current modes of observer engagement	2	August	32	9
Constituted bodies and support teams	2	August	27	5
Administrative and operational arrangements and financial support	2	July	20	26

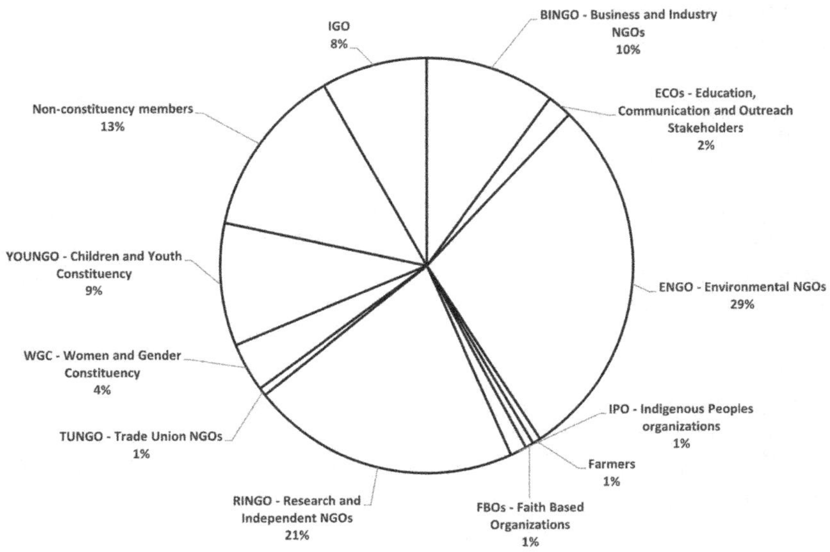

Figure 3.2a *Focus group constituency*

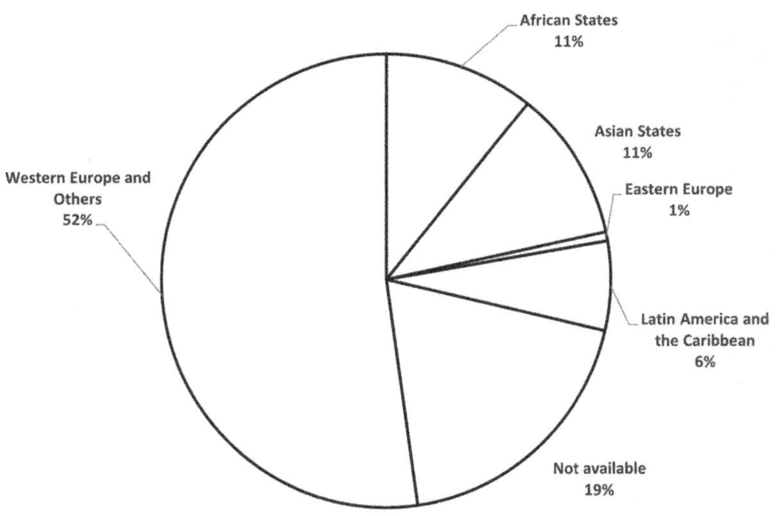

Figure 3.2b *Regional distribution*

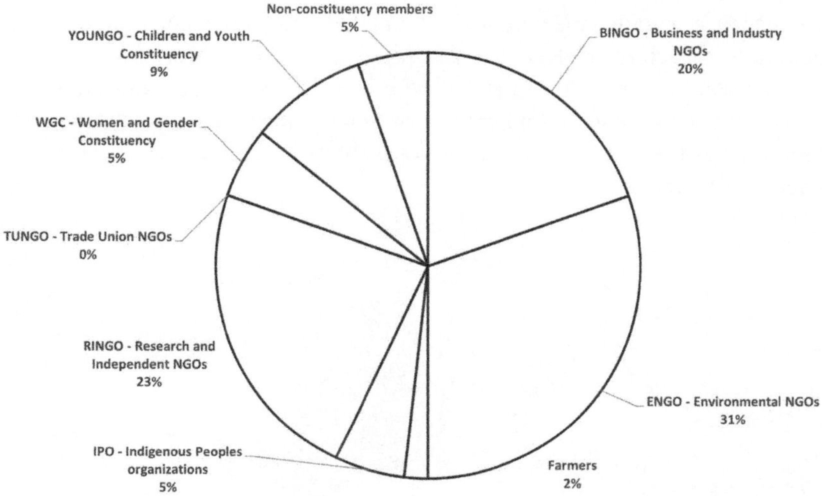

Figure 3.3a *Written submissions constituency*

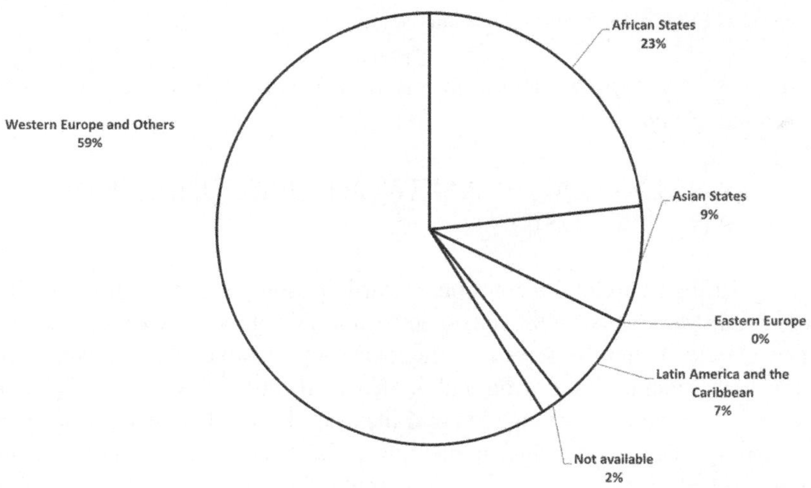

Figure 3.3b *Regional distribution*

the general constituency and regional distribution of admitted organisations (Figure 3.4 and Figure 3.5).

Phase three entailed the definition of tangible action points that can be taken forward by all actors involved, the assessment of additional work necessary for the successful completion of the review process, and a shared understanding of the limitations. It should be noted that this chapter's analysis excludes this last phase, as the authors were either not involved or had limited involvement in the implementation of it.

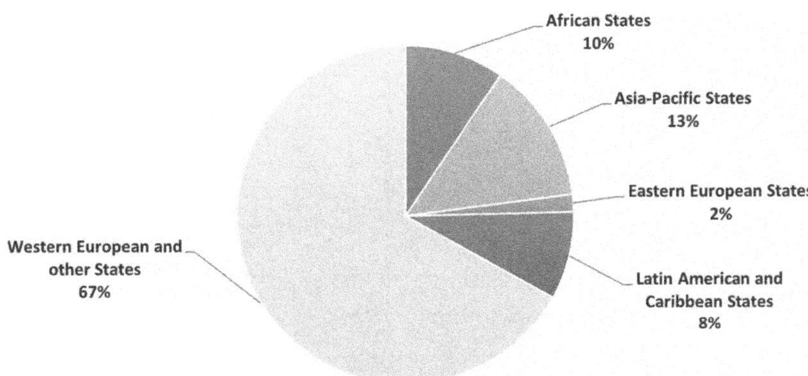

Source: UNFCCC (n.d.), 'Statistics on admission webpage'.

Figure 3.4 Admitted organisations as observers to the UNFCCC process by regional group

3 ANALYTICAL FRAMEWORK: PARTICIPATION AND INCLUSION

Distinguishing between the concepts of participation and inclusion forms the basis of our framework for the retrospective analysis of the review process, and it permits advancing the scholarly understanding of stakeholder engagement in IOs by extending theory from public management to the domain of global governance. Whereas participation and inclusion have often been considered overlapping terms, with inclusion referring to the extent to which participation is open to and representative of socioeconomic diversity, Quick and Feldman (2011) employ these terms to refer to two distinct dimensions of stakeholder engagement (Table 3.2). The goal of *participation* is to 'increase public input orientated primarily to the content of programmes and policies' (p. 272) through, for example, inviting many stakeholders to participate, making the

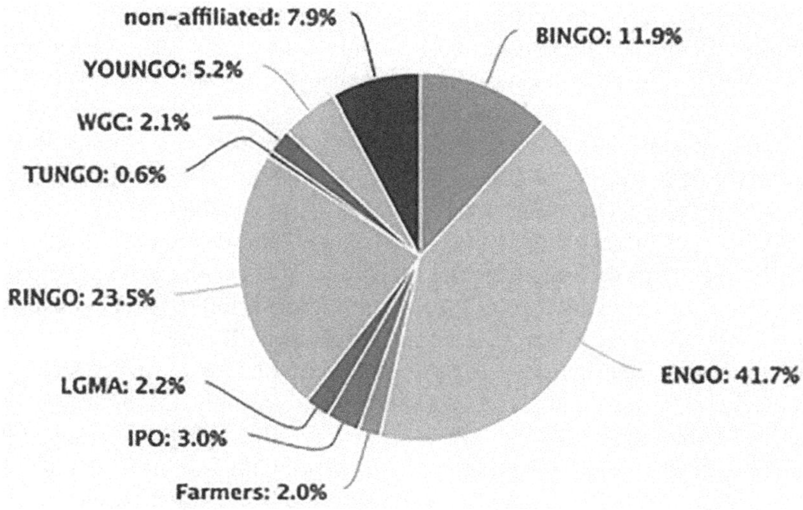

Source: UNFCCC (n.d.), 'Statistics on admission webpage'.

Figure 3.5 Constituency affiliation of admitted NGOs

Table 3.2 Participation and inclusion

Participation	Inclusion
• Oriented to increasing the level of *input* • Seeking high participation rates • Broadly accessible process • Collecting input to inform specific decisions	• Focus on building community capacity to *implement* the decisions • Aimed at creating relationships and networks among people, across different issues, throughout time • Extensive and continuous framework for interaction

Source: Adapted from Quick & Feldman (2011)

process broadly accessible and representative, collecting stakeholder inputs, and feeding them into policy decisions.

For Quick and Feldman, the goal of *inclusion* is to make connections between people, among issues, and over time, in order to create a community with the capacity to implement the decisions taken and tackle related issues. Quick and Feldman's understanding of inclusion is distinct from the common understanding of the notion as relating to the openness and representativeness of a process and should instead be understood as relating to the empowerment of its participants. This expansive goal is not easily broken down into a checklist of actions, since it depends on an 'ongoing framework for interaction' (p. 274).[5]

Framing stakeholders as the providers of *input* or as the *implementers* of decisions seems apt in the present context of a paradigm shift in the UNFCCC from a primary focus on intergovernmental negotiations intended to deliver a global framework agreement on climate change – in which stakeholders were called upon to provide inputs to the negotiations but generally operated on the periphery – to a post-Paris era focused on implementation and characterised by 'hybrid multilateralism' (Bäckstrand et al., 2017, Kuyper et al., 2018) that brings together state and non-state actors (Biniaz, 2020; Hale, 2016; Obergassel et al., 2022; Walker et al., 2021). Attention is increasingly turning towards the actions taken by stakeholders, who now operate at the 'very core' (Hale, 2016) of the regime as the driving force in implementing the transition to a net-zero world in line with the regulatory framework agreed by governments.

In this new era in the UNFCCC process, greater levels of *inclusion* will be required. There have been calls for a change in mindset around the purpose of COPs, from acting primarily as a negotiation space to instead acting as a platform for learning and community-building (Mar et al., 2023) and for the establishment of a comprehensive, long-term stakeholder framework that should be collaborative (i.e., co-owned by participating stakeholders) and catalytic (i.e., broker new relationships and/or establish a learning facility to improve stakeholders' capacity to make an impact) (Chan et al., 2015). That being said, others have pointed out that the UNFCCC remains 'primarily intergovernmental' in nature (Biniaz, 2020: 6) and that a shift from regime-building to implementation does not signal the end of negotiations (Walker et al., 2021: 331). It seems likely that stakeholders' inputs will continue to be required by decision-makers, and so *participation* remains a relevant consideration.

The two objectives of the review process are reflective of these two dimensions of stakeholder engagement.

To collectively find concrete and implementable solutions for the secretariat, observers, and presiding officers to strengthen observer engagement in the UNFCCC *(participation)*.To provide a shared understanding of the constraints, opportunities, and evolving contexts in which they operate *(inclusion)*.In order

[5] Quick and Feldman's work is geared towards public engagement and governments' relationship with their public rather than stakeholder engagement in IOs. The types of stakeholders included in the former include towns or municipalities, as opposed to the more heterogeneous stakeholders found in the UNFCCC, characterised by fierce internal politics and unequal power dynamics that tend to be overlooked and over simplified (Allan, 2020).

to maximise inputs (*participation*), the review process was open to all observer organisations, fully remote in its implementation, operating across different time zones and with simultaneous interpretation upon request. In order to empower observers to implement not only the concrete solutions identified through the review process but, more broadly, to work together to achieve their shared goal of advancing the implementation of the Paris Agreement (*inclusion*), the review process aimed to improve observers' understanding of the constraints within which the secretariat operates and of their own distinct situations. Furthermore, through its co-creative and collaborative nature, it aimed to foster a framework for ongoing interaction and strengthen networks and relationships (*inclusion*).

4 METHODOLOGY

As highlighted by Bensimon (2007) and Zeichner (2007), practitioners' rich and in-depth experiences in the field continue to be an underused source of information that can promote innovation and organisational progress. This is especially true when it comes to IO-led stakeholder engagements, particularly in fully remote settings after the COVID-19 pandemic. Through a combination of analysis of primary data from the review process, interviews with CFPs, and the authors' personal reflections as practitioners in the process, this chapter aims not only to advance the state-of-the-art on stakeholder engagement at the UNFCCC, but also to offer valuable insights and advice for other IOs that may wish to embark on a similar consultative process to enhance representation and inclusion.

In order to best address the research objectives, the Accidental Ethnography (AE) methodology – a reflexive, interpretivist, and practical method of inquiry – was employed. AE utilises a practitioner-researcher awareness to explore the learning of a group, community, or organisation. The methodology incorporates data sources developed in situ with ethnographic methods, allowing for subtle nuances of the practitioner's personal experience (Levitan et al., 2020). This approach seemed particularly fitting – as practitioners working in the review process, we found ourselves in the unique position of understanding and being able to provide perspective and insights both from the observers' side (as the authors participated in the UNFCCC process as part of a constituency), as well as grasping the context and implications of implementation from the secretariat side. This chapterr stems from the effort to make explicit valuable tacit knowledge (Nonaka and Konno, 1998) from an angle that could prove useful for practitioners in addition to contributing to the academic literature.

The findings and discussions are the result of a tripartite method of data collection. The first consists of rigorous thematic coding of primary data from the review process, namely the outcomes of a total of 20 focus group meetings, held between July and September 2022, and 72 written submissions, out of which four major clusters of cross-cutting issues emerged. The second method of data collection consisted of six CFPs interviews, covering five out of the nine constituencies.[6] The 30-minute-long, semi-structured interviews were conducted during February and March 2023, and addressed the first two phases of the review process, in which the authors were involved as practitioners. The interviews sought to determine which elements of the review process were (in)effective and to explore possible ways to improve similar processes in the future. Every interview was recorded, transcribed, and coded. The third method of data collection consists of the personal reflections and experiences of the authors as practitioners in the process. This data informed the subsequent section on lessons learnt (Table 3.3).

Table 3.3 Constituency Focal Points (CFPs) interviewed

Interviewee	Constituency (refer to the list earlier in this chapter)
CFP 1	BINGO
CFP 2	ENGO
CFP 3	RINGO
CFP 4	RINGO
CFP 5	Farmers*
CFP 6	YOUNGO*

Note: * indicates under-resourced constituency

5 SUBSTANTIVE OUTCOMES OF THE REVIEW PROCESS

The review process's aim was to collectively and constructively find solutions to the challenges actors face in ensuring meaningful, inclusive, fair and transparent observer engagement in the UNFCCC process, based on a mutual understanding of stakeholders' mandates, responsibilities, and constraints. Discussions were structured to consider these challenges, foster a mutual understanding of constraints and opportunities, and explore potential

[6] All CFPs were contacted for an interview, but some constituencies, including some of the most under-resourced and under-represented ones, did not respond, and therefore we are not able to include their insights in the study.

solutions. Four major clusters of cross-cutting issues emerged from the focus group discussions and the inputs provided through written submissions as key elements to strengthen observers' engagement in the UNFCCC.

5.1 Quality of engagement

Observers reinforced that simply registering for and attending the COP does not constitute meaningful engagement, i.e., the possibility for observers to inform and influence decision-making, convey concerns, and contribute positively to the process with their expertise and experience. They also aim to network and build awareness and alliances, and work collaboratively towards solutions. Engagement opportunities are finite in number (speaking slots, side event slots, registration quota, meeting space, access to negotiation meeting rooms, etc.). Therefore, as the scale of participation increases, the piece of the 'participation pie' observers can expect to receive becomes smaller, causing frustrations and increasing the burden on the secretariat's resources. In other words, a greater number of observers participating in UNFCCC sessions can actively work against the quality of their engagement.

These difficulties experienced by observers at UNFCCC meetings are compounded by a feeling that their contributions fail to result in real impact and influence. Access to government delegates is challenging to secure at the COP on account of the multiple competing pressures exerted on them by the negotiating process. Even when observers are able to find the opportunity to sit down and interact with negotiators, they often find that their positions are fixed, having been formulated and agreed upon at the national and group levels in the months prior to the COP. Engagement with decision-makers during the pre-negotiation stage, for example, during the domestic policy-setting process and particularly when governments are developing national climate targets and plans, offers observers a more effective opportunity to inform and influence both domestic policy and international negotiating positions.

Many participants of the review process expressed concerns and frustrations stemming from the rules of procedure at formal UNFCCC sessions. Rule 6 highlights the Party-driven nature of the process and stresses that those participating 'as observers' do so without the right to vote. While presiding officers may encourage Parties to allow enough time for observers to speak, they are unable to impose such constraints upon them. As a result, observers are only allowed to make statements once Parties' statements have finished. Changes to the rules of procedure to allow for more meaningful observer engagement would require a decision by Parties and therefore fall beyond the purview of the secretariat and the review process. Observers can, however, approach governments that are sympathetic to their plight and advocate for these changes.

Within the UNFCCC, multiple opportunities for engagement exist throughout the year, including Regional Climate Weeks (RCWs), the Marrakech Partnership for Global Climate Action (MP/GCA), and the meetings of the various constituted bodies that carry forward the work of the UNFCCC in areas including adaptation, finance, capacity-building, and loss and damage. These are not subject to the rules of procedure of formal UNFCCC sessions and operate with their own procedural rules, generally with fewer restrictions on observer participation. Several focus group participants reported that these modes of engagement offered broader and deeper stakeholder engagement, including more meaningful opportunities for interaction with government negotiators in a less-pressured environment.

5.2 Access, inclusion and representation

A heightened focus on the quality of observer participation does not preclude consideration of the quantity of different groups of observers that participate in the UNFCCC process. In spite of the record level of observer participation, a closer examination of the figures reveals a number of excluded or under-represented groups. In most cases, this results from financial and logistical barriers to participation, which disproportionately affect the most marginalised in society who often experience the earliest and most severe impacts of climate change. These findings echo the OECD-led '2018 IO Survey', illustrating that the major challenges IOs perceive in engaging stakeholders involve reaching out to unaware or under-represented stakeholders, and engaging effectively with marginalised stakeholders (OECD, 2021).

Developed country observers, for example, far outnumber developing country observers in UNFCCC sessions (Figure 3.4). Other representational deficits that require addressing include the gender imbalance in observer participation, the limited participation of Indigenous Peoples, currently representing only 3% of NGO observers (Figure 3.5), and the lack of inclusion of people with disabilities. Although progress has been made in making UNFCCC sessions more disabled-accessible, work remains to be done, for example, to make the COPs more inclusive for those whose disabilities are not visible.

Some of the most frequently raised issues were the insufficient quota being assigned to observer organisations and a lack of predictability surrounding observer quota allocation that prevents effective planning. There are two main factors that determine the allocation of quota to observer organisations. The first is the physical constraints of the COP venue, which has reached capacity in recent years, or even exceeded it, resulting in a poorer overall quality of participation. The second is the Party-driven nature of the UNFCCC process, whereby governments do not have limitations on their delegation sizes. When allocating a quota for observers, the secretariat must operate with a buffer that is sufficient to allow for governments to accommodate their delegates, who may continue to be nominated throughout the session. Based on the venue size and the expected number of government delegates, the secretariat must estimate the remaining quota that can be allocated to observers and distribute it in the most equitable manner possible.

5.3 Financial and logistical constraints

Financial and logistical barriers to observer participation were another key concern that was raised in almost all of the focus groups, along with the request for the provision of financial resources to help observers with the increasing costs associated with attending the COPs. The secretariat does not have a dedicated budget to sponsor observer participation. When the issue was raised with Parties under the formal negotiations on this topic, both developed and developing country Parties opposed the idea of establishing a trust fund for observer participation. Nevertheless, a lack of consensus among the negotiating Parties and a lack of resources on the part of the secretariat do not prevent observers from approaching sympathetic Parties bilaterally for voluntary funding or from searching for observer-led solutions to the financial barriers they face. Some focus group participants proposed setting up innovative schemes such as crowdfunding.

Obtaining visas is a logistical barrier to participation that de facto results in the exclusion of many developing country observers from UNFCCC sessions. The visa application process and the cost of visas are sovereign matters that can only be decided by the host government. The secretariat may only provide recommendations to the host country on the subject of visas and on logistical issues including the provision of affordable accommodation, transportation, and catering.

The possibility for virtual/hybrid participation, introduced as a response to the COVID-19 pandemic, was mentioned time and again as a positive development. Enhancing all forms of remote participation was highlighted as a potential enabler for better access, representation, and inclusion of observers. However, remote participation is no 'silver bullet'. Underrepresented groups are often precisely those who suffer from limited or inadequate access to technology and other financial and logistical resources. Therefore, virtual-only participation should not be seen as a replacement for in-person participation. Organisers should be wary of creating a potential 'two-tier access system' (i.e., in-person and online). Finally, it is also important to make accessible information on which modalities/opportunities for virtual engagement are available.

5.4 Lack of understanding of the processes, actors, and available engagement opportunities

Multilateral negotiations are defined by their size and complexity (Zartman, 1994), rendering the process confusing and difficult to navigate. The scale and scope of the climate change mandate further intensify this problem. Particularly for newcomers, the complexity of the UNFCCC process and jargon pose challenges in identifying how and when to engage, and what to expect as outcomes of engagement. The need to build observers' procedural and institutional capacity as a means of facilitating more meaningful engagement and managing expectations was a cross-cutting concern.

The system of NGO constituencies can likewise appear confusing to observers who have recently joined the process. NGO constituencies are self-formed and self-governing; as a result, each constituency operates with its own set of procedures and governance structures. This can pose a barrier for observer organisations to know how to effectively engage with constituencies, and for the different constituencies to coordinate among themselves. Cross-constituency collaboration brings benefits and is to be encouraged, both to help constituencies work towards their shared objectives in delivering the Paris Agreement as well as furthering the goals of the Convention. It can help constituencies navigate their shared challenges, for example, by pooling their resources and dividing labour.

One shared challenge reiterated during the focus groups concerns capacity-building for new members. Some constituencies, observer organisations and other external actors provide workshops, training sessions, explanatory materials, and other resources to help newcomers understand UNFCCC processes, language, actors, and opportunities for engagement. Combining these resources could allow for a more extensive range of capacity-building materials for observers and avoid potential duplication of labour among heads of observer organisations and CFPs, who are often overworked as they generally perform their functions on a voluntary basis on top of their day jobs. This is certainly the case during the COPs when they become inundated with requests for assistance from new members who are engaging for the first time. A division of capacity-building labour at the COP and the timely provision of accessible capacity-building resources in advance of the COPs would help to alleviate this situation and enhance observers' ability to meaningfully engage in the process. Pooling the different existing resources and sources of information into a centralised platform could also facilitate access to information for both newcomers and seasoned observers. Finally, pairing different admitted organisations together in a 'buddy system' for specific amounts of time could offer the opportunity not only for information and resource sharing, but for improving, interconnecting, and scaling up observer networks.

Table 3.4 provides a visual overview of the possible outcomes of the review process to strengthen observer engagement. For each suggested action, it indicates the actor(s) responsible for its implementation, including those actions that would require consensus from the negotiating Parties, thereby falling beyond the scope of the review process. It should be noted that this is a non-exhaustive summary of those outcomes considered most relevant by the

Table 3.4 Highlighted actions to strengthen observer engagement

Action to strengthen observer engagement	Secretariat	Observers	Parties (beyond scope of the review process)
Increase interaction with decision-makers during the pre-negotiation stages	–	X	–
Amend the rules of procedure to facilitate more meaningful observer engagement	–	–	X
Promote observer engagement throughout the year (e.g., Regional Climate Weeks)	X	X	–
Improve disability access at UNFCCC sessions	X	-	-
Explore options to increase quota and predictability by decoupling observer access and Party/Blue Zone access	X	X	–
Create a dedicated budget for observer participation	–	–	X
Develop bilateral/ innovative funding models for observer participation	–	X	–
Improve remote/hybrid participation options	X	–	–
Explore options for cross-constituency collaboration	–	X	–
Develop observers procedural/ institutional capacity, e.g., through timely provision of accessible resources via a centralised platform	X	X	–
Implement a "buddy system' between admitted observer organisations	–	X	–

authors to the readers of this chapter. A complete list of action points coming out of the review process can be found on the UNFCCC website.[7]

6 LESSONS LEARNT AND REFLECTIONS ON THE IMPLEMENTATION OF THE REVIEW PROCESS

Based on data from CFP interviews and from our own personal reflections, this section draws together key learnings from implementing the process to strengthen observer engagement in the UNFCCC. Elements that could be replicated in similar consultative processes include the provision of preparatory materials and the use of interactive online tools to facilitate discussions. While the fully remote implementation sought to open up the process, it failed to overcome a number of barriers to participation. The co-creative nature of the process was generally appreciated, but organisers should be aware that different groups of observers have different levels of capacity to contribute to such initiatives in line with their level of resources and be mindful of the need to balance a flexible process with clear expectation management regarding its parameters and eventual output.

6.1 Focus group materials, tools and facilitation

Before every substantive discussion during *phase two* of the process, three sets of preparatory materials were provided for each agenda item. These were emailed to the registered participants for the focus groups and made available on the web page to inform those submitting written inputs. The first set of documents consisted of 'info-sheets', short documents aimed at providing further context to the agenda items' questions and helping trigger the participants' thinking. Each info-sheet presented the background information and the guiding questions, as well as outlined any relevant responses provided by observers in the initial expression of interest survey. The second set of preparatory documents consisted of 'infographics', a one-page document containing all the relevant data, statistics, and visuals to refer to during the focus group discussions. Finally, guiding principles informing participants of the modalities of the focus groups and their expected conduct were also circulated.

CFPs and observers appreciated the guiding questions provided before every session, the interactive tools, and the facilitation style of the focus groups. Focus group sessions were two hours long and took place on Zoom.

[7] https://unfccc.int/process-and-meetings/parties-non-party-stakeholders/non-party-stakeholders/overview/process-to-strengthen-observer-engagement-in-the-unfccc.

Miro, a digital collaboration platform, was utilised as an interactive tool to promote discussion and brainstorming, integrating the guiding questions from the info-sheets in its layout. Live captioning was always activated, and simultaneous interpretation was provided on request through the support of the UN Volunteers platform.

6.2 Remote participation is no silver bullet

Proponents of online participatory technologies (OPTs) contend that they can help draw in more citizens, engage a more varied population, gather local knowledge, and aid in consensus building, as noted by Afzalan and Muller (2018). Yet, the same concerns voiced by focus group participants regarding the broader UNFCCC process also apply at the level of implementing the review process: under-represented and/or under-resourced organisations and groups are precisely the ones that tend to have poor or insufficient access to technology, as well as other financial and logistical resources. While beneficial in many ways, OPTs and remote participation are not a silver-bullet solution and should not be considered a substitute for in-person engagement.

Despite being entirely carried out in a remote modality, the review process suffered from a low participation rate. A first survey sent out to the 3,047 admitted observer organisations requesting an expression of interest in participating in the review process received only 304 responses, a 10% response rate. Out of those responses, 283 individuals registered for participation in focus groups. A total of 20 focus group meetings were held between July and September 2022, with the total participation of 157 representatives from admitted organisations. This clearly indicates that virtual access alone does not solve participation barriers, especially for under-represented and under-resourced groups, who did not benefit from any increase in participation vis-à-vis their representation in formal UNFCCC sessions.

6.3 Co-creative element and continuous feedback

As previously outlined, a fundamental aspect of the review process was its co-creative nature. While the review was open to all 3,047 admitted organisations and interested parties, in view of the limited timeframe, the secretariat team worked in close collaboration with the CFPs, as they represented the majority of the admitted NGO observers, and with five IGO representatives who had shown interest. Comments and feedback were sought in the drafting of a 'background note' aimed at assisting observers to better prepare for the review process by outlining the key issues of concern relating to observer engagement in the UNFCCC. The same approach was used to develop the agenda items to be addressed in *phase two*, in order to pinpoint those concerns and challenges that resonated with the majority of observers. Additionally, a presentation was provided to the CFPs by the secretariat team before each step of the review process to go through what was envisaged and to provide the space to incorporate any potential comments.

This method was intended to promote a sense of accountability and ownership among all those concerned, but it received mixed signals. During the interviews, some CFPs said that they appreciated the involvement at each stage from the very beginning, while others expressed a desire for further involvement in the co-creative side and reported feeling like they were simply informed of the next steps. There were others who did not participate in the meetings and later reported that the consultation process felt overwhelming.[8] Naturally, these reactions were contingent on the heterogeneous capacity of the different constituencies.

6.4 Diverse levels of process experience and capacity

A significant element that emerged from the interviews is that smaller and under-resourced constituencies rarely have the time to think about the broader process and make high-level procedural considerations, having to prioritise substantive contributions to their workstreams. In addition to the need to channel their limited amount of time and resources in the most effective way, this can largely be attributed to a lack of procedural and institutional capacity, as one CFP explained: 'We don't have many people who have enough consistent experience of attending sessions. Most of my constituency, even those from the Global North, have no idea how the system works. So they wouldn't have felt like they had anything to contribute to the discussion [in the review process]'.[9]

Phase 2 was characterised by an unforeseen high barrier to entry, as (similarly to the broader UNFCCC process) it required a specific level of understanding and experience in the UNFCCC to meaningfully participate. Thinking about the broader process, as required by the review process, represents a level of engagement that not all constituencies and other non-affiliated observer organisations have the experience and/or capacity to undertake, especially when dealing with a limited time frame and tight deadlines.

The review process aimed to be as inclusive as possible, involving all 3,047 admitted observer organisations in *phase two*. This approach was necessary and appreciated by many, but it brought some challenges. When joining the

---

[8] Some CFPs only became involved in the review process towards the end of phase 2 and did not have the possibility to provide feedback on its overall structure and delivery.

[9] All quotes from the CFPs were obtained during interviews and later anonymised, as described in section 4.

focus groups, it was clear that the participants had varying levels of experience and different motivations to contribute to the process; some observers were interested in providing their active contribution to the action points, while some participants were recently admitted and simply eager to learn about the UNFCCC process and interact with the secretariat for the first time. As the participants were assigned slots based on their time zone and availability rather than their experience level, the unfolding of every focus group session was highly unpredictable, posing limitations on the facilitation of the sessions and on the value that each participant could expect to derive from them. One of the CFPs argued that 'in some discussions, even if it was great to see different members, some of them did not have the necessary background', adding 'it requires a certain level of experience and understanding of the process to contribute. You don't want to go into conversation with participants that lack their basics'.[10]

6.5 The capacity-building paradox

Throughout the review process, in focus groups, as well as discussions with CFPs, the need for more resources and capacity-building efforts was often reiterated, especially for under-resourced and under-represented groups. Yet, when it came time for observers to provide input for the secretariat to create said resources, observers found they did not have enough capacity or time to follow up. Similarly, when the resources were provided, under-resourced groups with limited capacity reported they were not able to actually benefit from said resources, and in some cases, they reported being overwhelmed by the sheer quantity and complexity of documents and materials to go through.

The review process was delivered and implemented on top of an increasingly complex process and numerous demanding intersessional engagements. As stated by the CFP of an under-resourced constituency, 'it was a whole lot of information to absorb and process. Phase 2 really exposed us as a constituency about how seriously incapacitated we are. I cannot even say anything about Phase 2 because we couldn't even manage to follow the process as Focal Points'.

We found that the heterogeneity of the observer community manifests itself in a diverse set of needs specific to individual constituencies and organisations. While the secretariat attempted to provide resources seeking to address specific demands for under-resourced constituencies and groups, these same

[10] This reflects only the opinion of the interviewed CFPs. At the moment of writing, feedback from the participants from admitted observer organisations is not available.

actors with less capacity were the ones that benefited the least from the secretariat's efforts and even found them overwhelming. To offer a concrete example, at the early stages of *phase two,* in an effort to compensate for capacity limitations and ensure the representation, a CFP proposed that the secretariat allot resources to collect inputs via individual interviews with a representative group of members from under-represented and under-resourced constituencies. This proposal was made in light of the fact that members of such constituencies may have experienced difficulties in following the schedule of focus groups, overcoming technical barriers to remote participation, or in providing inputs in one of the six UN languages. Resources were mobilised, and the secretariat requested a list of names of individuals from these constituencies. Due to different constraints, however, none of the constituencies were able to

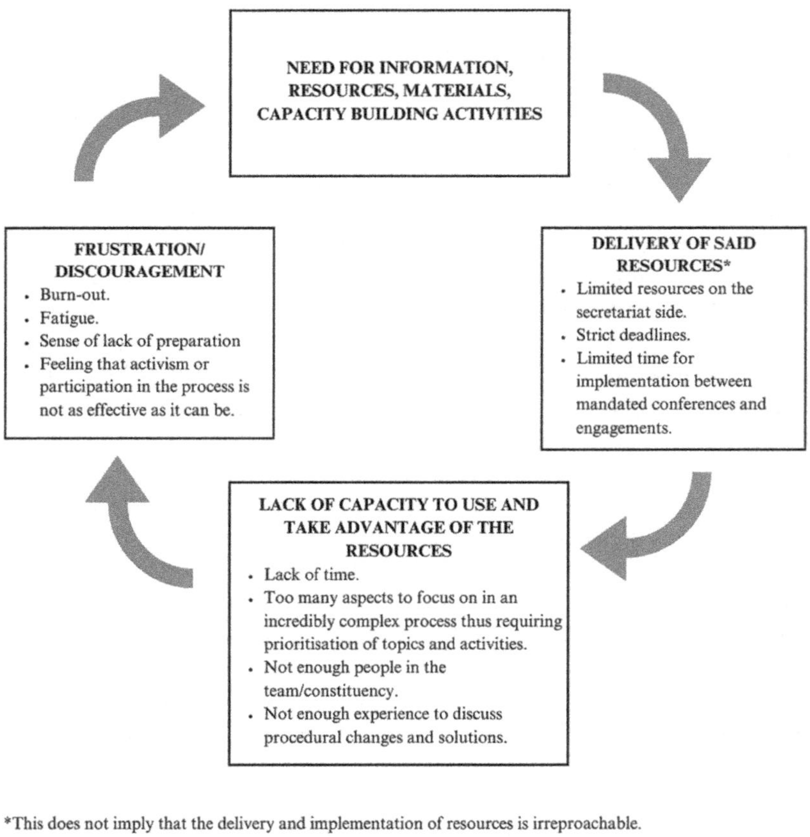

Figure 3.6 Capacity-building paradox in under-resourced constituencies

produce any list. We refer to this predicament as a 'capacity-building paradox' (Figure 3.6).

When asked about potential solutions, one CFP proposed that the UNFCCC secretariat should speak to all constituencies to understand their needs and subsequently tailor the resources to the different groups.
What is often not acknowledged, or even known, is that the Observer Relations Team (ORT) itself experiences a shortage of resources, especially considering the growing scale of admitted organisations. Although the quantity of admitted observer organisations continues to rise, this is not matched with an increase in resources for the secretariat to manage these stakeholders (Figure 3.7).

Consequently, the ORT, not unlike the rest of the secretariat, often relies on consultants and individual contractors to carry out its mandate, bound to the budget allocated to each division assigned by the Parties. Relying on a high turnover of temporary workers leads to a lack of institutional memory and, as a result, compromises the efficiency and effectiveness of an organisation's performance (Urbancova and Linhartová, 2011).

6.6 Expectation management

As the process was flexible and co-creative in nature, some interviewees noted that it was difficult to visualise it and understand what the final outcome would consist of. One CFP stated that 'many of them [the constituency members] did not understand where the process was coming from, why is this important for them to engage, what can they contribute and where is this eventually leading up to'. While this flexibility was necessary to address emerging needs and make necessary changes throughout the review process, it meant that there were no strict boundaries or parameters on specific topics, which led to the review process 'sprawling'. As one CFP stated, it attempted to be 'too many things for too many people'.

It is necessary to clearly define the scope of the consultations from the outset and to manage participants' expectations regarding how the process will advance and what it is capable of delivering. To mitigate the issue, it has been suggested by CFPs and participants, in hindsight, that a tailored messaging strategy to 'market' the review process would have improved participation numbers and possibly helped manage frustrations. As one CFP stated, 'it makes such a difference how you communicate it. There are many organisations that are just new or don't know how to engage on a continuous basis that don't have the understanding and for those you really have to communicate really well what you need from them and why they should engage'.

For a number of years, the question of how to manage 'conflicts of interest' has risen in prominence, driving contestation between different groups of observers (Bäckstrand et al., 2017). This question relates to the participation

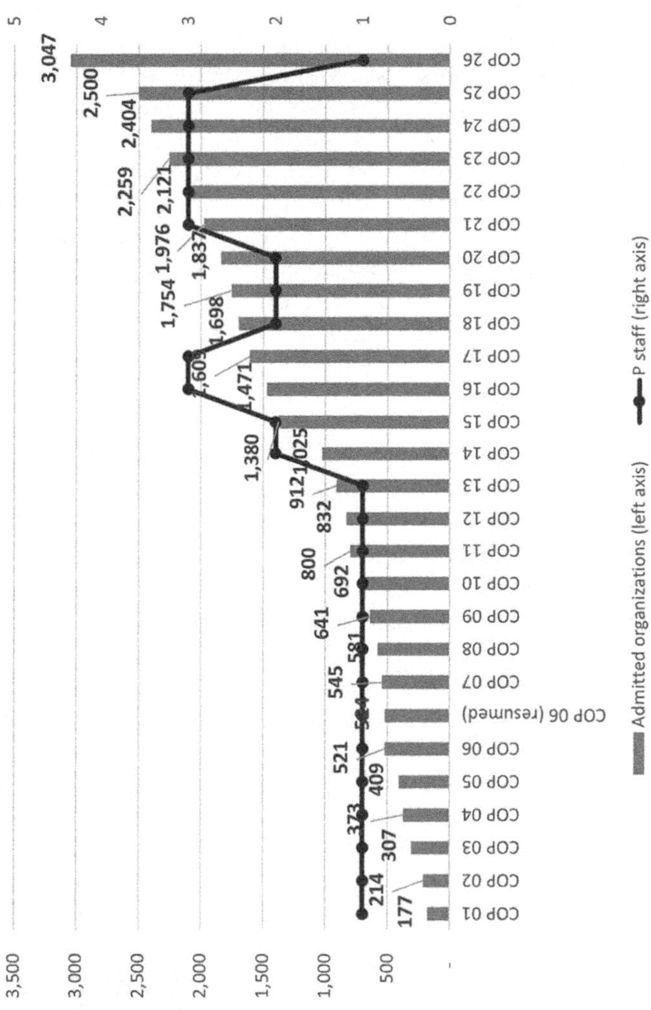

Source: UNFCCC (2022), 'Background note: Process to strengthen observer engagement in the UNFCCC'

Figure 3.7 Historical growth of observer admission and resources on observer support function

in UNFCCC sessions of observer organisations whose interests run counter to those of the goals of the Convention, such as fossil fuel lobbies, and the fear that these actors may use their presence at the COP to actively undermine progress. Several groups of observers have called for a conflict-of-interest policy to address this issue. Positions among its proponents vary, with some calling for the development of a transparency framework to disclose observers' potential conflicts of interest, and others calling for the exclusion of certain actors, ranging from representatives of fossil fuel interests to the entire business community. This latter position has led to tensions and suspicion between the business and industry constituency and those constituencies calling for such a mechanism.

It should be noted that the rules for the admission of observer organisations are set out in the Convention and subsequent guidance from Parties and that any amendments to the rules of procedure that would allow for the exclusion of admitted organisations would require a decision to be taken by consensus by the negotiating Parties, thereby falling beyond the scope of the review process. This was communicated to participants of the review process, who were urged to focus their discussions on the development of a transparency framework for observer participation. Nevertheless, certain interventions in the focus groups and comments from CFP interviews suggest that the secretariat's efforts to manage expectations had not been successful - advancing the agenda to exclude businesses from the UNFCCC remained the primary goal of this review process for certain constituencies. One of the CFPs stated that

> we [the CFPs] would have needed more guidance from the secretariat in terms of what is really plausible and what is the mandate of this observer review process. I felt that there were no parameters, even though I think you tried to give them, for certain groups. This is how very quickly you end up in a very confrontational discussion and I think this could have been avoided with strict parameters so that everyone understands clearly what is possible to do.

Consultations continued between the secretariat and different groups of observers throughout the first half of 2023, and in June 2023 they resulted in an agreement on a transparency framework to render potential conflicts of interest more visible. All participants are now required to declare their affiliation and are requested to specify the nature of their relationship with the organisation (McGrath, 2023).

7 DISCUSSION

When it comes to *participation* (i.e., increasing inputs from stakeholders to better inform the decision-making process), the review process can be viewed as a partial success.[11] A large volume of inputs was collected and used to influence policy decisions taken by the UNFCCC secretariat. Several concrete action points to strengthen observer engagement had already been taken ahead of COP 27, with many more in the pipeline.[12] Many stakeholders were invited to participate, and steps were taken to make the process as open and accessible as possible. Yet, participation rates were lower than anticipated and reflected the same representational deficits found in the broader UNFCCC process.

On *inclusion* (i.e., building the capacity of the community to implement the decisions, including by strengthening networks and building a framework for interaction over time), we left the review process with the impression that this goal had not been fully achieved. The review process aimed to build stakeholders' institutional capacity and understanding of the UNFCCC process, yet the diverse levels of experience that participants brought to the table made this challenging in practice. Efforts were made to nurture a spirit of collaboration between stakeholders during *phases 1* and *2* of the review process; yet the confrontational discussions on conflicts of interest that took place at the end of *phase 2* seemed to move this process backward, even if, ultimately, they laid the groundwork for the adoption of the transparency framework.

Our experiences in the review process suggest that organisers of similar initiatives should carefully consider participation and inclusion as two distinct dimensions of stakeholder engagement, and the interaction between the two, when planning and administering the process. For the review process, both dimensions were indispensable. Between the two components, the participation component was the primary purpose, and inclusion was a secondary but necessary component to complete the former. Participants needed to share a

[11] It should be emphasised that every IO stakeholder engagement effort is highly specific to the context, the sets of problems and challenges, and purpose of stakeholder participation (Bryson et al., 2013). This study pertains to a specific organisation with unique characteristics, and therefore caution should be exercised in applying the findings to other contexts. We discuss the findings of our particular case in light of the framework of participation and inclusion proposed at the beginning of this chapter and reflect on the possible implications for similar future processes. We also draw some parallels between the two previous sections, which deal respectively with suggestions for strengthening observer engagement in the UNFCCC and the lessons learnt on a much smaller scale through our implementation of the review process. We conclude by returning to the framework of participation and inclusion as a way of reflecting on the evolution of observer engagement in the UNFCCC process and its possible future.

[12] For more details, refer to the 'Process to Strengthen Observer Engagement' on the UNFCCC website.

common level of capacity (*inclusion*) in order to ensure meaningful discussions, quality inputs, and equitable representation (*participation*).

Differing levels of capacity among participants gave rise to two main problems. First was the problem of under-representation among those groups of stakeholders with fewer resources to invest in the review process. Given its own resource constraints, the secretariat is not able to plug the resource gap that gives rise to a 'capacity-building paradox'. The second capacity-related problem concerns the participants' divergent levels of experience in the UNFCCC process, which sometimes hindered the ability of the focus groups to deliver concrete and deliverable action points. Here, there are steps that could be taken to level the playing field of participants' capacities to engage in consultations on procedural and institutional questions relating to stakeholder engagement. One option could be to run a shorter, more targeted process among those key stakeholders with extensive experience in the UNFCCC. Another option could be to separate the process into two stages: first, a round of capacity-building whereby participants would acquire a baseline level of understanding of the UNFCCC process and the constraints within which the secretariat operates, followed by a round of focus groups to provide concrete inputs and develop action points. A third option would be to group participants according to their level of experience in the UNFCCC process, which would allow for tailored delivery of the focus groups.

The conflation of participation and inclusion in what is often broadly defined as public engagement creates misgivings and leads to inefficiency (Quick and Feldman, 2011). Indeed, stakeholders may go to great lengths to contribute to policies and decision-making efforts only to feel unheard or sense their involvement to be unproductive and fruitless. This sense of dissatisfaction can often lead to participation burnout and overall lack of trust in said process. In the climate space, said feelings are in many cases added to a pervasive sense of climate anxiety and hopelessness as witnessed especially in Indigenous and youth participants (Thew, Middlemiss, and Paavola, 2022; Yona, et al., 2020; MacKay, Parlee, and Karsgaard, 2020). Just as the review process tried to be '*too many things to too many people*' in terms of the substantive topics it covered, it also perhaps tried to achieve too much in terms of combining participation and inclusion. We advise organisers of similar initiatives to plan their implementation strategy with their goal (participation/inclusion/both) clearly in mind, and to communicate from the outset to participants what is expected of them, and what they can expect in return.[13]

[13] In line with the key principles of stakeholder engagement outlined in the Compendium of International Organisations' Practice (OECD, 2021).

While each stakeholder engagement effort is specific to its own context, we were struck by a number of parallels between the issues identified by participants on stakeholder engagement in the UNFCCC and those issues we identified when reflecting on our own experiences as part of the team responsible for implementing the review process, as a small-scale example of a stakeholder engagement initiative. First, the make-up of participants in the review process is remarkably similar to the make-up of stakeholders one can expect to see at a COP. Specifically, Indigenous peoples, young people, and developing country stakeholders suffer from a lack of representation, owing to resource and capacity constraints. While remote participation has been touted as a possible remedy, both in the review process and in the broader UNFCCC process, those under-represented and under-resourced organisations and groups are precisely the ones that tend to have poor or insufficient access to technology. Until this gap in resources and capacity is plugged – or some other solution is found to address the 'capacity-building paradox' – organisers' well-intentioned efforts may prove counterproductive, contributing to fatigue or even burnout among these overstretched groups.

A further parallel that can be drawn between both processes of stakeholder engagement is the low rate of take-up that characterises engagement opportunities in the UNFCCC outside of the COPs. Participation rates in the review process were lower than expected, but the engagement and response rate are consistent with other surveys and activities carried out by the UNFCCC secretariat,[14] especially those that do not directly relate to participation in COPs. This mirrors the findings from the review process regarding the numerous engagement opportunities that exist throughout the year in the UNFCCC process for stakeholders, which remain underutilised, while the focus remains squarely on the oversubscribed COPs.[15] A number of complementary explanations are possible: first, relating to the aforementioned capacity and resource constraints faced by many stakeholders and the resulting need for prioritisation; second, relating to a lack of awareness and a need for improved communication and coordination between the secretariat and NGO constituencies and their members; and third, a psychological element that relates to the underlying attractiveness of the high-profile COPs as a mode of engagement. Further research and action on this issue are to be encouraged, particularly given that COPs are not necessarily the most effective investment of stakeholders' limited resources.

---

[14] We refer here to surveys that we have administered or are familiar with through our time working within the Communications and Engagement division.

[15] For reference, the Subsidiary Body 56th session in June 2022 counted 5,053 registered participants, in comparison with COP 27, which counted 33,449 registered participants.

These parallels between the two processes of stakeholder engagement – very different in their size and objectives – suggest that multi-stakeholder processes do share certain fundamental qualities, regardless of their diverse contexts, perhaps by virtue of being, in essence, human processes. This, in turn, seems to justify the selection of an analytical framework from outside of the fields of international relations or global governance. Whether applied to local town hall meetings or global climate change conferences, insights on organisational goals and human behaviour seem to hold. This points to tremendous untapped potential in the fields of organisational behaviour and stakeholder theory, where a wealth of relevant research findings has been amassed over several decades. We call for a broadening of the theoretical horizons when studying IOs and for scholars of global governance to turn their attention to these interdisciplinary fields and translate knowledge so that it may be applied to improve the effectiveness and inclusiveness of IOs.

8 CONCLUSION

This chapter aimed to set out the lessons learnt from the process to strengthen observer engagement in the UNFCCC, both substantively and in terms of process management, from our practitioner perspective, having been involved in its design and delivery, and through the conceptual lens of Quick and Feldman's (2011) distinction between participation (i.e., increasing public inputs to inform decisions) and inclusion (i.e., creating a community with the capacity to implement decisions and tackle related issues). The substantive outcomes of the review process reveal a number of pain points for stakeholder engagement in the UNFCCC and possible remedial actions that can be taken by the secretariat or by observer organisations.

Although stakeholders participate in UNFCCC sessions in unprecedented numbers, there are concerns that quantity can undermine quality. On the one hand, annual COPs are oversubscribed – stakeholders struggle to find the space to carry out their activities and achieve their objectives, and governmental decision-makers struggle to find the time for meaningful, two-way interaction with stakeholders. On the other hand, a plethora of under-subscribed modes of engagement exist throughout the year, offering opportunities for higher-quality interactions with decision-makers and governed by rules of procedure that are more permissive in allowing stakeholders to participate in meaningful ways. Stakeholders may consider reorienting their strategy away from the COP and towards alternative fora in the UNFCCC, and the secretariat may consider options to raise awareness and promote engagement beyond the COP. It is also possible that this incongruence relates to a major underlying issue that came to light both in substantive discussions in the review process and in its implementation – resource and capacity constraints faced by groups of stakeholders that impose limits on their engagement and cause them to prioritise participation at the COP.

The 'capacity-building paradox' we observed, whereby under-resourced groups of stakeholders lack the capacity to benefit from the opportunities that are made available for them, applies just as well to the broader lack of engagement in the UNFCCC beyond the COPs as it does to our experiences of trying to engage certain constituencies in the review process. Until this paradox is addressed, either through the provision of adequate resources or through another creative solution, those wishing to engage stakeholders in IOs should consider the 'quality over quantity' maxim: avoid multiplying processes, initiatives, and other calls for engagement, which risk resulting in participation fatigue or even burnout among those with the least capacity to manage the additional workload, and instead focus resources on tailoring a smaller quantity of engagement efforts to the specific needs of different groups of stakeholders.

Further guidance that we can offer to those considering similar processes of stakeholder consultations in other IOs is to consider whether their goal is participation, inclusion, or, if both, how these different sets of objectives may interact and potentially impede each other. The review process aimed to collect inputs on possible action points (participation) and build a shared understanding among the stakeholder community and between stakeholders and the secretariat as a basis for future implementation (inclusion). Yet, in attempting to tackle both objectives in a single process, overall effectiveness was undermined: without a common level of understanding, it was difficult to engage in meaningful discussions on technical and procedural questions that required prior knowledge of and experience in the UNFCCC.

Although participation may seem to precede inclusion as a dimension of stakeholder engagement, for an exercise of this nature, it is necessary to first ensure participants share a common understanding of the UNFCCC process and of the practical, legal, and logistical constraints within which the secretariat operates to ensure the quality of the inputs received, the co-production of workable solutions, and ultimately, the delivery of real change. With the number of stakeholders participating in the UNFCCC projected to increase year-on-year, there is a fundamental need to manage expectations and create a shared understanding of what the UNFCCC can and cannot deliver in order to avoid disillusionment that risks undermining the legitimacy of the world's leading institution dedicated to combating climate change. This chapter aims to contribute to this effort.

ACKNOWLEDGMENTS

Our deepest gratitude goes to Megumi Endo for her invaluable guidance and expertise, which played a pivotal role in conducting this study. We extend special thanks to Sofia Shellard and Kathleen Mar for their instrumental feedback and insights, which enriched our research. Additionally, we are grateful to the Constituency Focal Point participants for their rich and thought-provoking interviews, and we sincerely acknowledge the reviewers for their constructive feedback, shaping this chapter into its best form.

REFERENCES

Allan, J. (2020), *The New Climate Activism: Ngo Authority And Participation In Climate Governance*, University of Toronto Press, Toronto Buffalo London, ISBN: 978-1-4875-2584-2.

Afzalan N., Muller B. (2018), Online participatory technologies: opportunities and challenges for enriching participatory planning, *Journal of the American Planning Association*, 84:2, 162–177.

Bäckstrand, K., Kuyper, J. W., Linnér, B. & Lövbrand, E. (2017), Non-state actors in global climate governance: from Copenhagen to Paris and beyond, *Environmental Politics*, 26:4, 561–579.

Bäckstrand, K., Kuyper, J. and Nasiritousi, N. (2021), From collaboration to contestation? Perceptions of legitimacy and effectiveness in post-Paris climate governance, *Earth System Governance,* 9, 1–11.

Bensimon, E. M. (2007), The underestimated significance of practitioner knowledge in the scholarship on student success, *The Review of Higher Education*, 30:4, 441–469.

Biniaz, S. (2020), After Madrid, W(h)ither the COP?, Sabin Center for Climate Change Law.

Chan, S. et al. (2015), Reinvigorating international climate policy: a comprehensive framework for effective nonstate action, *Global Policy* 6(4), 466–473.

Bryson, J., et al. (2013), Designing public participation processes: from theory to practice, *Public Administration Review*, 73(1), 23–34.

Hale, T. (2016), 'All hands on deck': The Paris agreement and nonstate climate action. *Global Environmental Politics* 16(3), 12–22.

Kuyper, J. W., Bäckstrand, K. & Schroeder, H. (2018), Non-state actors in hybrid global climate governance: justice, legitimachy and effectiveness in a post-Paris era, *WIREs Climate Change,* 9:e497.

Levitan, J., Carr-Chellman, D., & Carr-Chellman, A. (2020), Accidental ethnography: a method for practitioner-based education research, *Action Research*, 18(3), 336–352.

MacKay, M., Parlee, B., & Karsgaard, C. (2020), Youth Engagement in Climate Change Action: Case Study on Indigenous Youth at COP24, *Sustainability*, 12, 6299.

Mar, K. A., Schäpke, N., Fraude, C., Bruhn, T., Wamsler, C., Stasiak, D., Schroeder, H., & Lawrence, M. G. (2023). Learning and community building in support of collective action: toward a new climate of communication at the COP. *WIREs Climate Change, December 2022*, 1–12.

McGrath, M. (2023, June 16). Climate Change: UN to unmask fossil fuel lobbyists at climate talks. *BBC News*. See https://www.bbc.com/news/science-environment-65917660.

Nonaka, I., & Konno, N. (1998), The concept of 'Ba: building foundation for knowledge creation, *California Management Review*, 40, 40–54.

Obergassel et al. (2022), From regime-building to implementation: Harnessing the UN climate conferences to drive climate action. WIREs Climate Change, 13(6), e797. https://doi.org/10.1002/wcc.797

OECD (2021), 'Compendium of International Organisations' Practices: Working Towards More Effective International Instruments', OECD Publishing, Paris, https://doi.org/10.1787/846a5fa0-en.

Quick, K. S., & Feldman, M. S. (2011), Distinguishing participation and inclusion, *Journal of Planning Education and Research*, 31(3), 272–290.

Thew, H., Middlemiss, L., & Paavola, J. (2022) 'You need a month's holiday just to get over it!' Exploring young people's lived experiences of the UN climate change negotiations. *Sustainability*, 14, 4259.

UNFCCC (1992), United Nations Framework Convention On Climate Change. United Nations, FCCC/INFORMAL/84 GE. 05–62220 (E) 200705, Secretariat of the United Nations Framework Convention on Climate Change, Bonn, Germany, pp. 24, https://unfccc.int/resource/docs/convkp/conveng.pdf.

UNFCCC (2022), 'Background note: Process to strengthen the observer engagement in the UNFCCC', https://unfccc.int/documents/510800 (accessed 18 April 2023).

UNFCCC (n.d.), 'Statistics on admission webpage', https://unfccc.int/process-and-meetings/parties-non-party-stakeholders/non-party-stakeholders/statistics-on-non-party-stakeholders/statistics-on-admission (accessed 18 April 2023).

UNFCCC (2023), 'Provisional List of Registered Participants', https://unfccc.int/documents/634488 (accessed 8 January 2024).

Urbancova, H., & Linhartová, L. (2011), Staff turnover as a possible threat to knowledge loss, *Journal of Competitiveness*, Issue 3/2011, 84–98.

Walker, H., Monheim, K., Ohler, F., Jepsen, H., & Lundgren, M. (2021), 'Conclusion: The Landscape of Multilateral Agreement in Paris and Beyond' in H. Jepsen et al. (eds) *Negotiating the Paris Agreement*. Cambridge University Press.

Yona, L. et al. (2020), Applying a leverage points framework to the United Nations climate negotiations: The (dis)empowerment of youth participants, *Elem Sci Anth*, 8: 36.

Zartman, W.I. (Ed.) (1994) *International Multilateral Negotiation: Approaches to the Management of Complexity*. Jossey-Bass.

Zeichner, K. (2007). Accumulating knowledge across self-studies in teacher education. *Journal of Teacher Education*, 58(1), 36–46.

4. Rule-making in the African Union: current challenges and the way forward

Femi Amao, Michèle Olivier and Konstantinos D. Magliveras

1 INTRODUCTION

The African Union (AU), created at the dawn of the twenty-first century, is one of the largest regional international organisations in terms of member States (presently 55 members). It also has a long tradition of creating regional rules and norms, primarily through the negotiation and conclusion of treaties going back to the establishment of the AU's predecessor, the Organisation of African Unity (OAU) in 1963. Some of these treaties were quite progressive, expanding international rule-making to areas not covered elsewhere, e.g. the Convention on the Conservation of Nature and Natural Resources (1968, revised in 2013), and the African Charter on Human and Peoples' Rights (1981), with the additional Protocols on the Rights of Women (2003), of Older People (2016), of Persons with Disabilities (2018) and on the Rights of Citizens to Social Protection and Social Security (2022). The AU is an interstate organisation with limited provision for formal non-state involvement in decision-making. This is, however, changing as evidenced by the expressed need to build partnerships with civil society and the establishment of the Pan-African Parliament (PAP), which would ensure full participation of African peoples in the continent's development and economic integration.

The OAU spearheaded the nascent contribution of the continent to global governance and international law. Understanding its role and contribution would provide a useful background to the African regional approach and perspective on international rule-making and the changes introduced by the AU. A significant number of the rules that form the corpus of AU law and several treaties that have impacted international law can be traced back to OAU activities. The OAU, in its 39 years of existence (1963–2002), adopted twenty-two treaties with varying legal significance on the regional and international planes. It is, therefore, pertinent to understand its decision-making process and examine the extent of inclusivity or stakeholder engagement, if any. This would inform how the AU has advanced and improved its rule-making processes. Devising and enhancing a process that facilitates representation and inclusion of stakeholders (e.g., groups marginalised in terms of ethnicity, religion, race, geographical location) enhances legitimacy and acceptance of rule-making. Moreover, the role of external stakeholders is examined as they may have impacted the processes directly or indirectly.

As recently argued (Amao, Olivier & Magliveras (eds) 2021), an AU legal system has already been formed and is presently evolving into a norms-based regional/continental law, especially with regard to economic and political integration. However, OAU/AU rule-making is a topic not adequately investigated in the literature, and a paucity of in-depth examination limits a proper understanding of the way it has developed over the years and is presently progressing.

Even though the AU Constitutive Act and its Protocols forming part of its constitutional order (e.g., the Protocol on PAP, the Protocol on the African Court of Justice, the Protocol on the Peace and Security Council) do not refer to AU law *per se*, they do provide for a process of rule-making that is binding upon member states. Several AU organs are directly or indirectly involved in the process. Moreover, the challenges and problems that the continent continues to face should be properly addressed through applying African solutions within the capabilities of member states.

It is notable that decision-making in the AU is rather opaque. The lack of clear textual guidance on the powers of AU organs to take binding action is out of sync with the often-expressed goal to create a unified and strong Africa. The rule of law in the governance and decision-making processes does not appear to be a priority concern for the member states as evidenced by practice. Only rarely is the legal basis of adopted resolutions provided, while records of voting are not published. Moreover, the work of the AU Commission, the organisation's secretariat, is mostly underreported. Equally, the outcomes of the meetings of the Permanent Representatives' Committee, the organ representing member states within the AU's institutional structure and facilitating communication between the AU and member states' capitals, are apparently not published.

It is, therefore, not straightforward which stakeholders influence the rule-making process and to what extent. For many years now, several third states and international organisations ('non-AU stakeholders') have had a significant input in continental political, economic, and security matters. They include traditional external partners (the UN family, the EU, the USA, the UK, France, etc.), but also more recent partners of note, such as the BRIC countries that have made the greatest inroads. Finally, it is not widely publicised that for many years now, more than 50% of the AU budget has been financed by non-AU stakeholders. The degree of their (direct or indirect) impact on AU's affairs and more specifically on rule-making has never been adequately reviewed and assessed.

2 THE ORGANISATION OF AFRICAN UNITY AND RULE-MAKING

2.1 Background

The Organisation of African Unity (OAU) was established within the ambit of Article 53 of the Charter of the United Nations (1945), which allows the establishment of regional organisations with the potential to contribute to international rule-making. It is important to understand the original nature of the OAU. The OAU Charter did not create a political union or establish a 'United State of Africa', which was the aim of some of the major proponents for the establishment of a continental body (Amao, Olivier, Magliveras (eds) 2021). The idea to create a political union was rejected at the OAU Charter's negotiations in 1964 (Elias 1965, pp. 243–267). It did not, therefore, involve a transfer of sovereign powers to a supranational body because of opposition from members. Consequently, it was not surprising that the OAU's configuration limited its impact on international rule-making.

In that context, the OAU was generally regarded as a platform for intergovernmental cooperation. This perception would have significant ramifications for the OAU's rule-making capacity and process. In addition, the OAU Charter was anchored on the key principle of non-interference, which by implication affirmed the member states' absolute sovereignty, including in the legislative sphere. Its implication was explained by Maluwa as follows:

> With its emphasis on the related principles of sovereign equality of Member States, respect for the sovereignty, territorial integrity and independence of States and non-interference in the internal affairs of States, the OAU was clearly intended to be a loose organization for voluntary cooperation between African States, with no supra-national authority. As such, the OAU fell squarely within the typology of international organizations … (Maluwa 2012, p. 28)

It follows that the approach to rule-making within the OAU was predominantly a platform for one major group of stakeholders, that is, member states. An attempt to review the Charter to make it more functional and relevant to modern Africa, including rule-making, was initiated in 1980 with the establishment of the OAU Charter Review Committee. However, until it ceased to exist in 1996, the review exercise made no significant impact on its practice and procedure (Maluwa 2004, p. 28).

Even though the OAU was not conceived as a legislative body by its founding treaty (Maluwa 2004, p. 233), it has been suggested that through the adoption of multilateral treaties and resolutions, it was actively engaged in creating normative rules, some of which can be regarded as forming part of the rules of international law. The creation of these normative rules could be considered as rule-making by the OAU (Maluwa 2020, p. 233). Furthermore, Maluwa suggested that in some areas of practice, the OAU did not originally set out to create new international law, but it did so by 'purposely giving certain rules and principles a specifically regional African orientation' (Maluwa 2004, p. 232). Therefore, the Africanisation of rules and principles could also be seen as part of OAU rule-making, a practice that not only contributed to international law but also mapped new boundaries in rule-making (Maluwa 2004, p. 234).

The OAU contributions in rule-making were primarily driven by the political organs given their roles under its Charter. These were the Assembly of Heads of State and Government (Assembly) and the Council of Ministers. The functions and practice of the Assembly under the OAU Charter suggest that it provided a platform for discussion and deliberations, which usually led to conclusions that could potentially be operationalised at a later stage (Cervenka 1969, p. 45). Instructively, under Article X of the OAU Charter, the conclusions reached by the Assembly had to be registered as resolutions, except where they related to appointments and other organisational matters. Under Article X(2), resolutions were adopted by a two-thirds majority.

The next pertinent question is the legal status of the resolutions as 'rules' emanating from the OAU. The Charter itself did not provide guidance as to their legal status or implications. However, they were generally accepted as recommendations addressed to member States (Cervenka 1969, p. 45). From that perspective, it has been contended that the resolutions did not impose any legal obligations upon them (Cervenka 1969, p. 45). Similarly, Maluwa argued that the resolutions were not legally binding as such and had the nature of 'hortatory soft law only' (Maluwa 2002, p. 99). Nevertheless, (Cervenka 1969, p. 46) provided two key caveats to these views. First, although the resolutions addressed to member States were not legally binding, they provided an important avenue for bringing the weight of public opinion from the continent and the world to bear upon the member States. The platform provided a forum for discussion, which led to the development of recommendations on matters of common concern to the continent (Cervenka 1969, p. 46). In addition, Cervanka identified some important exceptions to the non-binding nature of OAU resolutions. These were situations where Assembly resolutions and decisions could potentially have a binding effect, including situations where it was exercising its power to decide on the OAU Charter's interpretation (by two-thirds majority). Second, the Assembly's decisions on admitting new Members (by a simple majority) and approving amendments to the Charter (by two-thirds majority) also had a binding effect (Cervanka 1969, p. 46). These examples show how Assembly practices could lead to rule-making that may be binding on member States.

This practice of the Assembly can be contrasted with resolutions from the OAU Council of Ministers. The Council, composed of the foreign ministers from member States, had the primary responsibility of implementing Assembly decisions. The Assembly's deliberations usually resulted in resolutions determined by a simple majority. Council of Ministers' resolutions were required to be submitted to the Assembly for approval under Article XIII of the Charter. It has been observed that '[t]he limited powers of the Council indicate clearly that its resolutions are mere recommendations, imposing no legal obligations on the Members of the Council' (Cervenka 1969, p. 51). However, it is arguable that once these resolutions were approved by the Assembly, and if they fell within the exceptions discussed above in relation to the Assembly, they could also have binding effect.

2.2 The example of the OAU Convention Governing the Specific Aspects of Refugee Problems in Africa (1969)

An examination of the process that initiated and drafted the Refugee Convention is an instructive example in understanding the OAU approach to rule-making. The main driver was to put in place a Convention regarding refugees on the continent given the prevailing situation after independence and the continuing struggle for independence that had led to significant displacement of people (Abebe et al. 2019, pp. 1–15). At the time, under the relevant multilateral treaty, the 1951 Refugee Convention, individuals connected with these struggles may not have been able to claim refugee status as they would not have been covered by the Convention's definition of refugees. Indeed, when the 1951 Convention was negotiated, only four African independent states were UN member states: Egypt, Ethiopia, Liberia, and South Africa. Of them, only Egypt participated in the drafting of the 1951 Convention, thereby limiting the continent's influence in shaping it. On the other hand, this fact shows the limitations in the Convention addressing all of the germane issues relating to refugees in Africa, hence the need to address the peculiarity of the refugee situation in Africa through specialised rules.

Against this backdrop, in 1964 the OAU Council of Ministers (equivalent to the Executive Council in the AU) constituted a commission of representatives from ten member states, later renamed the 'OAU Commission of Ten on Refugee Problems in Africa'. It had its first meeting in Addis Ababa in 1964 and in its report recommended that the OAU 'draft a special convention on the status of African refugees' (Mukirya 2004, p. 85). That recommendation led to the production of three drafts, which culminated three years later in the

Protocol to the 1951 Convention relating to the Status of Refugees (the 1967 Protocol) (Mukirya 2004, p. 85). However, certain member states (e.g., Nigeria and Uganda) felt that the 1967 Protocol did not sufficiently address the refugee problem as envisaged.

The Council of Ministers decided that it was necessary to put in place a more comprehensive instrument. It is notable that the OAU took a wider approach to consultation regarding the Convention. In partnership with the Dag Hammarskjöld Foundation, the UN Economic Commission for Africa (ECA), and UNHCR, it convened a major conference on the legal, economic, and social aspects of African refugee problems in Addis Ababa in 1967 (Betts 1967). Thus, the conference brought together what was thought to be the key relevant stakeholders in constructing rules relating to the peculiarities of the refugee problem in Africa. The outcome was the recommendation that a new refugee definition be adopted specifically for Africa. Significantly, this was the first time that the international rules regarding refugees under the 1951 UN Convention were officially acknowledged as potentially insufficient in addressing the specific situation in Africa, for instance the status of freedom fighters, as the existing definition of refugees would not have covered them.

What the OAU Refugee Convention shows is that the OAU, as an international organisation, was able to use its rule-making process to address a challenge that was specific to the continent and also leverage engagement with external stakeholders. Though the process was initially dominated by member states, the OAU and its membership decided to engage with international stakeholders, including the Dag Hammarskjöld Foundation, UNECA, and UNHCR, in producing the OAU Refugee Convention.

The approach adopted to rule-making with regard to the OAU Refugee Convention laid the groundwork for the adoption of rules governing Internally Displaced Persons (IDPs) in Africa. The rules are contained in the AU Convention for the Protection and Assistance of Internally Displaced Persons in Africa (Kampala Convention), adopted in 2009 and entered into force in 2012. Importantly, it is the first regional legal framework to address the issue of internal displacement in Africa. The Convention broadly makes provision for the protection and assistance of IDPs on the continent. IDPs are defined therein as persons or groups of persons who have been forced to flee or leave their homes or places of habitual residence as a result of armed conflicts, generalised violence, human rights violations, or natural or human-made disasters, among other reasons. The rules created in the Kampala Convention strongly complement and reinforce the OAU Refugee Convention by addressing IDPs within national borders while the latter covers those who have crossed international borders.

And in 2018, the AU adopted a model law to provide guidance to member states on how to protect and assist IDPs within their respective borders. This is the AU Model Law for the Implementation of the AU Convention for the Protection of and Assistance to Internally Displaced Persons (African Union 2018; African Union 2009). The model law, inter alia, provides a comprehensive legal framework for addressing the needs of IDPs, including the establishment of national laws and policies, the identification and registration of IDPs, the protection of their rights, and the provision of assistance and support.

3 RULEMAKING IN THE AFRICAN UNION

3.1 Background

3.1.1 Transforming the OAU into the AU: a new approach to rule-making or old wine in new bottles?

The raison d'être for the establishment of the OAU was to consolidate and lead the movement toward decolonising and to harness Africa's resources within a united vision of an independent Africa, thus bringing an end to the misfortunes suffered under colonialism. African independence was set up to occur within the colonial demarcated frontiers, creating new nation states imposed by the departing colonial powers, reflecting European interests instead of African linguistic, historic, and cultural realities (Meredith 2005, p. 1). The notion of modern statehood, not familiar to Africa prior to colonisation, thus became one of the realities that an independent Africa inevitably embraced and an important building block in the politics and architecture of future continental cooperation. An intellectual leader of the time, Nkrumah's prioritising of the 'political kingdom' (Pierre 2012, Chapter 2) in the liberation struggle against colonialism meant that political independence with the concomitant sovereignty, territorial integrity, and non-interference took precedence over matters such as socio-economic prosperity. The notion of *uti possidetis* (Dugard 2005, pp. 130–131) was accepted by the International Court of Justice in the *Frontier Dispute Case* (International Court of Justice 1986, p. 554) where it commented that '[T]he maintenance of territorial status quo in Africa is often seen as the wisest course, to preserve what has been achieved by peoples who have struggled for their independence, and to avoid a disruption which would deprive the continent of gains achieved by much sacrifice' (p. 567). This principle was indeed reflected in the OAU purposes and principles and became embedded in post-colonial African intellectual discourse (Ibhawoh 2020, p. 35). The widespread internal tensions and rivalries afflicting most African states after independence re-endorsed the idea that only a strong centralised state would provide the stability needed to develop and prosper (Meredith 2005, p. 175), hence the rise and popularity of so-called one-party states. Consequently, the influence of non-state African stakeholders outside of the ruling party was excluded from decision-making. The principles of good governance and political tolerance needed to help democracy take root in culturally diverse states were compromised at the behest of strong leaders backed up often by military power.

As in the case of the OAU, the AU principles and objectives clearly reflect this thinking (sovereignty, territorial integrity, non-interference, respect for colonial borders) with relatively weak provisions for continental governance and organisational decision-making (Olivier 2015). At the same time, lip service is paid to the ideals of African Unity, Pan Africanism, and one Africaness or negritude (Ome 2014) as expressed by African intelligentsia such as Leopold Senghor. With colonialism out of the way, African leaders were challenged by the daunting task of making their political kingdoms prosper and delivering on promises of development, education, medical care, and land. As these efforts floundered, corruption, conflicts, and political dictatorships flourished with an OAU, which represented only the political elite of member states and possessed limited powers and appetite to intervene in domestic affairs. Gradually, the realisation took root that economic development, democratic governance, and respect for human rights go hand in hand and that some level of transparency, accountability, and external scrutiny in the domestic affairs of a sovereign state should be permitted. Calls for an African renaissance, first articulated by Cheikh Anta Diop in a series of essays between 1946 and 1960 (Nicol 1979, pp. 3–11) and further popularised by former President of South Africa Thabo Mbeki during his tenure as Deputy President of South Africa in 1997, prompted a different way of thinking. This was followed by the establishment of the African Peer Review Mechanism (APRM) (2003), a tool for sharing experiences, reinforcing best practices, identifying deficiencies, and assessing capacity-building needs to foster policies, standards, and practices that lead to political stability, high economic growth, sustainable development, and accelerated sub-regional and continental economic integration. The APRM followed the New Partnership for Africa's Development (NEPAD) (2001) aimed at making way for a new approach to advance African development under the AU. Yet African leaders, preoccupied with staying in power, are still in the pound seats and vested interests remain a stumbling block in turning away from the AU's core values protecting absolute sovereignty as a cloak for lack of accountability, corruption, and authoritarianism. The discussion below will illustrate the extent to which the AU's founding treaties make way for an empowered continental organisation using law as a tool to improve governance and accelerate development.

3.2 How are the OAU and the AU different?

The OAU Charter is a document speaking to the realities of its time and not a complex legal text. More than thirty years later, African states have achieved independence, and priorities have now shifted to security, economic development, democracy, and human rights with the adoption of the AU Constitutive Act in 2000. The purposes of the Constitutive Act retain many of its predecessors' purposes as objectives but move well beyond. The preamble specifically refers to a range of stakeholders: 'Guided by our common vision of a united and strong Africa and by the need to build a partnership between governments and all segments of civil society, in particular women, youth, and the private sector, in order to strengthen solidarity and cohesion among our peoples.'

Comparing the OAU Purposes (art II OAU Charter) with the AU Objectives (art 3, Constitutive Act), the AU has a list of fourteen objectives compared to the OAU's five. Overlapping objectives/purposes relate to the ideals of African unity and solidarity; defending sovereignty, territorial integrity, and independence; and the encouragement of international cooperation. (OAU Charter, arts II, III; Constitutive Act, arts 3, 4) The OAU's purpose to eradicate all forms of colonialism is not repeated by the AU for obvious reasons. The purpose to coordinate and cooperate to achieve a better life for Africans (art II(b) OAU Charter) does not appear as such in the Constitutive Act, although the underlying sentiment is present but refined in objectives dealing with political and socio-economic integration (art 3(c)); and the promotion of cooperation to raise the living standards of Africans (art 3(k)). New objectives introduced by the AU cover regional integration (art 3(c)); peace and security (art 3(f)); the promotion of democratic principles and good governance (art 3(g)); the promotion and protection of human rights; participation in the global economy and the international stage (art 3(i)); sustainable development (art 3(j)); coordination between Regional Economic Communities (RECs); and development through science and technology (art 3(m)). Thus, although moving on from the eradication of colonialism, some key tenets are retained but the AU's objectives cover a much broader spectrum (Magliveras 2021, pp. 39–43).

3.2.1 Comparing the OAU organs with those of the AU

Compared to the OAU's four organs, the Constitutive Act provides for at least nine organs (the Assembly may also decide to establish additional organs) with a range of executive and administrative powers but also some powers at legislative and judicial levels. The purposes of the organs are to give effect to the organisation's objectives in accordance with the stipulated principles. The AU Assembly is essentially the OAU's Assembly of Heads of State and Government (supreme organ of both institutions) where the seat of power is vested. The AU Executive Council is similar to the OAU Council of Ministers. The OAU Secretariat and Commission of Mediation, Conciliation, and Arbitration are not mentioned by name. In addition, the AU adds the Pan-African Parliament; the Court of Justice; the Commission; the Peace and Security Council (replacing the Permanent Representative Committee by the

Protocol on Amendments to the Constitutive Act of the African Union, 2003); Special Technical Committees; the Economic, Social and Cultural Council (ECOSOCC); and the Financial Institutions. The Constitutive Act makes no provision for direct participation by non-state stakeholders in the Assembly and the Executive Council. The remaining organs, particularly the specialised technical committees and ECOSOCC, will inevitably depend on sourcing outside expertise to execute their functions. In the case of ECOSOCC, article 22 of the Constitutive Act specifically states that it is an 'advisory organ composed of *different social and professional groups* of the member states of the Union' (own emphasis).

The Constitutive Act contains provisions on the decision-making powers of the various organs that will be discussed below, also pointing to comparable powers of AU organs where applicable. Specific provisions on decision-making should be interpreted with due regard to the AU Objectives (art 3) and Principles (art 4) as the various organs are responsible for their execution.

Only the Assembly and the Executive Council possess externalpowers, meaning powers that could by implication bind member states. The Assembly, as supreme organ, for example, has the power to determine AU policies; take decisions on reports and recommendations coming from the other organs; monitor the implementation of policies and decisions and ensure compliance by all member states; and give directives to the Executive Council on the management of conflicts, emergencies, and the restoration of peace (Constitutive Act, art 9 (a), (b), (e), and (g)).

The remaining powers focusing on internal matters of the organisation will not be discussed. The powers of the OAU's Assembly were more basic: to discuss matters of common concern and to coordinate and harmonise the general policy of the OAU (OAU Charter, art 8).

The AU Assembly is backed up by the Executive Council, which is also responsible for policymaking with the power to make decisions (by consensus) on policy matters in several common interest areas (art 13). It appears that final decisions in most matters will lie with the Assembly, with the Executive Council acting as a monitor for implementation of policies adopted by the Assembly. The OAU's equivalent Council of Ministers had a similar support function, being entrusted with the implementation of the decisions of the Assembly and coordinating inter-African cooperation in accordance with the instructions of the Assembly. These are very broad and open-ended. What is interesting is that although the OAU Charter contains very little substantive detail and explicit provisions on decision-making, there is frequent reference that functions should be carried out in accordance with the provisions of the Charter (art VIII), Secretary-General and Secretariat (art XVIII), and Specialized Commissions (art XXII). It is presumed that Assembly policy and the purposes of the OAU played a central role in determining powers.

There are limited provisions empowering the AU to take decisions directly binding on member states, but the Constitutive Act is more direct in matters of internal governance of the organisation compared to the OAU. However, for the AU to execute its mandate under the preamble, objectives, and principles, some implied norm-creating capacity will be needed. (See, for example promoting and protecting human rights, democratic institutions, good governance and the rule of law (art 4(m)), and intervention in member states under grave circumstances (art 4(h).) This has led to an emergent African Union law (Amao, Olivier, Magliveras (eds), 2021). The newly added provision on the imposition of sanctions to be determined by the Assembly against member states that default in payments of contributions to the AU budget and where member states fail to comply with AU decisions and policies significantly adds to the Assembly's decision-making powers (AU Constitutive Act, art 23).

Important new principles added to the mandate of the AU can be found in Articles 4 (h), (j), and (p): intervention in a member state pursuant to a decision of the Assembly under grave circumstances, namely war crimes, genocide, and crimes against humanity; intervention on request of member states in order to restore peace; and condemnation and rejection of unconstitutional changes of government. These principles, however, are not matched to specific powers of the Assembly and the Council, leaving many questions as to scope and responsibility.

Given the open-ended and vague nature of substantive decision-making powers of the various AU organs, the Preamble, in addition to the 'objectives' (art 3) and 'principles' (art 4), should be used as a tool for treaty interpretation. The Preamble calls for a united and strong Africa determined to promote and protect human rights, democratic institutions, good governance, and the rule of law. This creates the expectation that the organs will be empowered to give effect to these ambitions (Olivier 2021). The Preamble underlines the importance for governments to build partnerships with all segments of civil society, in particular women, youth, and the private sector. This provision was expanded by the Protocol on Amendments to the Constitutive Act, adding as new objectives to ensure the effective participation of women in decision-making and inviting and encouraging the full participation of the African Diaspora in the building of the AU (Protocol on Amendments to the Constitutive Act 2003, art 3 (i) and (q)). These provisions would hopefully lead to broader and inclusive consultation informing inclusive decision-making (Amao 2021, pp. 47–48).

3.2.2 New organs with decision-making capacity introduced by the AU

The PAP (Protocol on Amendments to the Constitutive Act (2003), art 3(i) and (q)) is the organ foreseen by the Constitutive Act (art 17) that would ensure full participation of African peoples in the development and economic integration of Africa. The eventual goal is to establish a body with law-making powers, elected by universal adult suffrage representing all the peoples of Africa. (Protocol Establishing the African Economic Community relating to the Pan-African Parliament (2001), art 2.) Wider stakeholder participation is therefore at the core of PAP, which, pending the adoption of an amending Protocol, has only consultative and advisory powers. This was followed by the Protocol to the Constitutive Act of the AU relating to the Pan-African Parliament (Malabo Protocol 2014) that clearly endorses the imperative and urgent need for African unity and the commitment to democratic principles and popular participation, yet does not provide for any real legislative powers. Neither will PAP members be directly elected from member States. Each AU member state shall be represented by five members elected by the respective national parliaments or other deliberative bodies from outside their membership. The legislative powers provided for by the Malabo Protocol are severely qualified. The PAP shall, in addition to debating, discussing and making proposals, be limited to propose model laws on subject areas determined by the Assembly or on subjects/areas it would like to suggest for consideration and approval by the Assembly. It will be a case where the supposedly democratic legislature is subordinate to the heads of state and government composing the Assembly. Despite the limited legislative powers granted by the Malabo Protocol, only 15 states have ratified the Protocol as of March 2025, falling short of the 28 ratifications needed to bring it into force. In its present form, the PAP is an advisory body that fails to provide a platform for ordinary Africans to participate in shaping continental governance.

The African Commission on Human and Peoples' Rights (ACHPR), a quasi-judicial body established under the African Charter on Human and Peoples' Rights that came into force in 1986, is charged with monitoring the promotion and protection of human and peoples' rights of all African peoples (African Charter, art 30). Members of the Commission are Africans elected based on reputation, integrity, impartiality, and competence and serving in their personal capacity (art 31). Article 45 of the African Charter specifies the mandate of the ACHPR using broad language such as the promotion and protection of human rights, collection of documents, research, organisation of seminars, dissemination of information, and formulation of rules and principles that governments may follow; international cooperation in the field of human rights; and interpretation of the Charter and other tasks. No mention is made of granting the power to take binding and enforceable decisions. It may receive communications from both State Parties about Charter violations by other State Parties (art 47) and from individuals and NGOs who are not necessarily aggrieved parties (art 55). The ACHPR has established itself as a human rights watchdog by interpreting the African Charter; by considering interstate and other complaints; and by analysing the reports submitted by State Parties on their implementation of the African Charter and other African human rights conventions (Olivier 2015).

As far as the AU's judicial organs are concerned, the African Court on Human and Peoples' Rights, established in 1998 under the OAU, and the African Court of Justice, established by the 2003 Protocol on the African Court of Justice, were combined to form a single court, namely the African Court of Justice and Human Rights, by the Protocol on the Statute of the African Court of Justice and Human Rights in 2008. This Protocol has not yet achieved the required fifteen ratifications to enter into force. Once operational, the merged Court will enjoy jurisdiction to hear cases and provide advisory opinions on the interpretation and application of the Constitutive Act, AU human rights treaties, AU decisions, and questions of international law (art 28). Once African states have mustered the political will to bring this Court into operation, it will provide a robust enforcement mechanism presently lacking.

The African Court on Human and Peoples' Rights, which is presently still operational, has a more limited jurisdiction compared to the merged Court. It has jurisdiction to deal with human rights matters and cases, as well as disputes regarding the interpretation and application of the African Charter, the Protocol to the African Charter on Human and Peoples' Rights on the Establishment of an African Court on Human and Peoples' Rights, and any other relevant human rights instrument (Protocol to the African Charter on Human and Peoples' Rights on the Establishment of an African Court on Human and Peoples' Rights, 2004 arts 3 and 4). Under Article 4 of the Protocol, the Court may, at the request of an AU member state, any AU organ, or any African organisation recognised by the AU, provide an opinion on any legal matter relating to the African Charter or other relevant human rights instruments, provided that the subject matter of the opinion is not related to a matter under examination by the ACHPR. Of the present 34 state parties to the Protocol, only seven have deposited the declaration accepting the jurisdiction of the Court to receive cases from individuals and non-governmental organisations. The low level of ratifications and declarations threatens to limit the Court's role as a human rights watchdog within the AU (Naldi 2021, 319).

A new and important advisory organ is the African Union Commission on International Law (AUCIL), which was established under Article 5(2) of the Constitutive Act of the AU. The Statute of the AUCIL, adopted by the Assembly at the Twelfth Session in 2009, includes the objectives of 'codification and progressive development of international law in the African continent with particular attention to the laws of the Union as embodied in the treaties of the Union, in the decisions of the policy organs of the Union and in African customary international law arising from the practice of Member States'.

Further objectives are to propose model laws, treaties, and the formulation and analysis of state practice.

The Peace and Security Council (PSC), added as an AU organ by the Protocol on Amendments to the Constitutive Act of the African Union in 2003, is designated as 'the standing decision-making organ for the prevention, management, and resolution of conflicts'. To achieve the objectives to promote peace and prevent conflicts, a comprehensive array of powers is granted to the PSC (Protocol relating to the Establishment of the Peace and Security Council of the African Union 2003, art 7). The PSC is mandated to act on behalf of member States, which in turn agree to accept and implement its decisions.

The PSC Protocol re-endorses the right of the AU to intervene in a member state pursuant to an Assembly decision (Constitutive Act, art 4(h)) in respect of grave circumstances, namely war crimes, genocide, crimes against humanity, and to restore peace and stability where the legitimate order is under threat (arts 4 (j) and (k)). If operative, these provisions have the potential to grant powers to the Assembly that could be compared with the UN Security Council.

4 AFRICAN UNION RELATIONS WITH EXTERNAL STAKEHOLDERS AND THE PARTNERSHIP WITH THE OECD

4.1 The AU's over-reliance on external stakeholders

As was the case with the OAU, the AU has relied on external stakeholders primarily to fund its activities and programmes, to be assisted in their implementation, and to receive expertise and skills. The AU has promoted diplomatic relations with an increasing number of external stakeholders. Arguably, the drafters of the Constitutive Act realised that the continent had been kept away from the globalised international community and that reversing this negative situation required their support (in AU parlance they are invariably called 'international partners'; President of the Italian Republic 2024). Article 3 of the Constitutive Act (the AU's objectives) asserts this argument. The following three provisions are of direct bearing: the AU shall encourage international cooperation in accordance with the UN Charter and the Universal Declaration of Human Rights (Constitutive Act, art 3(e)); shall establish the necessary conditions which enable the continent to play its rightful role in the global economy and in international negotiations (art 3(i)); and shall work together with the relevant international partners to eradicate preventable diseases and promote good health on the continent (art 3(n)).

As with other regional international organisations, a balance must be maintained between, on the one hand, engaging with external stakeholders and reaping the benefits of close cooperation and, on the other hand, the risk of over-reliance. Arguably, the AU has not maintained this balance, which has shifted (permanently?) towards dependency. This is best exemplified by the Report, which in 2016 the AU Assembly asked Paul Kagame, the President of Rwanda, to prepare on how the AU should be reformed to create a system of governance capable of addressing the continent's challenges. According to the Kagame Report, there were two relevant challenges. First, the AU was neither financially independent nor self-sustained but had to rely on external stakeholders' funding. Second, its programmes had to be financed in a sustainable manner and, at the same time, reliance on external partners had to be reduced. However, '[T]his level of dependence on external partner funds raises a fundamental question: How can member states own the African Union if they do not set its agenda?' (African Union 2017, p. 14; Amao and Olivier 2021).

The Report revealed a troubling reality that has never been seriously discussed by member states. But it is also a complicated reality: the very large financial assistance that the AU receives from external stakeholders as well as its requests for expertise and skills may come with strings and conditions attached. For example, African countries may have to buy goods and services only from these external stakeholders. Moreover, this long-lasting situation could possibly lead to a dictation of policy. Even though there is no clear evidence of the latter, two relevant examples will be given. First, the request made in 2022 by the Peace and Security Council (PSC) to the AU Commission to develop an 'effective collaborative mechanism' for strengthening the AU regime on sanctions specifically 'in collaboration with the UN stakeholders and … UN Security Council Permanent Members' (AU PSC 2022, para. 8). Arguably, this example shows that the AU's appeal to the expertise of international partners might very well influence the process of rule-making as regards sanctions specifically. Second, the Assembly's statement during its Twenty-Eighth Ordinary Session that 'external parties' shall only be invited to participate in its sessions (invariably referred to as 'Summits', which now take place once yearly) 'on an exceptional basis and for a specific purpose determined by the interests of the [AU]' (AU Assembly, 2017: para. 5(c)(iv)). As also explained above, considerable rule-making takes place in the Assembly, including the adoption of protocols to existing OAU/AU treaties, the adoption of new treaties, the approval of policy instruments (e.g., common positions, model laws), etc. Therefore, one reading of said Decision is that the Assembly wanted to restrict intervention by non-AU stakeholders in the AU's work. These two examples were specifically chosen because they illustrate opposite situations, leading to the conclusion that the AU is rather unclear as to the influence/impact it is prepared to accept from international partners.

Figures from the AU's regular budgets (operating budgets and programme budgets; the budgets for peace support operations are set separately) during the last ten years confirm the over-reliance on external stakeholders. Thus, in

Financial Year (FY) 2014 the regular budget was 308 million USD and 50% was covered by 'international partners'; in FY 2016 it increased to 417 million USD with 60% covered from outside Africa, while in FY 2017 a staggering 74% was contributed by external stakeholders (the budget was 439 million USD). Even though the AU Assembly had resolved that by 2022 the whole operational budget, 75% of the programme budget, and 25% of the peace operations budget should be funded by member States (African Union Assembly 2015, para. 2), it proved unrealistic and was extended to 2025 (African Union Executive Council 2021, para. 14). However, the FY 2023 budget had already shown that it could not be achieved, forecasting that dependency on external stakeholders will continue *ad infinitum*. In particular, seventy-seven percent of the programme budget was expected from international partners, while the peace operations budget (252 million USD) was to be funded in full by them (AU Executive Council 2022B, para. 45). As also testified by the budget for FY 2024 (AU Executive Council 2023B, para. 4) and the Annual Procurement Plan 2024 (African Union Commission 2024), without non-African emoluments, the AU would probably be unable to carry out its activities and programmes. To the best of one's knowledge, no other regional international organization is so dependent upon external funding.

4.2 AU relations with external stakeholders and the 'Need to speak with one voice'

That the AU pursues relations with many external stakeholders (African Union Commission 2014) could be explained by the need for external funding as well as for the transfer of knowledge, skills, and experience, including in the area of rule-making and legal drafting. However, several member states, as well as RECs, have pursued their own dealings with external stakeholders (e.g., the Southern Africa Development Community (SADC) with the European Union (SADC-EU 2021)), which may not align with the AU's needs and priorities. Furthermore, certain states have increasingly transacted with and within Africa, primarily for economic and commercial reasons, lured by the continent's vast natural resources and its rising middle class (Melber 2022). To counter this development, traditional African partners, such as the EU and the USA, have shown a renewed interest (Huliaras and Magliveras 2008) and increasingly pledge more funds for Africa and its people: the conclusions of the Sixth EU-AU Summit (February 2022) and the US–Africa Leaders Summit (December 2022) are clear evidence.

In December 2017, the African Union Partnerships Coordination and Interactive Platform (AU-PCIP) was established to rationalise relations with the rest of the world. The following year, the Head of AU-PCIP said that 'the cooperation between Africa and its partners has mainly been a donor-recipient driven relationship that is skewed in favour of the donors [but] Africa wants … [p]artnerships that will be based on equality, accountability, mutual respect, efficiency, ownership and win-win cooperation'. And to achieve this goal while avoiding duplication of efforts, African states 'need to speak with one voice' (Madueke 2018). The reference to 'one voice' was in line with the objective in the Constitutive Act article 3(d), namely that the AU will promote and defend common positions on behalf of the continent and its people. Thus, the AU should be the only party to negotiate and transact with international partners, a view echoed in Aspiration 7 of Agenda 2063 (titled 'Africa as a strong, united, resilient and influential global player and partner'), which regards collaboration with international partners as a key objective in re-orienting AU partnerships and making them inclusive of the continent's economic, political, and social transformation. This will be achieved by strengthening common perspectives on external partnerships and by 'speaking with one voice' on priorities and global matters. To that end, an 'Africa's Partnership Strategy and Policy Framework' has been developed but not finalised (Apiko 2021; AU Executive Council 2023A, paras. 91 et seq.). It appears that member states want to have a far more inclusive role in these matters. This is inferred by the Assembly's reaffirmation of the right of all members to participate in statutory meetings relating to partnerships with external stakeholders (AU Assembly 2020, para. A(5)).

There are presently nine AU formal partnerships: (a) League of Arab States (LAS). Given that ten out of the twenty-two LAS member states are from Africa, relations with LAS have always been strong: the OAU supported the Palestinian cause (cf the African Committee on the Question of Palestine) (OAU Assembly, 1973) and the AU has endorsed the Palestinians' 'legitimate struggle against the Israeli colonial occupation' (AU Assembly, 2021); (b) EU; (c) South America; (d) India; (e) South Korea; (f) Turkey; (g) China; (h) USA; and (i) Japan. Even though these partnerships (developments on which are reviewed by the Executive Council (AU Executive Council 2022A, paras. 37–64; AU Executive Council 2023A, paras. 94–103)) are not directly linked to rule-making, it is submitted that the joint conclusions reached at summit meetings with the respective partners might result in AU action akin to rule-making. For example, at the Sixth EU-AU Summit, the two sides committed themselves, inter alia, to address domestic tax base erosion and tax transparency, to fight money laundering and terrorism financing, and to promote accountable and transparent governance (EU-AU Summit 2022). The AU should adopt the necessary instruments and/or revise existing ones to give effect to these commitments, and one could expect that it will be influenced by the relevant EU norms and rules.

This list of formal partnerships does not include the very close and multifaceted AU-UN collaboration, which goes back to OAU's founding (OAU

Assembly 1965). It has been enhanced through the work of the UN Economic Commission for Africa and, in the area of peace and security, through the United Nations Office to the African Union (UNOAU), established under UN General Assembly Resolution 64/288 on 1 July 2010 (UN Security Council 2022). Currently, there are more than thirty UN entities represented at the AU (African Union Commission & New Zealand Ministry of Foreign Affairs and Trade 2023, pp. 198–201). Finally, while not a formal collaboration, relations with BRICS are important on account of the AU having formal partnerships with two members (China and India), the membership of the Republic of South Africa, and of the Russian involvement in African affairs going back to the 1960s when the continent was a Cold War theatre (Swift 2003, pp. 90–91).

4.3 AU relations with the OECD and the still unfinished road towards a partnership

Although the OECD includes members from Europe, North and South America, and the Asia-Pacific region, no African state has joined it. However, several African states participate as members in OECD entities and initiatives, including the following two. First, the OECD Development Centre. Created in 1961 as an independent platform for knowledge sharing and policy dialogue between the OECD and developing economies, presently South Africa (since 2006); Egypt (2008); Mauritius and Morocco (2009); Senegal (2011); Cabo Verde (2011); Côte d'Ivoire and Tunisia (2015); Ghana (2015); Togo (2019); and Rwanda (2019) participate. South Africa is one of OECD's five Key Partners (OECD 2022A: 11). Second, the MENA-OECD Initiative on Governance and Competitiveness for Development. Established in 2005 to foster policies for sustainable and inclusive growth (OECD 2016), its scope was augmented in 2021 to address long-term socio-economic development opportunities and peace-building objectives in conflict-affected economies (OECD 2021); presently Algeria, Egypt, Libya, Mauritania, and Tunisia participate. Moreover, African states are parties to several OECD treaties and legal instruments, including the Convention on Mutual Administrative Assistance in Tax Matters (1988) and Amending Protocol (2010), and the Convention on Combating Bribery of Foreign Public Officials in International Business Transactions (1997). Finally, in 2014, an AU-OECD MOU was signed (renewed in 2016) principally on economic and social development that has resulted in joint activities in the areas of statistics, taxation, extractive industries, and so on.

African states and RECs have always been interested in engaging with the OECD, but also OECD members have also pursued expansive relations with Africa, especially through the OECD Regional Programmes (OECD, 2017, para. 24; OECD Secretary-General, 2018). Thus, in October 2021, when the OECD Council celebrated the 60th year of operation, it adopted the (first)

OECD Global Relations Strategy, which includes Africa as a target region (OECD 2022B, 15), and the 60th Anniversary Vision Statement, which calls for the engagement with the AU to be enhanced (OECD Council 2021, 5). Arguably, the time was ripe to upgrade relations with the AU and establish a partnership. The OECD Secretary-General prepared a working document for the June 2022 Ministerial Council to 'narrow down the scope and define the main pillars of the partnership' (OECD 2022A, 7), aiming 'to build an impactful partnership based on trust, mutual understanding, and enhanced co-operation on an equal footing, to address mutually agreed priorities' (OECD 2022A, 4). In the framework of this Council meeting, the 21st International Economic Forum on Africa took place under the theme 'Africa in the emerging global economic order', where the intention to upgrade collaboration through a strong and equal partnership based on trust and mutual understanding was announced. Devised as a mechanism for institutional coordination, it will initially specify the strategic goals, priorities, and main areas of work. This collaboration will take more concrete form through a bilateral MOU, which will evolve the sectoral cooperation as presently laid down in the 2014 and 2016 MOUs. This MOU, which will integrate operational modalities and the governance mechanism for AU/OECD dealings (OECD Council 2023, para. 29), has not yet been yet concluded.

5 CONCLUSION: POLICY RECOMMENDATIONS

The AU, now in its twenty-third year of operation, can no doubt be credited with enhancing the status of the African continent on the world stage and accelerating cooperation amongst African states in vital areas such as peace and security, democratic governance, human rights, and economic and trade relations. As the largest regional international organisation in terms of member states, it strives towards progressively realising an ambitious set of stated goals and aspirations, culminating in a long-term development blueprint expressed by Agenda 2063. While the AU has taken significant strides forward, its decision-making procedures are not inclusive of all potential stakeholders, its resolutions do not enjoy the binding nature they should, and its governance structures should improve. A significant factor hampering progress is the slow pace of member states' implementation and observance of its often very ambitious legal instruments. Here AU law provides an important tool. As the present chapter's authors have argued, a distinct AU legal system has developed and could greatly assist in implementing, enforcing, and facilitating the progress that Africa so desperately seeks (Amao, Olivier, and Magliveras, eds, 2021).

Apart from African leaders' reluctance to observe supranational commitments and follow AU rules and norms, the lack of adequate funding for programmes and activities remains a major problem. Like the OAU, the AU has relied on funding received from external stakeholders. While such reliance does not necessarily result in dependence, often the lines between the two are not very discernible. To operate independently and to give a voice to 'African solutions to African problems', continued operational dependence on foreign funding should be limited. Undoubtedly, international organisations are ready to support the AU, offer valuable know-how, and transfer skills. To that end, the OECD could have an important role to play. After all, several of its 38 member states engage with Africa as a whole (apart from those which are also EU members, suffice it to mention Japan, South Korea, the USA, and Great Britain), being as it were AU 'external stakeholders'. An inter-connected Africa with a population almost equal to that of China or India and a fast-rising middle class could offer diverse collaboration opportunities with multilateral institutions like the OECD.

But to do so, the AU must be fully equipped and fit both institutionally and procedurally. Therefore, the Constitutive Act should be urgently revised to cover, inter alia, economic integration, sustainable development, transcontinental networks and infrastructure, and relations with external stakeholders. Finally, the African Court of Justice should become operative; the role of the PAP should be seriously upgraded; the Peace and Security Council should become a proper organ; and the Statutes of the African Investment Bank and the African Development Bank should enter into force.

BIBLIOGRAPHY

Abebe, A, Abebe, T.T. and Sharpe, M. 2019, 'The 1969 OAU Refugee Convention at 50' ISS Africa Report 2019 No. 19: 1–15.

African Peer Review Mechanism, <https://au.int/en/organs/aprm> accessed 28 February 2024.

African Union, April 2022, <https://au.int/sites/default/files/treaties/7806-sl-Protocol_to_the_Constitutive_Act_of_the_African_Union_Relating_to_the_Pan-African_Parliament.pdf> accessed 28 February 2024.

African Union, 2017, 'The Imperative to Strengthen our Union: Report on the Proposed Recommendations for the Institutional Reform of the African Union', Report presented at the Second Retreat of Heads of State and Government of the African Union, Addis Ababa, 27 January, <https://static.pmg.org.za/Kagame_Report.pdf> accessed 28 February 2024.

African Union, 2009, African Union Convention for the Protection and Assistance of Internally Displaced Persons in Africa (Kampala Convention) <available at https://au.int/en/treaties/african-union-convention-protection-and-assistance-internally-displaced-persons-africa> accessed 8 February 2025.

African Union, 2018, Model Law for the Implementation of the African Union Convention for the Protection of and Assistance to Internally Displaced Persons in Africa, <https://www.refworld.org/legal/modellaw/au/2018/en/120774> accessed 8 February 2025.

African Union Commission, 2014, Report on Multilateral Cooperation with respect to Africa's Strategic Partnerships, EX.CL/802(XXIV)iv, January.

African Union Assembly, 2015, Decision on the Scale of Assessment and Alternative Sources of Financing the African Union, Assembly/AU/Dec.578(XXV), 15 June.

African Union Assembly, 2017, Decision on the Outcome of the Retreat of the Assembly of the African Union on the Institutional Reform of the African Union, Assembly/AU/Dec.635(XXVIII), 31 January.

African Union Assembly, 2020, Decision on Multilateral Cooperation, Assembly/AU/Dec.762(XXXIII), 10 February.

African Union Assembly, 2022, Declaration on the Situation in Palestine and the Middle East, Assembly/AU/Decl.1(XXXV), 6 February.

African Union Commission, 2024, Annual Procurement Plan 2024, 1 January <https://au.int/sites/default/files/documents/43419-doc-AUC-Annual_Procurement_Plan_2024-01-01–1.pdf> accessed 28 February 2024.

African Union Executive Council, 2021, Decision on the Report of the Joint Sitting of the Ministerial Committee on Scale of Assessment and Contributions and the Committee of Fifteen Ministers of Finance (F15), EX.CL/Dec.1119(XXXVIII), 4 February.

African Union Executive Council, 2022A, Decision on the Reports of the Sub-Committees of the Permanent Representatives' Committee (PRC), EX.CL/Dec.1143(XL), 3 February.

African Union Executive Council, 2022B, Decision on the Reports of the Sub-Committees of the Permanent Representatives' Committee (PRC), EX.CL/Dec.1168(XLI), 15 July.

African Union Executive Council, 2023A, Decision on the Reports of the Sub-Committees of the Permanent Representatives' Committee (PRC), EX.CL/Dec.1189(XLII), 16 February.

African Union Executive Council, 2023B, Decision on the African Union Budget for 2024, EX.CL/Dec.1217(XLIII), 14 July.

African Union Peace and Security Council, 2022, 1100th Meeting, Communiqué on Sanctions and Enforcement Capacities: Deterrence Against Unconstitutional Changes of Government, PSC/PR/COMM.1100 (2022), 15 August.

African Union Commission & New Zealand Ministry of Foreign Affairs and Trade, 2023, African Union Handbook, Addis Ababa, Ethiopia and Wellington, New Zealand <https://au.int/en/handbook> accessed 28 February 2024.

Amao, O. 2021, 'Framing AU Law through the Lenses of International Constitutionalization and Federalism', in O. Amao, M. Olivier and K. Magliveras (eds), *The Emergent African Union Law*, Oxford University Press, Oxford, 45–62.

Amao, O., M. Olivier and K. Magliveras (eds), 2021, *The Emergent African Union Law*, Oxford University Press, Oxford.

Amao, O. and M. Olivier, 2021, 'AU Law and Its Future: Reform and the Kagame Report', in O. Amao, M. Olivier and K. Magliveras (eds), *The Emergent African Union Law*, Oxford University Press, Oxford, 459–466.

Apiko, P. 2021, 'Getting Partnerships Right: The Case for an AU Strategy', European Centre for Development Policy Management, Discussion Paper No. 313, November, <https://ecdpm.org/work/getting-partnerships-right-the-case-for-an-au-strategy> accessed 28 February 2024.

Betts, T.F. 1967, 'Conference on the Legal, Economic, and Social Aspects of African Refugee Problems', *The Journal of Modern African Studies*, 5, 4, 561–564.

Cervenka, Z. 1969, *The Organisation of African Unity and its Charter*, C. Hurst & Company, London.
Charter of the Organization of African Unity, 1963.
Charter of the United Nations, 1945.
Constitutive Act of the African Union, 2000.
Dugard, J. 2005, *International Law A South African Perspective*, 3rd edition, Juta, Lansdowne, South Africa.
Elias, T.O. 1965, 'The Charter of the Organization of African Unity', The American Journal of International Law, 59, 2, 243.
EU–AU Summit, 2022, 6th European Union – African Union Summit: A Joint Vision for 2030, Final Declaration, 18 February.
Huliaras, A. and Magliveras, K. 2008, 'In Search of a Policy: European Union and U.S. Reactions to the Growing Chinese Presence in Africa', European Foreign Affairs Review, 13, 399–420.
Ibhawoh, B. 2020, 'Seeking the Political Kingdom', in A.D. Moses, M. Durant and R. Burke (eds), *Decolonization, Self-determination and the Rise of Global Human Rights Politics*, Cambridge University Press, Cambridge, doi:10.1017/9781108783170.
International Court of Justice, Frontier Dispute Case, Judgment, 1986 ICJ Reports 554.
Madueke, 2018, Opening Statement by Dr. Madueke, Head of African Union Strategic Partnerships, African Union Commission, at the 2nd Annual Conference of AU-PCIP, Accra, Ghana, 20–22 November, <https://au.int/sites/default/files/speeches/35399-sp-opening_statement_by_dr_madueke.pdf> accessed 28 February 2024.
Magliveras, K. 2021, 'The Implications of AU Law: Conceptual Analysis with Emphasis on the Institutional Consequences', in O. Amao, M. Olivier and K. Magliveras (eds), *The Emergent African Union Law*, Oxford University Press, Oxford, 30–45.
Maluwa, T. 2002, 'International Law-Making in Post-Colonial Africa: The Role of the Organization of African Unity', Netherlands International Law Review, 49, 1, 81–103.
Maluwa, T. 2004, 'The OAU/African Union and International Law: Mapping New Boundaries or Revisiting Old Terrain' Proceedings of the Annual Meeting, 98 American Society of International Law 232.
Maluwa, T. 2020, 'Reassessing Aspects of the Contribution of African States to the Development of International Law Through African Regional Multilateral Treaties', Michigan Journal of International Law, 41, 327.
Maluwa, T. 2012, 'The Transition from the Organisation of African Unity to the African Union' in Abdulqawi A. Yusuf and Fatsah Ouguergouz (eds), *The African Union: Legal and Institutional Framework: A Manual on the Pan-African Organization*, Martinus Nijhoff, Leiden, 28.
Melber, H. 2022, 'Africa's Middle Classes', Africa Spectrum, 57, 2, 204–219.
Meredith, M. 2005, *The State of Africa – A History of the Continent Since Independence*, Simon and Shuster, London.
Naldi, G. 2021, 'The Contribution of AU Human Rights Agreements to an Emergent AU law', in O. Amao, M. Olivier and K. Magliveras (eds), *The Emergent African Union Law*, Oxford University Press, Oxford, 319-334.
New Partnership for Africa's Development (NEPAD), <https://www.nepad.org/> accessed 28 February 2024.
Nicol, D. 1979, 'Alioune Diop and the African Renaissance', African Affairs, vol 78, no 310, 3–11 <https://www.africabib.org/query_a.php?pe=!242258980!&SR=3> accessed 28 February 2024.

Nyanduga, B. and T. Mukirya, 2004, 'Refugee Protection Under the 1969 OAU Convention Governing the Specific Aspects of Refugee Problems in Africa', German Yearbook of International Law, 47, 85.

OAU Assembly, 1965, Relations Between the Organization of African Unity and the United Nations, AHG/Res.33 (II), 26 October.

OAU Assembly, 1973, Resolution on the Continued Occupation by Israel of Part of the Territory of the Arab Republic of Egypt, AHG/Res. 70(X), 28 May.

OECD, 2016, Tunis Declaration, 4 October, <https://www.oecd.org/mena/ministerial/Declaration_Tunis_MENA_Ministerial_2016_EN.pdf> accessed 4 February 2024.

OECD, 2017, Ministerial Council Statement, 'Making Globalisation Work: Better Lives for All', 8 June, <https://one.oecd.org/document/C/MIN(2017)9/FINAL/en/pdf> accessed 28 February 2024.

OECD, 2021, Ministerial Declaration, 1 April, <https://www.oecd.org/fr/sites/mena/Ministerial-Declaration-2021.pdf> accessed 28 February 2024.

OECD Council, 2021, Trust in Global Cooperation – The Vision for the OECD for the Next Decade, C/MIN(2021)16/FINAL, accessed 28 February 2024

OECD, 2022A, The Secretary-General's Report to Ministers on the Implementation of the OECD Global Relations Strategy, C/MIN(2022)3, 1 June, <https://www.oecd.org/mcm/SG-Report-Implementation-OECD-Global-Relations-Strategy.pdf> accessed 28 February 2024.

OECD, 2022B, Meeting of the OECD Council at Ministerial Level, Paris, 9–10 June, Towards an OECD-Africa Partnership, <https://www.oecd.org/mcm/2022-OECD-Africa-Partnership-EN.pdf> accessed 28 February 2024.

OECD Council, 2023, Meeting of the OECD Council at Ministerial Level, Paris, OECD-AFRICA Partnership, 7–8 June.

OECD Secretary-General, 2018, The OECD's Mutual Engagement with Africa: Progress and Next Steps, Meeting of the Council at Ministerial Level, 30–31 May, C/MIN(2018)9, <https://one.oecd.org/document/C/MIN(2018)9/en/pdf> accessed 28 February 2024.

Olivier, M.E. 2015, 'The Role of African Union Law in Integrating Africa', South African Journal of International Affairs, vol 22, issue 4, 513–533.

Olivier, M.E. 2021, 'Conceptualizing AU Law within the Constitutional Framework of the AU', in O. Amao, M. Olivier and K. Magliveras (eds), *The Emergent African Union Law*, Oxford University Press, Oxford, 11–29.

Ome, E.M. 2014, 'Negritude: Leopold Sedar Senghor's Search for African Heritage and Identity', Sophia: An African Journal of Philosophy, vol 15, no 1, 47–54.

Pierre, J. 2012, *The Predicament of Blackness: Postcolonial Ghana and the Politics of Race*, University of Chicago Press, Chicago.

President of the Italian Republic, 2024, Remarks by the President of the Italian Republic on the occasion of the dinner in honour of the Heads of State and Government and other Dignitaries attending the Italy-Africa Summit, 28 January, <https://www.quirinale.it/elementi/107127> accessed 28 February 2024.

Protocol Establishing the African Economic Community relating to the Pan-African Parliament, 2001.

Protocol on Amendments to the Constitutive Act, 2003.

Protocol on the African Court on Human and Peoples' Rights, 1998.

Protocol relating to the Establishment of the Peace and Security Council of the African Union, 2003.

Protocol to the African Charter on Human and Peoples' Rights on the Establishment of an African Court on Human and Peoples' Rights, 2004.

Protocol to the Constitutive Act of the African Union relating to the Pan-African Parliament, 2014 (Malabo Protocol).

SADC-EU, 2021, Joint Communique SADC – EU Ministerial Political Dialogue, 16 June, <https://www.eeas.europa.eu/delegations/mauritius/joint-communique-sadc-eu-ministerial-political-dialogue-16-june-2021_und_en> accessed 28 February 2024.

Swift, J. 2003, *The Palgrave Concise Historical Atlas of the Cold War*, Palgrave Macmillan, London.

UN General Assembly, Convention Relating to the Status of Refugees, 28 July 1951, United Nations, Treaty Series, Vol. 189, p. 137.

UN Security Council, 2022, Strengthening the partnership between the United Nations and the African Union on issues of peace and security in Africa, including the work of the United Nations Office to the African Union – Report of the Secretary-General, S/2022/643, 25 August.

PART II

Engagement with private actors

5. Private sector participants in international rule-making: governance models

Melissa J. Durkee

1 INTRODUCTION

Who should be entitled to participate in international rule-making processes? What rights should those participants have? With respect to participants who represent the private sector, there are no easy answers. For example, should the World Coal Association help shape treaty texts addressing climate change? Should Philip Morris International, a tobacco industry leader, contribute to rules about tobacco control? In these contexts, for-profit contributions would seem to be obviously detrimental to the lawmaking tasks at hand. However, Boeing and Airbus, leading aircraft manufacturers, could be responsible partners for rule-making on aircraft financing, and Lixil, a global sanitation products company, might be well positioned to help UNICEF develop sanitation policy guidelines for governments in Eastern and Southern Africa. As these examples make clear, a more inclusive approach to stakeholder participation in rule-making presents a governance challenge for international organisations. One of the key factors for organisations to consider is how to respond to the business community.

This chapter was prepared for a volume titled: 'Improving Inclusiveness of IO Rulemaking'. The framing of this project assumes that international organisations make rules, and their rule-making processes should be more inclusive. Both premises are well-founded. Many different international organisations develop many kinds of international instruments (OECD 2021; Alvarez 2006; White 2017). They create model rules and non-binding standards, convene treaty conferences, and generate other normative products. Some of this rule-making is 'informal' (Pauwelyn et al. 2012); at other times, rules are incorporated into treaties, implemented at the domestic level, or both (White 2017). Because these international rule-making processes can shape international and domestic laws or create standards or policy benchmarks, many kinds of stakeholders seek to offer input. Theories of democratic legitimacy and administrative process affirm the importance of offering various stakeholders opportunities to offer input into the making of rules to which they will be subject (de Burca 2008; Esty 2006; Kingsbury et al. 2005; MacDonald 2008; Peters 2009; Stewart 2014; von Bogdandy et al. 2010). Incorporating stakeholder input produces more effective rules and increases their likelihood of acceptance.

A more inclusive approach to stakeholder participation, however, requires international organisations to determine which stakeholders should participate in a rule-making process and what opportunities they should have to offer their perspectives. This governance challenge is particularly acute in the context of for-profit actors, given the potential for their participation to create both significant benefits and harms (Berman 2017; Durkee 2016, 2017; Charney 1983). Since business actors and their many forms of representatives frequently do participate or seek to participate in rule-making processes (Berman 2017, 2022; Durkee 2016, 2017, 2023), any successful governance model for stakeholder participation in international rule-making must address the business community. To put it another way, the point is not to propose increased engagement with private sector actors as a novel pathway to more inclusive rule-making processes. Rather, this contribution recognises that engagement with business actors is already a current reality for many organisations. It proposes that international organisations that wish to update their stakeholder participation models to improve their inclusiveness should consider how for-profit actors will interact with those updated models and employ opportunities to participate.

Accounting for the business community in a stakeholder governance model presents a tension. On the one hand, for-profit groups can sometimes present unique challenges for a rule-making process, so rule-makers must specifically address their unique characteristics and roles in the process (Berman 2022). On the other hand, there is often no crisp dividing line between business groups and other groups (Braithwaite & Drahos 2000; Durkee 2017), so a successful governance process cannot rely on strict categories and divisions between kinds of groups and develop different rules for different groups.

This chapter proposes that two different governance models could realistically resolve this tension, either separately or in combination: first, a 'roundtable' model would allow an organisation to exert more control over the kinds of input it receives in its rule-making process and, in turn, would allow stakeholders to offer more meaningful forms of input. The tradeoff is that a roundtable model forces the organisation to make its own choices about which stakeholders should be included in the rule-making process, which will inevitably exclude participants who could offer meaningful perspectives. This can create effectiveness and legitimacy concerns. Second, a 'public' model would minimise an organisation's gatekeeping function and ensure that anyone who wants to participate in a rule-making process can do so while keeping these participants at arm's length to minimise the potential for undue influence. This approach would maximise transparency and ensure that all stakeholders can be heard, but could also reduce the impact of stakeholder engagement and fail to reap some benefits that an inclusive process would otherwise create. An organisation could choose to pursue these models in combination, with, for example, a multistakeholder insider group helping to set the agenda, leading to a public notice and comment period at a later stage of the rule-making process.

The chapter proceeds as follows. First, it offers a balanced assessment of the potential benefits and risks of including for-profit actors in a stakeholder participation process. Then it offers context, describing the state of play with respect to incorporating stakeholders in the rule-making process, and reviewing several models for how organisations include or exclude for-profit actors. This section reviews frameworks developed by the International Labour Organization (ILO), the Economic and Social Council (ECOSOC), the United Nations Framework Convention for Climate Change (UNFCCC), and the World Health Organization (WHO). Third, the chapter evaluates the distinct features of these participation frameworks, considering the difficult challenge of identifying and segregating private sector perspectives. Finally, the chapter identifies two ideal type governance models and the tradeoffs each model represents.

2 WHY INCLUDE OR EXCLUDE FOR-PROFIT ENTITIES?

Any stakeholder participation process must balance the beneficial aspects of a more inclusive process with the potential harms of opening up a rule-making process to outsiders. For example, openness to public input can increase popular trust in a rule, but it may decrease trust if the process seems ineffective or tainted by undue influence. Any stakeholder governance model will need to weigh these benefits and harms, regardless of the composition of participants in the rule-making process. Yet, private sector participation can heighten concerns about capture, outsized or undue influence, and the legitimacy and transparency of a process. Different governance models will offer trade-offs, as regulators use different strategies to strike a balance between capturing potential benefits and avoiding harms. Understanding the unique benefits and harms that private sector participants can bring to a rule-making process will help regulators strike the governance balance more effectively.

2.1 Reasons to include for-profit entities

The reasons to include for-profit participants in an international rule-making process build on the reasons to include other kinds of actors. One well-established framework for describing the value of stakeholder participation is input and output legitimacy (Keohane & Nye 2002). Rules are produced with 'input' legitimacy when they are developed through a rule-making process with good procedures, including deliberation, opportunities for participation, and transparency (Reiser & Kelly 2011 1016). Allowing participation by those who have some stake in the outcome of a rule-making process can increase the quality of deliberation as well as the perception of fairness and responsiveness. Welcoming input from a variety of sources can also help foster input legitimacy because hearing from a diversity of stakeholders can create a balanced process that airs countervailing interests (Abbott & Snidal, 2009). Rules have 'output' legitimacy when they are 'effective, fair, well-ordered' and accomplish the goals they are meant to address (Reiser & Kelly 2011, 1015–16). Building on contributions offered by those with relevant technical, professional, community, or personal expertise can improve the substantive success of rules (Abbott & Snidal 2009). Thus, instruments that emerge from a process that includes stakeholder input are likely to be more effective in content and more accepted by the communities they seek to regulate.

Including private sector participants in a rule-making process can facilitate both input and output legitimacy. Just like any other stakeholder group, private sector groups that participate in a rule-making process are more likely to perceive the resulting rule as 'effective, fair, and well-ordered' (Reiser & Kelly 2011 1015). They are also able to contribute to the usefulness of the rule by providing specialised expertise (Block-Lieb & Halliday 2017; Charney 1983; Durkee 2016). Private standard-setting bodies have long relied on the expertise of private sector entities for this reason (Büthe & Mattli 2011). The participation of the private sector, like that of other stakeholders, can balance the deliberative process by ensuring that different interests are represented. In addition, including private sector groups can blunt later lobbying campaigns at the domestic level, which can improve the effectiveness of the rule by facilitating domestic implementation and compliance (Braithwaite & Drahos 2000). Enabling participation by private sector groups can also potentially enhance transparency and foster domestic acceptance of a rule by allowing those groups to disseminate information about the rule and the rule-making process to others in the business community. For example, trade and industry groups might inform their memberships about the rule-making process and its results (Dadush 2017).

The OECD's Compendium of International Organisations' Practices ('IO Compendium') offers a slightly different terminology for evaluating the benefits of stakeholder participation (OECD 2021). In the IO Compendium's formulation, the reasons to include stakeholders are both principled and practical. The principled reason is that stakeholder engagement is central to good governance. As the IO Compendium articulates this, stakeholder participation is a 'fundamental determinant of public trust, process legitimacy, and rule credibility' (OECD 2021). The practical reason is that stakeholder engagement produces better rules. It does so by 'broadening the evidence base' for those rules, 'increasing [their] responsiveness' to perceived needs, and 'fostering a sense of ownership, confidence, and trust' in both international organisations and the rules they produce (OECD 2021). Private sector participation can help organisations to do all of these things.

2.2 Reasons to limit participation of for-profit entities

The reasons to exclude or limit the participation of for-profit participants in rule-making processes arise out of the unique challenges and risks their participation presents. To begin, the IO Compendium notes the 'risk of capture of the engagement process by those who have sufficient resources to exert influence' (OECD 2021, 80). As noted above, capture and undue influence concerns are at their height in the context of private sector interests. These concerns relate to whether an organisation can pursue its mission without getting derailed by special interests or by other distractions or destabilising forces. An organisation subject to undue influence or capture could begin to pursue the mission of certain special interests at the expense of its own mission. As the literature observes, and as the prior section describes, organisations can sometimes foster their missions by engaging with business groups. But private sector participation can also push an organisation away from its core agenda. Berman (2022, 232) described 'legal, subtle' forms of capture that are 'increasingly prevalent in international rule-making', such as information capture, representational capture, and resource capture.

For-profit participation in rule-making has been criticised as 'dilut[ing] member-state control' over decision-making (Kelly 2011, 111–12), causing over-representation of well-resourced representatives from geopolitically powerful states, and exacerbating the difficulties organisations have in engaging with more marginalised stakeholders (Willets 2011). If all non-state groups are admitted into a rule-making process on equal terms, groups with more resources will tend to dominate (Wagner et al. 2011). While international participatory processes are understudied (Berman 2017), research focusing on domestic contexts shows that industry and trade associations wield outsized influence (Hackney 2015). In particular, research on domestic lobbying groups in the United States has demonstrated that these groups do tend to dominate over other groups (Hackney 2015; Wagner et al. 2011). In the international context, trade associations with fossil fuel industry members have been able to send thousands of delegates to conferences of the parties of the UNFCCC, including large numbers of representatives from the International Emissions Trading Association, the International Chamber of Commerce, the World Coal Institute, and the International Gas Union, among others (Durkee 2023). The overwhelming presence of trade associations and other representatives from the fossil fuel industry may have discredited or limited the impact of the COP, at least in public opinion. Greta Thunberg memorably illustrated this point in a tweet: 'I don't know about you, but I sure am not comfortable with having some of the world's biggest villains influencing and dictating the fate of the world' (Thunberg 2021). Taken together, these representational imbalances can harm input legitimacy and regulatory trust (Bratspies 2009; Tyler, 1990).

In addition to concerns with capture and representational imbalances, a third challenge with the participation of for-profit groups in rule-making processes is the issue of transparency. These different concerns are related as for-profit groups can sometimes try to avoid an appearance of capture or over-representation by engaging in a participatory process less transparently. As I have described in prior work, major multinational corporate actors sometimes advance their positions without attribution through the mouthpieces of academic, third world, or grassroots organisations (Durkee 2017). As one example among many, tobacco industry insiders transformed the International Tobacco Growers' Association (ITGA) 'from an underfunded and disorganized group of tobacco farmers into a highly effective lobbying organization', which obtained both ECOSOC accreditation and observer status at the Food and Agriculture Organization (FAO) (Durkee 2017: 241) Documents revealed that the tobacco industry intentionally sought to exploit the group's apparent 'integrity and independence', and used it as a 'front for our third world lobby activities at WHO'.

As Keohane & Nye have observed, transparency is an important component of input legitimacy (2002). It also facilitates output legitimacy, or the effectiveness of rules, because it allows decision-makers to weigh the credibility of the information they receive. Non-transparent participation by for-profit groups (such as through purportedly independent academics or NGOs) can make it harder for rule makers to perform both of these legitimacy-related tasks: ensuring they are hearing from a representative range of perspectives and evaluating the credibility and utility of the perspectives they receive.

Finally, for-profit participation in rule-making can also create less useful rules, and thus rules with less output legitimacy. In particular, business participation has been critiqued as degrading the overall information economy in the rule-making process. This has been notably apparent in the context of coordinated private sector campaigns, like those against tobacco and sugar control at the WHO, where powerful industries flooded the Organisation with sponsored academic research, misleading 'third world' perspectives, and other low-value information (Durkee 2017: 241, Berman 2022). These input and output legitimacy deficits can cast doubt on the international rule-making process itself and the organisations convening that process. Private sector participation in rule-making processes can thus harm public trust not only in the products of the rule-making process but also in the international organisations engaged in rule-making.

2.3 Weighing the factors

There are potential benefits and risks that arise from an inclusive stakeholder process regardless of the kinds of stakeholders who participate in the process. In large part, the benefits and risks of including for-profit stakeholders in a process are the same in kind as the benefits and risks of including other kinds of actors. There is no bright line that separates 'stakeholder participation' and 'interest group lobbying', even though stakeholder participation has a positive valence and lobbying a negative one. Lobbying is associated with capture and undue influence, whereas stakeholder participation is associated with responsive and representative governance (Durkee 2018). Lobbying is perceived to harm legitimacy, while stakeholder participation is said to improve it. Business groups can be stakeholders, and excluding them can harm the legitimacy and effectiveness of rules/rule-making. Developing a balanced process requires sensitivity to these potential benefits and harms.

3 THERE IS NO STANDARD APPROACH TO INCLUDING FOR-PROFIT ENTITIES IN DECISION-MAKING PROCESSES

There is significant variation among international organisations as to what kind of rules the organisations produce, how they conduct their rule-making processes, and how these processes welcome or exclude participation by various actors. The variation extends to how formalised the rules of process are, and even the terminology organisations use to describe the various actors who seek to participate in rule-making. Among these many kinds of variation, there is also no standard approach to business participation in international rule-making. This section describes this lack of standardisation and offers a few examples of kinds of participation frameworks.

3.1 Diverse rule-making processes

First, international organisations make rules of various kinds. The IO Compendium defines 'international rule-making' as 'the design, development, implementation, and enforcement of international instruments developed by international organisations' or their secretariats, 'regardless of their legal effects or attributes' (OECD 2021, 19). Those international instruments are, in turn, defined as both 'legally binding requirements that are meant to be directly binding on members [of an organisation] and non-legally binding requirements that may in some cases be given binding value through transposition in domestic legislation or recognition in international legal instruments; and statements of intent or guidance' (OECD 2021, 19). International organisation rule-making thus concerns a broad range of different kinds of normative products including 'treaties, legally binding decisions, non-legally binding recommendations, model treaties or laws, declarations, international technical standards, statements of intent or any other guidance' (OECD 2021, 19).

Just as the products of an international rule-making process are diverse, so are the rule-making processes themselves, and this includes a diverse range of ways that organisations engage with stakeholders. The IO Compendium lists eight modalities, including specific consultation procedures; opportunities for commentary from the general public; invitations to specific stakeholders to help develop instruments or to help implement, disseminate, monitor, or evaluate them; advisory groups or expert committees; processes to give certain groups status to engage regularly with a body; and invitations to participate in meetings of a governing body (OECD 2021).

One point of commonality amid this significant diversity is that 'all IOs engage stakeholders to ensure the quality of their instruments, although to varying degrees' (OECD 2021, 86; OECD 2019; OECD 2016). This trend appears to be increasing as international organisations have perceived a variety of benefits from stakeholder engagement, including input and output legitimacy, leading to greater regulatory trust. Stakeholder participation at a minimum holds instrumental value in that it can create better, and more accepted, rules.

Despite a greater openness to stakeholder input across international organisations, there is very little standardisation across organisations for how to engage with stakeholders. There is no standard model of engagement, no set of best practices, and organisations even show significant variation in the terminology they use to describe their stakeholder engagement process and the actors that participate in it (Durkee 2018; OECD 2021). Many have not formulated or published a comprehensive approach to dealing with stakeholders.

There is even variation within organisations when it comes to stakeholder participation models. The IO Compendium recommends organisations adopt 'whole-of-organisation' approaches to standardise their internal processes and render them predictable and transparent (OECD 2021, 80–81). This would, in turn, increase legitimacy and the ultimate success of the instruments the organisations produce. The volume in which this chapter appears has been commissioned to offer lawmakers insights about how to develop this whole-of-organisation approach, and to encourage some standardisation in participation frameworks across organisations.

3.2 Diverse stakeholder inclusion models

While there is little consistency between international organisations as to how they incorporate stakeholder input in rule-making processes, there are some prominent examples of whole-of-organisation approaches. These models can help illuminate the variation in possible approaches to for-profit participants. Four models are particularly salient, in that they offer a spectrum of potential approaches. The spectrum extends between, on one end, organisations that offer for-profit actors very robust opportunities to participate in their rule generation processes as full members of the organisation and, on the other end, organisations that carefully constrain the participation of for-profit actors to avoid the possibility of undue influence. Between these two extremes, there are a variety of middle-ground approaches.

International Labour Organization. The ILO is a unique example of an organisation that incorporates for-profit actors as full members and full participants in the work of the organisation. The ILO's 'tripartite' structure includes workers, employers, and state parties as full participants (ILO 2023b). '[T]rade unions and employers' organisations ... are placed on an almost equal footing with states in all the bodies of the ILO, and in particular in the Governing Body' (Louis 2019, 44–45). With respect to the rule-making that is the subject of this volume, employers' organisations hold a right to vote on all the forms of labour standards the ILO produces: international labour conventions, recommendations, resolutions, and declarations. The ILO's unique structure may be explained by the fact that its labour rights mission requires support from the business community. Another explanation is that the ILO is the first and oldest of the United Nations-affiliated organisations, originally founded in 1919 under the League of Nations system (ILO 2023a). Later, the United Nations created more distinct lines of separation between intergovernmental organisations and other transnationally active groups, and thus did not develop more organisations with this tripartite structure. That trend may be reversing in the twenty-first century as the United Nations has begun to encourage public-private partnerships and develop multi-stakeholder organisations that include national representatives, non-governmental organisations, and business actors on equal footing (Abbott & Gartner 2012; Kell 2017).

United Nations Economic and Social Council. ECOSOC's accreditation procedure offers a significant entry point for non-state actors who wish to participate in the work of the United Nations and, specifically, one of the ways that actors can gain access to various rule-making procedures. The UN Charter's Article 71 provides that 'The Economic and Social Council may make suitable arrangements for consultation with non-governmental organisations which are concerned with matters within its competence.' Article 71 has served as a 'de facto charter for NGO activities' (Charnovitz 2006, 357), but the UN Charter has no similar mention of a working relationship with other entities, like business entities.

ECOSOC has exercised its Article 71 authority by developing an accreditation procedure. Its rules define a 'non-governmental organisation' as '[a]ny international organisation which is not established by intergovernmental agreement'. The definition reflects ECOSOC's principal concern at its founding, which was to draw a distinction between *inter*governmental organisations (such as the United Nations itself) and *non*governmental groups (Hobe 2012; Charnovitz 1997). ECOSOC has since updated the consultation procedure to stipulate that consultative groups must be organised as non-profit entities and that they must have some basic indicia of responsiveness to their memberships (e.g., a democratically adopted constitution and representative policy-making process) (U.N. 2003 & 2004). Organisations that receive consultative status are categorised into tiers (general, special, and roster), with different levels of access afforded to each (Spiro 2007). Accreditation through the ECOSOC procedure entitles organisations to UN grounds passes, press releases, and access to treaty-making conferences and other events. Accredited groups can make written presentations and sometimes offer input from the floor during negotiation sessions.

Because ECOSOC requires that accredited groups be non-profits, it would seem to exclude the business community from consultative status, and thus access to rule-making procedures through the ECOSOC consultation mechanism. However, while ECOSOC procedures exclude individual businesses, *associations* of businesses have always consulted with the United Nations through this accreditation procedure. In fact, the International Chamber of Commerce was one of the first associations with consultative status (Tully 2007). Industry and trade organisations, which advocate on behalf of profit-oriented entities, are usually non-profits, so these groups are not barred from accreditation. Many do hold consultative status with ECOSOC. For example, as of this writing, approximately 6,500 organisations hold consultative status with ECOSOC, and about 11% of these have selected 'Industry and Business' as an area of expertise and field of activity (U.N. 2025). Among these are groups representing multinational oil and gas companies, financial services, construction, lumber, automotive industries, railways, nuclear power, and coal.

While there is no consistent blueprint that international organisations use to govern the participation of non-state stakeholders, the ECOSOC accreditation regime is one of the most influential because of its authorisation by the U.N. Charter, longevity, role as a boilerplate for other accreditation systems, and incorporation into other participation systems that require ECOSOC accreditation as a prerequisite (Durkee 2017, 223–24; Charnovitz 1997 & 2006). Like ECOSOC, many other organisations admit 'non-governmental' groups that are registered as non-profits, but they do not exclude traditional lobbying groups (industry and trade organisations), so long as those groups are non-profits and can articulate purposes concordant with the mission of the relevant organisation (Durkee 2017).

World Health Organization. The World Health Organization's procedures for regulating the participation of for-profit actors fall to the opposite end of the spectrum from that of the International Labour Organization and recent multi-stakeholder organisations, as described above. In other words, far from accepting for-profit actors on equal terms as state or non-profit participants (the ILO approach), or from accepting all non-profits on equal terms, whether or not they advocate for business agendas, the WHO has explicitly tried to restrict the participation of any group that speaks on behalf of a for-profit entity (WHO 2016; Berman 2022). This is so, despite the fact that the WHO's accreditation system quite explicitly models itself after the ECOSOC system, with a parallel Article 71 in the WHO constitution. The new approach responds to the WHO's embattled history with private sector influences, including its experience with concerted lobbying efforts by the tobacco, pharmaceutical, and agribusiness industries around attempted regulations (Berman 2022). Thus, in 2016, the WHO adopted a Framework of Engagement with Non-State Entities (FENSA, The Framework). The Framework erects a separate set of rules for 'private sector entities' and 'international business associations' than for 'nongovernmental organisations', with additional safeguards in place for engagement with the private sector (WHO 2016).

The Framework's safeguards are meant to guard against conflicts of interest that might have negative impacts on the 'WHO's integrity, independence, credibility and reputation; and public health mandate' (WHO 2016). The WHO declared that it would no longer 'engage with the tobacco industry', the arms industry, or any nonstate actors that advance those industries' work, and it would 'exercise particular caution' when engaging with other entities whose policies or activities are 'negatively affecting human health and are not in line with WHO's policies, norms and standards' (WHO 2016).

To carry out these policies, FENSA broadly defines 'private sector entity' to include commercial enterprises as well as 'international business associations ... that do not intend to make a profit for themselves but represent the interests of their members, which are commercial enterprises' (WHO 2016). In addition, the category includes other entities or associations that are not sufficiently independent from their commercial sponsors. The WHO takes upon itself the task of determining if an entity should be categorised as a private-sector entity given that it is the recipient of 'undue influence' from commercial entities through financing, participation in decision-making, or otherwise (WHO

2016). For example, other NGOs, philanthropic foundations, or academic institutions may be categorised as private-sector entities and thus also be subject to the WHO's new provisions on engagement with this type of entity. To equip its gatekeepers with sufficient information to determine which entities might have such private-sector relationships, all would-be consultant organisations are required to provide detailed information on their membership, legal status, objectives, governance structure, assets, income and funding sources, affiliations, webpage, and other data so that the WHO can conduct its own due diligence (WHO 2016; Berman 2022). The WHO's due diligence process is explicitly aimed at determining why an organisation seeks access and what interests it may have. Along with FENSA, the WHO established an electronic tool for managing engagement that contains a register of nonstate actors and identification of potential conflicts of interest (Berman 2022).

WHO's reforms are innovative in that they regulate different nongovernmental entities differently, attempting to erect separate influence pipelines for public-interest NGOs on the one hand and, on the other, for private-sector entities and any others that might be unduly influenced by those private-sector entities. The Food and Agriculture Organisation has implemented similar reforms, separating business representatives from groups it calls 'Civil Society Organisations' (FAO 2013). The business, or 'private sector', groups are defined as 'all sectors of the food, agriculture, forestry and fisheries systems' including 'enterprises, companies or businesses ... private financial institutions; industry and trade associations; and consortia that represent private sector interests' (FAO 2000). These groups are not permitted to obtain formal status or accreditation but may engage with the FAO in 'policy dialogue' among other things (FAO 2000).

United Nations Framework Convention for Climate Change. One last model is worth a brief mention. Like WHO's FENSA, the UNFCCC also erects distinctions between different kinds of groups – specifically between different kinds of NGOs. These categories include 'research and independent NGOs (RINGOs'), business and industry NGOs ('BINGOs'), environmental NGOs ('ENGOs'), local NGOs, Indigenous Peoples organisations ('IPOs'), local government and municipal authorities ('LGMAs'), islanders, trade unions, and faith-based groups' (Tully 2005). The categories do not affect the amount of access a particular organisation receives when accredited but rather are designed to help organisations coordinate with each other and help the UNFCCC communicate in a coordinated fashion with them (Tully 2005). Unlike the WHO's FENSA, therefore, the UNFCCC does not separate groups into tracks to separately regulate the access of these groups or to single out for-profit groups for special safeguards.

4 THE CHALLENGE OF DEFINING AND SEGREGATING FOR-PROFIT INFLUENCE

Profit-driven perspectives can appear in a rule-making process in many forms. This is a very significant challenge that must be confronted by international organisations seeking to develop a trusted, effective rule-making process. That is, business influence in a rule-making process can take many guises. These influences can emerge most obviously from for-profit entities and their trade and industry group representatives. But for-profit perspectives can also be aired by non-profit groups, experts and academic institutions, national delegations, philanthropic foundations, and other sources. These influences can be overt or covert. They can be part of a concerted influence campaign, or not. A principal challenge for-profit entities present for rule-making processes is therefore that their perspectives are hard to define, segregate, and regulate separately. Any realistic stakeholder governance model must account for the fact that for-profit perspectives cannot easily be isolated within a process.

Nevertheless, the governance challenge is significant: regulating for-profit input *too little* can expose a rule-making process to undue influence and capture, but regulating it *too much* can drive that influence underground, making the process less transparent, effective, and trusted. The standard models for incorporating stakeholder input can fall prey to one or another of these challenges.

4.1 Stakeholder types and links

Many different kinds of actors participate (or seek to participate) in the rule-making processes that international organisations convene. The IO Compendium has developed a taxonomy of stakeholder groups as shown in Figure 5.1.

As this figure makes clear, there are at least two kinds of self-evidently for-profit actors among the 'actors regarded by stakeholders by IOs'. These are private sector entities and international business organisations. Private sector entities are individual entities – such as multinational corporations or other business entities – speaking on their own behalf. International business organisations are usually organised as non-profit entities within a domestic jurisdiction (Dadush 2017; Reiser & Kelly 2011). They exist to serve their memberships in various ways, including by advocating for a common industry or sector-specific perspective before domestic and international governance bodies (Dadush 2017).

For-profit perspectives are not, however, confined to these two self-evidently business-oriented categories. The IO Compendium's taxonomy of stakeholder

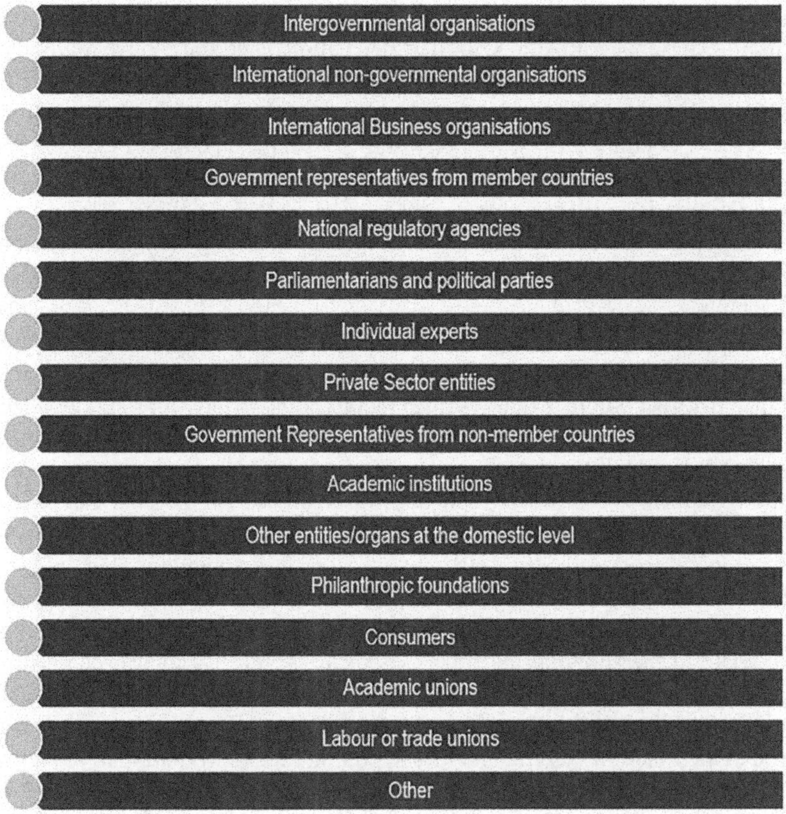

Source: OECD 2021.

Figure 5.1 Actors regarded as stakeholders by IOs

groups is useful in that it offers an expansive view of the varieties of actors that may participate in a rule-making process. The taxonomy's categories should not, however, be viewed as fully distinct or separate. Rather, they are permeable, overlapping, and susceptible to cross-influence.

This is certainly the case when it comes to for-profit stakeholders. For-profit perspectives can be aired through many of the other groups listed in the taxonomy. Here are a few examples of the blurring and overlapping between for-profit actors and other groups:

Governmental delegations sometimes include industry representatives. The International Maritime Organization (IMO) was recently subjected to critique for failing to adopt greenhouse gas emissions standards or other climate change policies. A report by Transparency International attributed this in part to the fact that '[m]ember states are able to appoint employees of corporations, including shipping companies, to their delegations, and these have dominated some delegations. These delegates can actually determine "their government's position on IMO policy" and "are not subject to conflict of interest rules nor to a code of conduct"' (Psaraftis & Kontovas 2020). One report claimed that 'the Marshall Islands, the flag with the world's third-largest fleet in the world, is represented in part by International Registries Inc. (IRI), a US-based private shipping company' (Psaraftis & Kontovas, 2020). Moreover, there is no requirement that the industry affiliations of these national delegates be made transparent.

There is no natural dividing line between 'private sector' NGOs and NGOs organised to advance other interests. Non-governmental organisations can be organised to accomplish many different missions. Many commentators use the terms 'NGO' or 'civil society' to refer to non-profit organisations composed of individual members who share a moral or ideological commitment to the organisation's distinctive purpose (Charnovitz 2006). This can lead to an understanding that 'public interest' or 'civil society' groups are in a separate category from industry associations or trade associations, but this is a relatively recent distinction (Durkee 2023). Both kinds of groups (private sector and public interest) can be organised as non-profits, and both can seek to participate in the rule-making processes of many international organisations on equal terms. For example, the IMO has granted consultative status to 'well-established environmental organisations such as Greenpeace International, World Wide Fund for Nature, and Friends of the Earth International' as well as trade and industry associations such as 'Cruise Lines International Association and Oil Companies International Marine Forum' (Psaraftis & Kontovas 2020). As previously discussed, many trade and industry associations have an accreditation at ECOSOC alongside other kinds of groups. While trade and industry associations have not received sustained attention as actors in international governance (Berman 2017), they are nevertheless present in many forums alongside other NGO groups.

Individual experts, academic institutions, philanthropic organisations, and consumer groups can also be used overtly or covertly for business interests. For example, when the WHO sought to develop the Framework Convention on Tobacco Control, the organisation became the target of an 'elaborate, well-financed, sophisticated, and usually invisible' campaign by tobacco industry groups to discredit and impede it (WHO 2000). To conduct this campaign, powerful multinational companies hid behind 'tobacco company-created front groups and trade unions that had obtained consultative status at the WHO' (WHO 2000). As one example among many, tobacco industry insiders transformed the International Tobacco Growers' Association (ITGA) 'from an underfunded and disorganized group of tobacco farmers into a highly effective lobbying organization' in order to serve as a 'front for [their] third world lobby activities at WHO' (WHO 2000). Industry insiders infiltrated the group to benefit from its 'integrity and independence,' and sought to use the group to 'capture the moral high ground' (WHO 2000). To conduct this campaign, industry insiders caused ITGA to seek and obtain accreditation at the WHO and FAO and to oppose or undermine the WHO's tobacco control activities before those organisations as well as the World Bank and the United Nations Conference on Trade and Development. In connection with this campaign, the tobacco industry also created NGOs and research groups, with innocuous titles like the Center for Indoor Air Research, Institute for International Health and Development, and Associates for Research in the Science of Enjoyment (WHO 2000). The WHO's report noted that it found 'such a considerable body of evidence pointing to use of other organisations with undisclosed relationships to tobacco companies, that it [sic] likely that the committee has identified only a small proportion of the organisations that have such undisclosed relationships' (WHO 2000). Indeed, the tobacco industry campaign itself is just one of many instances of 'astroturf activism' in international governance (Durkee 2017), where major corporate actors act covertly, through apparently grassroots organisations or other actors.

For-profit groups sometimes use multiple access points to influence a process. In the context of the IMO, in addition to serving on governmental delegations, powerful industry groups have used observer and consultative status to access the process (Psaraftis & Kontovas 2020). In the context of concerted campaigns at the WHO, industry representatives also used multiple points of access (WHO 2000; Berman 2022).

4.2 A categorical approach to inclusion/exclusion

The links between private sector groups and other groups, and definitional difficulties, make it challenging for international organisations to take a categorical approach to identifying and separately regulating private sector perspectives. For example, the ECOSOC stakeholder accreditation model described previously in this chapter distinguishes between non-profit and for-profit groups and permits accreditation only of non-profits (ECOSOC 1996). At first glance, this distinction would seem to exclude for-profit perspectives from the kinds of access afforded through accreditation. This is not the case. Business groups regularly access United Nations processes through ECOSOC accreditation, in both overt and covert ways.

First, and most simply, industry and trade associations are fully eligible for accreditation alongside other non-governmental organisations. Indeed, just like other non-governmental organisations, international business organisations tend to be registered in domestic jurisdictions as non-profit entities, feature a membership bonded by some common interest, and participate in international rule-making processes in order to advocate for that common interest of their membership. The clear difference is the composition of the memberships of the two groups, which, in the case of international business organisations, is a set of business groups classified by region or sector. The ECOSOC accreditation rules do not, however, stipulate what interests accredited groups may or may not represent, so long as the group can articulate 'aims and purposes' that support the work of the United Nations. Rather, the accreditation rules focus on whether groups seeking accreditation are registered as non-profits drawing their funding from their membership, whether they have a representative process of governance, and whether their representatives are accountable to the membership (ECOSOC 1996). Industry and trade groups that exist to lobby for the interests of their business membership can satisfy these criteria. Indeed, business groups constitute about 10% of groups accredited with ECOSOC. These groups include, for example, the World Coal Association, which announces an explicit lobbying objective: to 'deepen and broaden understanding amongst policymakers and key stakeholders of the positive role of coal.'

Second, the 'non-profit' criteria do not exclude 'astroturf' groups, or groups that have been influenced by or captured by business interests. The term 'astroturf' has been used to describe groups that appear to be grassroots social movement groups but are in fact, mouthpieces for covert business agendas. As Braithwaite and Drahos (2000) have noted, businesses sometimes create groups that appear to be grassroots citizens' groups with names like 'Citizens for Sensible Control of Acid Rain' (created by coal and electricity companies), 'Consumers for World Trade' (formed by an industry coalition), or the 'National Wetlands Coalition' (a tool of US real estate developers). Such groups can satisfy ECOSOC's accreditation criteria. In addition to forming 'astroturf' groups, businesses can capture existing groups through donations, partnerships, and NGO board representation. There are well-documented instances of powerful industry interests covertly using NGO surrogates to advance agendas at the international level. ECOSOC's accreditation criteria do not screen for this kind of influence.

Third, non-profit status is obtained domestically when a group registers as such with the relevant domestic agency. When international organisations like ECOSOC rely on for-profit or non-profit status to identify and segregate business influences, they have to rely on domestic-level regulators to screen non-profit registrants. As Reiser and Kelly (2011) have shown, domestic officials often have little capacity to evaluate whether an organisation is a legitimate non-profit or maintains any accountability to its stated mission.

In sum, the non-profit criterion does not successfully segregate and exclude for-profit influences in a stakeholder participation process. Rather, those for-profit influences can enter overtly through industry and trade associations, covertly through NGO influence or capture, or haphazardly through inconsistent or under-reviewed domestic non-profit entity registrations. As a final note, in addition to the fact that the non-profit criterion may be unsuccessful as a descriptive matter, it also may not be the best choice as a matter of policy: it forces actors to organise as non-profit groups and gain access only through those groups. This excludes individuals and individual businesses, whose participation may otherwise be beneficial for the reasons summarised earlier in this chapter.

4.3 An alternative to categories

Because the categorical approach to identifying and segregating business input, such as through the 'non-profit' label, is unsuccessful due to the deep links between business actors and other groups, organisations may seek a more nuanced approach. The WHO offers an example. It developed a comprehensive set of guidelines on engaging with the private sector, FENSA, as described earlier in this chapter. The FENSA guidelines anticipate the fact that the boundaries between different kinds of stakeholders in a rule-making process are permeable, overlapping, and susceptible to cross-influence, and the guidelines try to anticipate all the different ways that for-profit perspectives could be delivered within a rule-making process. So, for instance, the framework includes not just commercial enterprises and non-profit international business associations, but also other entities and associations (NGOs, philanthropic foundations, or academic institutions) with close links to private-sector sponsors.

The challenge with this more nuanced, or non-categorical, approach is that it raises the gatekeeping burden for rule makers. The WHO has assumed the burden of determining if an entity should be categorised as a private-sector entity since it is the recipient of 'undue influence' from commercial entities through financing, participation in decision-making, or otherwise. All groups who seek accreditation with the WHO must provide detailed information on their membership, legal status, objectives, governance structure, assets, income and funding sources, affiliations, webpage, and other data. The WHO has also established an online registry to catalogue different groups and to try to identify potential conflicts of interest. The WHO's resource-intensive due diligence process is explicitly aimed at determining why an organisation seeks access and what interests it may have. While these goals would seem to solve the problems the categorical approach does not, they raise a question about whether it is really feasible for officials to discover and determine what interests a group represents. This is especially the case considering the limited bandwidth of gatekeepers and the potential for very significant links between for-profit and non-profit groups. Moreover, stakeholder groups are not static and are subject to changing influences and partnerships. Will gatekeepers have enough information and bandwidth to effectively assess 'undue influence'? One clear risk is that attempting to eliminate conflicts of interest could send those interests underground. The process could produce a cat-and-mouse game where motivated corporate actors could use ever-more-covert methods of hiding influence. Indeed, this approach incentivises business groups who would act covertly to go to greater lengths to hide their links with the groups seeking access to the rule-making process. Gatekeepers must thus continuously assess whose interests an actor truly represents, and this duty is ongoing. A non-categorical approach to identifying actors with profit motives therefore requires a very high level of due diligence by gatekeepers.

Second, and adding to the gatekeeper burden, the WHO's more nuanced approach creates definitional problems around what constitutes 'undue influence'. Does this include corporate donations to a foundation? Or the presence of an NGO board member who previously worked at a multinational corporation? Or in-kind donations? Finally, this approach exposes the organisation to potential legitimacy complaints if its analysis is over- or under-inclusive, excluding groups that do not perceive themselves as linked to the private sector or including groups that others perceive as 'tainted' by the private sector.

In sum, the *categorical* approach imposes a formidable burden on institutional gatekeepers, especially because NGOs often have close links and partnerships with the corporate world, and well-resourced and motivated business actors can seek all potential avenues of influence. Yet a *non-categorical* approach might fail to identify and segregate private sector influences because of failures in capacity.

5 GOVERNANCE MODELS

International organisations could resolve the dilemma for-profit stakeholders present by moving away from an approach that divides those private sector or for-profit actors from others. Instead, two different governance models could realistically help organisations meet their stakeholder inclusiveness goals: a roundtable model or a public comment model.

A *roundtable* model would, I propose, allow an organisation to exert more control over the kinds of input it receives in its rule-making process and would, in turn, allow stakeholders to offer more meaningful forms of input. The roundtable model borrows from the innovations of new multi-stakeholder projects like GAVI, the Vaccine Alliance, UNAids, and UN Women, which welcome business groups as full participants in multi-stakeholder processes (Abbott & Gartner 2012; Durkee 2018). These organisations do so to capture the various contributions those private actors can offer, like financial resources, access to populations or groups, or voluntary compliance within their scope of operations. The trade-off is that a roundtable model forces the organisation to make its own choices about which stakeholders should be included in the rule-making process, which will inevitably exclude participants who could offer meaningful perspectives. This can create effectiveness and legitimacy concerns.

A *public comment* model would minimise an organisation's gatekeeping function and ensure all actors who want to participate in a rule-making process can do so, but this governance model would keep these participants at arm's length to minimise the potential for undue influence. Such a model would accept input from all sources, presuming that groups will advance a diversity of special interests, some profit-motivated, and some unrelated to profit. Potential conflicts-of-interest issues could be mitigated by a structured process drawing from domestic models such as administrative notice-and-comment procedures or lobbying laws requiring disclosures and implementing other protections. For example, OECD lobbying guidelines, which are directed at decision-makers at the national and sub-national levels, recommend that all stakeholders – 'the private sector and the public at large' – should have 'fair and equitable access to participate in the development of public policies' (OECD 2022). The guidelines emphasise disclosure, including the objectives and beneficiaries of lobbying activities, and recommend that all stakeholders should have access to information about lobbying (OECD 2022). This public comment approach would maximise transparency and ensure that all stakeholders can be heard, but could also reduce the impact of stakeholder engagement and fail to reap some benefits that an inclusive process would otherwise create.

The choice, then, is to

1. Refrain from policing the representativeness or for-profit links of participants and use regulatory tools like disclosure and transparency (public comment model), or
2. Build participatory multistakeholder structures that permit a smaller number of hand-selected representatives to participate more robustly in the rule-making process (roundtable model).

The first model would improve administrability by avoiding admission criteria meant to enhance representativeness and accountability but not successfully doing that. It would instead borrow domestic regulatory strategies focusing on registration and publicly available disclosure. Organisations would not assess a group's motives and influences and instead put all entrants on an equal playing field. Lawmakers would be charged with assessing the value of the input on its own terms for its expertise or other functional value. This approach would give public access but would not try to balance perspectives in any kind of representative process.

The second model would improve administrability, but in a different way. It would decrease the number of representatives who are permitted to participate but enable organisations to try to select groups who should be indispensable to the process. In reducing the number of participants, this model could offer stakeholders more robust opportunities to provide input, such as speaking rights or even a voting stake in the rule-making process. This structure would not likely be the right choice for all international organisations, but it could be a promising reform for some, particularly in areas where collaboration with private-sector entities is likely to produce better, more effective, or more broadly accepted legal rules.

Which strategy will be most successful for a given organisation will depend on how well those collaborations help the organisation carry out its mission. Organisations that draw substantially on private-sector assistance – for expertise, voluntary compliance, or financial support – may be more likely to benefit from the roundtable model. Indeed, the multistakeholder models identified earlier (UNAids, UN Women, and GAVI, the Vaccine Alliance) adopt a roundtable format in order to engage robustly with industry partners or groups that work with affected populations. Future efforts in tech, such as regulating cybersecurity, data privacy, AI, or content moderation, may similarly benefit from a roundtable model for stakeholder engagement. Organisations that require substantial support and buy-in from national governments for the results of the rule-making process may be best advised to use public comment structures that safeguard intergovernmental control. For example, in areas implicating national security, territorial delimitation, or other matters of sovereign prerogative, or requiring detailed domestic implementing regulations, governments may not accept the result of a roundtable process and organisations should opt for a public comment model.

These models are rough archetypes, and there are more nuances to explore elsewhere and to work out over time. For example, organisations like the United Nations Commission on International Trade Law (UNCITRAL) may fall in a middle-ground area between these approaches because these organisations are caught in a bind: On the one hand, they need governmental support in order to obtain domestic implementation of the rules they produce. On the other hand, these organisations benefit from private-sector expertise and buy-in to produce more useful and more accepted rules. Should UNCITRAL adopt the roundtable model or the public comment model? Perhaps it and other middle-ground organisations would still be better off with the categorical approach (ECOSOC) or its more nuanced variation (FENSA). Understanding the limitations of those models should nevertheless ensure that they are implemented with attention to their risks and challenges, and that these models do not become default options. That is, the ECOSOC and FENSA approaches should not become a more general blueprint for stakeholder engagement in circumstances where the roundtable or public comment model would be more suitable.

6 CONCLUSION

While private sector participants can make valuable contributions to international organisation rule-making – helping international organisations make more effective or more accepted rules – they can also pose unique challenges. These challenges stem from the capacity of private sector groups to imbalance a process, exert undue influence over rule-makers, or reduce the quality of information flow. For these reasons, a whole-of-organisation approach to stakeholder inclusion should consider how it will apply to private sector actors.

This chapter has illustrated the tension international organisations must resolve in order to develop a principled approach to private sector contributions. On the one hand, private sector participants in a rule-making process offer distinct benefits and risks. On the other hand, it is challenging to define, distinguish, and segregate the actors that offer private sector perspectives.

The bottom line, as this chapter has proposed, is that organisations often cannot realistically divide private sector interests from those of other groups. Instead, stakeholder participation frameworks could follow one of two more realistic patterns:

1. A 'public comment' process that is open to all participants on equal terms in a transparent, arm's-length manner; or
2. A 'roundtable' process that includes a smaller, hand-selected group of participants who are likely to represent the interests at issue in the rule-making process.

These models are ideal types, and there is certainly room for variation and middle paths. However, either of these models should address difficulties presented by the often-substantial engagement of private sector actors in stakeholder participation processes.

REFERENCES

Abbott, K. and D. Gartner (2012), 'Reimagining participation in international institutions', *Journal of International Law and International Relations*, Vol. 8, University of Toronto, Toronto, pp. 1–35.

Abbott, K. and D. Snidal (2009), 'Strengthening international regulation through transnational new governance: Overcoming the orchestration deficit', *Vanderbilt*

Journal of Transnational Law, Vol. 42/2, Vanderbilt University, Nashville, pp. 501–578.

Alvarez, J. (2006), *International Organizations as Lawmakers*, Oxford University Press, Oxford, https://doi.org/10.1093/acprof:oso/9780198765639.001.0001.

Berman, A. (2017), 'Industry, regulatory capture and transnational standard setting', *AJIL Unbound*, Vol. 111, pp. 112–118, https://doi.org/10.1017/aju.2017.29.

Berman, A. (2022), 'Between participation and capture in international rule-making: The WHO framework of engagement with non-state actors', *European Journal of International Law*, Vol. 32/1, Oxford University Press, Oxford, pp. 227–254, https://doi.org/10.1093/ejil/chab014.

Block-Lieb S. and T. Halliday (2017), *Global Lawmakers: International Organizations in the Crafting of World Markets*, Cambridge University Press, Cambridge, https://doi.org/10.1017/9781316941508.

Braithwaite, J. and P. Drahos (2000), *Global Business Regulation,* Cambridge University Press, Cambridge, https://doi.org/10.1017/9780521780339.

Bratspies, R. (2009), 'Regulatory trust', *Arizona Law Review*, Vol. 51/3, The University of Arizona, Tucson, pp. 575–631.

Büthe, T., and W. Mattli (2011), *The New Global Rulers: The Privatization of Regulation in the World Economy*, Princeton University Press, Princeton.

Charney, J. (1983), 'Transnational corporations and developing public international law', *Duke Law Journal*, Vol. 32/4, Duke University, Durham, pp. 748–788.

Charnovitz, S. (1997). 'Two centuries of participation: NGOs and international governance', *Michigan Journal of International Law*, Vol. 18/2, The University of Michigan Law School, Ann Arbor, pp. 183–286.

Charnovitz, S. (2006), 'Nongovernmental organizations and international law', *The American Journal of International Law,* Vol. 100/2, Cambridge University Press, Cambridge, pp. 348–372.

Dadush, S. (2017), 'The internal challenges of associational governance', *AJIL Unbound*, Vol. 111, pp. 125–129, https://doi.org/10.1017/aju.2017.30.

de Burca, G. (2008), 'Developing democracy beyond the state', *Columbia Journal of Transnational Law*, Vol. 46/2, Columbia Law School, New York City, pp. 221–278.

Durkee, M. (2016), 'The business of treaties', *UCLA Law Review*, Vol. 63/2, UCLA Law School, Los Angeles, pp. 264–321.

Durkee, M. (2017), 'Astroturf activism', *Stanford Law Review*, Vol. 69/1, Stanford University, Stanford, pp. 201–268.

Durkee, M. (2018), 'International lobbying law', *The Yale Law Journal,* Vol. 127/7, The Yale Law Journal Company, Inc., New Haven, pp. 1742–1826.

Durkee, M. (2023), 'Industry groups in international governance: A framework for reform', *Journal of Human Rights and the Environment*, Vol. 14/1, Edward Elgar Publishing, Cheltenham, pp. 4–26, https://doi.org/10.4337/jhre.2023.01.01.

ECOSOC (1996), Resolution 1996/31. Consultative Relationship between the United Nationsand non-governmental organizations, 49th plenary meeting, 25 July 1996.

Esty, D. (2006), 'Good governance at the supranational scale: Globalizing administrative law', *The Yale Law Journal,* Vol. 115/7, The Yale Law Journal Company, Inc., New Haven, pp. 1490–1562, https://doi.org/10.2307/20455663.

FAO (2000), *Principles and Guidelines for FAO Cooperation with the Private Sector*, Food & Agriculture Organization of the United Nations, Rome, http://www.fao.org/3/a-x2215e.pdf

FAO (2013), *Strategy for Partnerships with Civil Society Organizations*, Food & Agriculture Organization of the United Nations, Rome, http://www.fao.org/docrep/018/i3443e/i3443e.pdf.

Hackney, P. (2015), 'Taxing the unheavenly chorus: Why section 501(c)(6) trade associations are undeserving of tax exemption', *Denver Law Review*, Vol. 92/2, Denver University, Denver, pp. 265–324.

Hobe, S. (2012), 'Article 71', in *The Charter of the United Nations: A Commentary*, Vol. 2, 3rd edn, Oxford University Press, Oxford, pp. 1788, https://doi.org/10.1093/law/9780199639779.001.0001.

ILO (2023a), 'History of the ILO', International Labour Organization, Geneva, Origins and History, http://ilo.org/global/about-the-ilo/history (accessed May 19, 2023).

ILO (2023b), 'Structure', International Labour Organization, Geneva, http://ilo.org/global/about-the-ilo/who-we-are (accessed May 19, 2023).

Kell, G. (2017), 'Relations with the private sector', in *The Oxford Handbook of International Organisations,* Oxford University Press, Oxford, pp. 730–753, https://doi.org/10.1093/law/9780199672202.003.0002.

Kelly, C.R. (2011), 'The politics of legitimacy in the UNCITRAL working methods', in *The Politics of International Economic Law*, Cambridge University Press, Cambridge, pp. 106–130.

Keohane, R.O., and J.S. Nye (2002) 'The club model of multilateral cooperation and problems of democratic legitimacy', in *Power and Governance in a Partially Globalized World*, Routledge, London, pp. 219–244.

Kingsbury, B., N. Krisch and R. Stewart (2005), 'The emergence of global administrative law', *Law and Contemporary Problems*, Vol. 68/3, Duke Law, Durham, pp. 15–61.

Louis, M. (2019), 'Who decides? Representation and decision-making at the International Labour Organization', *International Development Policy*, Vol. 11, pp. 40–58, https://doi.org/10.4000/poldev.3000

Macdonald, T. (2008), *Global Stakeholder Democracy: Power and Representation Beyond Liberal States,* Oxford University Press, Oxford, https://doi.org/10.1093/acprof:oso/9780199235001.001.0001.

OECD (2016), *International Regulatory Co-operation: The Role of International Organisations in Fostering Better Rules of Globalisation*, OECD Publishing, Paris, https://dx.doi.org/10.1787/9789264244047-en.

OECD (2019), *The Contribution of International Organisations to a Rule-Based International System: Key Results from the Partnership of International Organisations for Effective Rulemaking*, OECD Publishing, Paris, https://www.oecd.org/gov/regulatory-policy/IO-RuleBased%20System.pdf.

OECD (2021), *Compendium of International Organisations' Practices: Working Towards More Effective International Instruments*, OECD Publishing, Paris, https://doi.org/10.1787/846a5fa0-en.

OECD (2022), *Lobbying in the 21st Century: Transparency, Integrity and Access*, OECD Publishing, Paris, https://legalinstruments.oecd.org/public/doc/256/256.en.pdf

Pauwelyn, J., R. Wessel and J. Wouters (eds) (2012), *Informal International Lawmaking*, Oxford University Press, Oxford.

Peters, A. (2009), 'Membership in the global constitutional community', in *The Constitutionalization of International Law*, Oxford University Press, Oxford, pp. 153–262, https://doi.org/10.1093/acprof:oso/9780199543427.003.0005.

Psaraftis, H.N., and C.A. Kontovas (2020), 'Influence and transparency at the IMO: the name of the game', *Maritime Economics & Logistics* Vol. 22, Springer Nature, Switzerland, pp. 151–172, https://doi.org/10.1057/s41278-020-00149–4.

Reiser, D. and C. Kelly (2011), 'Linking NGO accountability and the legitimacy of global governance', *Brooklyn Journal of International Law*, Vol. 36/3, Brooklyn Law School, Brooklyn, pp. 1011–1073.

Schweitz, M. (1995), 'NGO participation in international governance: The question of legitimacy', *Proceedings of the ASIL Annual Meeting*, Vol. 89, Cambridge University Press, Cambridge, pp. 415–420, https://doi.org/10.1017/S0272503700084846.

Spiro, P. (2007), 'Non-governmental organizations and civil society', in *The Oxford Handbook of International Environmental Law,* Oxford University Press, Oxford, pp. 770–790, https://doi.org/10.1093/oxfordhb/9780199552153.013.0033.

Stewart, R. (2014), 'Remedying disregard in global regulatory governance: accountability, participation, and responsiveness', *The American Journal of International Law,* Vol. 108/2, Cambridge University Press, Cambridge, pp. 211–270.

Thunberg, Greta, @GretaThunberg (8 Nov. 2021), "There are more delegates at COP26 associated with the fossil fuel industry than from any single country' I don't know about you, but I sure am not comfortable with having some of the world's biggest villains influencing & dictating the fate of the world', https://twitter.com/gretathunberg/status/1457761013932175368?lang=zh-Hant.

Tully, S. (2005), 'Commercial contributions to the climate change regime: who's regulating whom?', *Sustainable Development Law & Policy*, Vol. 5, American University, Washington DC.

Tully, S. (2007), *Corporations and International Lawmaking*, Brill, Leiden.

Tyler, T. (1990), *Why People Obey the Law*, Yale University Press, New Haven.

U.N. (2003), 'UN system and civil society: An inventory and analysis of practices', background paper for the secretary-general's Panel of Eminent Persons on United Nations Relations with Civil Society, United Nations, New York City, https://unece.org/DAM/env/pp/ppif/UN%20SYSTEM%20AND%20CIVIL%20SOCIETY.doc. (accessed 19 May 2023).

U.N. (2004), 'We the peoples: Civil society, the United Nations and global governance', report of the Panel of Eminent Persons on United Nations-civil society relations, United Nations Document, 58th Session, Agenda Item 59, United Nations, New York City, https://digitallibrary.un.org/record/523950? (accessed 19 May 2023).

U.N. (2025), Advanced Search for Civil Society Organizations, United Nationals Department of Social and Economic Affairs, https://esango.un.org/civilsociety/displayAdvancedSearch.do?method=search&%20%20sessionCheck=false (accessed 1 April 2025).

WHO (2016), 'Framework of engagement with non-state actors', World Health Assembly Document, WHA69.10, Agenda Item 11.3, World Health Organization, Geneva, https://apps.who.int/gb/ebwha/pdf_files/wha69/a69_r10-en.pdf. (accessed 19 May 2023).

von Bogdandy A., R. Wolfrum, J. Bernstorff, P. Dann and M. Goldmann (2010), *The Exercise of Public Authority by International Institutions: Advancing International Institutional Law,* Beiträge zum ausländischen öffentlichen Recht und Völkerrecht, Vol. 210, Springer Berlin, Heidelberg, https://doi.org/10.1007/978-3-642-04531–8.

Wagner, W., K. Barnes and L. Peters (2011), 'Rulemaking in the shade: An empirical study of EPA's air toxic emission standards', *Administrative Law Review*, Vol. 63/1, American Bar Association, Chicago, pp. 99–158.

White, N. (2017), 'Lawmaking', in *The Oxford Handbook of International Organizations,* Oxford University Press, Oxford, pp. 559–580.

WHO (2000), 'Tobacco company strategies to undermine tobacco control activities at the World Health Organization', Report of the Committee of Experts on Tobacco Industry Documents, World Health Organization, https://iris.who.int/handle/10665/67429.

Willets, P. (2011), *Non-Governmental Organizations in World Politics: The Construction of Global Governance,* Routledge, Abingdon.

6. How should IOs engage with private actors in global climate and energy governance?

Kaho Yu, Xinchuchu Gao and Xuechen Chen

1 INTRODUCTION

The past decade has witnessed the increasingly crucial role played by International Organisations (IOs) in global governance (see Introductory chapter). In the field of climate and energy governance, IOs such as the Organisation for Economic Co-operation and Development (OECD), the United Nations (UN), and the International Energy Agency (IEA) are leading global climate mitigation efforts. With their extensive research-based knowledge, apolitical nature, and capability to serve as platforms for collaboration, IOs are playing a unique role in coordinating global efforts and responses to the climate challenge. However, to maximise their impact, IOs should ensure the inclusiveness of a diverse range of actors, including states, private actors, and the general public (see chapter 2). Among multiple stakeholders, engagement with private actors – particularly multinational corporations and small- and medium-sized enterprises (SMEs) involved in energy business and investment – is considered key to global climate and energy governance. Their operations can influence emissions control and the development of low-carbon solutions. Yet, including the private sector in global climate governance is not without risks given the concerns over the legitimacy of involving commercially driven entities with differing priorities.

In line with the overall theme of this edited volume, this chapter contributes to the discussion of how to improve the inclusiveness of IOs' rule-making processes. It will provide telling examples of how IOs play a crucial role in supporting the private sector's engagement in global climate governance while also addressing the perceived risks that have, until now, restrained IOs from further engagement with the private sector. This chapter is structured as follows: The second section reviews the global landscape of climate and energy governance and demonstrates the importance of the private sector's participation. The third section focuses on three key strategies that can enhance engagement between IOs and private actors while also mitigating the perceived risks that have thus far hindered broader collaboration. The fourth section summarises the key findings of the chapter, highlighting critical points and recommendations.

2 THE GLOBAL LANDSCAPE OF CLIMATE GOVERNANCE: THE IMPORTANCE OF MOVING BEYOND THE STATE-CENTRIC GOVERNANCE ARCHITECTURE

2.1 The global climate governance architecture: state of play

The global climate governance architecture has primarily been built on the basis of intergovernmental negotiations within the United Nations (UN) framework. Formal UN talks on climate change took off with the decision of the World Meteorological Organisation and the United Nations Environment Programme to set up the Intergovernmental Panel on Climate Change (IPCC) in 1988. The creation of the IPCC marked a significant advancement in incorporating scientific insights into addressing climate change, enhancing public understanding of global warming science, and stressing the need for diplomatic talks. Immediately after the release of the IPCC's first assessment report in 1990, the United Nations General Assembly adopted a resolution to launch formal negotiations for an international instrument to address climate change. During the 1992 Rio Conference on Environment and Development, these negotiations were concluded, resulting in a final agreement known as the United Nations Framework Convention on Climate Change (UNFCCC). The UNFCCC was designed so as not to put extra burdens on developing nations. Developing countries were exempt from all of the UNFCCC's obligations except filing reports on their emissions (Victor, 2011). In 1995, at the first meeting of the Conference of the Parties to the UNFCCC (COP 1) in Berlin, the parties decided that commitments outlined in the Convention were insufficient to meet emission reduction objectives. As a result, they agreed to initiate another round of negotiations to create a 'protocol or another legal instrument' to catalyse 'appropriate action for the period beyond 2000' (UNFCCC, 1995). This round of negotiations ended with the 1997 Kyoto Protocol.

To better achieve emission reduction objectives, the Protocol included legally binding emissions targets for developed countries, focusing on the six major greenhouse gases. Similar to the UNFCCC, the targets and timetables set by the Kyoto Protocol did not extend to developing countries. However, for the first time, the Kyoto Protocol highlighted that non-governmental support was crucial to the Protocol's effective implementation (Kuyper et al., 2018).

Furthermore, the Protocol explicitly assigned a role to private actors in the transfer of environmentally sound technologies and stressed their participation in activities such as the Clean Development Mechanism (CDM) and Joint Implementation (JI). By facilitating the participation of private actors in the international carbon market through CDM and JI, the Kyoto Protocol enabled them to actively engage in the fight against climate change.

However, with the development of emerging economies and the rise of their greenhouse gas (GHG) emissions, the differences between developed and developing countries and their consequent responsibilities to address climate change were challenged. Developed countries questioned the allocation of GHG emissions allowances and pressured emerging economies to reduce them (Jiang and Li, 2020). Developing countries, on their side, emphasised their lack of capability to reduce emissions without hindering economic development. In 2001, the withdrawal of the United States from the Kyoto Protocol further exacerbated the deadlock within the UN-led, state-centric architecture of global climate governance.

In response to this crisis, the 2009 UN Climate Conference in Copenhagen adopted a more inclusive rule-making process by incorporating more non-state and sub-state actors. The Copenhagen summit was a pivotal moment in global climate politics, signifying that improving the inclusiveness of IO's rule-making was finally put on the agenda (Bäckstrand and Kronsell, 2015). Subsequently, the 2015 UN Paris Climate Change Conference further facilitated and institutionalised the participation of non-state actors. Differing from the Kyoto Protocol, the Paris Agreement did not set specific emission reduction goals for parties. Instead, the Agreement outlined ambitious overall climate change targets and urged parties to contribute through their nationally determined contributions. This transition from internationally regulated climate governance under the Kyoto Protocol to party-determined contributions under the Paris Agreement coincided with a proliferation of public-private partnerships (Widerberg and Pattberg, 2017). As Hale stated, the Paris Summit clearly recognised the benefits of linking climate actions by cities, businesses, and civil society to the multilateral treaty regime (Hale, 2016). The increasing involvement of non-state actors was evidenced in the significant number of non-state participants at the Paris Summit. Indeed, 8,000 out of 28,000 participants were registered as non-state actors (Lövbrand et al., 2017). Among them, 1,300 non-state actors joined the 'Paris Pledge for Action' and committed to act to reduce greenhouse gas emissions to a safe level (Streck, 2020). Moreover, in the COP decision accompanying the Paris Agreement, non-state stakeholders were acknowledged as critical contributors to the goal of limiting global warming to below 2°C or even 1.5°C (UNFCCC, 2016).

In the post-Paris Agreement era, an increasingly diverse landscape of non-state actors participating in the global climate governance has become evident

(Sinclair, 2017). The number of non-state and sub-state climate commitments and initiatives has experienced remarkable growth. Illustrative examples include the Compact of States and Regions, the European Union Covenant of Mayors, and the Global Covenant of Mayors for Climate and Energy. In July 2023, the 'Non-State Actor Zone for Climate Action (NAZCA)', hosted by the UNFCCC, documented a diverse array of non-state actors (NAZCA, 2023). This included 11,354 cities, 282 regions, 15,590 companies, 1,654 investors, and 3,443 organisations (NAZCA, 2023). These figures underscore the significant emergence of climate pledges made by various non-state and sub-state actors, highlighting their growing involvement and dedication to combating climate change.

2.2 Why IO's engagement with private actors matters

The discussion above demonstrates the growing recognition of the need to involve non-state and sub-state actors and make global climate governance more inclusive. Within this wide range of non-state actors, private actors are now considered critical contributors to addressing global environmental problems. To begin with, the private sector is the de facto implementer of climate standards, as highlighted in chapter 2. While governments and IOs typically set forth regulations and targets for emission reduction, it is primarily the private sector, particularly companies like oil and gas corporations, that significantly influences the escalation of emissions (Victor, 2011). Therefore, the effectiveness of emission reduction policies is closely linked to the compliance of these private actors. Without their active participation and commitments to reducing emissions, it becomes challenging to achieve the desired climate goals.

In essence, including private actors in the process of shaping measures and regulations to address climate challenges is crucial. This increases the likelihood of gaining private actors' support to comply with the regulations in the long run. The establishment of private initiatives, such as carbon-trading systems like the World Bank's Prototype Carbon Fund (PCF), exemplifies the benefits of public-private partnerships. Through such partnerships, private actors gain a stake in setting rules and regulations of climate actions, making it more likely that they will comply with emission reduction schemes (Levy & Jones, 2009).

Second, private actors possess key resources, including capital, expertise, and political influence, which are essential in determining the effectiveness of international environmental regimes. Private investments geared towards climate initiatives are a key component of global climate finance. There has long been an awareness that public funding aimed at fulfilling environmental and climate commitments falls short (Clark et al., 2018). For instance, in the Copenhagen Accord of 2009, developed countries committed to jointly mobilising USD 100 billion annually by 2020 to address the needs of developing countries for Convention implementation (UNFCCC, 2010). However, it is estimated that less than half of the 'new and additional' total development finance (including flows from official aid, multilateral contributions, and export credits) has materialised (Mitchell et al., 2021). Bridging the gap in climate finance to achieve sustainable development goals necessitates the crucial involvement of private sector investment (Park, 2022).

Apart from providing investment and capital required for climate actions, private actors play a role as knowledge brokers, providing technical knowledge and expertise in innovation to find solutions to specific climate change and energy problems. Often, private firms know best how to control emissions at the lowest cost, thereby proactively participating in technical panels in the negotiation process of many international environmental regimes (Andrade and de Oliveira, 2015). For instance, oil and gas companies frequently share their knowledge and expertise about carbon capture and storage technologies with policymakers at both national and international levels (Nasiritousi, 2015: 52). Other examples of bringing private actors together to formulate regulations and standards include the Greenhouse Gas Protocol Corporate Accounting and Reporting Standard, Verified Carbon Standard, and the American Carbon Registry (Streck, 2020). Therefore, private actors have an increasingly formal voice in making climate standards by providing relevant knowledge and expertise (Levy and Newell, 2004).

Private actors can also use their industrial influence to impact the formation, function, and maintenance of global environmental regimes in both direct and indirect ways. For instance, they can directly participate in the global climate regime as industrial members. Crucially, private actors benefit from a huge political advantage because they do not rely on government funding. Private actors' influence can also be indirect. Particularly, multinational corporations hold forms of structural power in the global economy. In the context of globalisation, national states tend to pursue policies that are more acceptable to corporations to maintain or attract more investment. This allows multinational corporations to exert an indirect influence on domestic climate policies. As Falkner has pointed out, private actors' role in directing investments is bound to give them an important position in international environmental politics (Falkner, 2007).

2.3 The potential risks of including private actors in the global climate regime

Yet the growth of private sector actors' participation in different stages of IO rule-making also raises some concerns (see chapter 1). First, private actors' participation can be problematic if it lacks legitimacy, as their involvement is primarily motivated by economic profits rather than the public interest. During the initial phase of global climate change negotiations, private actors primarily opposed the development of climate change regulations due to concerns about potential threats to their competitiveness. However, the landscape has evolved, and nowadays, an increasing number of private actors view climate regulations as opportunities for technical innovation and business profits. Despite this shift, there remains a clear division among private actors, each holding distinct preferences regarding climate governance. For instance, the fossil fuel industry has historically impeded progress in climate talks (Si et al., 2023). On the other hand, industries supportive of addressing climate change, such as green energy providers and technology companies, have actively advocated for more stringent climate regulations aligned with their business interests. In other words, private actors are not homogeneous in their interests and actions. Critics therefore express concerns that the involvement of private actors in global climate governance could lead to the prioritisation of pro-business agendas (OECD, 2021). This might result in inadequate attention to the pressing environmental and social challenges posed by climate change, potentially compromising the broader public interest.

Additionally, the lack of comprehensive and transparent data reporting on the implementation of private actors' climate commitments raises concerns about their accountability. Various studies have highlighted that a lack of data transparency hampers an assessment of climate actions (Hsu et al., 2016). For instance, in 2012, ten years after the 2002 World Summit on Sustainable Development, around 43% of the 'Partnerships for Sustainable Development' did not produce accountable results (Pattberg et al., 2013). Similarly, only 44% of actions launched at the 2014 UN Climate Summit have established monitoring arrangements, making it difficult to track their progress and impact (Chan et al., 2018). Another example is that, despite encouraging commitments towards climate goals, only just over half (56%) of New York Declaration on Forests (NYDF) endorsers have disclosed their progress to the public. Given these challenges, there is a growing consensus that relying solely on voluntary disclosure of data reporting on private actors' climate commitments will not be sufficient to address the climate challenge (Chan et al., 2018). Hsu and her colleagues therefore point out that national government actions are required to facilitate non-state actors' implementation of their climate commitments (Hsu et al., 2016).

In summary, the participation of private actors in global climate regimes has sparked controversy. As Andrade and de Oliveira have stated, it remains unclear whether private actors' involvement is 'a bane or a boon to global environmental governance' (Andrade and de Oliveira, 2015: 382). Nonetheless, the private sector continues to play a crucial role in addressing emerging climate risks, emphasising the necessity for their inclusive participation within IOs.

The following section will discuss ways in which IOs could enhance their interactions with private actors.

3 THREE WAYS IN WHICH IOs COULD IMPROVE THE INCLUSIVENESS OF PRIVATE ACTORS

As global climate and energy challenges grow increasingly complex, the importance of improving the inclusiveness of private actors has become evident. Effective collective actions between these entities are crucial, as private actors, especially multinational corporations and SMEs in the energy business and investment sectors, can influences emissions control and the development of low-carbon solutions. The performance of IOs is highly dependent on the inclusiveness of these private actors. Their participation is vital in driving the energy transition and promoting sustainable development, underscoring the need for IOs to engage with them actively. However, the question remains how to encourage the private sector to participate in international organisations or, more broadly global energy and climate governance. This section delves into three key strategies to enhance IOs' inclusiveness of private actors, ultimately contributing to a more efficient and coordinated approach to addressing climate and energy challenges.

3.1 Demonstrate clearer business relevancy

While IOs are established on public good mandates rather than commercial objectives, many have showcased business-relevant capabilities that can incentivise private sector partnerships. These include enhancing market and capital access, risk mitigation, crisis management, and R&D and knowledge sharing. They are not only important to multinational corporations but also to smaller players in the market, such as SMEs, that are less resourceful but still impactful as a group in the global climate agenda. It is essential for IOs to clearly communicate the business relevance of their functions to encourage private sector participation in global climate agenda and better align their profit-driven objectives with sustainable practices. Some IOs have already exemplified these advantages.

3.1.1 Market access and network

Cooperating with IOs could provide private actors with enhanced market access and network opportunities. As discussed below, some IOs are designed to facilitate market entry by providing companies with relevant information, contacts, and support, as well as by advocating for policy frameworks that encourage sustainable investments. This is particularly relevant for companies operating in the renewable energy sector or offering low-carbon technologies and services.

The International Trade Centre (ITC), a joint agency of the United Nations and the World Trade Organisation, is one such organisation that supports SMEs in developing countries. It provides market intelligence, advisory services, technical assistance, and capacity-building services to help companies navigate complex international markets (ITC, 2023). By working with the ITC, companies can strengthen their knowledge about the latest environmental regulatory frameworks and sustainability reporting requirements adopted in their targeted markets, especially the emerging ones. Companies in the renewable energy and low-carbon sectors can also identify and seize new business opportunities in emerging markets, thereby expanding their global footprints and increasing their competitiveness (ITC, 2023).

IOs also aim to promote cross-border cooperation and facilitate partnerships between companies across multiple countries. For example, the United Nations Industrial Development Organization (UNIDO) runs the Global Cleantech Innovation Programme (GCIP) to build entrepreneurship ecosystems for innovative cleantech solutions. It provides a coordination platform for cleantech startups and SMEs to exchange best practice ideas with a global network of investors and R&D experts from more than 15 countries (UNIDO, 2025). It is designed to forge international partnerships and identify investable cleantech solutions as a way to address environmental challenges together with the private sector.

Beyond mere market access, IOs have the potential to offer private actors funding opportunities, thereby assisting them in overcoming the financial barriers commonly associated with R&D investments. Numerous international financial institutions, such as the World Bank, along with regional development banks, such as the Asian Development Bank and the Inter-American Development Bank, have established various long-term programmes to provide financial support to private sector actors. Utilising a range of financial instruments, including loans, grants, guarantees, and technical assistance, these institutions assist companies in overcoming financial obstacles that hinder investment in innovative cleantech solutions. Such support creates an environment for bolstered investments in R&D, enhancing production capabilities, and commercialising innovative technologies in the renewable energy and low-carbon industries.

Another example is the Green Climate Fund (GCF), one of the world's largest climate funds with over 200 partners. It is dedicated to funding initiatives promoting low-emission and climate-resilient development in developing countries. To stimulate investment, GCF created the Private Sector Facility (PSF), providing concessional instruments, including loans, equity investments, and risk mitigators. PSF strategically focuses on five areas: financial institutions, project finance, climate funds, climate markets, and climate innovations. According to its latest Strategic Plan, the GCF private sector strategy aims to catalyse private climate finance by taking more risks in climate-related projects and de-risking conservative sources of finance (GCF, 2020). By collaborating with the GCF, private entities have the opportunity to secure financing for avant-garde climate and energy ventures, enabling them to broaden their market footprint and explore new avenues for growth (Reyes and Schalatek, 2021).

3.1.2 Risk mitigation

Another advantage private actors can derive from collaboration with IOs is risk mitigation, particularly concerning climate change and energy-related risks. These threats could be far-reaching, potentially undermining businesses' financial stability, day-to-day operations, and reputation. Private actors have the opportunity to tap into extensive databases, analytical tools, and specialised resources that could enable them to identify, assess, and manage these risks more effectively.

For instance, the UNFCCC's Task Force on Climate-Related Financial Disclosures (TCFD) has developed recommendations on the disclosure of companies' climate risk-related information as a way to support investors, lenders, and insurers in better capital allocation (Meyer, 2022). By adopting these recommendations, a company could enhance its risk management and strategic planning, staying ahead of climate risks from extreme weather to environmental regulatory changes.

IOs could also equip private actors with access to early climate risk warning systems, empowering them to make data-driven decisions in their daily operations and investments. For example, the IFC's Performance Standards on Environmental and Social Sustainability stand as a global benchmark for managing environmental risks of projects in the private sector (IFC, 2012). It establishes the importance of improving the environmental performance of a commercial project through disclosure of risk information and consultation with local communities. Since a variety of financial institutions also use the Performance Standards, compliance with them could increase a company's credibility with investors and stakeholders. Similarly, the World Meteorological Organization (WMO) provides climate services, data, and insights, including climate forecasts and early warning systems. These climate-related resources help businesses anticipate and prepare for potential climate-related impacts on their operations (WMO, 2020).

3.1.3 Crisis management

Crisis management is another critical area where IOs can support private actors. Since climate change can trigger crises such as natural disasters, political instability, and supply chain disruptions on a regional and global scale, the private sector requires a global governance approach to deal with these threats. As such, the multilateral platform of an IO is well-placed to help private actors establish and maintain effective crisis communication strategies. This is expected to foster transparency, consensus building, and stakeholder collaboration during critical situations. Leveraging the expertise and platforms of IOs, private actors would be better positioned to navigate the complex landscape of crisis management and minimise the potential impacts on their operations, reputation, and financial stability.

Indeed, the history of IOs managing global energy crises is extensive. The International Energy Agency was created after the first major oil crisis in the 1970s and was mandated to coordinate and improve emergency supply measures (Colgan, 2009). It established emergency response mechanisms such as the Coordinated Emergency Response Measures (CERM) to address supply disruptions (Colgan, 2009). It is a rapid mechanism designed to help IEA member countries respond collectively to disruptions in oil supplies, ensuring the stability of global energy markets. Participation in the IEA's emergency response system allows private actors in the energy sector to obtain information, support, and coordination tools to manage energy supply disruptions, ensuring operational continuity.

Another example is the United Nations Office for Disaster Risk Reduction (UNDRR). It works closely with the private sector to develop disaster risk reduction strategies for crises, such as the COVID-19 pandemic (UNDRR, 2021). To increase mobilisation in the private sector, the UNDRR coordinates the Private Sector Alliance for Disaster Resilient Societies (ARISE), a network of private sector partners committed to implementing the Sendai Framework for Disaster Risk Reduction 2015–2030.[1] Through ARISE, companies can access resources, best practices, and collaboration opportunities to strengthen their disaster resilience and contribute to global risk reduction efforts. Similarly, the United Nations Global Compact provides resources and guidance to aid companies in integrating responsible business practices into their crisis response strategies. Better crisis management helps them maintain trust and credibility with stakeholders during times of uncertainty (Orzes and Moretto, 2020).

3.1.4 R&D promotion and knowledge sharing

Innovative R&D in energy transition and cleantech solutions requires heavy investment. Collaborating with IOs enables private actors to tap into additional

---

[1] See ARISE website, available at https://www.ariseglobalnetwork.org/explore.

funding and financial information for the development and execution of innovative solutions to climate and energy challenges. IOs play a pivotal role in diverting capital to private actors that are able to identify and demonstrate R&D innovation opportunities. R&D support from IOs can also equip private actors, especially smaller private players, with a competitive edge in the market by staying informed about the latest technological advancements and trends in the climate and energy sectors. Access to avant-garde research and development facilitates private actors in adapting their business models, investing in contemporary technologies, and crafting innovative products and services that resonate with dynamic market demands.

An example is the International Renewable Energy Agency (IRENA). Through its Innovation and Technology Centre (IITC), IRENA facilitates the formation of partnerships between public and private actors to accelerate the development and deployment of clean energy technologies (IRENA, 2016). Furthermore, IRENA has developed guidelines for better cooperation with the private sector, thereby fuelling innovation in key areas of the renewable energy sector, such as deploying renewable energy mini-grids (IRENA, 2016).

Collaboration with IOs could facilitate sharing knowledge and technology between private actors and stakeholders. As essential intermediaries, IOs could link private actors with relevant information, expertise, and technological solutions to help them overcome climate and energy challenges. By actively engaging in knowledge and technology exchange initiatives, private actors could access cutting-edge innovations, thereby improving their internal capabilities and enhancing their transition.

An example in this regard is the International Energy Agency's Technology Collaboration Programmes (TCPs). TCP is designed to facilitate international cooperation among governments and industries on energy technology research, development, and deployment. It involves over 6,000 experts globally from almost 300 public and private organisations across 55 countries. Through these collaborative efforts, private actors can collaborate with governments, research institutions, and other industry players to advance the research and, more importantly the commercialisation of energy technologies (IEA, 2023a).

3.2 Involve the private sector in standards and agenda-setting

IOs' inclusiveness of the private sector can be enhanced by involving companies in shaping agendas and standards related to climate issues. By taking an active role in developing these standards, private actors may gain the opportunity to understand their ramifications better, thus becoming more willing to contribute to policies more aligned with their interests and capabilities. One benefit of this cooperation with IOs is improved compliance with international standards and best practices. It equips private actors with the foresight to adapt to regulatory changes and emerging market trends and, more importantly, maintain their competitive advantage. Furthermore, compliance with these international standards can also pave the way for new business opportunities, especially in a broader environment where sustainable practices are becoming increasingly important to investors, customers, and other stakeholders (WEforum, 2022). This collaborative commitment to shaping and complying with international standards could also contribute to a unified and measurable approach to climate challenges.

Many IOs have played instrumental roles in creating and promoting standards, guidelines, and frameworks related to climate and energy governance. These tools can guide private actors in aligning their operations with global sustainability goals, demonstrating their commitment to responsible business practices. For example, the International Organization for Standardization (ISO) develops and publishes various standards relevant to sustainable development, such as the ISO 14001 and ISO 50001 standards (Currey, 2023). These standards are widely used in energy management systems and carbon pricing instruments. They help private actors improve environmental performance, reduce energy consumption, and enhance their credibility with investors, customers, and other stakeholders.

Other than improved compliance, engagement with these IOs also allows private actors to receive guidance to better understand global sustainability requirements. Many of these standard-setting IOs have established capacity-building programmes and technical assistance to help private actors implement international standards and best practices in their operations. For example, the United Nations Global Compact, a voluntary initiative seeking to advance universal sustainability principles, has developed several frameworks, such as the CEO Water Mandate and Caring for Climate, to encourage businesses to embed sustainability into their business strategy. It provides library resources, from SDG guidelines to joint research reports with multinational corporations, to help the private sector align their operations with the Compact's principles on sustainability (UN Global Compact, 2023).

Another example of an IO promoting standard compliance in the private sector is the United Nations Environment Programme's Finance Initiative. It provides training and capacity-building programmes for financial institutions to integrate environmental, social, and governance (ESG) factors into their decision-making processes. These programmes are designed to help private actors strengthen their internal capacity to manage climate- and energy-related risks and opportunities, promoting sustainable finance. One more example is the Global Reporting Initiative (GRI), which provides a comprehensive sustainability reporting framework that enables businesses to measure and communicate their economic, environmental, and social performance. Adhering to GRI guidelines could enhance transparency and accountability, which can draw the interest of investors increasingly aware of sustainable best practices.

3.3 Institutionalise stakeholder engagement with the private sector

Inclusiveness of the private sector can be strengthened by institutionalising stakeholder engagement with private actors. This approach establishes a structured framework for collaboration, ensuring continuity and long-term commitment from both IOs and private actors. It fosters mutual trust and creates a coordinated approach to address climate and energy challenges. Many IOs consider this approach as both contributing to better quality of the rule-making process and as a fundamental determinant of trust (OECD, 2016). Moreover, it serves as a mechanism to align private sector interests with global sustainability goals, allowing for the integration of policies and practices across different sectors and regions. By creating a stable environment for cooperation, institutionalised stakeholder engagement can lead to more impactful and enduring partnerships that contribute significantly to the global fight against climate change and promote sustainable energy development. The sections below summarise three ways of institutionalising stakeholder engagement with the private sector and fostering a more inclusive rule-making process.

3.3.1 Establish membership networks targeting private actors

IOs often function as platforms for dialogue and cooperation, bringing together diverse stakeholders, including governments, businesses, civil societies, and academia. Participating in these forums allows private actors to share knowledge, forge partnerships, and collaborate on initiatives that advance their climate and energy objectives. To further manage and encourage regular participation of the private sector, some IOs have created membership networks for them. To strengthen transparency and accountability, most IOs have put in place mechanisms to collect feedback from stakeholders on their cooperation, activities, and standard settings (OECD, 2016). The pre-existing coordination mechanisms embedded in these networks have become particularly important when there is a need to manage global energy crises, such as the supply shortage after the Ukraine crisis broke out in 2022 (Larkin, 2022).

For example, the IEA actively involves the private sector in its activities, such as through its Energy Business Council (EBC) (IEA, 2023b). The EBC operates as a dialogue platform between IEA member countries and leading industry representatives, attracting interest from a broad range of companies, from fossil fuel companies to renewable energy producers, automakers, and financial institutes. It aims to foster conversations about key energy issues and market trends. EBC meetings and events allow the IEA to incorporate the insights and experiences of private actors into its formulation of energy strategies.

Another example is the Clean Energy Ministerial (CEM), a global forum hosted by the IEA that promotes collaboration between governments, businesses, and other stakeholders to accelerate the transition to clean energy. Through initiatives such as the Corporate Sourcing of Renewables Campaign, the CEM connects private actors with policymakers and market participants, enabling them to work together to increase the adoption of renewable energy in the private sector. Regular high-level meetings in the CEM have normalised the involvement of private actors to address climate and energy challenges and capitalise on emerging opportunities in the sustainable energy market.

3.3.2 Involve the private sector in policy-making

An OECD report (2016) points out that the successful design and implementation of regulations serving the public interest requires contributions from those subject to the regulations (OECD, 2016). Involving private actors in the policymaking process in IOs can help establish a sense of ownership and responsibility that incentivises them to participate more actively in implementing these policies and regulations (OECD, 2016). While private actors benefit from enhanced insights into the regulatory landscape and opportunities to influence policies affecting their operations, IOs can simultaneously draw on their expertise, resources, and unique perspectives. Furthermore, this inclusive approach can help overcome potential barriers to cooperation, such as mistrust, misunderstanding, or conflicting priorities. As private actors become more engaged in the policymaking process, they will likely develop a deeper understanding of the objectives and limitations IOs face. Similarly, IOs may also be more attuned to the needs and concerns of the commercial world. This mutual appreciation is essential for driving more effective and sustainable policy outcomes safeguarding the interests of both IOs and private actors. Ultimately, it fosters more collective actions between the public and private sectors to address global issues (OECD, 2015).

For example, the Carbon Pricing Leadership Coalition (CPLC), an initiative led by the World Bank and the International Monetary Fund (IMF), brings together governments, businesses, and civil society to promote the adoption of carbon pricing policies. By actively participating in the CPLC, private actors can share their insights and experiences that are useful in designing effective carbon pricing mechanisms and play an essential role in shaping the development of carbon markets.

3.3.3 Establish structured training programmes targeting the private sector

Structured training programmes bridge IOs and the private sector, filling knowledge gaps, enhancing skills, and fostering collaboration. Through these programmes, IOs demonstrate their commitment to engaging with the private sector and acknowledge their essential role in driving sustainable development. This proactive approach sends a strong message to private actors that IOs value their contributions and are willing to invest in their capacity building collectively.

Structured training programmes also enable IOs to gain insights into the nuanced needs, challenges, and opportunities private actors face. They allow IOs to tailor their support and engagement strategies more effectively, ensuring their initiatives and policies are relevant, practical, and finely tuned to the private sector's requirements. Moreover, these training programmes create platforms for networking and collaboration, enabling public and private actors to share knowledge, experiences, and best practices. This helps cultivate trust and understanding, which are essential for establishing long-lasting partnerships and collaboration on shared projects.

Several IOs have provided capacity-building support to private actors in the climate and energy domains. For example, the IEA provides a range of resources and training programmes to improve energy efficiency and promote the adoption of clean energy technologies. One of them is the Energy Efficiency Training Weeks, which gathers experts from the public and private sectors across multiple countries to share knowledge and best practices in energy efficiency policy, management, and technology.[2] Similarly, the Clean Energy Solutions Center, an initiative of the Clean Energy Ministerial, supports governments and private sector actors in developing and implementing clean energy policies. Through its 'Ask an Expert' service, the Solutions Center links private actors with experts who can provide tailored technical assistance on diverse clean energy subjects, such as policy design, financing mechanisms, and technology assessment.[3]

The United Nations Environment Programme (UNEP) also offers various capacity-building initiatives designed to help businesses transition towards more sustainable practices. One of them is the Global Environmental Management Initiative, which provides a range of practical guidance materials

---

[2] See IEA's Energy efficiency policy in emerging economies training week, https://www.iea.org/events/energy-efficiency-policy-in-emerging-economies-training-week.

[3] See Clean Energy Solutions Centre 'Ask an expert', https://www.cleanenergyministerial.org/initiatives-campaigns/clean-energy-solutions-center/#ask-an-expert/.

including best practices guides, benchmarking tools, and case study reports. These resources enable businesses to identify and implement effective environmental management strategies tailored to their needs and circumstances. Another example at UNEP is the Green Industry Platform, a multi-stakeholder partnership promoting green industry practices within manufacturing and related sectors. This platform provides private actors access to training programmes, workshops, and technical assistance, as a way to build their capacity in areas such as resource efficiency, cleaner production, and circular economy strategies. The Green Industry Platform also acts as a hub for knowledge sharing and collaboration among its members, cultivating a cooperative environment where companies can learn from each other's experiences and jointly develop innovative solutions to common challenges (United Nations Environment Programme, 2019). Membership in this platform is inclusive and open to any business, corporation or industry trade association committed to fostering environmental sustainability and EHS excellence.

4 CHALLENGES AHEAD FOR IO

Despite efforts in place to improve inclusiveness, IOs still encounter challenges in engaging effectively with the private sector. These challenges stem from concerns about the legitimacy of involving commercially driven private actors, as well as communication barriers arising from differing priorities. As mentioned above, private participation in global climate regimes can be problematic because of a lack of legitimacy, as their involvement is primarily motivated by economic profits rather than the public interest. In contrast, IOs are established on public good mandates, and their objectives may not always align with or even clash with the priorities of the private actors. Over-relying on private actors for funding or expertise also risks IOs' autonomy on sustainability goals. There are chances of private capture where the commercial interests of private actors could unduly influence the agenda of IOs, undermining their public good mandates (OECD, 2021).

To incentivise commercially driven businesses to comply with global sustainability standards, IOs need to establish clear benefits for compliance, such as improved market access, brand reputation, or consumer trust. Simultaneously, there should be penalties or consequences for non-compliance. This 'carrot-and-stick' approach aims to motivate private actors to align their practices with international standards. However, the lack of comprehensive and transparent data reporting on the implementation of private actors' climate commitments hampers an assessment of private actors' climate actions.

While IOs have provided platforms for knowledge sharing and research cooperation, concerns about commercial sensitivities could limit the scope and transparency of these collaborations. Building trust and transparency through more open communication can help address these concerns about sharing sensitive information and promote effective partnerships between IOs and private actors. Additionally, the complexity of sustainability standards established by IOs can be a barrier for private actors. As Laughland and Bansal (2011) pointed out, the lack of universal rules for sustainable sourcing and the multitude of metrics and frameworks embedded in these standards can make it difficult for companies to adjust their business models. Misunderstandings can also lead to accusations of greenwashing, further complicating the relationship between IOs and the private sector. IOs could work on simplifying sustainability standards and establishing clearer guidelines to make them more accessible to a wider range of industries.

These challenges are key considerations for improving IOs' inclusiveness of the private sector, and overcoming them requires a collaborative effort. By offering clear incentives, promoting more open and effective communication, and simplifying complex sustainability standards, IOs and private actors can work together more effectively to mitigate climate challenges.

5 CONCLUSION

In the post-Paris Agreement era, an increasingly diverse landscape of nonstate actors participating in the global climate governance reflects the importance of greater inclusiveness in international organisations, as discussed in the Introductory chapter. In particular, private actors are considered critical contributors to global efforts in mitigating climate challenges due to their status as de-facto implementers of climate actions and their possession of key resources, including market access, expertise, and political influence.

Improving IOs' inclusiveness of the private sector relies on tackling the complexities of climate change and progressing toward a sustainable, low-carbon economy. The performance of IOs is highly dependent on the inclusiveness of affected stakeholders, from multinational companies to SMEs, to operate properly. This chapter proposes three approaches through which IOs can enhance their collaboration with private actors to effectively address climate-related challenges. First, IOs need to demonstrate clearer business relevancy of their functions. This involves providing enhanced market and capital access, alongside aiding in risk mitigation, crisis management, R&D, and knowledge sharing. Second, IOs need to strengthen partnerships with private actors in shaping agendas and standards. This can empower private actors to grasp these standards better, ensuring improved compliance in the long run. Third, IOs should institutionalise their engagement with private actors by creating membership networks tailored to private actors, incorporating private actors into policy-formulation processes, and establishing structured training initiatives targeted at private actors. These actions could improve IOs' inclusiveness of private actors, setting the stage for sustained progress in climate mitigation efforts.

However, the chapter also acknowledges certain limitations in improving the inclusiveness of private actors. These include issues concerning the legitimacy and accountability of private actors, as well as communication barriers. To overcome these challenges, it is critical to establish clear incentives, foster open and efficient communication channels, and simplify sustainability standards. By collectively addressing these constraints, IOs and private actors can work towards mitigating the challenges posed by climate change.

In the future, it is recommended that IOs continue to explore innovative ways to foster collaboration with private actors. By leveraging their combined resources, expertise, and influence, IOs and private actors can proactively tackle the emerging issues of climate change.

REFERENCES

Andrade, J.C.S. and J.A.P. de Oliveira (2015) The role of the private sector in global climate and energy governance. *Journal of Business Ethics*, 130(2),375–387.

Bäckstrand, K. and A. Kronsell (2015) *Rethinking the Green State: Environmental Governance towards Climate and Sustainability Transitions*, Routledge, London.

Chan, S. et al. (2018) Effective and geographical balanced? An output-based assessment of non-state climate actions. *Climate Policy*, 18(1), 24–35.

Clark, R. et al. (2018) Bridging funding gaps for climate and sustainable development: Pitfalls, progress and potential of private finance. *Land Use Policy*, 71, 335–346.

Colgan, J. (2009) *The International Energy Agency: Challenges for the 21st century*, Global Public Policy Institute, https://www.gppi.net/media/Colgan_2009_The_International_Energy.pdf (accessed 4 April 2023).

Currey, A. (2023) *CICS' Quick guide to ISO 50001, the new energy management system standard*, https://www.sustainabilityexchange.ac.uk/files/cics_quick_guide_to_iso_50001.pdf (accessed 2 May 2023).

Falkner, R. (2007) *Business Power and Conflict in International Environmental Politics*, Palgrave Macmillan, Basingstoke.

GCF (2020) Updated Strategic Plan for the Green Climate Fund 2020–2023, https://www.greenclimate.fund/document/updated-strategic-plan-green-climate-fund-2020–2023 (accessed 1 Aug 2023).

Hale, T. (2016) '"All on Desk": The Paris Agreement and Nonstate Climate Action', *Global Environmental Politics*, 16(3), 12–22.

Hsu, A. et al. (2016) Track climate pledges of cities and companies. *Nature*, 532(7599), 303–306.

IEA (2023a) About the TCP, https://www.iea.org/programmes/technology-collaboration-programme (accessed 1 Aug 2023).

IEA (2023b) *Energy business council dialogue among the IEA, the business community and policymakers*, International Energy Agency, https://www.iea.org/about/structure/energy-business-council (accessed 1 May 2023).

IFC (2012) *IFC performance standards on environmental and social sustainability, International Finance Corporation*, https://www.ifc.org/wps/wcm/connect/

topics_ext_content/ifc_external_corporate_site/sustainability-at-ifc/publications/publications_handbook_pps (accessed 6 April 2023).

IRENA (2016) *Policies and regulations for private sector renewable energy mini-grids*, IRENA, https://www.irena.org/-/media/Files/IRENA/Agency/Publication/2016/IRENA_Policies_Regulations_minigrids_2016.pdf (accessed 2 May 2023).

ITC (2023) Business, https://intracen.org/business (accessed 1 August 2023).

Jiang, S. and J. Li (2020) Global climate governance in the new era: Potential of business actors and technological innovation. *Chinese Journal of Population, Resources and Environment,* 18(1), 165–171.

Kuyper, J.W., B.O. Linnér and H. Schroeder (2018) Non-state actors in hybrid global climate governance: justice, legitimacy, and effectiveness in a post-Paris era. *Wiley Interdisciplinary Reviews: Climate Change*, *9*(1), e497.

Larkin, A. (2022) IEA strengthens focus on clean energy in ministerial meeting, *Energy Global*, https://www.energyglobal.com/special-reports/04042022/iea-strengthens-focus-on-clean-energy-in-ministerial-meeting/ (accessed 5 May 2023).

Laughland, P and T. Bansal (2011) The top ten reasons why businesses aren't more sustainable. *Ivey Business Journal*, https://iveybusinessjournal.com/publication/the-top-ten-reasons-why-businesses-arent-more-sustainable/ (accessed 1 May 2023).

rLevy, D.L., and C.A. Jones (2009) 'Business strategies and climate change', in Selin, H. and S.D. VanDeveer (Eds) *Changing climates in North American politics: Institutions, policymaking, and multilevel governance*, MIT Press, Cambridge MA.

Levy, D.L. and P.J. Newell (Eds) (2004) *The Business of Global Environmental Governance*, MIT Press, Cambridge MA.

Lövbrand, E. et al. (2017) Making climate governance global: how UN climate summitry comes to matter in a complex climate regime. *Environmental Politics*, 26(4), 580–599.

Meyer, M. (2022) *What is the TCFD and why does it matter*, Deloitte, https://www2.deloitte.com/ch/en/pages/risk/articles/tcfd-and-why-does-it-matter.html (accessed 25 April 2023).

Mitchell, I., E. Ritchie and A. Tahmasebi (2021) Is climate finance towards $100 billion 'new and additional'. Center for Global Development: Washington DC, https://www.cgdev.org/sites/default/files/PP205-Mitchell-Ritchie-Tahmasebi-Climate-Finance.pdf (accessed 22 April 2023).

Nasiritousi, N (2015) *Shapers, Brokers and Doers: The Dynamic Roles of Non-State Actors in Global Climate Change Governance*, Linköping Studies in Arts and Science No. 667, Linköping University Electronic Press, Linköping.

NAZCA (2023) *Global Climate Action*, https://climateaction.unfccc.int (accessed 6 June 2023).

OECD (2015) Improving service provision: Drawing on collective action theory to fix incentives, https://www.oecd.org/dac/accountable-effective-institutions/Governance%20Notebook%203.5%20Tembo.pdf (accessed 5 March 2024).

OECD (2016) *International Regulatory Co-operation: The Role of International Organisations in Fostering Better Rules of Globalisation*, OECD Publishing, Paris, https://doi.org/10.1787/9789264244047-en (accessed 5 March 2024).

OECD (2021) 'Compendium of International Organisations' Practices: Working Towards More Effective International Instruments. OECD Publishing, Paris.

Orzes, G. and A. Moretto (2020) The impact of the United Nations Global Compact on firm performance: A longitudinal analysis. *International Journal of Production Economics,* 227(4), 107664.

Park, J. (2022) How can we pay for it all? Understanding the global challenge of financing climate change and sustainable development solutions. *Journal of Environmental Studies and Sciences* 12, 91–99.

Pattberg, P. et al. (eds) (2013) *Public–Private Partnership for Sustainable Development: Emergence, Influence and Legitimacy*, Edward Elgar Publishing, Cheltenham.

Reyes, O., and L. Schalatek (2021) *GCF private sector finance in focus 2: MSMEs, Heinrich-Böll-Stiftung*, https://us.boell.org/sites/default/files/2022-03/hbs%20Washington_GCF-PrivateSector2_MSME%20briefing_final.pdf (accessed 3 May 2023).

Si, Y., D. Desai, D. Bozhilova, S. Puffer, & J.C. Stephens (2023) Fossil fuel companies' climate communication strategies: Industry messaging on renewables and natural gas. *Energy Research & Social Science*, 98, 103028.

Sinclair, G. F. (2017) *To Reform the World: International Organisation and the Making of Modern States*, Oxford University Press, Oxford.

Streck, C. (2020) Filling in for governments? The role of the private actors in the international climate regime. *Journal for European Environmental & Planning Law*, 17(1), 5–28.

UN Global Compact (2023) Explore our enhanced library, https://unglobalcompact.org/library (accessed 01 Aug 2023).

UNDRR (2021) *Annual report 2021, United Nations Office for Disaster Risk Reduction*, https://www.undrr.org/publication/undrr-annual-report-2021 (accessed 5 April 2023).

UNFCCC (1995) Report of the Conference of the Parties on its first session, held at Berlin from 28 March to 7 April 1995, Addendum. FCCC/CP/1995/7/Add.1, https://unfccc.int/resource/docs/cop1/07a01.pdf (accessed on 2 May 2023)

UNFCCC (2010) *Report of the Conference of the Parties on its Fifteenth Session, Held in Copenhagen from 7 to 19 December 2009. Addendum: Part Two: Action Taken by the Conference of the Parties at its Fifteenth Session*, https://unfccc.int/sites/ default/files/resource/docs/2009/cop15/eng/11a01. Pdf (accessed 6 June 2023).

UNFCCC (2016) *Decision 1/CP.21. Adoption of the Paris Agreement FCCC/CP/ 2015/10/Add.1.*, https://unfccc.int/resource/docs/2015/cop21/eng/10a01.pdf (accessed on 3 May 2023).

UNIDO (2025) Global Cleantech Innovation Programme, https://www.unido.org/GCIP (accessed 08 Feb 2025)

United Nations Environment Programme (2019) *Two new platforms offer the latest knowledge on green finance and green business, UN environment programme*, https://www.unep.org/news-and-stories/press-release/two-new-platforms-offer-latest-knowledge-green-finance-and-green (accessed 16 April 2023).

Victor, D (2011) *Global Warming Gridlock: Creating More Effective Strategies for Protecting the Planet*, Cambridge Press, Cambridge.

WEforum (2022) *Why sustainability is crucial for corporate strategy*, https://www.weforum.org/agenda/2022/06/why-sustainability-is-crucial-for-corporate-strategy/ (accessed 1 May 2023).

Widerberg, O. and P. Pattberg (2017) Accountability challenges in the transnational regime complex for climate change. *Review of Policy Research*, 34(1), 68–87.

WMO (2020) *State of climate service: Risk information and early warning system, World Meteorological Organization*, https://library.wmo.int/doc_num.php?explnum_id=10385 (accessed 06 April 2023).

7. The involvement of private actors in transnational rule-making: the case of securities regulation

Antonio Marcacci

1 INTRODUCTION

The International Organization of Securities Commissions – IOSCO – is the only international organisation that brings together public securities regulators from around the world. Although being driven by public authorities, IOSCO actively involves private actors in its standard-setting process. Cornerstone of IOSCO's commitment towards private actors' participation is the 2005 IOSCO Consultation Policy and Procedure. While being formally in force for almost 20 years, the 2005 Procedure has only actually been used after the 2008 financial crisis, when IOSCO's standard production dramatically increased. An analysis of the private-sector input received so far reveals the legal nature of the stakeholders that actively contribute to the Organization's standard-setting. In particular, this chapter sheds light on IOSCO's efforts to collect private actors' input with a view to obtaining specific information and knowledge that, on the one hand, would make its standards more effective, and, on the other hand, would bring in specific insights with regard to the understanding and evaluation of standards' implementation on the part of the industry. The three case studies examined in this chapter reveal the importance of acquiring high-quality feedback from the private sector. IOSCO does this to gain a deeper understanding of technical issues and then adopt meaningful global standards that are able to function in the real world and not just on paper. Based on such analysis, the chapter concludes that IOSCO's approach represents a successful practice in terms of stakeholders' inclusion in a very technical field. Nevertheless, some significant challenges still remain on the table. In particular, the chapter identifies room for improvement with regard to the participation of civil society representatives. While it is widely known that civil society representatives do not have the means and resources that the industry has, their input is still equally important. As a result, their ability to meaningfully contribute to IOSCO consultations should be enhanced. This is a challenge that IOSCO might take up in the near future by leveraging its capacity-building programmes.

2 THE INTERNATIONAL ORGANIZATION OF SECURITIES COMMISSIONS: IOSCO

2.1 Overview

IOSCO was officially established in 1983, and its Secretariat has been in Madrid since 1999 (Bismuth 2011, pp. 294, 324–325). IOSCO is not based on a public international law treaty but is, instead, incorporated under Spanish law as an association of public utility.[1] From an internal viewpoint, IOSCO is governed by its own By-Laws (IOSCO 2011), which define the organisation's governance. Over time, IOSCO has been able to grow both in size and in quality. Its membership currently covers 'more than 95% of the world's securities markets in more than 130 jurisdictions' (IOSCO 2021a). Its standard production has achieved a high level of sophistication and political importance, as I have analysed elsewhere (Marcacci 2022). In particular, the 1998 *Objectives and Principles of Securities Regulation* have become the global yardstick in the field, used by other international organisations – such as the IMF, the World Bank, and the FSB – to conduct monitoring and assessment activities (Jordan 2014). The 2002 Multilateral Memorandum of Understanding (MMoU) represents the 'international benchmark for cross-border co-operation' (IOSCO 2021g) between securities regulators (Austin 2017). Especially after the 2008 global financial crisis, IOSCO has produced a large set of non-binding, soft-law standards covering a wide spectrum of securities regulation (Marcacci 2022).

2.2 Membership

IOSCO Membership is split into three categories. First, Full Members. These are national administrative authorities in charge of supervision over national securities markets (IOSCO 2021h). The key requirement to become an ordinary member is to be an MMoU signatory. Full Membership implies a wide range of supervisory and enforcement powers that allow a national agency to cooperate with its foreign peers (Marcacci 2022). Second, Associate Members.

---

[1] Ley 55/1999, de 29 de diciembre, de medidas fiscales, administrativas y del orden social, Boletín Oficial del Estado, 30 diciembre 1999, n° 312, p. 46095, n° 24876.

These are subjects of public but supranational, subnational, or intergovernmental nature, alongside 'other governmental bodies with an appropriate interest in securities regulation' (IOSCO 2021a). For instance, the European Union Authority for Securities Markets, ESMA, is an IOSCO Associate Member (Conac 2015). Third, Affiliate Members. This is a residual category that includes 'self-regulatory organizations, securities exchanges, financial market infrastructures, international bodies other than governmental organizations with an appropriate interest in securities regulation, investor protection funds and compensation funds, and other bodies with an appropriate interest in securities regulation' (IOSCO 2021a). The Affiliate Members category is particularly important for this chapter because private sector entities can apply for affiliate membership. For instance, according to the official website of IOSCO,[2] both the International Swaps & Derivatives Association and the European Fund and Asset Management Association are affiliate members.

2.3 Governance

In terms of internal governance, IOSCO is organised as follows. Formal powers belong to the Presidents Committee, which brings together the Heads of all Full Members – each of them with one voting right – and the Heads of all Associate Members – without voting rights (IOSCO 2011). The Presidents Committee meets once a year at the Annual Meeting (IOSCO 2021i). Although it 'has all the powers necessary or convenient to achieve the objectives of the Organization' rights (IOSCO 2011), the Presidents Committee is the de facto political venue where decisions already discussed and approved at the IOSCO Board level are finally passed. (Marcacci, 2022). The Board is, instead, the core decision-making body of IOSCO (IOSCO 2021f). It 'is constituted for a period of two years' (IOSCO 2011) during the IOSCO Biennial Meeting[3] and its members are chosen among the Organisation's Full Members,[4] thus

[2] IOSCO. 2021b. Affiliate Members Consultative Committee [Online]. Available at: https://www.iosco.org/about/?subsection=display_committee&cmtid=2 [accessed 24 September 2024].

[3] Article 25 of the By-Laws reads as follows: 'At an Annual Meeting held in every even-numbered year ("a Biennial Meeting"), the various Committees of the Organisation and the IOSCO Board hold elections for their various office-holders.'

[4] The Board also comprises two observers: the European Securities and Markets Authority, which represents the European Union in IOSCO and is an Associate Member; and the National Futures Association (NFA) as the current Chair of the Affiliate Members Consultative Committee. The NFA is a US self-regulatory organisation that brings together derivative markets operators. IOSCO. 2021b. Affiliate Members Consultative Committee [Online]. Available at: https://

public domestic authorities with full regulatory and enforcement powers. It currently comprises 35 securities regulators coming from all continents.[5] The Board adopts key IOSCO policies and operates through a network of internal standing Committees that cover all relevant areas,[6] in addition to ad-hoc, time-limited Task Forces that are established for specific topics.[7]

Three more internal bodies play a significant role within IOSCO. First, the Growth and Emerging Markets Committee (GEM), which gathers 90 Full Members from emerging economies and 24 non-voting associate members (IOSCO 2021e). It 'promote[s] the development and greater efficiency of emerging securities and futures markets by establishing principles and minimum standards, providing training programmes and technical assistance for members, and facilitating the exchange of information and transfer of technology and expertise' (IOSCO 2021e). Second, four Regional Committees,[8] which take care of specific regional topics and provide the Board with regional perspectives (IOSCO 2022). Third, and most importantly for this chapter, the Affiliate Members Consultative Committee (AMCC). The AMCC gathers 68 affiliate members that represent 'securities and derivatives markets and other market infrastructures, self-regulatory organisations (SROs), investor protection funds and compensation funds, as well as other bodies with appropriate interest in securities regulation' (IOSCO 2021b). AMCC Members

www.iosco.org/about/?subsection=display_committee&cmtid=2 [Accessed 24 September 2024]; IOSCO. 2021f. IOSCO Board [Online]. Available at: https://www.iosco.org/about/?subsection=display_committee&cmtid=11 [Accessed 24 september 2024].

5 At the time of writing, the Members are: Australia, the Bahamas, Bangladesh, Belgium, Brazil, China, DIFC Dubai, Egypt, France, Germany, Greece, Hong Kong, India, Ireland, Italy, Japan, Kuwait, Malaysia, Mauritius, Mexico, Morocco, Ontario, Peru, Quebec, Republic of Korea, Saudi Arabia, Singapore, Spain, Sweden, Switzerland, The Netherlands, Türkiye, the United Kingdom, and the United States of America. See IOSCO's official website.

6 Such as: Accounting, Auditing, and Disclosure; Secondary Markets; Market Intermediaries; Enforcement and the Exchange of Information and the Multilateral Memorandum of Understanding Screening Group; Investment Management; Credit Rating Agencies; Commodities Derivatives Markets; and Retail Investors. IOSCO. 2021i. Presidents Committee [Online]. Available at: https://www.iosco.org/about/?subsection=display_committee&cmtid=11 [Accessed 24 September 2024].

7 See interviews with IOSCO senior management in: Marcacci, A. 2022. *Transnational Securities Regulation. How it Works, Who Shapes it*, Cham, Springer, p. 59.

8 Africa/Middle-East Regional Committee; Asia-Pacific Regional Committee; European Regional Committee; and Inter-American Regional Committee.

can either have a public or private law nature. For instance, the International Swaps & Derivatives Association (ISDA) and the European Fund and Asset Management Association (EFAMA) are both members of the AMCC. Given its members' 'proximity with market participants' (IOSCO 2022), AMCC's input into IOSCO policy discussions is absolutely relevant.

2.4 Internal rule-making

The driving principle underpinning IOSCO's internal rule-making is consensus. The By-Laws officially affirm 'that the best means to achieve [...IOSCO's] aims is by fostering consensus' (IOSCO 2011). Within the IOSCO world, 'consensus is not equivalent to unanimity but, rather, to a "general understanding" around a common core, i.e., a meaningful result' (Marcacci 2022).[9] Significantly, this feature does not belong to IOSCO only, but it is the case in most International Organisations.[10] Interestingly, in case agreements cannot be achieved via consensus due to internal divisions, the IOSCO By-Laws allow a majority-based vote (IOSCO 2011). In particular, Resolutions approved by the Presidents Committee can be 'put to a vote' and 'must have the support of a majority of the members in attendance' to be adopted (IOSCO 2011). Similarly, the Board's decisions can be 'put to the vote and must have the support of the majority of the members in attendance' to be approved (IOSCO 2011). Significantly, in the case of 'a tie, the [Board's] Chairman [has] a casting vote' (IOSCO 2011). Interestingly, the same rules on internal standard-making decisions do not extend to standing committees and task forces, which operate in a more informal fashion (Marcacci 2022).

3 INPUT FROM PRIVATE ACTORS INTO IOSCO'S STANDARDS: THREE CASE STUDIES

Private actors can provide input to IOSCO standards via public consultations, and this section covers a description of the related internal procedure alongside the analysis of three case studies.[11]

[9] See interviews with IOSCO senior management in: MarcaccI, A. 2022. *Transnational Securities Regulation. How it Works, Who Shapes It*, Cham, Springer. p. 119.

[10] As analysed in: OECD (2016), International Regulatory Co-operation: The Role of International Organisations in Fostering Better Rules of Globalisation, OECD Publishing, Paris. Available at: https://doi.org/10.1787/9789264244047-en.

[11] Parts of section 3 and its subsections have previously been published in: A. Marcacci, *Transnational Securities Regulation – How it Works, Who Shapes It*,

3.1 The IOSCO Consultation Policy and Procedure

The procedure to submit comments is regulated by the 2005 IOSCO Consultation Policy and Procedure (IOSCO 2005). This is the official document directly addressing participation from private parties and gathering the 'views and comments from the international financial community' (IOSCO 2005). The Policy is divided into two parts, Consultation and Procedure. The first part lists the objectives that IOSCO pursues via public consultations and the elements that are taken into account when deciding whether and how to seek public comments. The first two goals focus on obtaining 'substantive input into IOSCO's work' and benefiting 'from the expertise of the international financial community' (IOSCO 2005). This is because some specific knowledge only develops in the private sector and may lead to 'alternative regulatory approaches', a facet strictly linked to understanding the 'impact, benefits and costs of any proposed standards and principles' (IOSCO 2005). The importance of private sector expertise is highlighted by the fact that consultations should be carried out when 'technical or industry-specific information is necessary' (IOSCO 2005). The two other goals regard the need to determine 'whether concern exists [that would] require a regulatory response' and 'assist persons who may be affected by proposed IOSCO standards and principles to modify their activities and/or processes, if necessary, by providing early notice of potential IOSCO standards and principles' (IOSCO 2005). In its Final Reports, while not addressing all comments on an individual basis, IOSCO explains how public comments were addressed or discloses the reasons why these were not addressed, as confirmed by the three case studies below.

The second part outlines the Procedure. In particular, each consultation must be transparently labelled as such on the cover page, contain a clear deadline, provide background information alongside the reasons why IOSCO seeks the opinion of the public, and, if necessary, specific questions. To ensure full publicity, all consultation reports and received comments are published on the IOSCO official website, with commentators' anonymity granted if requested. Concerning the nature of the commentators, these are usually private sector associations, large financial institutions, clearing houses, self-regulatory organisations, trading venues like stock exchanges, and – far more rarely – civil society representatives and even individuals with particular expertise in the field.

The following sections deal with three case studies: hedge funds, retail structured products, and ESG ratings and data products providers. The 2009 hedge funds case was chosen because this was the first public consultation IOSCO had ever done. It is important to begin with this case to understand the first steps taken by IOSCO in terms of standard-setting inclusion. I chose the retail products and ESG ratings cases because they contain input from consumer associations and representatives of civil societies, in addition to comments from the industry. Scanning the comments publicly available on IOSCO's website, these consultations appear to be two of the very few cases with concrete input from non-industry representatives. Importantly, being from 2009, 2013, and 2021, the three cases cover the entire time-lapse of public comments so far. As a result, analysing these three consultations helps understand IOSCO's limits in terms of inclusion and puts forth some propositions to ameliorate the current landscape.

3.2 Hedge funds

Although the Consultation Policy and Procedure was adopted in 2005, the first set of public comments published on IOSCO's official website dates to 2009. The topic was hedge fund oversight, one of the most relevant for financial market supervision. IOSCO's work on hedge funds was carried out in the aftermath of the 2008 global financial crisis (GFC) with the aim to 'support the initiatives [of] the G-20' (IOSCO 2009a, p. 5). Although the original plan covered more generally 'unregulated financial entities', IOSCO heightened its focus on hedge funds due to the 'G-20's particular interest' in the topic (IOSCO 2009a, p. 5). As a matter of fact, scarce regulation of entities like hedge funds was viewed as one of the contributing causes of the 2008 GFC, although IOSCO had clarified that the GFC was 'not actually a "hedge fund crisis"' (IOSCO 2009a, p. 31). Scarce regulation was coupled with 'no consistent or agreed-upon definition' at the global level of what a hedge fund is (IOSCO 2009b, p. 4).

This led IOSCO to issue the 'Hedge Funds Oversight – Consultation Report' in March 2009. The purpose was to provide, first, a description of the hedge funds' operating environment with particular regard to regulatory risks; then an illustration of IOSCO's recommendations in the field; and, finally, the establishment of 'possible principles and actions that may serve to mitigate these risks' (IOSCO 2009b, p. 17). In particular, the consultation highlighted the following overarching features meant to help define an investment scheme as a hedge fund:

- borrowing and leverage restrictions, typically included in collective investment schemes related regulation, are not applied; many (but not all) hedge funds use high levels of leverage;

- significant performance fees (often in the form of a percentage of profits) are paid to the manager in addition to an annual management fee;
- investors are typically permitted to redeem their interests periodically, e.g., quarterly, semi-annually or annually;
- often significant 'own' funds are invested by the manager;
- derivatives are used, often for speculative purposes, and there is an ability to short sell securities;
- more diverse risks or complex underlying products are involved.

(IOSCO, 2009a, pp. 6–7)

While the definition is wide open, specific features can be detected. First of all, the key issue of high leverage, which implies particularly risky strategies. This is corroborated by the use of derivatives and other complex products, coupled with fund managers' proprietary trading. Second, higher performance fees would usually refrain the average retail investor from chipping into such funds. Here, the sophisticated profile of hedge fund investors also emerges in their freedom to redeem their interests periodically. Given this scenario, it comes as no surprise that the comments received on the *Consultation* were mainly from industry representatives, with only four contributions from regulators (Jersey, Malta, and the Cayman Islands) and exchanges (London) with a clear interest in the field.

The subsequent Hedge Funds Oversight – Final Report was published in June 2009, and it took into full account the comments received on the March Consultation. In particular, the comments were used to delineate the following high-level principles:

1. Hedge funds and/or hedge fund managers/advisers should be subject to mandatory registration.
2. Hedge fund managers/advisers which are required to register should also be subject to appropriate ongoing regulatory requirements relating to:
   a. Organisational and operational standards;
   b. Conflicts of interest and other conduct of business rules;
   c. Disclosure to investors; and
   d. Prudential regulation.
3. Prime brokers and banks which provide funding to hedge funds should be subject to mandatory registration/regulation and supervision. They should have in place appropriate risk management systems and controls to monitor their counterparty credit risk exposures to hedge funds.
4. Hedge fund managers/advisers and prime brokers should provide to the relevant regulator information for systemic risk purposes (including the identification, analysis and mitigation of systemic risks).
5. Regulators should encourage and take account of the development, implementation and convergence of industry good practices, where appropriate.
6. Regulators should have the authority to co-operate and share information, where appropriate, with each other, in order to facilitate efficient and

> effective oversight of globally active managers/advisers and/or funds and to help identify systemic risks, market integrity and other risks arising from the activities or exposures of hedge funds with a view to mitigating such risks across borders.
>
> (IOSCO 2009b, pp. 8–9)

Given the nature of the commentators, key points frequently raised were, first, the need to avoid over-regulation – 'a [proportionate] mixture of direct and indirect regulation' – and second, the necessity to recognise that hedge funds, on the one hand, play an important role in global finance given their focus on risks, and, on the other hand, did not (primarily) cause the GFC (IOSCO 2009b, p. 17). Given the global nature of the hedge fund industry, the need for cooperation between authorities and regulatory convergence also emerged from the feedback received (IOSCO 2009b, p. 18). In addition, an important point was raised about retail investors. Although hedge funds are usually acquired by institutional investors, commentators highlighted the increasing accessibility of retail investors via 'funds of hedge funds or allocation of traditional funds assets in hedge funds' (IOSCO 2009b, p. 17). As a result, the necessity to increase transparency for the benefit of less sophisticated investors was brought up.

Going into more detail, respondents clearly pointed out that conflicts of interest in the form of compensation structures cross all financial sectors, not only hedge funds. In particular, they made a case for hedge fund managers' remuneration structure being already 'align[ed with] the interests of managers and investors, mitigating the relevant conflicts' (IOSCO 2009b, p. 18). For instance, this point was raised by the Standards Board for Alternative Investments (SBAI), known then as the Hedge Fund Standards Board, a non-profit association of asset managers and allocators (IOSCO 2009b, p. 18; Standards Board for Alternative Investments – SBAI 2023).

In terms of risk management, some respondents seemed to take quite a defensive approach. First, they pointed out that hedge funds mostly resort to financial leverage less than other market players. Second, since investors in hedge funds are usually sophisticated, they can autonomously request additional information concerning risk management. Third, risks posed by hedge funds' counterparties should be taken into full account. Such points were particularly raised by the Managed Fund Association (MFA), which represents the alternative asset management industry at the global level (IOSCO, 2009b 18; MFA, 2023). The Asset Management Association Switzerland – at that time known as the Swiss Funds Association – also made a case for obtaining information from counterparties such as prime brokers and banks, while fully supporting the proposition of stronger risk management controls at the hedge fund level (IOSCO 2009b, p. 18). The Asset Management Association Switzerland is the industry organisation of the Swiss asset management industry (Asset Management Association Switzerland 2023).

In terms of regulatory strategy, all respondents agreed on a 'direct regulation' approach. However, most of them favoured direct regulation of managers rather than that of funds themselves. Importantly, the *Association Française de la Gestion financière* (AFG) – which represents the French investment management industry (AFG 2023) – made the crucial point that direct regulation of fund managers may fail in terms of retail investor protection as many hedge funds are incorporated in offshore financial centres, thus making retail investors increasingly vulnerable (IOSCO 2009b, p. 19).

Finally, in terms of supervision, many commentators broadly agreed on IOSCO's proposals. Convergence was particularly strong on the requirement for the proportionate establishment of independent internal functions – Compliance and Risk Management – as a second line of defence (IOSCO 2009b, p. 20). For instance, this was endorsed by the *Bundesverband Alternative Investments e.V.* (BAI), which represents the asset class- and product-spanning of Alternative Investments in Germany (BAI 2023). Very interestingly, some respondents did not agree on the proposition to introduce minimum capital requirements due to the fact that, first, hedge funds are not depository institutions, and second, they 'target sophisticated investors who understand the risks involved with their investments' (IOSCO 2009b, p. 21). One of those respondents was CompliGlobe, a US company that provides regulatory advisory services (CompliGlobe 2023).

This first-ever set of public comments on an IOSCO open consultation shows that market operators have a strong interest in playing t a part in transnational rule-making. Although technical and, thus, difficult to understand for non-experts, the preferences of the industry at that time were clear.. Chief among all was the fear of over-regulation driven by the post-GFC normative zeal. Here, IOSCO is to be praised for two reasons. First, it provided aggregate answers to all comments. Second, it took into account the feedback received when drafting the six high-level principles. What was clearly missing, however, was input from retail investors and civil society representatives. Although the interests of retail investors are mentioned, these were conveyed by industry associations rather than consumer organisations.

3.3 Retail structured products

The vast majority of IOSCO documents deal with wholesale securities markets, which means that the interests of retail investors are addressed somewhat indirectly. One of the few consultations tackling the welfare of retail investors was the April 2013 *Regulation of Retail Structured Products – Consultation*

Report (IOSCO 2013a). Structured products are complex investment solutions that 'embed ... a derivative that provides economic exposure to reference assets, indices or other economic values' (IOSCO 2013a, p. 3).[12] Although sometimes traded on trading venues, structured products are often manufactured and sold over-the-counter (IOSCO 2013a, p. 3). Retail structured products are those structured products sold to retail investors. The main interest that drove IOSCO to address this topic concerned the regulatory challenges posed by such products to retail investors. Such challenges were, in particular, the average investor's understanding of the products' design, the products' suitability and disclosure, the likelihood of mis-selling, and the post-sale controls (IOSCO 2013a, p. 4).

To address this matter, IOSCO established an ad-hoc Working Group. The Working Group issued an Organisation-level Survey on retail structured products in mid-2012, in which 26 IOSCO Members took part. Some common features emerged from the Survey, in particular the general absence of precise statutory definitions of 'retail investor' and 'structured product'. This definitional gap could affect the measuring of related market size, making comparative analyses more difficult. Another common feature was the identification of financial institutions (banking and other financial institutions) as key manufacturers/issuers of retail structured products. Very often, distributors were also issuers or their affiliates, which inevitably increased the likelihood of conflicts of interest to the detriment of retail investors. Concerning the investors, only three respondents provided data on the demographics. However, some common characteristics emerged, such as high income and being either a younger (below 42) or an older investor (above 55). Concerning the product drivers, most respondents pointed out profit for the supply-side and portfolio diversification and yield for the demand-side. The latter represented evidence that investors willing to acquire structured products have a preference for higher risks (IOSCO 2013a).

As for domestic regulation, disclosure and marketing regulatory standards emerged asthe preferred regulatory approach for almost all respondents. While disclosure is a constant feature of securities laws, regulation of marketing material is especially important to avoid false or misleading communications. Almost all respondents had introduced mandatory suitability assessments

12 In more detail, the Report states that: 'Structured products are compound financial instruments that have the characteristics of combining a base instrument (such as a note, fund, deposit, or insurance contract) with an embedded derivative that provides economic exposure to reference assets, indices, or portfolios. In this form, they provide investors, at predetermined times, with payoffs that are linked to the performance of reference assets, indices or other economic values' (IOSCO 2013a. Regulation of Retail Structured Products – Consultation Report, pp. 6–7).

that investment firms must conduct before selling a structured product to a retail investor. Slightly fewer respondents had established domestic registration obligations followed by supervisory review of products' prospectuses. The same number of respondents had already been already empowered with some product intervention powers, such as the temporary prohibition of a product (IOSCO 2013a).

After the survey, a Round Table was held in November 2012. The Round Table brought together financial institutions issuing retail structured products, law firms providing legal advice to financial institutions on retail structured products, derivative industry associations, and consumer groups (IOSCO 2013a, p. 1). A general point raised at the Round Table was that yield-based products were enticing due to the then-low-interest-rate environment. In particular, credit-linked products were more popular among high-net-worth investors. In addition, although a trend toward simpler products could be observed, this did not implying less risky solutions. Another very interesting takeaway from the Round Table was the suggestion that issuers and distributors should have different duties. While issuers should have a more general obligation to define target markets, distributors should be responsible for determining whether a product is suitable for a specific investor (IOSCO 2013a). Last, but definitely not the least, consumer representatives made the clear point 'that certain investors have difficulty understanding the most simple of structured products' (IOSCO 2013a, p. 21).

Concerning potential regulatory options, views regarding how intrusive regulation should be were mixed. Some attendees were in favour of a stronger regulatory approach, while others feared an increase in costs. Although the IOSCO document does not reveal *who* said *what*, it is quite intuitive that consumer representatives would likely want a more penetrating approach, while the industry would prefer a lighter touch. Some support was expressed for a more encompassing approach, such as consistent regulation across types of wrappers and a value-chain focus throughout the existence of a product (IOSCO 2013a, p. 22). Typical investors' concerns were raised, such as the risks of mis-selling, the need to carry out suitability assessments, the shortcomings of disclosure, the promotion of informed decision-making by investors, investor education, the importance of product testing, and the problem of conflicts of interest in the distribution chain. However, some points could also originate from *within* the industry, such as the (harsher) responsibilities of distributors vis-à-vis those of issuers (IOSCO 2013a).

On the basis of the Survey's results and the Round Table's takeaways, a public consultation systematised a set of regulatory options – a Toolkit – that IOSCO members could consider when addressing retail structured products in their home jurisdictions. While the goal was to enhance retail investor protection, the Toolkit was designed to be sufficiently flexible to adapt to different regulatory landscapes. Importantly, IOSCO attuned the Toolkit with its Suitability Principles, crafted to address the distribution of complex financial products – which include structured products – to retail and non-retail customers (IOSCO 2013c). The Toolkit comprised the following 15 elements: (i) Regulatory Arbitrage; (ii) Value Chain Focus; (iii) Intended Investor Identification and Assessment; (iv) Use of Financial Modelling; (v) Product Approval Processes; (vi) Product Standards; (vii) Disclosure Standards Generally; (viii) Short-Form or Summary Disclosure; (ix) Costs and Fees; (x) Use of Fair Value Assessment; (xi) Hypothetical Scenarios; (xii) Backtesting; (xiii) Enhancement of Informed Investment Decision Making; (xiv) Distribution Channel Considerations; and (xv) Post-Sales Practices.

Most of the responses to the consultation were from industry (22 out of 28), one from an investor advocacy group, two from government agencies, and three from individuals. All respondents agreed on two points. First, the fact that inter- or intra-jurisdictional regulatory arbitrage is a serious problem. Second, the necessity to have a summary conveying key product information. Still, in terms of disclosure, almost all respondents agreed about asking regulators to set issuer disclosure standards, while taking into account the risk of overreliance on disclosure (IOSCO 2013b).

Other responses were mixed. In particular, mixed answers were given on whether a value-chain approach to retail structured products would be useful. On the contrary, most of the respondents agreed on the necessity of requiring internal approval processes for issuers. Mixed responses were also given on whether disclosure of disaggregated costs would be useful as disaggregated costs are difficult to understand and are not useful for retail investors (IOSCO 2013b).

Some other points were endorsed by most of the commentators For instance, most respondents agreed on the need to require issuers and distributors to assess end markets and to disclose hypothetical scenarios. While the first requirement would potentially reduce mis-selling, the second would help investors understand the products. Here, the advocacy group and one individual put forth the advantages of a probabilistic approach vis-à-vis the drawbacks of a simplistic scenario analysis/valuation matrix, viewed as a marketing rather than a transparency tool (Academics et al. 2013; Barone 2013). On the same topic, another individual emphasised the necessity to disclose worst-case scenarios (Barnard 2013). Most respondents also agreed to reject some of the propositions. Most of them first agreed on the non-necessity to disclose issuers' internal product modelling to investors, given the lack of substantial benefit to the latter. Second, a general understanding was achieved on the non-necessity to pre-approve products because it would shift risks onto the regulators' and investors' shoulders. Finally, most of the respondents agreed that regulators should not set product standards since it would be 'morally hazardous, ... reduce product innovation and hinder competition' (IOSCO 2013b).

This case study shows the various perspectives conveyed by the different stakeholders. The survey results show that, while sharing several commonalities, regulators cope with different levels of market development and investors' sophistication. This brings about different solutions, some of them innovative and likely to be transplanted into other (fairly similar) jurisdictions. The outcomes of the round table are even more diverging. Here one can distinguish some sort of cleavage between the stances of the industry and those of consumer associations. The same emerges in the responses to the public consultation, as the critical points on scenarios raised by individuals and the investor advocacy group show. While IOSCO is to be praised for taking into account all comments and trying to strike a fair balance between the different viewpoints, the type of comments received is clearly lopsided. Indeed, the voice of civil society representatives looked far weaker than that of the industry, and this was to some extent reflected in the final regulatory outcome (see, for instance, Regulatory Tool 11 on hypothetical scenarios).

3.4 ESG ratings and data products providers

Climate change has become a source of public concern in recent years. Vast financial resources are necessary to modify current production infrastructures, and public finances alone cannot cope with such a burdensome task. The financial sector is asked to play a critical role, and civil society is increasingly willing to channel funds towards 'green' solutions. Nevertheless, it is not an easy task to achieve a shared understanding of what 'green' is. With the purpose of guiding financial institutions and investors in the green maze, some firms have been providing environmental, social, and governance (ESG) ratings and data products.[13] Unfortunately, without a standardised yardstick, ratings and data

---

[13] '"ESG data products": refer to the broad spectrum of data, including raw data where appropriate, and related products in the sustainable finance area that are marketed as providing information on an entity, a financial instrument or a product, a company or an industries' ESG profile, characteristics or exposure to ESG, climatic or environmental risks whether or not they are explicitly labelled as "ESG data products". "ESG ratings": refer to the broad spectrum of ratings and related products in the sustainable finance area that are marketed as providing an assessment of an entity, a financial instrument or a product, a company ESG profile, or characteristics or exposure to ESG, climatic or environmental risks, whether or not these are explicitly labelled as "ESG ratings"' (IOSCO 2021c. Environmental, Social and Governance (ESG) Ratings and Data Products Providers - Consultation Report, p. 47). 'In addition to the increasing range of

products diverge from each other to the point that comparison between them is extremely difficult, if not impossible. This is where IOSCO jumped in.[14]

In July 2021, IOSCO issued a new Consultation Report on *Environmental, Social and Governance (ESG) Ratings and Data Products Providers,* seeking feedback from the industry and civil society. A fact-finding exercise underpinned the Consultation Report. This exercise was conducted with ESG ratings and data products providers, users of ratings and products, and firms subject to ESG ratings or data products. It consisted of a series of roundtables with market participants held in December 2020 and a questionnaire organised in January 2021. Several points emerged from the fact-finding exercise. First, a lack of substantial clarity and common understanding on definitions, including basic definitions. Second, a lack of transparency concerning the methodologies employed in ratings and data products. Third, the divergence among ratings and data products is coupled with 'uneven coverage of products offered', which makes investment strategies difficult to unfold. Fourth, ratings and data product providers hold conflicts of interest when they simultaneously provide consultation services to firms subject to their review. Fifth, communications and information exchange with firms subject to ESG ratings and data products should be strengthened (IOSCO 2021c, p. 5).

The July 2021 consultation report provides an overview of the market for ESG ratings and data products (chapter 1) and of the current practices of ESG ratings and data products providers (chapter 2). Subsequently, it conveys viewpoints about users of ESG ratings and ESG data products (chapter 3) and parses the interactions between firms subject to ESG ratings or data products and ESG ratings and data products providers (chapter 4). Finally, the consultation identifies areas for improvement and puts forth some recommendations addressed not only to securities markets regulators but also to ESG ratings and data products providers, users, and firms subject to providers' review (chapter 5). Tellingly, IOSCO has thoroughly considered the takeaways from the fact-finding exercise when drafting its recommendations (IOSCO 2021c, pp. 5–6).

The November 2021 Final Report on ESG leverages the July Consultation Report and lists IOSCO's ten recommendations for regulators about ESG

ESG ratings and data products, some ESG ratings and data products providers also offer other ESG products and services. These include, inter alia: ESG indices; consulting services such as portfolio analysis, advisory services to companies for ESG strategy development; provision of certification and second-party opinions; regulatory reporting assistance for companies and financial market participants' compliance with new sustainability regulations; and advisory services to companies on ESG ratings improvement techniques' (Ibid., p. 16).

14 For a recent analysis of ESG topics and IOSCO standards, see: Marcacci 2023.

ratings and data products; for ratings and products providers; for market participant users of ratings and products; on how ESG ratings and data products providers could consider interacting with entities subject to assessment; and on how covered entities could consider interacting with ESG ratings and data products providers (IOSCO 2021d).

Responses were numerous, including non-profit organisations. An overall agreement was reached among the respondents on the necessity to develop regulatory frameworks on ESG ratings and data product providers (Recommendation No. 1). Usual features of securities regulation should be reproduced in this area, such as conflicts of interest, transparency, disclosure, and the like. Some respondents from the industry pointed out that regulation should take a 'proportionate approach in order not to stifle innovation and competition beneficial to the markets and to the mitigation of the underlying environmental impacts' (S&P Global 2021). Similarly, most respondents agreed on making efforts towards wider transparency and internal consistency of providers' methodologies (Recommendation No. 2). Nevertheless, industry representatives pointed out the limits set by proprietary information to the disclosure of data sources (IOSCO 2021d).

General consensus was also registered on IOSCO's propositions to require providers, on the one hand, to ensure that 'their decisions are, to the best of their knowledge, independent and free from political or economic pressures' (Recommendation No. 3) and, on the other hand, to avoid a situation where their 'activities, procedures or relationships may compromise or appear to compromise the independence and objectivity of' their products (Recommendation No. 4). Here, voices from civil society pointed out the need for providers to adopt clear 'internal policies and processes to avoid any conflict of interest';some even suggested that asking providers to be free from political or economic pressures is '[i]mpossible and [i]mplausible' (WWF 2021; Harrington, 2021).

Likewise, there was a wide consensus about requiring providers to ensure a high level of transparency and disclosure, which would include their methodologies and internal processes (Recommendation No. 5). While one respondent highlighted the need to provide, ex ante, an exhaustive list of items to be disclosed, most commentators pointed out the need for 'sufficient quality to allow stakeholders to have a reasonable sense of what the rating was intending to measure and how they approached this measurement' (IOSCO 2021d, p. 51). Here, in particular, an individual correctly highlighted that 'there would need to be a balance between what information ESG ratings and data products providers are willing to publish, given the commercial proprietary nature of methodologies, and the usefulness of that information' (Whitecross 2021). Similar comments were raised about Recommendation No. 6. This concerns the adoption of policies and procedures to 'protect all non-public information received from or communicated to providers by any entity'. Here, IOSCO has accepted the request coming from some industry voices that data confidentiality arrangements between providers and entities should be in place (IOSCO 2021d, p. 52).

Most of the respondents agreed on asking market participants to execute due diligence on ESG ratings and data products before making an investment decision (Recommendation No. 7). Interestingly, one civil society representative raised doubts about the usefulness of this recommendation. This is because 'financial market participants [...] might not have the expertise to conduct due diligence on the ESG ratings and data products that they use in their internal processes' (Friends of the Earth (HK) 2021, p. 7). However, another civil society representative highlighted that 'increased transparency by ESG ratings and data product providers on the methodologies of their products [would] enable investors to conduct this due diligence in full' (Principles for Responsible Investments (PRI) 2021, p. 7). Importantly, IOSCO decided not to include further details on its recommendation since 'existing regulatory frameworks may already cover some of these aspects' (IOSCO, 2021d, p. 52).

Most respondents agreed on the recommendations concerning the interactions between providers and the entities subject to their assessment. Here again, divergences between the industry positions and those of the civil society representatives emerged. For instance, one market player emphasised the higher costs for smaller entities and proposed that providers use all publicly available information before reaching out to assessed firms (Hermes Equity Ownership Services Limited 2021, p. 11). A civil society representative also raised the same point, adding that 'providers could also consider the best common timing to liaise with companies and not ask for information all year round' (WWF 2021). However, another civil society representative suggested that providers publicly disclose their internal information gathering processes and that domestic regulators provide guidance on this point (Friends of the Earth (HK) 2021, p. 8).

Finally, wide consensus was reached on recommendation number 10, concerning the assessed entities' opportunity to 'streamlin[e] their disclosure processes for sustainability-related information to the extent possible' (IOSCO 2021d, p. 53). Here, both industry and civil society representatives seemed to agree on this suggestion. Interestingly, one civil society representative added that assessed entities 'should also try to disclose any gaps or limitations in the current disclosure they recognise and how they plan to address them in the next reporting cycle' (WWF 2021, p. 5).

Although IOSCO could not incorporate all comments in its final Recommendations, it has extensively used the input from industry and civil society representatives. In particular, IOSCO has been able to give room to input from civil society representatives, as clearly emerges in the Final Report.

Nevertheless, IOSCO could not incorporate every comment. Indeed, IOSCO finds itself having to carry out a sort of diplomatic task, striking a balance between the various interests at stake.

4 CONCLUSION

IOSCO appears to be fully committed to involving private actors in its standard-making procedure for two key reasons. First, stakeholders have specific technical information and knowledge that can only be developed in the private sector. This representsan extraordinary source when it comes to adopting meaningful standards, able to achieve the expected regulatory goals in the real world. Through their input, IOSCO stakeholders can adjust the contours of the policy propositions coming from regulatory authorities or even propose alternative solutions. Second, IOSCO stakeholders can provide their specific insights with regard to the understanding of standards' implementation on the part of the industry. Against this backdrop, the 2005 Consultation Policy and Procedure represent the cornerstone of IOSCO's commitment towards private actors' participation. Although formally in force for almost 20 years, the Procedure was used only after the 2008 crisis, when IOSCO was given new tasks and its standard production dramatically increased (Marcacci 2022). This was the point in time when input from the private sector and civil society began to be viewed as necessary.

There are several ways Full Members can take part in the Organization's life. First of all, Full Members can join standing committees and temporary task forces (Marcacci 2022), and contribute to IOSCO's standard-setting via ad hoc surveys/questionnaires such as those described here on structured products. To a lesser extent, member private actors can contribute to the Organization's normative production via the Affiliate Members Consultative Committee. However, non-member private actors can only rely on the 2005 Policy. As a result, this appears to be especially important for those private actors from local civil societies. As a matter of fact, the analysis of the private-sector input carried out here reveals that most of the stakeholders who actively contribute to the Organization's standard-setting are global firms and industry organisations rather than consumer associations and civil society representatives.

The case studies examined here suggest that IOSCO takes on several of the guiding principles of the IO Compendium relating to stakeholder engagement[15] and itsapproach represents a successful practice in terms of stakeholders'

[15] See OECD (2021), Compendium of International Organisations' Practices: Working Towards More Effective International Instruments, OECD Publishing, Paris. Available at: https://doi.org/10.1787/846a5fa0-en. p. 83 et seq.

qualitative and quantitative inclusion. This is illustrated by the amount and sophistication of industry organisations' input into IOSCO standard-setting. IOSCO's strong commitment towards inclusion also emerges in the additional ways employed to receive feedback from the private sector. The Round Table in the structured product case and the fact-finding exercise in the ESG case provide substantial evidence of IOSCO's strong commitment. Nevertheless, input from civil society, in particular retail investor associations, is still poor. The case study on retail structured products, while proving IOSCO's commitment towards investors' welfare, also shows that consumers' voices are far weaker than those in industry. This is, to some extent, reflected in the final regulatory outcome. The very recent case of ESG Ratings and Data Products Providers seems to be the first with more comments from civil societies. The ESG case might be the first of a new wave, but it is too early to tell.

Although IOSCO is fully committed to considering private actors' input in its normative production, there is still room for improvement when it comes to consumer associations and civil society representatives. As for the former, IOSCO could offer its affiliate membership and a seat at the Affiliate Members Consultative Committee to the most representative consumer associations around the globe. Not only would the institutionalisation of consumers' perspectives enhance the quality of IOSCO's standards, but it would also provide further, relevant insights. In addition, IOSCO could adopt specific capacity-building programmes directed at consumer associations and civil society representatives. Such programmes would aim at enhancing civil society's ability to meaningfully contribute to the IOSCO consultations by reducing the existing resource gap with the industry. Tellingly, IOSCO could use the insights from civil society to better address potential litigation risks that arise from regulatory failures, a topic that directly affects consumers.

DISCLAIMER

The views expressed in this chapter are those of the author and do not necessarily represent the views of his current and/or past employers.

REFERENCES

Academics, Consumers Associations, Unions and Other Representatives of Investors' Interest (2013), Response to the Consultation by the Board of the International Organization of Securities Commissions (IOSCO) on the project and the work undertaken by the Working Group on Retail Structured Products of the Task Force on Unregulated Markets and Product [Online]. Available at: https://www.iosco.org/library/pubdocs/434/pdf/Academics,%20consumers%20associations,%20unions%20and%20other%20representatives%20of%20investors'%20interest.pdf (accessed 24 August 2023).

Asset Management Association Switzerland 2023. Portrait [Online]. Available at: https://www.am-switzerland.ch/en/ueber-uns/portraet (accessed 24 August 2023).
Association Française de la Gestion Financière – AFG 2023. Nous connaître [Online]. Available at: https://www.afg.asso.fr/lafg/, (accessed 24 August 2023).
Austin, J. 2017. Insider Trading and Market Manipulation: Investigating and Prosecuting Across Borders, Cheltenhem, Edward Elgar.
Barnard, C. 2013. Your Ref: Comment letter on Consultation Report - Regulation of Retail Structured Products [Online]. Available at: https://www.iosco.org/library /pubdocs/434/pdf/Mr%20Chris%20Barnard,%20Germany.pdf [Accessed 24 September 2024].
Barone, L. 2013. Comment on Consultation Report – Regulation of Retail Structured Products [Online]. Available at: https://www.iosco.org/library/pubdocs/434/pdf/Mr %20Luca%20Barone.pdf (accessed 24 September 2024).
Bismuth, R. 2011. La coopération internationale des autorités de régulation du secteur financier et le droit international public, Bruxelles, Bruylant.
Bundesverband Alternative InvestmentS E.V. – BAI. 2023. About us [Online]. Available: https://www.bvai.de/en/about-us/about-us (accessed24 September 2024).
Compliglobe 2023. About CompliGlobe. Available: https://compliglobe.com/about -compligobe/ (accessed 24 September 2024).
Conac, P.-H. 2015. The European Union's Role in International Economic Fora – Paper 6: The IOSCO. Committee on Economic and Monetary Affairs – European Parliament.
Friends Of The Earth (HK). 2021. Friends of the Earth (HK) response to IOSCO's consultative report 'Environmental, Social and Governance (ESG) Ratings and Data Products Providers' [Online]. Available: https://www.iosco.org/library/pubdocs/690 /pdf/Friends%20of%20the%20Earth%20(HK).pdf (accessed 24 September 2024).
Harrington, W. J. 2021. William J. Harrington response to IOSCO's consultative report 'Environmental, Social and Governance (ESG) Ratings and Data Products Providers' [Online]. Available: https://www.iosco.org/library/pubdocs/690/pdf/ William%20J.%20Harrington.pdf (accessed 24 September 2024).
Hermes Equity Ownership Services LimiteD. 2021. Hermes Fund Managers Limited response to IOSCO's consultative report 'Environmental, Social and Governance (ESG) Ratings and Data Products Providers' [Online]. Available at: https://www .iosco.org/library/pubdocs/690/pdf/Hermes%20Fund%20Managers%20Limited .pdf (accessed 24 September 2024).
International Organization Of Securities Commissions – IOSCO 2005. IOSCO Consultation Policy and Procedure.
International Organization Of Securities Commissions – IOSCO 2009a. Hedge Funds Oversight – Consultation Report.
International Organization Of Securities CommissionsI – IOSCO 2009b. Hedge Funds Oversight – Final Report.
International Organization Of Securities Commissions – IOSCO 2011. By-Laws of IOSCO. Madrid.
International Organization Of Securities Commissions – IOSCO 2013a. Regulation of Retail Structured Products – Consultation Report.
International Organization Of Securities Commissions – IOSCO 2013b. Regulation of Retail Structured Products - Final Report.
International Organization Of Securities Commissions – IOSCO 2013c. Suitability Requirements With Respect To the Distribution of Complex Financial Products.

International Organization Of Securities Commissions – IOSCO. 2021a. About IOSCO [Online]. Available at: https://www.iosco.org/about/?subsection=about_iosco (accessed 24 September 2024).
International Organization Of Securities Commissions – IOSCO. 2021b. Affiliate Members Consultative Committee [Online]. Available at: https://www.iosco.org/about/?subsection=display_committee&cmtid=2 (accessed 24 September 2024).
International Organization Of Securities CommissionS – IOSCO 2021c. Environmental, Social and Governance (ESG) Ratings and Data Products Providers – Consultation Report.
International Organization Of Securities Commissions – IOSCO 2021d. Environmental, Social and Governance (ESG) Ratings and Data Products Providers – Final Report.
International Organization Of Securities Commissions – IOSCO. 2021e. Growth and Emerging Markets Committee [Online]. Available at: https://www.iosco.org/about/?subsection=display_committee&cmtid=8 (accessed 24 September 2024).
International Organization Of Securities Commissions – IOSCO. 2021f. IOSCO Board [Online]. Available at: https://www.iosco.org/about/?subsection=display_committee&cmtid=11 (accessed 24 September 2024).
International Organization Of Securities Commissions – IOSCO. 2021g. Multilateral Memorandum of Understanding Concerning Consultation and Cooperation and the Exchange of Information (MMoU) [Online]. Available at: https://www.iosco.org/about/?subsection=mmou (accessed 24 September 2024).
International Organization Of Securities CommissionS – IOSCO 2021h. Ordinary Members of IOSCO.
International Organization Of Securities Commissions – IOSCO. 2021i. President's Committee [Online]. Available at: https://www.iosco.org/about/?subsection=display_committee&cmtid=11 (accessed 24 September 2024).
International Organization Of Securities Commissions – IOSCO 2022. Fact Sheet – February 2022.
Jordan, C. 2014. International Capital Markets: Law and Institutions, Oxford, Oxford University Press.
Managed Fund Association – MFA. 2023. About MFA [Online]. Available at: https://www.managedfunds.org/about-mfa/ (accessed 24 September 2024).
Marcacci, A. 2022. *Transnational Securities Regulation. How it Works, Who Shapes it*, Cham, Springer.
Marcacci, A. 2023. Global Finance and the Anthropocene: Regulatory Shifts and Prospective Effects, *European Business Law Review*, 34(4), 619–664.
OECD (2016), International Regulatory Co-operation: The Role of International Organisations in Fostering Better Rules of Globalisation, Paris, OECD Publishing. Available at: https://doi.org/10.1787/9789264244047-en.
OECD (2021), Compendium of International Organisations' Practices: Working Towards More Effective International Instruments, Paris, OECD Publishing, Paris. Available at: https://doi.org/10.1787/846a5fa0-en.
Principles For Responsible Investments (PRI). 2021. Principles for Responsible Investments (PRI) response to IOSCO's consultative report 'Environmental, Social and Governance (ESG) Ratings and Data Products Providers' [Online]. Available at: https://www.iosco.org/library/pubdocs/690/pdf/Principles%20for%20Responsible%20Investments%20(PRI).pdf (accessed 24 September 2024).
S&P Global. 2021. S&P Global Response to IOSCO Consultation Report on Environmental, Social and Governance (ESG) Ratings and Data Products

Providers [Online]. Available: https://www.iosco.org/library/pubdocs/690/pdf/S&P%20Global.pdf (accessed 24 September 2024).

Standards Board For Alternative Investments Available at: SBAI. 2023. About the SBAI [Online]. Available: https://www.sbai.org/about-the-sbai.html (accessed 24 September 2024).

Whitecross, R. 2021. Robin Whitecross response to IOSCO's consultative report 'Environmental, Social and Governance (ESG) Ratings and Data Products Providers' [Online]. Available: https://www.iosco.org/library/pubdocs/690/pdf/Robin%20Whitecross.pdf (accessed 24 September 2024).

Worldwide Fund for Nature (WWF). 2021. Worldwide fund for Nature response to IOSCO's consultative report 'Environmental, Social and Governance (ESG) Ratings and Data Products Providers' [Online]. Available \t: https://www.iosco.org/library/pubdocs/690/pdf/Worldwide%20fund%20for%20Nature.pdf (accessed 24 September 2024).

PART III

Civil society and citizens' participation

8. Citizen participation in regional organisations: perspectives from their founding treaties

María Rodríguez Alcázar

1 INTRODUCTION

The benefits of developing mechanisms for stakeholder engagement in the policy cycle are widely studied, especially at the national level. In the last decades, international organisations (IOs) from all over the world have developed a growing interest in their openness to citizens and non-governmental stakeholders, which can be seen with the creation of parliamentary bodies, or the institutionalisation of civil society organisations (CSOs) and profit-oriented actors in rule-making processes (Jetschke et al. 2017; Jetschke & Münch, 2020; Reinold 2019). However, the studies in this domain are limited and often confined to studying a single case or a limited number of cases, failing to depict a more comprehensive analysis of how these mechanisms are deployed in practice in a systematic way across organisations (Steffek & Kortendiek 2018). Furthermore, research is even more lacking in the case of regional organisations (ROs) (Jetschke et al. 2017), a particular type of IO that, depending on its degree of cooperation and institutionalisation (Lenz 2021), may resemble more the institutional setting and practices of a state. Some ROs have a clear objective of creating a community or *regional demos*, strengthening concepts of citizenship that relate to a geographical regional area.

This chapter proposes a structure to study citizen participation in ROs, referring both to the engagement of non-governmental stakeholders and citizens in ROs. This chapter offers an overview of the mechanisms for citizen participation in ROs according to their formal rules and founding treaties.

After reviewing the benefits of citizen participation in ROs, this chapter presents references to citizen participation in the founding treaties of ROs from 1945 to 2016. I analyse references to mechanisms for citizen participation in the treaties in three components: (1) the explicit recognition of civil participation in the treaties, (2) the access to information about decision-making in ROs provided in the treaties, and (3) the possibilities of direct participation for citizens in the policy cycle, both in terms of participation in regularly organised elections or through structured consultation procedures. For the three participation components analysed, this chapter offers descriptive statistics from a sample of 70 ROs.

Going one step further, this study not only presents the commitment of ROs through their founding treaties regarding citizen participation, but it also gathers data related to the implementation of access to information and direct elections. This information, which is not often collected, offers the possibility to contrast the *de jure* and *de facto* for the second and third components: access to information and participation in direct elections. The methodology and datasets used for the analysis are described in detail in section 3.

2 THE BENEFITS OF CITIZEN PARTICIPATION IN REGIONAL ORGANISATIONS

Citizen participation is increasingly recognised as a crucial component of good governance and effective and legitimate decision-making leading to the provision of public services. Across different frameworks in public administration theory, there is a common claim for citizens' active participation in policymaking processes (Scupola 2018). From an instrumental point of view, citizen participation enhances policy implementation (King & Stivers 1998), increases the responsiveness and effectiveness of the policies and public services provided (Guo & Neshkova 2013; Osborne 2020; Vigoda & Golembiewski 2001), and increases the efficiency of the administrations (Boyer et al. 2016; Brudney & England 1983).

Studies at the national level show that the organisations or administrations promoting citizen participation are more likely to be transparent and accountable with their own objectives, which ultimately increases their legitimacy and reliability towards internal and external partners (Bourgon 2007; King & Stivers, 1998; Leighninger 2020; Piotrowski 2017; Sørensen & Torfing 2018).

Similarly, studies on global governance show citizen participation as a way of strengthening democratic processes, acting as a complement to representative democracy, and increasing trust in institutions (Boyer et al. 2016; Leighninger 2020). Scholars like Scholte (2020) claim that citizen participation can counter the pitfalls in global democracy provoked by contemporary globalisation and the lack of accountability in global policymaking.

Scholars on policymaking at international institutions and organisations also point to citizen participation as one of the key factors for good governance (Esty 2005; Kingsbury et al. 2005; Ryngaert & Wouters 2004). From the literature in this field, it can be deduced that citizen participation is a catalyst for the effectiveness of organisations and institutions.

Citizen participation affects all cooperation areas and has a further impact on the policies developed by the ROs (Reinold 2019). Previous research in the field of trade agreements illustrates the impact of citizen participation on decision-making processes through officially established consultation mechanisms, such as the Domestic Advisory Groups (Drieghe et al. 2021; Potjomkina et al. 2021). Similarly, in the field of fiscal policy, increased public debate with stakeholders made governments more accountable in terms of fiscal transparency (Okonjo-Iweala & Osafo-Kwaako 2007).

It comes as no surprise that international organisations from all over the world have developed a growing interest in their openness toward non-governmental stakeholders and citizens (Tallberg et al. 2013). Examples of this are the increasing commitment to creating parliamentary bodies with representatives directly or indirectly elected by the citizens (as in the European Union, MERCOSUR, or the African Union); including CSOs in the policy-making processes of the ROs (Jetschke et al. 2017; Jetschke & Münch 2020; Reinold 2019) or developing consultation mechanisms and processes, such as the Conference on the Future of Europe (EU 2022).

The OECD, with its work on stakeholder engagement, aims to systematically shed light on the participation of different agents across IOs. However, there is still little systematic knowledge about the mechanisms for citizen participation that are in place in different IOs in the world and their historical evolution. Research in this field is limited and, for the most part, qualitative and focused on the case of one or just a couple of IOs (see e.g., Mattheis 2014; Reinold 2019). An existing database, introduced in the next section, allows us to analyse the state of *de jure* citizen participation in IOs, focusing on regional organisations[1] (ROs).

3 METHODOLOGY

In this chapter, I delve into the commitments of ROs regulating citizen participation by analysing the presence of mechanisms and formal procedures for non-governmental stakeholders and citizen engagement in the ROs' founding treaties and their amendments. I also analyse the implementation of those commitments through access to information and ad hoc and structured participation in decision-making.

This chapter's understanding of citizen participation is based on Baum's definition (2001). In his work, 'citizens' are either individuals or organised

[1] Jetschke and colleagues define an RO as 'any organization that: a) is constituted by at least two member states who define membership on a regional basis [e.g., African, Latin American]; (b) is multipurpose in character; c) has some institutional framework for meetings and decision-making' (2017, p. 8).

communities, and 'participation' can range between observation and power. This chapter conceptualises the organised communities of citizens in two categories, referred to as non-governmental stakeholders: (i) non-governmental organisations or not-for-profit organisations, such as civil society organisations, and (ii) profit-oriented actors, such as business or private sector organisations. Therefore, the definition of citizen participation used in this chapter encompasses not only citizens – as individuals or inhabitants of a particular place (OECD, 2022) – but also non-governmental stakeholders – as any interested or affected party, including civil society organisations, private sector entities, academic or labour unions, or other non-governmental agents included in the definition of stakeholders by the OECD Compendium of International Organisations' Practices (2021).

When it comes to participation, this study follows the continuum proposed by Arnstein's Ladder of Citizen Participation (1969), moving from non-participation or tokenism to degrees of citizen participation in eight different steps. One of its limitations is that the model was specifically designed to explain participation at the local level; therefore, its application to ROs may require adapting the descriptions of each rung. In order to create the adaptation, this project works with the OECD guidelines on how to engage stakeholders in international organisations (2021), where stakeholder engagement is defined as an extensive spectrum of practices, starting from the dissemination of information and solicitation of consultation to participatory collaboration, coproduction, co-decision, and partnership.

The first part of this study focuses on the formal rules allowing citizens to take part in the RO policy cycle. This *de jure* or formal conception of participation mechanisms is limited to the formal characteristics defined in the founding or amending treaties of ROs. I acknowledge that there are other formal characteristics defined by international agreements of lower scope (such as protocols, rules of procedure, administrative decisions, etc.), but there is, to date, no database that can be used to track their provisions, especially for smaller ROs, which is a bias recognised in the literature (Sommerer & Tallberg 2017). The second part of the chapter goes a step further, examining the practice of two mechanisms put into practice by some ROs: the accessibility of information about meetings and the development of direct elections.

3.1 Information and data

3.1.1 De jure or regulation in founding treaties

There is a reduced number of datasets coding information related to IOs' institutional design and containing information about citizen inclusiveness. This limits the quantitative analysis that can be produced in this field. There are several authors interested in data gathering around some indicators of institutional design for regional organisations (see Abbott & Snidal 2001; Haftel & Alexander 2006; Hooghe & Marks 2015; Jetschke et al. 2017; Koremenos et al. 2001; Lenz et al. 2022). Therefore, this analysis relies on the dataset created by the Comparative Regional Organisation Project (CROP) (Jetschke et al. 2017), which is one of the most comprehensive existing datasets for studying institutional characteristics of IOs. It focuses on a particular kind of IOs, the ROs, which are those defining their membership on a geographical regional basis. The CROP dataset provides extensive details on the contents of the treaties of ROs from 1945 to 2016 in hundreds of items. In total, it contains information from 276 founding documents of ROs and major amendments to them. The database contains information on most aspects of the institutional architecture of ROs, as well as on their areas of cooperation.

Therefore, this analysis works with 70 organisations, and over 30 of their predecessors, that correspond with ROs composed of Member States from a particular continent. A full list of them and their abbreviations can be found in Appendix 8.1. In total, this chapter presents the analysis of 235 founding treaties of ROs. Appendix 8.2 shows the list of the analysed treaties per RO.

The data results are often presented in four geographical areas throughout the chapter in order to capture the evolution in different areas of the world. The 70 ROs analysed comprise 18 from Africa, 18 from the Americas, 15 from Asia, and 19 from Europe.

One of the biggest advantages of the CROP database is that it often contains multiple treaties per organisation, as well as information on whether the subsequent treaties are addendums or replace an older treaty. This allows us to track how the *de jure* institutional design of an RO changes over time. The granularity of the CROP database enables us to identify the relationship of citizen participation with other relevant variables in the institutional design of ROs.

The CROP is presumably the only project coding fields related to citizen participation from RO treaties. In particular, the CROP dataset includes a section on 'Representation of Interests', which encompasses information about the participation of individual citizens, non-governmental actors, and profit-oriented actors. From this dataset, I also use the information collected on the election method of the different organs, such as the parliamentary organ. For this chapter, the CROP dataset has been revised vis-à-vis the original treaties in relation to citizen participation.[2]

In this chapter, some observations and descriptive information derived from the analysis of this updated dataset are presented, operating within a time

[2] The original CROP dataset is available upon request to the CROP team. For this research, some corrections have been implemented after the revision with the original texts. The file used for the analysis is available upon request.

frame that starts in 1945 and ends in 2016. The names used to refer to the ROs correspond to the last name given in the treaties to their successor RO, regardless of the official name of the RO at any moment in time.[3]

The formal existence of processes or mechanisms is not enough, as it does not tell about the implementation of citizen participation (Best 2011), however, the institutional framework *enables* the work of the ROs (Koremenos et al. 2001) and its understanding is crucial to analyse the actual openness of these organisations.

3.1.2 De facto or implementation of the agreements

The lack of data about *de facto* citizen participation limits the possibility of analysing it in a quantitative way. In order to offer a contrast between the *de jure* and *de facto* for the two components analysed in this chapter, I collected additional data on two elements: the actual accessibility to deliberations and minutes from RO meetings, and the actual development of direct regional elections to parliamentary organs of the RO. With the information collected from primary sources, I verify whether the provisions and commitments included in the treaties are met in the practice of the ROs.

The operationalisation of these elements for the data collection is explained in the following sections. The poor accessibility and time required to collect information about these variables explain the limitations of the data available for qualitative research on this matter.

3.2 Operationalisation of the analysis

The structure used to analyse the formal or de jure citizen participation in RO treaties encompasses three components. The first requires analysing whether civil participation is mentioned at all in the founding treaties, as this may be a sign that the RO adopts a strategic and comprehensive approach to citizen participation, which is one of the key principles of stakeholder engagement in IOs defined by the OECD (2021).

The second component of the analytic structure is the accessibility of information related to decision-making in ROs, in particular through access to deliberations and meeting minutes. Access to information is defined as one of the lowest participation steps and as a prerequisite for a meaningful engagement level.

---

[3] The name of the RO and its predecessors can be tracked over the years on the website of the Regional Integration Knowledge System (UNU-CRIS, 2020): https://riks.cris.unu.edu/.

Lastly, the third component analyses the direct mechanisms for citizen participation in ROs, using two relevant modalities of participation in the life of an RO: first, the participation in regularly organised elections and, second, through structured consultation procedures.

In practical terms, in this study, *citizen participation* is operationalised by looking at the access to information and mechanisms for direct participation, such as elections for RO bodies, regulations for CSOs and profit-oriented actors' participation in the RO policy cycle. Additionally, it considers the existence of other mechanisms such as consultations, petitions, or referenda.

4 RECOGNITION OF CITIZEN PARTICIPATION IN REGIONAL ORGANISATIONS

The vast majority of the treaties do not include any mention of civil participation nor mechanisms to promote citizen engagement. This applies to 160 treaties, two-thirds of all the founding treaties of ROs analysed.

Only 78 treaties include any provisions related to citizen participation, which corresponds to 40 ROs. Of those 40 ROs, only 15 mention civil participation explicitly in their founding treaty (27 treaties). The rest include provisions related to citizen engagement mechanisms, such as public access to meetings or channels for collectives of civil society to get involved in policymaking, without explicitly referring to the terms 'citizen participation', 'civil engagement' or derivations of those.

However, there are four treaties that include a mention of civil participation – usually in the preamble of their treaties – but they do not include any other provisions developing this extent. This is the case for three ROs: the East African Community (EAC) in 2007 and 2009; the Southern African Development Community (SADC) in 2001; and the Organization for Security and Co-operation in Europe (OSCE) in 1990.

The next section delves into the evolution of citizen participation provisions in RO treaties over time.

4.1 Small steps for the inclusion of citizen participation

The inclusion of any provisions related to citizen participation in the founding treaties of ROs started in punctual European ROs in the 1950s, followed by a couple of ROs in Africa and Latin America during the 1960s. As Figure 8.1 depicts, it would not be until the 1990s that the inclusion of citizen participation provisions would be established as a trend. The pioneer ROs in including citizen participation in their founding treaties are described in the next paragraphs.

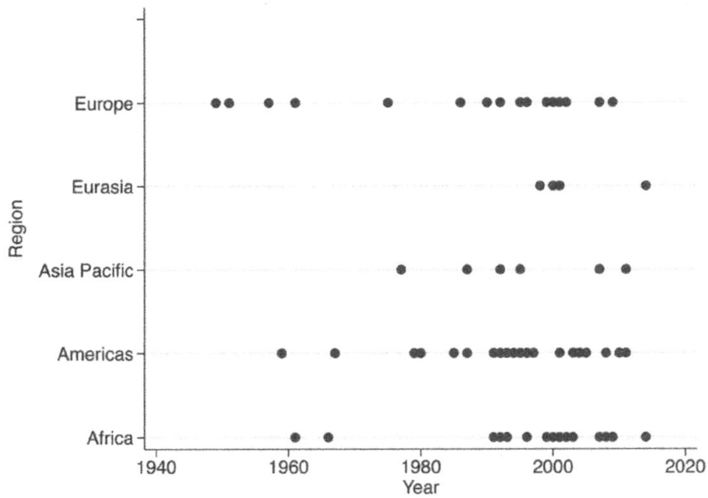

Figure 8.1 *Time evolution of ROs per region including any provision for citizen participation in their treaties*

An early precedent on the inclusion of provisions for citizen participation was the establishment by the United Nations, in 1945, that the Economic and Social Council (ECOSOC) would make suitable arrangements for consultation with non-governmental organisations which are concerned with matters within its competence (United Nations Charter 1945, art. 71). In consequence, the UN, through the ECOSOC, became the first IO allowing for the participation of non-governmental actors in an institutionalised way.

Only a couple of years later, in 1949, with the phrasing 'Unless the Consultative Assembly decides otherwise, its debates shall be conducted in public', the Council of Europe became the first RO to include references to mechanisms open to citizen engagement, even if limited (Statute of the Council of Europe 1949). In this case, it facilitated the accessibility of the meetings and deliberations of the Parliamentary Assembly. The Council of Europe was also the first RO to explicitly reference in its treaties the relationships with non-governmental international organisations. In particular, 'make[ing] suitable arrangements for consultation with international non-governmental organisations which deal with matters that are within the competence of the Council of Europe' (Appendix I – Statutory Resolution, 1951, para. E. iv).

This was followed two years later by the European Union, with the Treaty Establishing the European Coal and Steel Community (1951), hereinafter the 'Treaty of Paris', which created a parliamentary organ 'composed of delegates whom the parliaments of each of the member States shall be called upon to designate once a year from among their own membership, or who shall be elected by direct universal suffrage, according to the procedure determined by each respective High Contracting Party', which included the first mention of a possible direct election by universal suffrage of the members of that Assembly. That circumstance did not materialised, but it was the first inclusion of such a possibility in an RO treaty. The fact that the following treaty, the Treaty Establishing the European Economic Community (1957), hereinafter the'Treaty of Rome', was less ambitious, illustrates the non-linear journey that the RO treaties have followed. In that case, the Treaty of Rome was more pragmatic, designating to the Assembly the task of developing a proposal to make universal suffrage a reality. The first European elections to the European Parliament eventually took place in 1979.

When it comes to the recognition of non-governmental actors, the Treaty of Paris also recognised the participation of NGOs, yet referred mainly to the consultation with workers and consumers. It created a 'Consultative Committee' attached to the High Authority, that 'shall include producers, workers and consumers and dealers in equal numbers' (1951, art. 18). Similarly, the Treaty of Rome established a committee with representatives of some categories of economic and social life, mainly producers and workers, as well as companies (1957, arts 58 and 193).

Beyond Europe, the first provisions on citizen participation were adopted by the Organization of American States (OAS) in Latin America. In its Agreement Establishing the Inter-American Development Bank, the organisation recognised the existence of non-governmental entities and private firms that may interfere in the activity of the Bank (1959, arts 3.8a and 6.1). This was a stepping stone for the recognition of civil society actors. Additionally, the OAS Protocol of Buenos Aires recognised the importance of the contribution of organisations such as labour unions, cooperatives, and associations with a cultural, professional, profit, or community purpose to the life of the RO and its development process (1967, art. 43.g). It was the first time that such civil society organisations were named in RO treaties.

Similarly, in Africa, the 1961 Charter of the Union of African States recognised the establishment of a Coordinating Committee composed of political organisations, trade unions, women's movements, and youth movements (art. 5).[4] It is remarkable that the predecessor of the African Union mentioned two particular types of established organisations (political organisations and trade unions); however, when referring to women and youth, it did not refer to organisations, but rather to 'movements'. This may find its explanation in the level

4 Information referenced in CROP dataset (Jetschke et al. 2017).

of formalisation of civil society organisations at the moment of the signature of the agreement. In another instance, regarding the accessibility of meetings and deliberations, OCAM, the African and Malagasy Common Organisation, in its 1966 Charter offered the possibility of having some open sessions of the Conference's meetings (art. 7), which shows the interest in opening the deliberations to other agents.[5] However, the most prolific time for including references to civil participation in African ROs came from the 1990s, coinciding with what Gyimah-Boadi (1996) defined as the third wave of civil society in Africa, when civil society groups were more vocal in asking for space in democratic processes.

The time evolution in Figure 8.1 depicts that the Asian continent was the last to include any provisions related to citizen participation in the treaties of their ROs. The first mention of such activities appears in the Economic Cooperation Organisation (ECO) (Treaty of Izmir, 1977), followed a decade later by the Association of Southeast Asian Nations (ASEAN) with the Manila Declaration (1987). This late interest in civil society engagement mechanisms might be related to the tendency of institutions to engage with civil society actors in a less institutionalised and informal way in the region (Shivakoti 2020), or with the lack of interest of citizens and civil society organisations to engage with the ROs – because of their elitist approach of those, not connected to their needs or interests – argued by academists like Chandra (1999).

4.2 Explicit mention to civil participation

When looking at the evolution of the first mention of *civil participation*[6] in the treaties of ROs, two periods can be identified, with the time division around the year 2000 (Figure 8.2). This first explicit mention of civil participation can presumably be identified as the moment in which the recognition of citizen participation crystallised in the founding treaties of ROs. The graph is dominated by American ROs and, to a lesser extent, African and European ROs. No ROs from Asia explicitly mention civil participation in their founding treaties.

While in the 1950s small steps were made towards citizen participation or, at least, recognising civil societal actors, the term *civil participation* was coined in RO treaties long after the inclusion of any mechanisms for citizen participation. The pioneer RO including civil participation in its founding treaty was the Andean Community (CAN), with the Treaty Establishing the Andean Parliament(1979). The treaty also included the aim of the election of

[5] Information referenced in CROP dataset (Jetschke et al. 2017).

[6] In this analysis, it is not only the literal mention of the term 'civil participation' that is considered, but also other equivalent wordings such as 'citizen participation' or 'citizen engagement'.

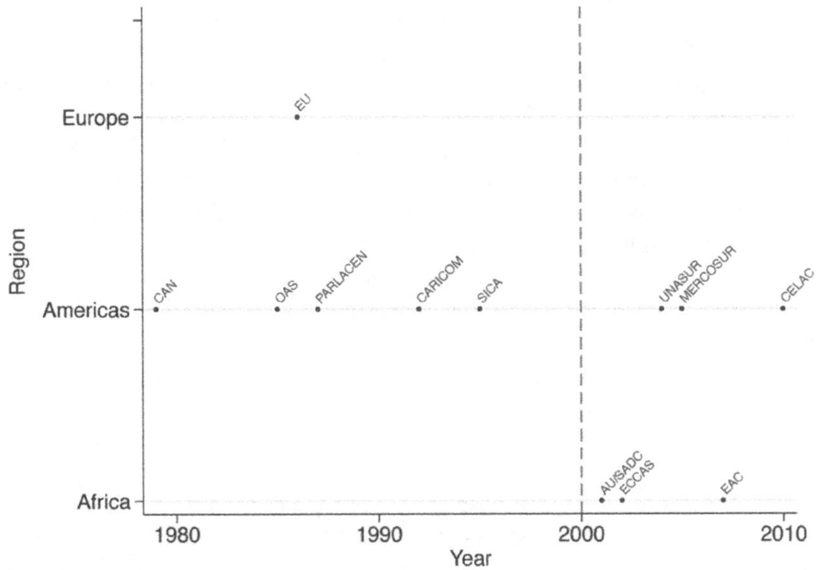

Figure 8.2 *First mention of civil participation in ROs*

the parliamentary organ by universal suffrage. The aim for universal suffrage was set in the general vision of participation as a prerequisite for the success of the RO, recognising the role of people's participation in the integration process, for the effective exercise of democracy and democratic values, the development of a common conscience of community and solidarity, and the promotion of human rights, freedom, peace, security, and stability.

The second RO, including direct reference to *civil participation,* was OAS, in the Protocol of Cartagena de Indias (1985). However, while this treaty mentioned civil participation, it did not specify any mechanisms to put it into practice. The wording recognised that the effective exercise of democracy should be furthered by sectoral participation mechanisms.

The first direct mention of citizen participation in the European continent can be found in the European Union (EU)'s Single European Act (1986), which aimed to include people participation in the integration process. This came 35 years after the first mention of the possibility of direct universal suffrage in European Parliament elections and consultations with several civil society actors, mainly enterprises and workers, in 1951 (Treaty Establishing the European Coal and Steel Community). This seems to point to the fact that *civil participation* was only included when this participation had crystallised as an idea inside the RO.

In Africa, the first mention of civil participation dates to 2001, when a prolific wave of civil society inclusion in the treaties took place (see Figure 8.1). It happened with the Protocol to the Treaty Establishing the African Economic Community Relating to the Pan-African Parliament of the African Union (AU), as well as with the Agreement Amending the Treaty of the Southern African Development Community (SADC). The former was promoted to ensure "the full participation of the African peoples in the economic development and integration of the continent' (2001), as well as for the promotion of peace, security, and stability, and the common conscience of community and solidarity. For the latter, the reasons that motivated the mention to civil participation were not specified. However, this was in the framework of establishing SADC National Committees with representatives of the government, private sector, civil society, NGOs, and workers' and employers' organisations (2001).

Of the 78 RO treaties that mention civil participation, 59 do not specify a purpose or justification for including greater mechanisms for participation. Across the world, and from those specifying their reasons, 75% include civil participation to improve the integration process (Table 8.1). Enhancing the effective exercise of democracy and democratic values, developing a common conscience of community and solidarity, and promoting values such as human rights, freedom, social justice, gender equality or good governance justifies the use of civil participation in half of the ROs. In the case of the African ROs, enhancing the effective exercise of democracy and democratic values is

Table 8.1 Percentage of ROs using justification for citizen participation

Category	Africa (4)	Americas (7)	Europe (1)	Asia (0)	Total
The participation of the peoples in the integration process	50%	86%	100%	N/A	**75%**
Enhance the effective exercise of democracy and democratic values	50%	43%	100%	N/A	**50%**
The development of a common conscience of community and solidarity	25%	57%	100%	N/A	**50%**
The general vision of participation as a prerequisite for the success of the RO	25%	57%	0%	N/A	**42%**
Promote peace, security and stability	25%	14%	100%	N/A	**25%**
Promote human rights, freedom, social justice, gender equality or good governance (sum)	25%	57%	100%	N/A	**50%**

more present than the other reasons, which are instead more common in Latin American ROs.

Five ROs consider civil participation as a prerequisite for the success of the RO: CAN, MERCOSUR, PARLACEN, UNASUR, and African Union. Except for the AU, these are all Latin American.

5 PUBLIC ACCESS TO DELIBERATIONS AND MINUTES IN RO MEETINGS

As a second focal point in the analysis, this chapter studies the presence of other mechanisms that can enhance the participation of citizens, such as public access to deliberations or meetings, as well as access to the minutes and protocols that regulate decision-making.

Only 15 ROs state in their treaties that they will offer public access to their meetings and deliberations. The time evolution shows that most of them included this possibility in their treaties from 1990 onwards (Figure 8.3). Again, the ROs from Asia show a lower representation, in line with the explanation given by Chandra (1999) that Asian organisations were more open to the participation and inclusion of non-governmental stakeholders after the financial crisis of 1997, due to the process of relative democratisation in the region.

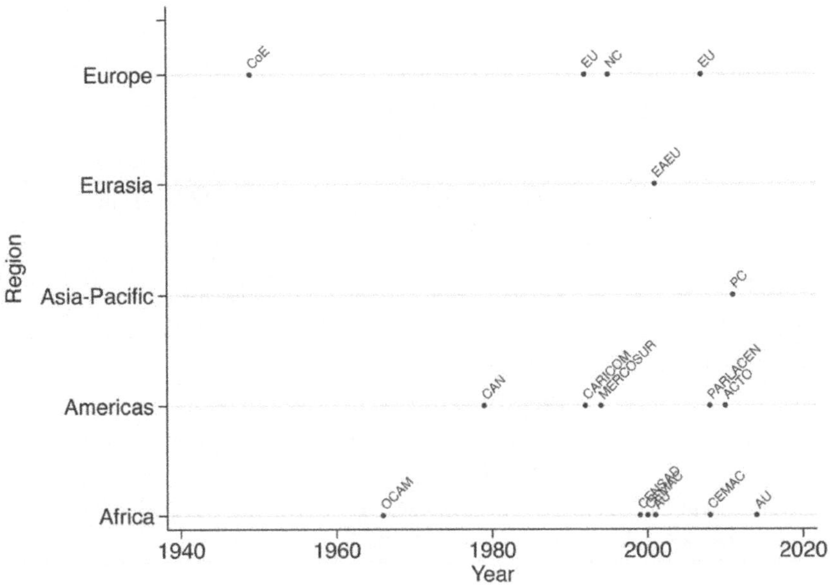

Figure 8.3 *ROs committed to give access to meetings and minutes*

When asked whether the access to information formulated in the founding treaty is linked to any particular organ of the RO, the findings of this analysis show that parliamentary organs are the ones most commonly offering public access to meetings and deliberations. In the case of public access to minutes, the most common organ that has been given that responsibility is the Council. Other ROs also include this provision for other organs (see Table 8.2). Seventy-one ROs did not specify which organs have access to public deliberations or meetings, which may mean that the provision was stated in a general way, as a principle that should apply to all the instances of the RO. The fact of providing a concrete mandate to one or several organs could create a direct responsibility for them to develop mechanisms to meet their treaty commitments.

It is relevant to mention that the measures of making minutes and deliberations accessible are not only related to the promotion of citizen participation but also to the transparency of ROs, which has increasingly been in the interest of IOs (OECD 2021). Once again, the Asian ROs are not very present in the picture, with the Pacific Community (PC) and the Eurasian Economic Union (EAEU) being the only ROs from the continent that include in their founding treaty the possibility of public access to meetings or minutes. Similar observations can be made regarding European ROs, of which only three commit to this accessibility of information in their founding treaties: the European Union (EU), the Council of Europe (CoE), and the Nordic Council (NC).

Table 8.2 *ROs regulating in their treaties public access to their meetings and deliberations or minutes per organ*

Organs	Public access to meetings and deliberations	Public access to minutes
Council (5)	EU, PC	MERCOSUR, EAEU, EU, CoE
Commission (3)	EU	CEMAC, MERCOSUR
General Secretariat (1)	CENSAD	–
Conference (3)	CENSAD, OCAM, PC	–
Parliament (7)	AU, CARICOM, PARLACEN, CE, EU, NC	CEMAC
Court of Justice and (3)	AU, COMESA, EAC	–
Dispute Settlement (2)	EAC	EAEU

Notes: Some of the categories are regrouped, including organs with similar functions that, in different ROs, might be called differently. The Committee at the CoE defines what needs to be shared in other organs.

I collected additional information to assess whether these *de jure* provisions related to giving public access to meetings and deliberations, as well as whether public access to meetings, are met in the practice of the ROs. Therefore, I collected evidence regarding whether the organs in practice offer the public information they committed to in their founding treaties. The results can be seen in Table 8.3 which shows in a combined way all the ROs that committed either to providing public access to the meetings or to their minutes. In order to compose the table, the interpretation of 'public access to meetings and deliberations' is access to agendas and live streams or recordings of the meetings. In the case of 'access to protocols and minutes', the information that has been analysed is whether the minutes with the decisions made by that organ were publicly accessible online.[7]

6 MECHANISMS FOR DIRECT PARTICIPATION OF CITIZENS IN ROs

The third aspect analysed in this chapter is the existence of mechanisms for the direct participation of citizens. When analysing the direct participation of citizens, I identify two main mechanisms put in place in ROs: the possibility of citizens directly electing representatives for any of the organs, and the engagement of non-governmental stakeholders through the policymaking cycle of the ROs. The provisions around these two topics will be analysed in depth in the following sections. Beyond these two categories, there are other mechanisms such as referenda, consultations, or petitions, whose analysis will be grouped in the last section on other mechanisms for direct citizen participation, which I anticipate are very rarely regulated in the founding treaties.

6.1 Elections to parliamentary organs in ROs

One of the main mechanisms for periodic participation in ROs is participation in elections in any of the organs of the RO. It suffices to take a quick look at the data to see that the only organ that is elected by citizens (directly or indirectly) is the parliamentary organ. Nineteen ROs recognise a parliamentary organ with members selected exclusively for it. There are three modalities for the selection of those representatives: (1) direct election by the citizens in universal elections; (2) indirect election by the National Parliament; and (3) selection by

---

[7] The verifications of information took place through online sources; hence, this analysis does not include a physical consultation of minutes in archives. Some ROs that did not offer directly accessible information online were contacted via email; however, no further information was received.

Table 8.3 De facto access to information about meeting in ROs committed to it

Organs	RO	Agenda	Minutes	Livestream
Council	EU	Accessible	Accessible	Accessible
Council	MERCOSUR	Accessible	Accessible	Non-accessible
Council	EAEU	Accessible	Accessible	Non-accessible
Council	PC	Accessible	Accessible	Non-accessible
Council	CoE	Accessible	Accessible	Non-accessible
Commission	EU	Accessible	Non-accessible	Non-accessible
Commission	CEMAC	See note 1	See note 1	See note 1
Commission	MERCOSUR	Accessible	Accessible	Non-accessible
General Secretariat	CENSAD	See note 1	See note 1	See note 1
Conference	CENSAD	See note 1	See note 1	See note 1
Conference	OCAM	See note 1	See note 1	See note 1
Conference	PC	Accessible	Accessible	Non-accessible
Parliament	AU	See note 1	See note 1	See note 1
Parliament	CARICOM	Non-accessible	Non-accessible	Non-accessible
Parliament	PARLACEN	Non-accessible	Accessible	Non-accessible
Parliament	CE	Accessible	Accessible	Accessible

Organs	RO	Agenda	Minutes	Livestream
Parliament	EU	Accessible	Accessible	Accessible
Parliament	NC	Accessible	Accessible	See note 2
Parliament	CEMAC	See note 1	See note 1	See note 1
Court of Justice	AU	No Accessible	Accessible	No Accessible
Court of Justice	COMESA	N/A	Accessible	N/A
Court of Justice	EAC	N/A	Accessible	N/A
Dispute Settlement	EAC	Non-accessible	Non-accessible	Non-accessible
Dispute Settlement	EEU	See note 1	See note 1	See note 1

Notes: 1. No information was available online nor has been provided via email to the researcher. 2. It was not possible to verify this information.

the national governments. Most ROs have experienced an evolution in the way their parliaments are composed (Figure 8.4).

It seems an intuitive evolution that the first parliamentary organs were characterised by indirect elections, meaning that the parliamentary organs of the Member States would elect the representatives at the regional parliaments. Only later did ROs developed the ambition to implement direct elections to the regional parliaments by citizen vote. However, this evolution has not always been straightforward. Table 8.4 shows the composition of the RO parliaments, indicating in bold the latest regulation. A back and forth regarding direct elections can be seen, with treaties recognising direct elections, and later treaties of the same RO reverting to indirect elections (e.g., CAN or EAEU). This may be related to the difficulty of implementing the elections in practice (in terms of organisational capacity and costs), but it might be related to voter turnout, with ROs not widely known to the citizens in the region, not given enough importance, or being considered 'far' from them (Stockemer 2017).

When looking at the composition of the parliament, two main options are found. On the one hand, eight ROs established in their history a parliamentary organ directly elected by the population, six in their most recent founding treaties. On the other hand, 18 ROs established a parliament composed of members elected by the national parliamentary organs, 13 in their most

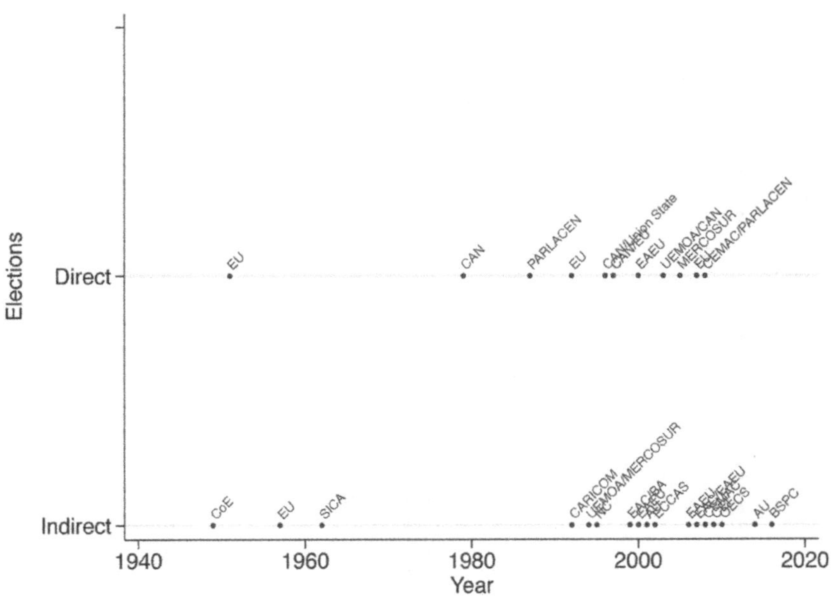

Figure 8.4 Elections of representatives by citizen vote to RO Parliament

Table 8.4 *RO Parliament by composition and region*

Region	Directly elected parliamentarians	Parliamentarians elected by national parliaments	Parliamentarians appointed by national government	Mixed indirect election national parliament and government	Not specified
Africa	**CEMAC** (2008), **UEMOA** (2003)	**AU** (2014), **CEMAC** (2008), **EAC** (1999, 2007), ECCAS (2002), UEMOA (1994)	–	–	AU (1991), CEMAC (1994), **ECOWAS** (1993), UEMOA (2003)
Americas	CAN (1979, 1996, 1997), **MERCOSUR** (2005), **PARLACEN** (1987, 2008)	**CAN** (2003), **CARICOM** (1992), MERCOSUR (1994), SICA (1962)	**OAS** (1985, 1992)	**OECS** (2010)	**UNASUR** (2008), **SICA** (1991)
Asia	EAEU (2000)	**EAEU** (2000, 2006, 2007)	–	–	EAEU (2001)
Europe	**EU** (1951, 1992, 1997, 2007), **Union State** (1996)	**BA** (1999), **BSPC** (2016), **BSEC** (1998), **CEI** (2009), **CoE** (1949), EU (1951,1957), **NC** (1995), **WNC** (1985)	–	–	CEI (2002), **BU** (2012), **WEU** (1984), **OSCE** (1990)

Notes: 1. In bold, the last treaty of a given RO. 2. In CAN (2003), AU (2014), EU (1951,1957) the end goal stated in the founding treaty is to develop direct citizen suffrage. 3. AU (1991), ECOWAS (1993), UEMOA (2003), UNASUR (2008), SICA (1991), CEI (2002), BU (2012), WEU (1984) derive the regulation of the Parliament to a protocol or another agreement. 4. MERCOSUR (2005) establishes that the election of representatives will take place by direct citizen suffrage; however, it establishes a transitionary measure, stating that 'in the first step of the transition, National Parliaments will establish how to designate their representatives'.

recent founding treaty. In only one case, the OAS, do the national governments appoint the members of the parliamentary organ, and in another, the OECS, it is a mixed organ with national parliamentarians and members appointed by the government, including representatives from the main opposition party. For some ROs, the composition of the parliament is not detailed in the founding treaty, but they delegate the regulation to a protocol or to another international agreement. The case of OSCE (1990) is quite exceptional, as it postponed the official establishment of the parliament to the development of a lower-scope agreement. In this case, by the resolution establishing the CSCE Parliamentary Assembly (OSCE 1991), also known as the 'Madrid Resolution'.

6.1.1 De facto development of direct elections in ROs

As what is included in the treaties may diverge from practice, I proceeded to check whether the direct elections included in the treaties effectively took place. In Table 8.5 the findings are summarised, and it is shown that elections do take place, but also, in some cases, no evidence could be found of that happening.[8]

6.1.2 Different trajectories of RO parliaments from founding treaties to practice

According to the information found, I can clearly state that elections effectively took place in the European and Latin American ROs that committed to that in their founding treaties. Even in the case of the Andean Community (CAN), where the regulation stated a transitional period in 2003 (Cartagena Agreement), direct elections for the RO parliament have indeed been in fact taking place in their Member States. The next paragraphs will delve into the cases of ROs holding direct parliamentary elections, offering more information about lower-scope agreements which regulate the functioning of their parliaments beyond their founding treaties.

Starting with the African ROs, the UEMOA Parliament was regulated in the Treaty Establishing the Creation of the Parliament of UEMOA (Traité portant création du Parlement de l'Union Économique et Monétaire Ouest Africaine, 2003). The treaty stated that the Members of the Parliament would be elected by universal suffrage every five years. The electoral procedure is delegated to an additional Act of Conference (art. 5). The instrument also established a transitionary measure, by which, pending their election by direct universal suffrage, the Members of Parliament are appointed by the National Parliaments

---

[8] It must be clarified that the fact of not finding evidence does not mean that those elections did not take place, but that the researcher involved could not access any information on this matter.

Table 8.5 De facto direct elections in RO Parliaments

Region	Directly elected parliamentarians	Evidence	Conclusions
Africa	**CEMAC** (2008)	No evidence found.	–
Africa	**UEMOA** (2003)	No evidence found.	–
Americas	**PARLACEN** (1987, 2008)	Last elections: 28 November 2021 (Honduras), 7 November 2021 (Nicaragua), 28 February 2021 (El Salvador), 5 July 2020 (Dominican Republic), 16 June 2019 (Guatemala), 5 May 2019 (Panama).	• Elections taking place regularly in all Member States • No simultaneous elections
Americas	**CAN** (2003)	Last direct elections: 18 October 2020 (Bolivia), 21 April 2021 (Peru), 7 February 2021 (Ecuador), 9 March 2014 (Colombia).	• Elections taking place in all Member States • No simultaneous elections
Americas	**MERCOSUR** (2005)	Direct elections in Argentina and Paraguay. Indirect elections in the rest (Brazil, Uruguay). New regulation in 2019 to re-establish indirect elections in all Member States, justifying the inequality that it generates.	• No simultaneous elections • Direct elections only held in some countries. In the rest, the representatives are elected indirectly by National Parliaments • Decision to go back to indirect elections • End goal: development of simultaneous direct elections
Asia	n/a	n/a	n/a
Europe	**EU** (1951, 1992, 1997, 2007)	Last election: from 6 to 9 June 2024 (all EU Member States). Taking place every five years since 1979.	• Simultaneous election • In all the Member States • Adaptation to national voting culture

(art. 31), which seems to be the procedure currently taking place. No evidence has been found of universal elections being held to elect the members of the UEMOA Parliament.

Similarly, in the CEMAC Treaty (Traité instituant la Communauté Economique et Monétaire de l'Afrique Centrale 1994), it was mentioned that the Parliament would be regulated in a different treaty. The treaty regulating the CEMAC Parliament (Convention Régissant le Parlement Communautaire 2008) was not developed until 2008. This regulation used the exact same phrasing as UEMOA's Treaty, stating that the Parliament would be composed by universal suffrage, that the electoral procedure would be agreed upon in an additional act of the Heads of the State Conference, and that while that happened, the members of the Parliament would be appointed by the National Parliaments (Traité portant création du Parlement de l'Union Économique et Monétaire Ouest Africaine, 2003). It seems evident that CEMAC inspired its regulation from that of UEMOA.

In Latin America, PARLACEN established direct elections with the Treaty on the Establishment of the Central American Parliament (1989), a commitment that was restated in 2008 in the revision of the treaty (Protocol Amending the Treaty on the Establishment of the Central American Parliament). In line with the regulation of this last treaty, elections for PARLACEN representatives are confirmed to have taken place in a non-simultaneous fashion in all PARLACEN Member States on a regular basis.

In the case of the Andean Community (CAN), for years its regulations included that the Parliamentary body would be directly elected by citizens (see Treaty Establishing the Andean Parliament, 1979; Trujillo Protocol, 1996; Additional Protocol to the Treaty Establishing the Andean Parliament, 1997). The rationale given in the treaties was that the Parliament is the organ that represents the peoples of the Andean Community and hence it shall be made up of representatives chosen by direct universal suffrage.

In 1997, with the Additional Protocol , CAN developed the work procedure of the Andean Parliament and stated the obligation of universal direct suffrage, aiming for a uniform procedure for all the States. However, it established as a backup option that the Member States would develop their own elections within a timeframe of five years and would inform the Parliament about the results. The Protocol also established that, as a transitionary measure before the direct elections are developed, the appointment of representatives will take place in the National Parliaments. This Protocol, however, did not include the procedure to develop CAN elections in practice. The truth is that the protocol was not put into practice (Insignares Cera, 2009 p. 327). The RO developed a temporary measure in 2003, to allow the Parliamentary body to be elected by the National Parliaments as a provisional measure until the Additional Protocol instituting direct elections was signed, which can be seen as a setback motivated by the difficulty of implementing the elections in practice (Cartagena Agreement, 2003, art. 42).

In 2004, the Andean Electoral Council was created. In the San Francisco de Quito Agreement (2004, para. 42), the National Parliaments were requested to develop elections for the Andean Parliament in their next electoral appointment. However, until 2015, there was no specific regulation to make these elections happen. In 2015, the General Rules of the Andean Parliament were adopted and amended in 2018 (CAN, 2018). Since then, direct elections have taken place in CAN member states, adapting to the national election rules and timing.

The case of CAN is similar to MERCOSUR's. The main difference is that the last MERCOSUR founding Treaty in 2005 clearly stated that the election of Members of the PARLASUR would be conducted by universal direct suffrage (Protocol Establishing the MERCOSUR Parliament). As with most of other ROs, it also established a transitionary measure in which the National Parliaments would indirectly appoint the representatives until direct elections are in place. Direct elections have been evidenced to take place in Argentina and Paraguay, whereas the rest of the MERCOSUR members continue selecting their representatives to the regional Parliament indirectly through the national parliaments.

The case of MERCOSUR is intriguing because, as a measure of equality in the organisation as well as reciprocity in rights and duties, a new Protocol was adopted in 2019, establishing what can be considered a setback in the democratisation of the RO (Additional Protocol That Modifies the Constitutive Protocol of MERCOSUR Parliament). The Protocol established that the PARLASUR will be composed of members of the National Parliaments 'until the MERCOSUR members of the parliament are elected simultaneously in all the Member States by direct, universal, and secret suffrage of the citizens' (2019, art. 1). The Protocol remarks on the fact that the direct election of the representatives must be simultaneous in all the States, in order to avoid imbalances in the citizen representation. The Protocol also establishes that the simultaneous universal, secret, and direct elections will happen on the 'day of the MERCOSUR citizen', with the aim of creating a common citizenship feeling, or *regional demos*.

Looking at Europe, the European Union was the first RO to develop a direct election to select the members of its Parliament. Its ambitious regulation in 1951 with the Treaty of Paris stating universal direct elections was toned down in the Treaty of Rome in 1957 with a more pragmatic proposal: calling for the Assembly to draw up a proposal for regulating the direct universal suffrage in accordance with a uniform procedure in all Member States. In the meantime, the parliamentary organ would be designated by the respective Parliaments indirectly. It was only in 1976 that the Council of Ministers issued the Act concerning the election of the Members of the European Parliament by direct universal suffrage (EU, 1976). It came after some attempts since 1960, where it was agreed that European integration could not succeed without direct citizen participation (Salm 2019). In 1978 the first European Parliament elections took place, which since then happen regularly and simultaneously in all the Member States. The debate is still open, as new steps are proposed in the concluding report of the Conference on the Future of Europe, where it is proposed to amend the EU electoral law to harmonise electoral conditions (voting age, election date, requirements for electoral districts, candidates, political parties, and their financing) and moving to a system of 'transnational lists', instead of national-lists (EU, 2022, para. 38.3).

As it can be seen, the trajectories of the different parliaments are diverse. A first conclusion is that region-wide elections are difficult to implement. This may be caused by different regulations and traditions in the member states (e.g., different voting days, different voting ages, and the cost and operational difficulties of organising the elections, which can be reduced if several votings merge on one date) or also the level of understanding or importance given by the citizens to the RO may create a fear of low voter turnout. According to the literature, voter turnout is higher when there is a lower geographical distance between citizens and the administrative capital (Stockemer 2017).

For some ROs, it has taken years for their regulations to be adopted. The path was never smooth for any of the ROs, and the actual implementation made them reconsider whether the system in place was serving the original purposes of the ROs. That was the case of MERCOSUR, which eventually came back to an indirect election of representatives. While some ROs seem to be working well with a non-simultaneous electoral system (such as PARLACEN or CAN), for others direct elections seem to be the road to take, even exploring ways to further homogenise the procedures in place, such as in MERCOSUR with the creation of Mercosur Citizen Day, dedicated to electing the representatives at the regional level.

6.2 Engagement of non-governmental stakeholders in the ROs policy cycle

When it comes to mechanisms that go beyond one punctual interaction, this chapter studies the engagement of non-governmental stakeholders in the life of the ROs. In practice, I operationalise this concept to include the mentions and regulations in the founding treaties of two groups of non-governmental stakeholders: Non-Governmental Organisations (NGOs) and profit-oriented actors.

Non-Governmental Organisations are usually referred to as NGOs in ROs treaties. However, a wide variety of names is also used in the treaties, such as Civil Society Organisations, non-profit organisations, or non-governmental stakeholders, groups, or bodies. Less frequently, also non-state actors, social partners, or third parties, among others. In the case of NGOs, there are several sub-groups specifically mentioned in the treaties. Among the most frequent ones, trade unions, women, youth, academic or epistemic communities, or special occupational groups can be found.

Similarly, profit-oriented actors are usually referred to as industry, business, private enterprises, commercial actors, and the private sector. To a lesser extent, they are simply companies, corporations, or firms.

From the total sample of 70 ROs or 235 treaties analysed, the data shows that 18 of these ROs mention both kinds of non-governmental stakeholders (NGOs and profit-oriented actors). Both groups are mentioned similarly in the treaties, with NGOs mentioned in 25 ROs, corresponding to 41 treaties, and profit-oriented actors in 28 ROs, corresponding to 44 treaties. Table 8.6 shows the distribution of ROs per continent referring to NGOs, profit-oriented actors, or both in their treaties.

Differently than in other variables analysed, Asian ROs are present in this category. ROs such as EAEU, ECO, MSG, PC, PIF, ASEAN, and LAS include in their founding treaties some mentions of CSOs or profit-oriented actors. This might be in line with the reflection proposed by Pétric, who argues the promotion of NGOs by international organisations in Asian countries during the post-soviet era (Pétric, 2005).

Table 8.6 ROs mentioning non-governmental stakeholders in their founding treaties

Region	Both NGOs and profit-oriented actors	NGOs only	Profit-oriented actors only
Africa (8)	AU, COMESA, EAC, ECOWAS, SADC	IGAD	CEMAC, UEMOA
Asia (7)	EAEU, ECO, MSG, PC, PIF	ASEAN	LAS
Europe (10)	BSEC, EU, RCC, SEECP	AC, CEI, CoE, OSCE	BU, EFTA
Americas (12)	OAS, SICA	ACS, LAIA, NAFTA	ALBA, AP, CAN, CARICOM, MERCOSUR, SELA, UNASUR

6.2.1 Institutionalisation of non-governmental stakeholders

When I study which ROs institutionalise the participation of NGOs or profit-oriented actors in any of their structures, that is, whether they develop formal structures or procedures for non-governmental stakeholders to engage in the life of the RO, only eight ROs regulate the participation of NGOs and seven of profit-oriented actors, out of 70 ROs analysed (Table 8.7).

The list of ROs seems surprising, due to its reduced extent, but also considering the results of the previous analysis. As an example, it is striking that organisations such as CAN, one of the ROs with the strongest emphasis on the participation of citizens, do not offer channels to make that participation possible in an institutionalised way. It would be interesting to understand better the case of this RO in a further qualitative study.

It must be mentioned that 34 treaties do not specify whether they institutionalise the participation of non-governmental stakeholders. The specific criteria for the accreditation of NGOs seem not to be usually included in the founding treaty. Some references redirecting to other protocols can be found. The same happens with the length of the mandate, the possibility of re-election, and the funding available for NGOs to participate. The main conclusion that can be derived from this information is that the institutionalisation of NGOs or profit-orientated actors is not usually formalised through the founding treaties, but rather through agreements of lower scope, such as protocols, rules of procedure or administrative decisions.

Table 8.7 ROs institutionalising non-governmental stakeholders' participation in their founding treaties

Region	Both NGOs and profit-oriented actors	NGOs only	Profit-oriented actors only
Africa (3)	AU,SADC	–	COMESA
Asia (1)	EAEU	–	–
Europe (4)	EU	AC, CoE, OSCE	–
Americas (2)	SICA	–	CAN

6.3 Other mechanisms for direct participation of citizens

When looking at the references in the treaties to mechanisms for the direct participation of citizens, it can be seen that the only mechanisms of direct participation mentioned or regulated in some treaties are the direct elections of any organ, the engagement through non-governmental stakeholders (developed in sections above), and petitions or complaints to an Ombudsperson body, an appointed official in charge of investigating complaints on the poor administration of the organisation for the benefit of citizens. These are mentioned only by a handful of ROs.

Looking at other forms of direct participation of citizens, there is only one RO that regulates in its founding treaty the possibility of submitting complaints from citizens to an organ that acts as an Ombudsperson. It is the case of the European Union through the European Parliament since the Treaty on European Union (1992), also known as the 'Treaty of Maastricht'. The EU is also the only RO in the world that regulates the possibility of submitting petitions by citizens through its current founding treaty (Treaty of Lisbon, 2007, art. new 16.2.d). In the case of the Council of Europe, there is a similar mechanism linked to one international agreement, the Revised European Social Charter (1996). This is the procedure for Collective Complaints to the Committee of Social Rights.

As a system similar to public consultation, the Eurasian Economic Union (EAEU) also regulates a procedure for citizens to directly submit comments and suggestions on all the draft decisions by the organs of the RO (Treaty on the Eurasian Economic Union, 2014, art. 111.4).

No other forms of direct citizen participation have been identified in the founding treaties, while this analysis specifically looked specifically for the regulation of referenda, plebiscites, legislative initiatives, or public consultations, beyond direct elections, engagement of non-governmental stakeholders, complaints, and petitions by citizens. The absence of regulation for these forms of participation in the RO founding treaties does not mean that they are not put into place in the organisations. A possible explanation for the lack of codification in the founding treaty could be that the practice is not yet fully established or well-spread across the RO. ASEAN showcases this with its Guidelines on Public Service Delivery, in which an analysis of the practices on citizen participation, accountability, and inclusiveness in the policymaking process in the Member States and neighbouring countries is presented, as well as a set of recommendations and indicators for ASEAN policymaking processes in all the departments of its administration (ASEAN, 2020a). This effort may lead to the incorporation of these practices in further revisions of the founding treaties.

However, how direct citizen participation is developed in ROs should be further studied in lower-scope agreements, which may be more prolific in regulating this matter. That is the case with public consultations in the European Union or MERCOSUR, which are being conducted in practice[9] despite not being regulated in the founding treaties of these ROs but by decision of the executive body of the RO or as part of the staff working guidelines. In the case of the European Union, consultations with relevant stakeholders in

9 Examples at the European Union (https://commission.europa.eu/about-european-commission/service-standards-and-principles/transparency/consultations_en) or MERCOSUR (https://www.ippdh.mercosur.int/consultas-publicas/).

policymaking are regulated by the Communication on 'Better regulation: Joining forces to make better laws' (2021) by the European Commission, and also by the Staff Working Document "Better Regulation Guidelines' (EU Commission 2021) by the EU Directorate-General. By Decision of its Council of Common Market, MERCOSUR introduced the possibility for private sector agents to participate in all their decisions, opening a consultation mechanism (1991). Similarly, by Decision of the aforementioned Council, the Unit to Support Social Participation was created in 2010, with the goal of opening a dialogue and consulting civil society organisations and social movements for policies and strategies to be developed (MERCOSUR 2010). While this is the case for consultations, it seems unlikely that referenda or plebiscites would be regulated in an instrument with a lower scope directly, as this possibility should be first allowed at the level of constitutional development or at the highest legal instrument (e.g., see Revised Code of Good Practice on Referendums by the Council of Europe (2022)).

Within this whole analysis of citizen participation from a *de jure* perspective, it can be seen that the ROs from Asia are once again less represented. This raises a question about the mechanisms to include citizen participation in the work of ROs in that area of the world. There may be different picture when looking at the informal engagements between institutions and civil society actors. along with further investigations into the patterns for citizen participation in the region. Even though the mechanisms are not regulated in the founding treaties, at least in ASEAN there is evidence of an interest in strengthening the 'efforts in building a people-oriented, people-centred' regional community, as declared by its Secretary General and evidenced in the guidelines for public servants in the last years (ASEAN 2020a, 2020b).

7 CONCLUSION

The first conclusion derived from this chapter is that the mechanisms for citizen participation are not widely spread across ROs. When looking at the founding treaties, these are only present in one-third of the existing ROs in the world. However, the fact that these mechanisms are not included in founding treaties does not mean that they are not developed by the ROs. Next steps in researching the *de jure* or formal characteristics of citizen participation must include a deeper analysis of lower-level agreements, such as protocols, rules of procedure or administrative decisions in ROs. This study is not possible in a systematic way, due to the lack of datasets coding this information.

The picture of the time evolution of mechanisms for citizen participation shows some changes in the way citizen participation was codified before and after the 2000s. It would be interesting to explore this finding in relation to other events taking place in the world, such as the expansion of the internet or the consolidation of the post-Soviet era. Some geographical differences can be found in the distribution of citizen participation mechanisms: ROs from Asia are less present, and when they developed any mechanisms for citizen participation, they did so later than ROs in other regions, seen in all the categories analysed. This can be related to a late formalisation of the engagement of institutions with civil society actors, explained by the remarked un-interested approach from the elites of the ROs, or by the own interest of the existing societal actors to be part of decision-making processes in the RO (Chandra 1999). When looking at the evidence of the actual practice of ROs, it can be seen how ROs in the Americas and Europe tend to deliver on the commitments included in their treaties. For most African ROs, there was not enough evidence found to assess this.

The analysis of direct parliamentary elections highlights the diversity of trajectories of the different RO parliaments. This points to the difficulty of implementing region-wide elections, due to the different regulations and traditions, but also due to the different levels of understanding of the RO in the different member states. The difficulties in implementation create the need to reconcile the ambition of ROs with their practice, with examples in which the regulation reverts to earlier stages, as was the case in MERCOSUR. Furthermore, this also sparks the debate on how relevant regional parliaments are in terms of competences and their link with the kind of representatives' selection process in place, which is a question that should be further studied.

When it comes to the institutionalisation of non-governmental stakeholders in the life of ROs, it seems that the founding treaties may not be the best instruments to focus on, as there are only a handful of ROs which include these kinds of mechanisms in their highest-level regulation. It is expected to find more regulations about this extent in agreements of lower scope. Similarly, it happens with other forms of direct citizen participation, such as petitions, consultations, or complaints. However, it is surprising not to find more references to the regulation of referenda or legislative initiatives, as these are commonly constitutional considerations that would be expected to have their regulations in the RO founding treaties.

It is convenient to remark that the analysis offered in this chapter reflects mostly only one side of the coin, the formal or *de jure* perspective. The study of the *de facto* practice of citizen participation in ROs may show a different picture, including informal mechanisms for engagement which are not codified. In the words of Tallberg and Sommerer (2017), 'it is plausible to assume that the data on formal access underestimate, rather than overestimate, the actual level of openness in IOs'. However, the highest-level regulation of ROs can serve as an enabler of the work of the RO and shows a clear commitment from them that can translate into developing a strategic and comprehensive approach towards citizen engagement.

ACKNOWLEDGEMENTS

The research project whose results are presented in this chapter has received funding from the 'la Caixa' Foundation (ID 100010434), under the agreement LCF/BQ/EU21/1189006. The author is grateful for it.

REFERENCES

Abbott, K. W., & Snidal, D. (2001). International 'standards' and international governance. *Journal of European Public Policy, 8*(3), 345–370. https://doi.org/10.1080/13501760110056013.

Additional Protocol to the Treaty Establishing the Andean Parliament (1997). https://www.wipo.int/wipolex/en/text/224740.

Agreement Amending the Treaty of the Southern African Development Community (2001). https://www.sadc.int/document/agreement-amending-treaty-2001-english-0.

Agreement Establishing the Inter-American Development Bank, C-15 (1959). https://www.oas.org/dil/treaties_C-15_Agreement_Establishing_the_Inter-American_Development_Bank_sign.htm.

Appendix I – Statutory Resolution the Statute of the Council of Europe, (51) 30 (1951). https://assembly.coe.int/nw/xml/rop/statut_ce_2015-en.pdf.

Arnstein, S. (1969). A ladder of citizen participation. *Journal of the American Institute of Planners*, 35(4), 216–224.

ASEAN. (2020a). *ASEAN Guidelines on Public Service Delivery.* https://asean.org/wp-content/uploads/2021/08/ASEAN-Guidelines-on-Public-Service-Delivery_Final_19Feb2021.pdf.

ASEAN. (2020b). *In Conversations with ASEAN Citizens. ASEAN: A Community of Opportunities for Al.* https://asean.org/wp-content/uploads/2021/08/In-Conversations-with-ASEAN-Citizens.pdf.

Baum, H. S. (2001). Citizen Participation. In N. J. Smelser & P. B. Baltes (Eds), *International Encyclopedia of the Social & Behavioral Sciences* (pp. 1840–1846). Pergamon.

Best, E. (2011). Assessing regional governance: an indicative framework for developing indicators. In P. De Lombaerde, R. Flores, L. Iapadre, M. Schulz (Eds), *The Regional Integration Manual.* Routledge, 2012. p. 1–23.

Bourgon, J. (2007). Responsive, responsible and respected government: Towards a new public administration theory. *International Review of Administrative Sciences, 73*(1), 7–26. https://doi.org/10.1177/0020852307075686.

Boyer, E. J., Van Slyke, D. M., & Rogers, J. D. (2016). An empirical examination of public involvement in public-private partnerships: Qualifying the benefits of public involvement in PPPs. *Journal of Public Administration Research and Theory, 26*(1), 45–61. https://doi.org/10.1093/jopart/muv008.

Brudney, J. L., & England, R. E. (1983). Toward a definition of the coproduction concept. *Public Administration Review, 43*(1), 59–65. https://doi.org/10.2307/975300.

CAN. (2018). *Reglamento General del Parlamento Andino (Rules of the Andean Parliament).* https://www.congreso.gob.pe/Docs/ParlamentoAndino/files/informes/reglamento_parlamento_andinoweb.pdf.

Chandra, A. C. (1999). The role of non-state actors in ASEAN. *Exchange, 167,* 94.

Codificación del Acuerdo de Integración Subregional Andino. Acuerdo de Cartagena. (Codification of the Andean Subregional Integration Agreement. Cartagena Agreement), (2003). http://www.sice.oas.org/trade/junac/decisiones/dec563s.asp.

Communication From the Commission to the European Parliament, the Council, the European Economic and Social Committee and the Committee of the Regions. Better regulation: Joining forces to make better laws, COM(2021) 219 (2021). https://eur-lex.europa.eu/legal-content/EN/ALL/?uri=COM:2021:219:FIN.

Convention Régissant le Parlement Communautaire (Convention Governing the Communitary Parliament) (2008). https://www.cemac.int/sites/default/files/inline-files/Convention_parlement.pdf.

Council of Europe. (2022). *Revised Code of Good Practice on Referendums*. https://www.venice.coe.int/webforms/documents/?pdf=CDL-AD(2022)015-e.

Drieghe, L., Orbie, J., Potjomkina, D., & Shahin, J. (2021). Participation of civil society in EU trade policy making: How inclusive is inclusion? *New Political Economy*, 1–16.

Esty, D. C. (2005). Good governance at the supernational scale: Globalizing adminsitrative law. *Yale Law Journal*, *115*(7), 1490–1563.

EU. (1976). *Act concerning the election of the representatives of the Assembly by direct universal suffrage*. https://eur-lex.europa.eu/eli/dec/1976/787(2)/oj.

EU. (9 May 2022). *The Conference on the Future of Europe. Report on the final outcome*. https://www.europarl.europa.eu/news/en/press-room/20220509IPR29102/the-conference-on-the-future-of-europe-concludes-its-work.

European Social Charter (Revised), (1996). https://rm.coe.int/168007cf93

Guo, H. (David), & Neshkova, M. I. (2013). Citizen input in the budget process: When does it matter most? *The American Review of Public Administration*, *43*(3), 331–346.

Gyimah-Boadi, E. (1996). Civil society in Africa. *Journal of Democracy*, *7*(2), 118–132.

Haftel, Y., & Alexander, T. (2006). The independence of international organizations: Concept and applications. *Journal of Conflict Resolution*, *50*(2), 253–275.

Hooghe, L., & Marks, G. (2015). Delegation and pooling in international organizations. *The Review of International Organizations*, *10*(3), 305–328. https://doi.org/10.1007/s11558-014-9194-4.

Insignares Cera, S. (2009). Las Elecciones Directas en el Parlamento Andino un Camino para Fortalecer su Papel Como Institución Promotora de la Integración. *Revista de Derecho*, *32*, 306–333.

Jetschke, A., & Münch, S. (2020). The existence of courts and parliaments in regional organizations: A case of democratic control? *Politische Vierteljahresschrift*, *61*(2), 309–333. https://doi.org/10.1007/s11615-020-00230-w.

Jetschke, A., Theiner, P., Marggraf, C., & Münch, S. (2017). *A bird's eye view of the elephants: The Comparative Regional Organizations Project*. Paper presented at the DVPW IR Conference, Bremen, October 4-6, 2017. Available at https://www.researchgate.net/publication/320244144_A_bird's_eye_view_of_the_elephants_The_Comparative_Regional_Organizations_Project (accessed 8 February 2025)

Jetschke, A., Theiner, P., Marggraf, C., & Münch, S. (2017). Comparative Regional Organizations Dataset. A survey of regional organizations' agreements (CROPDA I). edited by Comparative Regional Organizations Project. University of Goettingen. https://comparativeregionalorganizations.org/

King, C. S., & Stivers, C. (1998). Citizens and administrators: Roles and relationships. In C.S. King & C. Stivers, *Government Is Us*. Sage Publications, 49–69

Kingsbury, B., Krisch, N., & Stewart, R. B. (2005). The emergence of global administrative law. *Law and Contemporary Problems*, *68*(3/4), 15–61.

Koremenos, B., Lipson, C., & Snidal, D. (2001). The rational design of international institutions. *International Organization, 55*(4), 761–799. https://doi.org/10.1162/002081801317193592.

Leighninger, M. (2020). Teaching democracy in public administration: Trends and future prospects. *Journal of Deliberative Democracy, 6*(1), Article 1. https://doi.org/10.16997/jdd.100.

Lenz, T. (2021). Appendix A – The Dependent Variable 'RO institutionalization'', In T. Lenz, *Interorganizational Diffusion in International Relations: Regional Institutions and the Role of the European Union.* Oxford Academic (pp. 201–204) https://doi.org/10.1093/oso/9780198823827.005.0001.

Lenz, T., Ceka, B., Hooghe, L., Marks, G., & Burilkov, A. (2022). Discovering cooperation: Endogenous change in international organizations. *The Review of International Organizations,* 18, 631–666. https://doi.org/10.1007/s11558-022-09482–0.

Manila Declaration, (1987). https://asean.org/manila-declaration-philippines-15-december-1987/.

Mattheis, F. (2014). Comparing Regionalisms in the South and studying regional spaces – Conclusions. In F. Mattheis, *New Regionalism in the South – Mercosur and SADC in a comparative and interregional perspective,* Leipziger Universitätsvlg,246–254.

MERCOSUR. (1991). *SICE – Decisiones—MERCOSUR/CMC/DEC. N°04/91.* http://www.sice.oas.org/trade/mrcsrs/decisions/dec0491s.asp.

OECD. (2021). *Compendium of International Organisations' Practices: Working Towards More Effective International Instruments.* OECD. https://doi.org/10.1787/846a5fa0-en.

OECD. (2022). *OECD Guidelines for Citizen Participation Processes.* https://www.oecd.org/publications/oecd-guidelines-for-citizen-participation-processes-f765caf6-en.htm.

Okonjo-Iweala, D. N., & Osafo-Kwaako, P. (2007). *The Role of Civil Society Organizations in Supporting Fiscal Transparency in African Countries—Document for discussion.* Results for Development. https://www.r4d.org/wp-content/uploads/Ngozi-CSO_Paper_Revised_Version.pdf.

Osborne, S. P. (2020). The Evolution of Public Service Logic I. In S. P. Osborne, *Public Service Logic.* Routledge.

OSCE. (1990, November 21). *Charter of Paris for a New Europe.* https://www.osce.org/mc/39516.

OSCE. (1991). *Final Resolution Concerning the Establishment of the CSCE Parliamentary Assembly.* https://www.osce.org/files/f/documents/0/3/40791.pdf.

Pétric, B. (2005). Post-Soviet Kyrgyzstan or the birth of a globalized protectorate. *Central Asian Survey, 24*(3), 319–332. https://doi.org/10.1080/02634930500310402.

Piotrowski, S. J. (2017). The 'Open Government Reform' movement: The case of the open government partnership and U.S. transparency policies. *The American Review of Public Administration, 47*(2), 155–171. https://doi.org/10.1177/0275074016676575.

Potjomkina, D., Orbie, J., & Shahin, J. (2021). Forging their path in the Brussels bubble? Civil society resistance within the domestic advisory groups created under the EU trade agreements. *Cambridge Review of International Affairs,* 1–20.

Protocol amending the Treaty on the establishment of the Central American Parliament and other political organs, (2008). https://international.vlex.com/vid/protocol-amending-the-treaty-851201553.

Protocol of Amendment to the Charter of the Organization of American States, B-31 (1967). http://www.oas.org/dil/treaties_b-31_protocol_of_buenos_aires_sign.htm.

Protocol of Amendment to the Charter of the Organization of American States. Protocol of Cartagena de Indias, (1985). http://www.oas.org/dil/treaties_A-50_Protocol_of_Cartagena_de_Indias.htm.

Protocol to the Treaty Establishing the African Economic Community Relating to the Pan-African Parliament, (2001). https://au.int/en/treaties/protocol-treaty-establishing-african-economic-community-relating-pan-african-parliament.

Protocolo Adicional al Protocolo Constitutivo del Parlamento del MERCOSUR (Additional Protocol that modifies the Constitutive Protocol of MERCOSUR Parliament), (2019). https://www.mercosur.int/documento/protocolo-adicional-al-protocolo-constitutivo-del-parlasur/.

Protocolo Constitutivo del Parlamento del MERCOSUR (Protocol Establishing the MERCOSUR Parliament), (2005). https://www.parlamentomercosur.org/innovaportal/file/7308/1/protocolo_es.pdf.

Protocolo Modificatorio Del Acuerdo De Integracion Subregional Andino. Protocolo De Trujillo. (Amending Protocol to the Andean Subregional Integration Agreement. Trujillo Protocol), (1996). http://www.sice.oas.org/trade/junac/carta_ag/trujillo.asp.

Reinold, T. (2019). Civil society participation in regional integration in Africa: A comparative analysis of ECOWAS, SADC, and the EAC. *South African Journal of International Affairs*, *26*(1), 53–71.

Ryngaert, C., & Wouters, J. (2004). Good governance: Lessons from international organizations. in D. M. Curtin and R. A. Wessel (eds), *Good Governance and the European Union: Reflections on Concepts, Institutions and Substance* (pp. 69–106). Intersentia.

Salm, C. (2019). *European elections: A historical perspective.* European Parliamentary Research Service, https://www.europarl.europa.eu/RegData/etudes/ATAG/2019/637957/EPRS_ATA(2019)637957_EN.pdf (accessed on 8 February 2025).

San Francisco de Quito Agreement, (2004). http://www.sice.oas.org/Trade/Junac/XVacta_e.asp.

Scholte, J. A. (2020). After liberal global democracy: New methodology for new praxis. *Fudan Journal of the Humanities and Social Sciences*, *13*(1), 67–92. https://doi.org/10.1007/s40647-019-00265-3.

Scupola, A. (2018). Policy and process tracing of international digital transformation practices – Case Denmark. In *Policy and process tracing of international digital transformation practices – Case Denmark, Co-VAL [770356] 'Understanding value co-creation in public services for transforming European public administrations'* [Report].

Shivakoti, R. (2020). Asian Migration Governance. In G. Rayp, I. Ruyssen, & K. Marchand (Eds), *Regional Integration and Migration Governance in the Global South* (pp. 177–199). Springer International Publishing. https://doi.org/10.1007/978-3-030-43942-2_8.

Single European Act, (1986). https://www.europarl.europa.eu/about-parliament/en/in-the-past/the-parliament-and-the-treaties/single-european-act.

Sommerer, T., & Tallberg, J. (2017). Transnational access to international organizations 1950–2010: A new data set1. *International Studies Perspectives*, *18*(3), 247–266. https://doi.org/10.1093/isp/ekv022.

Sørensen, E., & Torfing, J. (2018). The democratizing impact of governance networks: From pluralization, via democratic anchorage, to interactive political leadership. *Public Administration*, *96*(2), 302–317. https://doi.org/10.1111/padm.12398.

EU Commission (2021). Commission Staff Working Document: Better Regulation Guidelines, SWD(2021)305, https://commission.europa.eu/system/files/2021-11/swd2021_305_en.pdf.

Statute of the Council of Europe, (1949). https://rm.coe.int/1680306052.

Steffek, J., & Kortendiek, N. (2018). Participatory governance in international organizations. In H. Heinelt, *Handbook on Participatory Governance*. Edward Elgar Publishing, pp. 203–224 https://doi.org/10.4337/9781785364358.

Stockemer, D. (2017). What affects voter turnout? A review article/meta-analysis of aggregate research. *Government and Opposition*, *52*(4), 698–722. https://doi.org/10.1017/gov.2016.30.

Tallberg, J., Sommerer, T., Squatrito, T., & Jönsson, C. (2013). *The Opening Up of International Organizations: Transnational Access in Global Governance*. Cambridge University Press. https://doi.org/10.1017/CBO9781107325135.

Traité instituant la Communauté Economique et Monétaire de l'Afrique Centrale (Treaty Establishing the Economic and Monetary Community of Central Africa), (1994). https://www.banque-france.fr/sites/default/files/media/2016/11/02/umac.pdf.

Traité portant création du Parlement de l'Union Économique et Monétaire Ouest Africaine (Treaty Establishing the Creation of the Parliament of the Economic and Monetary Union of West Africa), (2003). http://www.uemoa.int/fr/traite-portant-creation-du-parlement-de-lunion-economique-et-monetaire-ouest-africaine.

Tratado Constitutivo del Parlamento Andino (Treaty Establishing the Andean Parliament), (1979). http://www.sice.oas.org/trade/junac/carta_ag/parla_s.asp.

Treaty Establishing the European Coal and Steel Community, (1951). https://eur-lex.europa.eu/LexUriServ/LexUriServ.do?uri=CELEX:11951K:EN:PDF.

Treaty establishing the European Economic Community, (1957). http://data.europa.eu/eli/treaty/teec/sign/eng.

Treaty of Izmir, (1977). https://treaties.un.org/doc/Publication/UNTS/Volume%201655/v1655.pdf.

Treaty of Lisbon amending the Treaty on European Union and the Treaty establishing the European Community, 306 OJ C (2007). http://data.europa.eu/eli/treaty/lis/sign/eng.

Treaty on European Union, (1992). https://eur-lex.europa.eu/legal-content/EN/TXT/?uri=CELEX:11992M/TXT.

Treaty on the establishment of the Central American Parliament and other political organs., (1989). https://international.vlex.com/vid/treaty-on-the-establishment-851197106.

Treaty on the Eurasian Economic Union, (2014). https://www.wto.org/english/thewto_e/acc_e/kaz_e/wtacckaz85_leg_1.pdf.

MERCOSUR (2010). Unidad de Apoyo a la Participación Social, 65/10, Council of Common Market, MERCOSUR/CMC/DEC.65(10) . http://www.sice.oas.org/trade/mrcsrs/decisions/DEC6510_s.pdf.

United Nations Charter, (1945). https://www.un.org/en/about-us/un-charter/full-text.

UNU-CRIS. (2020). *Regional Integration Knowledge System (RIKS)*. UNU-CRIS. https://cris.unu.edu/riks.

Vigoda, E., & Golembiewski, R. T. (2001). Citizenship Behavior and the Spirit of New Managerialism: A Theoretical Framework and Challenge for Governance. *The American Review of Public Administration*, *31*(3), 273–295. https://doi.org/10.1177/02750740122064956.

APPENDIX 8.1: LIST OF ORGANISATIONS AND ABBREVIATIONS

AC	Arctic Council
ACC	Arab Cooperation Council
ACS	Association of Caribbean States
ACTO	Amazon Cooperation Treaty Organization
ALBA	Bolivarian Alternative for the Peoples of America – Predecessor: Bolivarian Alternative for the Americas
AMU	Arab Maghreb Union
AP	Pacific Alliance
ASEAN	Association of Southeast Asian Nations
AU	African Union – Predecessor: The Union of African States, Casablanca Group, Organisation Inter-Africaine et Malgache, Organisation of African Unity
BA	Baltic Assembly
BSEC	Organization of the Black Sea Economic Cooperation
BSPC	Baltic Sea Parliamentary Conference
BU	Benelux Community – Predecessor: Benelux Convention, Benelux Economic Union
CAN	Andean Community
CARICOM	Caribbean Community – Predecessor: Caribbean Free Trade Association, Caribbean Community, Caribbean Community and Common Market
CAU	Union of Central African States
CBSS	Council of the Baltic Sea States
CCTS	Organization of Turkic States – Predecessor: Cooperation Council of Turkic Speaking States
CE	Entente Council
CEI	Central European Initiative
CELAC	Community of Latin American and Caribbean States – Predecessor: Summit of Latin America and the Caribbean on Integration and Development
CEMAC	Central African Economic and Monetary Union – Predecessor: Central African Economic and Customs Union
CENSAD	Community of Sahel-Saharan States
CENTO	Central Treaty Organization
CEPGL	Economic Community of the Great Lakes Countries
CIS	Commonwealth of Independent States
CO	Caribbean Organization – Predecessor: Caribbean Commission
CoE	Council of Europe
COMECON	Council for Mutual Economic Assistance
COMESA	Common Market for Eastern and Southern Africa
CONDECA	Central American Democratic Community

CPS	Colombo Plan – Predecessor: Council for Technical Co-operation in South and South-East Asia
EAC	East African Community
EAEU	Eurasian Economic Community
ECCAS	Economic Community of Central African States
ECO	Economic Cooperation Organization – Predecessor: Regional Cooperation for Development
ECOWAS	Economic Community of West African States
EFTA	European Economic Area Agreement – Predecessor: European Free Trade Association
EU	European Union – Predecessor: European Coal and Steel Community, European Economic Community, European Communities
GCC	Cooperation Council for the Arab States of the Gulf
GUAM	Organization for Democracy and Economic Development – Predecessor: GUUAM, acronym for Georgia, the Republic of Uzbekistan, Ukraine, the Republic of Azerbaijan, and the Republic of Moldova.
IGAD	Intergovernmental Authority on Development – Predecessor: Intergovernmental Authority on Drought and Development
IOC	Indian Ocean Commission
LAIA	Latin American Integration Association – Predecessor: Free Trade Latin-American Association
LAS	League of Arab States – Predecessor: Arab League, Council of Arab Economic Unity, Arab Fund for Economic and Social Development, Arab Monetary Fund
LGA	Liptako-Gourma Integrated Development Authority
MERCOSUR	MERCOSUR
MRU	Mano River Union
MSG	Melanesian Spearhead Group
NAFTA	North American Free Trade Agreement
NC	Nordic Council
OAS	Organization of American States
OCAM	Common Afro-Malagasy Economic Organization – Predecessor: Union of African Malagasy States, African Malagasy Economic Cooperation Organization
OECS	Organization of Eastern Caribbean States
OSCE	Organisation for Security and Co-operation in Europe
PARLACEN	Central American Parliament
PC	Pacific Community – Predecessor: South Pacific Commission
PIF	Pacific Islands Forum – Predecessor: The South Pacific Bureau for Economic Cooperation, South Pacific Forum
RCC	Regional Cooperation Council
RO	Regional organisations
SAARC	South Asian Association for Regional Cooperation

SADC	Southern African Development Community – Predecessor: Southern African Development Coordination Conference
SCO	Shanghai Cooperation Organization
SEECP	South-East European Cooperation Process
SELA	Latin American and Caribbean Economic System – Predecessor: Latin American Economic System
SICA	Central American Integration System – Predecessor: Central American Common Market, Organization of Central American States
UEMOA	West African Economic and Monetary Union – Predecessors: African Monetary Union, West African Customs Union, West African Monetary Union, West African Economic Community
UNASUR	Union of South American Nations – Predecessor: Community of South American Nations
Union State	Union State of Russia and Belarus
WEU	Western European Union
WNC	West Nordic Council

APPENDIX 8.2: LIST OF TREATIES BY ROs ANALYSED

AC	Declaration on the Establishment of the Arctic Council (Ottawa Declaration)
ACC	Agreement on the establishment of the ACC
ACS	Convention establishing the Association of Caribbean States
ACTO	Treaty for Amazonian Cooperation
ACTO	Amendment Protocol
ACTO	Reglamento del Consejo Cooperacion Amazonica - CCA
ACTO	Reglamento de la Reunion de Ministros de Relaciones Exteriores
ACTO	Reglamento de la Comisión de Coordinación del Consejo de Cooperación Amazónica - CCOOR
ACTO	Reglamento del Secretaría permanente de la OCTA
ALBA	Agreement between Venezuela and Cuba
ALBA	Agreement for the Application of ALBA and TCP
AMU	Treaty instituting the Arab Maghreb Union
AP	Declaración Presidencial sobre Alianza del Pacífico
AP	Acuerdo Marco de la Alianza del Pacífico
ASEAN	Bangkok Declaration (ASA Treaty)
ASEAN	Bangkok Declaration I
ASEAN	Declaration of ASEAN Concord (Bali Concord)
ASEAN	Treaty of Amity and Cooperation
ASEAN	Agreement on the establishment of the ASEAN Secretariat
ASEAN	Manila Declaration
ASEAN	Protocol Amending the Treaty of Amity and Cooperation in Southeast Asia
ASEAN	Singapore Declaration
ASEAN	Declaration of ASEAN Concord (Bali Concord II)
ASEAN	ASEAN Charter
AU	African Charter of Casablanca
AU	Charter of the Union of African States
AU	Charte de Lagos
AU	Charter of the Organization of African Unity
AU	Treaty Establishing the African Economic Community
AU	Protocol on Relations between the African Economic Community and the Regional Economic Communities
AU	Constitutive Act of the AU
AU	Protocol to the AEC Treaty Relating to the Establishment of the Pan-African Parliament
AU	Protocol relating to the establishment of the Peace and Security Council of the AU
AU	Rules of Procedure of the Assembly of the Union
AU	Rules of Procedure of the Permanent Representatives' Committee

AU	Statutes of the Commission of the African Union
AU	Rules of Procedure of the OAU of Heads of State and Government
AU	Protocol of the Court of Justice of the African Union
AU	African Union Non-Aggression and Common Defence Pact
AU	Protocol on the Statute of the African Court of Justice and Human Rights
AU	Protocol on Amendments to the Protocol on the Statute of the African Court of Justice and Human Rights
AU	Protocol to the Constitutive Act of the African Union relating to the Pan-African Parliament
BA	Statutes of the Baltic Assembly
BSEC	Summit Declaration Istanbul
BSEC	Charter of the Organization of the Black Sea Economic Cooperation
BSEC	Additional Protocol of the Privileges and Immunities of the Organization of the Black Sea Economic Cooperation
BSPC	Rules of Procedure
BU	Convention for the establishment of an Economic Union between the two countries
BU	Treaty establishing the Benelux Economic Union
BU	Treaty revising the Treaty establishing the Benelux Economic Union
BU	Treaty establishing a Benelux Court of Justice
CAN	Acuerdo de Cartagena
CAN	Tratado constitutivo del Parlamento Andino
CAN	Treaty creating the Court of Justice of the Cartagena Agreement
CAN	Protocolo de Trujillo
CAN	Protocol of Cochabamba amending the Treaty Creating the Court of Justice
CAN	Additional Protocol to the Treaty Establishing the Andean Parliament
CAN	Sucre Protocol
CAN	Andean Subregional Integration Agreement Cartagena Agreement
CARICOM	CARIFTA - The Dickenson Bay Agreement establishing the Caribbean Free Trade Association
CARICOM	CARIFTA - The Georgetown Accord
CARICOM	Treaty estalishing the Caribbean Community
CARICOM	Agreement for the Establishment of an Assembly of Caribbean Community Parliamentarians
CARICOM	Agreement Establishing the Caribbean Court of Justice

CARICOM	Revised Treaty of Chaguaramas Establishing the Caribbean Community including the CARICOM Single Market and Economy
CAU	Charter of the Union of Central African States
CBSS	Copenhagen Declaration
CBSS	Terms of Reference of the Secretariat of the Council of the Baltic Sea States
CCTS	Nakhchivan Agreement on the Establishment of the Cooperation Council of Turkic Speaking States
CE	Charte
CE	Charte (Amended)
CE	Règlement Secrétariat Exécutif
CE	Règlement Conseil des Ministres
CEI	Guidelines and Rules of Procedure
CEI	Rules of Procedure of the CEI Parliamentary Dimension
CELAC	CALC - Latin American and Caribbean Unity Summit Declaration
CELAC	Procedures for the Organic Operation of CELAC
CELAC	Caracas Declaration
CEMAC	Brazzaville Treaty (UDEAC)
CEMAC	Traité instituant la Communauté Economique et Monétaire de l'Afrique Centrale (CEMAC)
CEMAC	Convention régissant la Cour de Justice
CEMAC	Convention Commission Interparlementaire
CEMAC	Convention régissant de la parlementaire Communaitaire de la CEMAC
CEMAC	Traité révisé de la CEMAC
CEMAC	Convention Regissant l'Union Economique de l'Afrique Centrale
CEMAC	Convention Regissant l'Union Monetaire de l'Afrique Centrale
CENSAD	Treaty on establishment of the community of Sahel Saharan States
CENSAD	Treaty on establishment of the community of Sahel-Saharan States with Annexes 1999
CENTO	Baghdad Pact
CEPGL	Convention establishing the Economic Communities of the Great Lake Countries
CIS	Alma-Ata Declaration
CIS	Charter of the Collective Security Treaty Organization
CO	CC - Agreement for the Establishment for the Caribbean Commission
CO	Agreement and Statute for the Establishment of the Caribbean Organization
CoE	Statute of the Council of Europe
CoE	European Social Charter

CoE	European Social Charter (revised)
COMECON	Charter of the Council for Mutual Economic Assistance
COMESA	Treaty Establishing the Common Market for Eastern and Southern Africa
CONDECA	La Comunidad Democratica Centroamericana
CPS	Constitution of the Colombo Plan
CPS	Rules for the Colombo Plan Council and Bureau
EAC	Treaty of East African Cooperation
EAC	Treaty for Establishment of the East African Community
EAC	Protocol on the Establishment of the East African Customs Union
EAC	Amended Treaty for the Establishment of the East African Community
EAC	Protocol on the Establishment of the East African Community Common Market
EAC	Protocol on Foreign Policy Coordination
EAEU	Agreement on the foundation of the Eurasian Economic Community
EAEU	Treaty on the establishment of the Eurasian Economic Community
EAEU	Rules of Procedure for the Interstate Council of the Eurasian Economic Community
EAEU	Statute of the Court of the Eurasian Economic Community
EAEU	Regulations on the Interstate Council of the Eurasian Economic Community
EAEU	Regulations on the interparliamentary assembly of the Eurasian Economic Community
EAEU	Regulations on the Secretariat of the Inter-parliamentary Assembly of the Eurasian Economic Community
EAEU	Treaty on the establishment of the Eurasian Economic Community
EAEU	Treaty on the Eurasian Economic Union
ECCAS	ECCAS Treaty
ECCAS	Treaty establishing the network of parliamentarians of the ECCAS
ECO	Regional Cooperation for Development (RCD) Treaty
ECO	Treaty of Izmir
ECO	Protocol amending the Treaty of Izmir
ECO	Treaty of Izmir (1996)
ECOWAS	Treaty of Lagos
ECOWAS	Protocol Relating to Mutual Assistance of Defence
ECOWAS	Revised Treaty of the Economic Community of West African States
EFTA	Convention establishing the European Free Trade Area
EFTA	Agreement on the standing committee of the EFTA States

EFTA	Agreement on a committee of members of parliament of the EFTA states
EFTA	Convention on the European Free Trade Area (Consolidated Version)
EU	ECSC - Treaty establishing the European Coal and Steel Community (Treaty of Paris)
EU	EEC – Treaty establishing the European Economic Community (Treaty of Rome)
EU	EC – Treaty establishing a Single Council and a Single Commission of the European Communities (Merger Treaty)
EU	EC – Single European Act
EU	Treaty on European Union (Maastricht Treaty)
EU	Treaty of Amsterdam
EU	Treaty of Nice
EU	Treaty of Lisbon
GCC	Charter of the Gulf Cooperation Council
GCC	Economic Agreement
GCC	Monetary Union Agreement
GCC	Statute of the Monetary Council
GUAM	GUUAM – Yalta GUUAM Charter
GUAM	Charter of Organization for Democracy and Economic Development
IGAD	Accord institutif de l'autorité intergouvernementale contre la sécheresse et pour le développement en Afrique de l'est
IGAD	Agreement establishing IGAD
IOC	General Cooperation Agreement (Victoria Agreement)
LAIA	LAFTA - Montevideo Treaty
LAIA	Treaty of Montevideo
LAS	Pact of the League of Arab States
LAS	Treaty of Joint Defense and Economic Cooperation
LAS	The Economic Unity Agreement
LAS	Arab Common Market
LAS	Agreement establishing the Arab Fund of Economic and Social Development
LAS	Arab Monetary Fund
LAS	Agadir Declaration
LAS	Agadir Agreement
LGA	Convention est. the statutes of the Liptako-Grouma Authority
LGA	Protocole d'accord revisee portant création de l'autorité de développement integre de la région du Liptako-Gourma
LGA	Convention révisée portant statuts de LGA
MERCOSUR	Mercosur Free Trade Agreement
MERCOSUR	Protocol of Brasilia
MERCOSUR	Ouro Preto Protocol
MERCOSUR	Olivos Protocol

MERCOSUR	Protocolo Constitutivo del Parlamento del Mercosur
MRU	Mano River Declaration
MSG	Trade Agreement among the Melanesian Spearhead Group Countries
MSG	Agreement Establishing the Melanesian Spearhead Group
NAFTA	North American Free Trade Agreement
NC	Treaty of Cooperation between Denmark, Finland, Iceland, Norway and Sweden
OAS	Charter of the OAS
OAS	Agreement establishing the Inter-American Development Bank
OAS	Protocol of Buenos Aires
OAS	Protocol of Cartagena de Indias
OAS	Protocol of Washington
OAS	Protocol of Managua
OCAM	Traité Instituant une Organisation Africaine et Malgache de Cooperation Economique (OAMCE)
OCAM	The Charter of the Union of African States and Malagasy
OCAM	Charter and Regulations of the Organisation Commune Africaine et Malgache
OECS	ECCM – Agreement Establishing the East Caribbean Common Market
OECS	Treaty establishing the Organisation of the Eastern Caribbean States
OECS	Revised treaty of Basseterre establishing the OECS Economic Union
OSCE	Helsinki Act
OSCE	Charter of Paris for a New Europe
PARLACEN	Treaty on the establishment of the Central American Parliament and other political organs
PARLACEN	Protocol to the Treaty on the establishment of the Central American Parliament
PC	Agreement establishing the South Pacific Commission (Canberra Agreement)
PC	Tahiti Nui Declaration
PIF	Agreement Establishing the South Pacific Bureau for Economic Cooperation
PIF	South Pacific Regional Trade and Economic Cooperation Agreement
PIF	Agreement Establishing South Pacific Forum Secretariat
PIF	Waigani Convention
PIF	Agreement Establishing the PIF Secretariat
PIF	Revised Agreement Establishing the PIF
RCC	Stability Pact for South Eastern Europe
RCC	Joint Declaration on the establishment of the RCC

SAARC	Declaration on South Asian Regional Cooperation
SAARC	SAARC Charter
SADC	SADCC – Declaration Southern Africa Towards Economic Liberalisation
SADC	Treaty of the Southern African Development Community
SADC	Protocol on Tribunals and the Rules of Procedure
SADC	Agreement on Amending the Treaty of the SADC
SCO	Declaration on the Establishment of the Shanghai Cooperation Organization
SCO	Charter of the Shanghai Cooperation Organization
SCO	Treaty on Long-Term Good Neighborliness, Friendship and Cooperation Between the Member States of the Shanghai Cooperation Organization
SEECP	Sofia Declaration on Good-Neighbourly Relations, Stability, Security and Cooperation in the Balkans
SEECP	Charter on Good Neighborly Relations, Stability, and Security (Bucharest Charter)
SELA	Panama Convention
SELA	Headquarters Agreement
SELA	Reglamento de la Secretaría Permanente
SELA	Arrangement aimed at improving the provisions of the Headquarters Agreement
SICA	ODECA – Charter of the Organization of Central American States (San Salvador Charter)
SICA	ODECA – Tratado Multilateral de Libre Comercio e Integracion Economica Centroamericana
SICA	CACM – Central American Economic Free Trade Agreement
SICA	ODECA – Charter of the Organization of Central American States
SICA	Tegucigalpa Protocol to the Charter of the Organization of Central American States
SICA	Protocolo al Tratado General de Integracion Economica Centroamericana (Protocolo de Guatemala)
SICA	Tratado de la Integracion Social Centroamericana (Tratado de San Salvador)
SICA	Enmienda al Protocolo al Tratado General de Integracion Economica Centroamericana (Protocolo de Guatemala) (2002)
UEMOA	Treaty Establishing a West African Monetary Union
UEMOA	Convention of the West African Customs Union
UEMOA	Treaty instituting the West African Economic Community
UEMOA	Traité de l'UMOA
UEMOA	Traité de l'UEMOA
UEMOA	Traité revisé de l'UEMOA
UEMOA	Traité portant création du parlement de l'UEMOA
UEMOA	Traité de l'UMOA

UNASUR	CSN – Declaración del Cusco sobre la Comunidad Sudamericanade Naciones
UNASUR	South American Union of Nations Constitutive Treaty
UNASUR	Reglamento General de UNASUR
Union State	Charter
WEU	The Brussels Treaty
WEU	Modified Brussels Treaty
WEU	Rome Declaration
WNC	Charter for Vestnordisk Rad

9. Informal institutions and formalised non-state actor engagement: analysing G7 and G20 outreach processes

Diane Schumann

1 INTRODUCTION

The number of informal arrangements and their importance in global governance has been rising. In fact, they have become so prominent that their existence 'reshuffles power and influence in world society, not only among states, ... but also between states and civil society' (Conzelmann 2012). States started to find ways to operate outside of existing formal structures, seeking more flexibility, effectiveness, and at the same time, less accountability. Operating without binding agreements, official charters and structures, however, typically means less inclusiveness for external stakeholders as there are no intuitive interfaces for non-member states or non-state actors. Nevertheless, two of the most influential informal intergovernmental institutions, the Group of Seven (G7)[1] and the Group of Twenty (G20), have developed extensive processes intended to increase their inclusiveness of various non-state actors. Both of these 'Gs' are surrounded by numerous so-called Engagement Groups, in which different sets of stakeholders meet and discuss policy recommendations.

Even though the informal G-system 'has traditionally demonstrated little systematic regard for public opinion' and 'the avenues of public participation, consultation, or input ... have been minimal' (Slaughter 2013), their Engagement Groups have come to play a routinised part in the Gs' annual calendar. This proliferation is even more perplexing when considering that these groups, while officially acknowledged by the respective G, are mostly self-organised and operate fairly informally themselves. Every year they have to

[1] The G7 became the G8 when Russia was a member between 1998 and 2014. In this article, the term G7 will be used as an overarching term, and G8 will be used to refer to the group in that respective time frame.

rebuild themselves and negotiate relations and support with their G-presidency. At the same time, they have become almost independent actors with a voice that even secured their existence in non-democratic host countries such as Saudi Arabia. Given the overall informal context, data on the Engagement Groups is not very accessible. Their websites are sometimes slowly updated and are annually overwritten without providing an archive, and their social media presence is incoherent. Detailed information on internal processes, such as leadership selection or funding, is not generally published. Hence, concise and summarising information on the processes is rarely available and warrants reconstructive efforts in this chapter.

The G7 and the G20 serve as valuable case studies to observe inclusiveness under informality as they both have assumed prominent roles as agenda-setters and global coordinators. Hence, this chapter focuses on understanding and reconstructing the practices of the Engagement Groups as well as their relation to the G7 and the G20, with a strong focus on the larger and very active civil society groups, the Civil7 (C7) and Civil20 (C20), answering the question how conditions of informality influence formalised non-state actor engagement. Research reveals two particular interdependencies that characterise these G-Engagement Groups and their capacities, which will be analysed within this study. First, Engagement Groups on the one hand rely on acceptance and institutionalisation into the G-process in order to receive financial support and direct personal interaction with G-representatives. On the other hand, it has become obvious that close relations can be used to control criticism and interfere with the Engagement Group process. Secondly, operating within a rotating presidency system means that there is a risk that presiding states misuse Engagement Groups as marketing tools, while this exact desire to promote a positive image has also turned out to advance civil society.

This chapter first introduces the concept of informality in global governance as well as the initiation and consolidation of the G7 and G20 and their role within global governance. The following section concentrates on the development of non-state actor relations with the two Gs and highlights how respective outreach processes became more formalised. The analysis then illustrates the development, varying degrees of formalisation, and institutionalisation of Engagement Groups under conditions of informality, counterintuitively indicating that informality has certain advantages when it comes to non-state actor participation. Results show that especially the civil society groups, C7 and C20, are torn between needing financial support and acceptance without being co-opted or silenced but that, at the same time, they are able to highlight or even progress the need for civic space even in non-democratic countries. For the presiding country, the importance of promoting a positive image seems to be a crucial part of the consolidation of the formalised non-state actor engagement within the informal G-system.

2 INFORMALITY IN GLOBAL GOVERNANCE

2.1 Informal institutions in global governance

Informality in global governance can refer to different aspects; it can describe the informality of institutions, within institutions, or around institutions (Westerwinter, Abbott, and Biersteker 2021), or in other terms, it can refer to the informality of actors, processes, or outcomes (Pauwelyn 2012). Here, the focus lies on informal intergovernmental organisations (IIGOs). An institution can be described as relatively informal when its norms, rules and social practices are rather implicit, and when compliance cannot be enforced against resistance (Daase 2009). IIGOs are further built around shared expectations about their purpose but lack the foundation of a formalised agreement. They have explicitly associated members participating in regular meetings but no permanent staff, headquarters, or an independent secretariat (Vabulas and Snidal 2013). Participation in informal arrangements often depends on particular resources and not on a formal mandate (Conzelmann 2012).

Informal arrangements in global governance have increased both in number and importance (Luckhurst, 2016). The rise of IIGOs started around the 1970s when their number increased from almost zero to around 30 in the early 2000s and up to 82 in 2014 (Vabulas and Snidal, 2013). Informality is also spreading to policy areas that were traditionally formalised, such as security (Daase 2009, p. 295). In a parallel development, the proliferation of formal intergovernmental organisations (FIGOs) slowed down. It seems that the perception of international cooperation becoming more and more 'gridlocked' kindled the rise of IIGOs as a way forward. Even though informal practices have at times been seen as a downfall of formal organisations, they can and should be seen as a way of innovating within existing rigid structures that cannot be easily reformed. The emergence of informal arrangements should therefore be perceived as 'a deliberate choice' or 'rational strategy' specifically chosen 'to deal with uncertainty and to recover freedom of action' (Daase 2009).

Early on, the advantages of informality were perceived to be 'simplicity, speed, flexibility, and confidentiality' (Aust 1986). Arrangements that are not based on formal treaties provide more leeway to adjust goals or strategies along the way, and can also be more easily abandoned (Vabulas and Snidal 2013). Especially in situations of high uncertainty, IIGOs can be conducive to establishing common understandings and coordination, without demanding strong commitments. Because they allow for more flexible involvement and composition of members or participants, they can become a door opener for negotiations. Actors can more easily come together informally, without the need to include all actors present in a FIGO and without having to adhere to existing rules or expectations. This also means it can be easier for actors to leave negotiations or to exclude others from negotiations for breaking norms (Bendiek and Neyer 2016). An example of the latter is the exclusion of Russia from the G8 following their invasion of Crimea in 2014 (Daase 2009). Including only actors who are 'seen as decisive for a resolution' and are willing to work on the issue could enhance effectiveness. Informal arrangements are also used to bypass FIGOs if these are blocked by vetoes (Conzelmann 2012; Rinke and Schneckener 2013). The lack of bureaucracy can enable shorter time frames, further decreasing overall transaction costs (Greven 2005). Additionally, due to the lack of a superordinate secretariat, member states are also not compromising their own authority and remain in control of information (Vabulas and Snidal 2013; Daase 2009). As there are no headquarters or independent staff, IIGOs often operate through summits, organised as meetings for the member states' heads of government. This offers state leaders informal and non-binding, but personal and regular opportunities for exchange. In-person meetings are thought to be able to build 'inter-personal familiarity, trust, and mutual confidence', which can be beneficial in times of crises or high uncertainty (Vabulas and Snidal 2013). A popular solution to facilitate these summits is the rotation of chairmanship among member states. Organisational tasks are assumed by national government officials or delegated to a formal organisation, handing them 'some temporary independent decision capacity', without fully reaching the characteristics of an independent bureaucracy (Vabulas and Snidal 2013).

However, informality has also raised legitimacy concerns, as negotiations are not typically accessible to outsiders, often remain undocumented, and results are neither binding nor based on transparent rules. IIGOs thus rely on their relatively higher output legitimacy; their potential gain in effectiveness and enhanced problem-solving capacity comes at the cost of decreased transparency and accountability and arguably also legitimacy, as they are not fulfilling the long-sought ideal of more democratic governance (Rinke and Schneckener 2013; Greven 2005; Daase 2016; Reh 2014).

2.2 The G-system in global governance

The G7/G8 and the G20 are among the most prominent and most influential IIGOs. Both of them emerged in times of financial crises with a strong economic focus and have since become fora discussing a broad variety of global issues, including finance, but also health, climate, and security. They are not based on a formal treaty, do not follow a constitution, and do not have a permanent secretariat, staff, or budget. Instead, the various summits and a plethora of preceding meetings are organised and headed by a presiding host country, which is rotated annually. Always intended to remain informal, both Gs lie at the 'more institutionalised end' of informality (Vabulas and Snidal 2013).

The G7 emerged 'as an informal nonbureaucratic forum of the leaders of the most advanced market-economy countries' in the 1970s (Hajnal 2018). The club format, as it is sometimes called, was supposed to more easily deal with and solve protracted economic issues and take over a coordinating and steering role in global economic governance (Conzelmann 2012). The common denominator among the participating states, apart from economic power, were the shared norms of democracy, market economy, and the value of human rights (Gstöhl 2012). The idea of creating a 'network of like-minded members' was somewhat softened when Russia was included in 1998, extending the format to the G8. Russia's membership was, however, suspended again following the annexation of Crimea in 2014 (Morin et al. 2019; Hajnal 1999). Originally meant to function as an ad hoc instrument to tackle the financial crisis, the format persisted and increased in scope, becoming 'well-choreographed routines' (Vabulas and Snidal 2013), involving an increasing network of ministers, civil servants, international organisations, and CSOs (Gstöhl 2012).

The G20 was initially formed at the level of finance ministers and central bank governors during the financial crisis in 1997/1998. Facing the next crisis ten years later, the format was elevated to heads of state level in November 2008 (Benson and Zürn 2019; Slaughter 2013; Wouters and van Kerckhoven 2011). The G20 roughly represents the 19 countries with the highest GDP, but their selection also carefully followed political interests, mostly of the United States. In total, the G20 represents a large majority of the 'world's gross product, trade, and economic growth and, importantly, 60% of the world's poor' (Cooper and Thakur 2013). The 20th member is the European Union (EU) and, as of 2024, the African Union (AU) is included as a new member with the goal of strengthening 'the agenda of the countries of the Global South' (G20 Brazil 22 January 2024). The first G20 summits in 2008 and 2009 consolidated the group's image as a crisis committee and, since then, the G20 has become one of the most prominent and most influential IIGOs (Benson and Zürn 2019; Roger 2020).

Elevating the G20 to leaders' level in 2008 was also a reaction to the criticism that the G8 was an 'unrepresentative clique' (Slaughter 2013). It had become clear that global issues could no longer be in the hands of 'an exclusive club of Western, industrialised countries' (Cooper and Antkiewicz 2010). In principle, all members within the G20 are equal, and the inclusion of emerging economies is described as 'a slow and incremental shift toward greater participation' (Wouters and van Kerckhoven 2011). The troika system, a coordination between the three presidencies of the past, present, and future, explicitly hands power to different members: 'After centuries of one-sided Western domination … new voices are being heard in global governance' (Cooper and Pouliot

2015). This way, the G20 can have a bridging function between 'the established North and the "rising" powerhouses of the global South' (Cooper 2010). Given the informal design, however, checks and balances that could ensure equality among the member states are lacking. Some authors hence point out that this could emphasise differences in status or reinforce existing power asymmetries, so that the middle powers who had hoped to gain more influence could still face disadvantages within G20 negotiation processes owing to the stronger bargaining power of the larger developed economies (Benson and Zürn 2019; Daase 2009; Cooper and Pouliot 2015). Larger heterogeneity of members also bears the danger that results will end up 'being inefficient and with little ambition', simply because they will always only reach the lowest common denominator (Bendiek and Neyer 2016). Furthermore, G20 policies still reach far beyond its member states and its decisions impact people that are not represented within the forum. As a result, smaller countries and those from regions that are less represented criticise the concentration of power and emphasise that agenda setting of global governance should happen within the UN (Cooper 2010; Luckhurst 2016).

The organisational setup of both Gs is relatively similar. The presidency rotates among the members in a specific order, and the presiding country is responsible for setting up a temporary secretariat. Close coordination within the troika ensures a degree of consistency and organisational learning despite the informality (Vollmer 1996). Most of the preparatory and administrative work is done by dedicated Sherpas – national governmental officers that form the Gs' consistent operational basis (Gstöhl 2012). Despite not having formal authority to enforce or implement their own policies, the G-fora gained decisive influence within global governance (Viola 2015). While the G-system was partially created as a space for informal, personal dialogue, it was also always motivated by the idea of coordinating and steering global governance (Slaughter 2021; Viola 2015). As a 'meta-authority' or 'global playmaker', especially the G20 found itself in a position to delegate between various existing (economic) international organisations and influence their agenda (Benson and Zürn 2019; Wouters and van Kerckhoven 2011).

Through this form of governance, defined as orchestration, the G20 is able to influence FIGOs without actually having any legally binding authority to do so (Viola 2015; Downie 2022). FIGOs then might partially and temporarily act as so-called intermediaries on behalf of the G20 (compare Abbott, Levi-Faur, and Snidal 2017). This does, importantly, not imply any form of coercion as there is no formal hierarchy. Instead, the mechanism works through 'shared regulatory objectives [and] intermediaries report to the G20, … on a voluntary basis' (Viola 2015). In-depth research by Downie shows that FIGOs are actually very willing to cooperate with the G20, suggesting that close cooperation is potentially advantageous for an organisation's reputation or overall legitimacy, based on financial considerations given the economic power of G-members, and it could also be rooted in a desire to, in turn, influence the G-agenda (Downie 2022; Wouters and van Kerckhoven 2011). In fact, 'G20' negotiators expressed frustration that IOs had too much influence … and some G20 working groups have sought to limit the role IOs play' (Downie 2022). Understanding this network structure of the G7 and G20 is important for the analysis of their outreach activities with non-state actors in the form of the various Engagement Groups (Cooper 2019).

3 THE G-SYSTEM AND NON-STATE ACTORS

3.1 Developing and formalising non-state actor relations

As IIGOs emerged on the global stage, non-governmental actors needed to adapt their advocacy strategies, and hence the initial rapprochement between the G7/G8 and the various non-state actors shows a learning curve. Especially CSOs might not have early on realised the 'power and importance of the G7 as a discrete entity' (Hajnal 2000). Non-state actor lobbying began to target the G7 in the 1980s. The first lobby groups were not CSOs but instead representatives from the realms of business, labour and agriculture. Early forms of lobbying mostly happened on a country-level basis and were not globally coordinated. The term 'NGO' was not used by the G7 in their official declarations until 1995 (Hajnal 2000). Non-state actor engagement towards the G8 solidified and became 'more sophisticated' around the turn of the millennium (Hajnal 2019). This period is also characterised by major contestation against the global economic institutions as embodiments of neo-liberal globalisation by social movements relating to the Alter Globalisation Movement (AGM). Major backlash against the G8 became visible in 2001, when between 70,000 and 200,000 protesters opposed the leaders' summit in Italy (Hajnal 2000). In light of these highly mediatised demonstrations, and under the immediate impression of the 9/11 attacks, the Canadian presidency invited civil society to a dialogue forum in 2002, marking the start of a more formal relationship between G8 and civil society (Hajnal 2019; Hack 2019). From here on out, with few exceptions, dialogue processes in the form of the Engagement Groups were regularly organised. Following the first civil society meetings, the engagement process of the G7/G8 was broadened and, as of 2023, the G7 entertains a total of six Engagement Groups (Business 7, Civil 7, Labour 7, Science 7, Women 7, and Youth 7).

The mutual learning process continued when the G20 was elevated to the leaders' level. Civil society actors had to develop a substantive network and obtain specific knowledge of the various opaque and multi-level working processes in order to achieve any kind of impact. G20 summits also became stages of large-scale and, at times violent demonstrations, as was the case in Hamburg in 2017 (BBC, 7 July 2017; Reuters, 5 July 2017). Diminishing protest activities in the subsequent years might not necessarily be caused by greater acceptance but rather by different protest cultures, more repressive governments, and the outbreak of the Covid-19 pandemic in 2020.

As of 2023, the G20 has officially recognised a total of 11 different Engagement Groups (see Table 9.1). The first group to be officially recognised was the Business 20 (B20) in Korea in 2010. Under the Korean presidency in 2010, the G20's agenda was markedly expanded with the inclusion of development and environmental issues. As these topics correspond to the typical concerns of CSOs, civil society action increased (Hajnal 2019). In the following year, the Labour 20 (L20) was founded by the International Trade Union Confederation (ITUC) and the OECD's Trade Union Advisory Committee (TUAC) as a space for trade unions. In 2012, the Think 20 (T20) was created for and by representatives of academic institutions and think tanks, and the Youth 20 (Y20) emerged as a forum for young people. Civil society actors were in the beginning mostly involved via demonstrations and protests (Koch 2016). An initial meeting on developing a civil society group was held in 2010 in Korea, where CSOs were able to consult with Korean Sherpas and government officials, but the Civil 20 (C20) was not initiated until 2013 (Hajnal 2019). Further Engagement Groups established and officially acknowledged were the Women 20 (W20) in 2015, Science 20 (S20) in 2017, Urban 20 (U20) in 2018,

Table 9.1 Development of G20 engagement groups

Year of recognition	Presiding country	Name of engagement group
2010	Korea	Business 20 (B20)
2011	France	Labour 20 (L20)
2012	Mexico	Think 20 (T20)
2012	Mexico	Youth 20 (Y20)
2013	Russia	Civil 20 (C20)
2015	Turkey	Women 20 (W20)
2017	Germany	Science 20 (S20)
2018	Argentina	Urban 20 (U20)
2022	Indonesia	Parliament 20 (P20)
2022	Indonesia	Supreme Audit Institutions 20 (SAI20) Religion 20 (not continued in 2023)
2023	India	Startup20

and finally the Parliament 20 (P20), the Supreme Audit Institutions (SAI20) in 2022, and the Start Up 20 in 2023. There is no official process for Engagement Groups to become acknowledged; it can either be a top-down process initiated by the respective presiding country or can happen through advocacy (interview C20 member, 20 October 2023).[2]

3.2 Dialogue fora as legitimation strategy in global economic governance

Today, all FIGOs engage with a diverse set of stakeholders to varying degrees. By utilising their stakeholders' expertise, they are looking to increase their trustworthiness and legitimacy as well as their responsiveness and policy implementation. These stakeholders can broadly be differentiated into governmental, commercial, and non-commercial actors (OECD 2021). Within the field of study of international organisations, this trend of increasing accessibility for civil society actors has become known as the 'opening-up' (Tallberg et al. 2013). This chapter aims to further the research on how this stakeholder inclusion works under conditions of informality. It focuses on non-governmental actors that are involved in the engagement processes of the G7 and G20, with a particular focus on civil society organisations (CSOs). CSOs are defined as 'non-profit, non-violent pressure groups that pursue certain public goals and that, directly or indirectly, seek to influence outcomes in international politics' (Dobusch and Quack, 2009). Civil society more broadly is understood as the overarching political sphere in which the norms and policies of governance can be challenged (Schnabel and Scholte 2003).

From the various modalities that exist to engage stakeholders (compare OECD 2021), especially international economic institutions have decided on the implementation of dialogue fora to create a space of interaction and engagement with civil society actors. Their implementation is understood as an explicit legitimation strategy towards this set of stakeholders. The study of legitimation strategies has a procedural perception of 'how IOs actively build their legitimacy' and is interested in how they try to actively intervene and shape the legitimacy beliefs among their various stakeholders (Lenz and Söderbaum 2023). Early such fora were implemented by the OECD in 2000, the WTO in 2002, and the World Bank and IMF in 2002. The inclusion of

[2] In addition to these officially affiliated groups, there are varying number of independent Engagement Groups. These groups either deliberately renounce official affiliation to maintain their independence, such as the G20 Interfaith Forum and Foundation 20, or they are advocating to eventually gain official recognition, such as the Values 20, or have been founded as a sign of dissatisfaction with the official groups, such as the Peoples 20 in 2023.

civil society actors was a novelty for international economic organisations who were, for a long time, able to primarily build their authority on their problem-solving capacities and expertise while doubting the relevant expertise of civil society (interview C20 committee member, 10 August 2021). Dialogue fora, in particular, are based on the idea of deliberative democracy and are seen as a reaction to widespread protest and the acceptance of civil society as a crucial legitimacy constituency. They are supposed to enable direct and regular engagement and open dialogue between critics and organisational representatives (compare Coni-Zimmer, Deitelhoff and Schumann 2023).

In this light, the official acknowledgement of the G-Engagement Groups is seen as a legitimation strategy, directly targeting the criticism of lacking accountability and greater inclusiveness of external stakeholders (Slaughter 2013; Koch 2016; Hilbrich and Schwab 2018; Slaughter 2015). Including a wider range of actors is supposed to repaint the Gs' image as 'an illegitimate and secretive club of wealthy states' by providing access to 'a wider array of perspectives and information' (Slaughter 2015). Outreach formats enable the inclusion of civil society groups that are affected by an institution's policies but are not otherwise represented within its decision-making policies, and can allow for the inclusion of civil society from countries that 'lack democratic structures and civic spaces' (Slaughter 2015; also compare OECD, 2021 for modalities of stakeholder engagement). Thus, theoretically, dialogue fora have the potential to increase an institution's inclusiveness and thus input legitimacy by enabling broader participation and inclusion of relevant perspectives and can also fulfil a credible monitoring and evaluative role (Koch 2019; Hilbrich and Schwab 2018).

Despite their longevity and seeming popularity, dialogue fora are also frequently subject to criticism. The idea of implementing participative fora is seen as a chance to make an institution appear accessible and representative without it actually having to implement changes. Researchers have often suspected dialogue fora to be a means of co-optation, criticising them for possibly becoming 'a sham ritual', a purely symbolic exercise in which participants could end up being restricted in 'their freedom to question and challenge' the organising institution (Slaughter 2015). The official inclusion of external voices could be used to create a controlled environment where criticism can be supervised and monitored (Slaughter 2015). The inclusion of a variety of external participants could also lead to a broader diffusion and amplification of an institution's ideas and policies, leading to a solidification and stabilisation of its specific ideas and policies. The Engagement Groups could thus be seen as 'efforts to entrench the existence of the G20 … in a way that enhances the legitimacy of the G20 without constraining its power and influence' (Slaughter 2019). Despite persistent criticism, the Engagement Group processes not only remain popular, but their number has been growing over the years, and high participation numbers confirm that stakeholders value the process enough to invest a considerable amount of financial and human resources to be part of the process (Luckhurst 2016).

4 NON-STATE ACTOR ENGAGEMENT UNDER CONDITIONS OF INFORMALITY

When the consolidation and disseminating influence of the G7 is described as paradoxical and puzzling (Fioretos 2019; Gstöhl 2012), and the G20 is perceived as 'a unique twenty-first century club' (Luckhurst 2016: 190), this certainly also accounts for the existence and flourishing of the various Engagement Group processes. First of all, the informal nature of the G-system, the lack of a dedicated outreach department or team means there is no intuitive interface to deal with non-state actors. Nevertheless, a whole network of outreach groups spans around the two Gs. These groups also developed, or copied, a similar informal operating structure to the Gs, which influences their organisational learning capacities, cohesion, and consequentiality. Additionally, the Engagement Groups' informality means that their processes also remain opaque and subject to change – every presidency in the end creates its own Engagement Group processes, and relationships and networks between stakeholders and institutional representatives have to be formed anew.

On the one hand, this lack of transparency and dedicated staff can make stakeholder engagement more complicated and less effective. On the other hand, rotating presidencies could also offer advantages. Dealing with governments instead of FIGO bureaucracies could mean that stakeholders can use existing networks for their advocacy. Holding summits in alternating countries can also increase the regional diversity of stakeholders who can actively engage. Additionally, a G-presidency comes with a lot of global (media) attention and presents an opportunity for a country to shape and promote its global reputation, and it will likely use the opportunity to present themselves as open and inclusive towards civil society (interview C20 Panellist, 22 January 2021; Cooper 2019).

The Engagement Groups are not permanently or formally institutionalised into the G-processes. Institutionalisation is seen as an important feature of a dialogue forum in order for it to be able to actually impact an institution's policies (Coni-Zimmer, Deitelhoff and Schumann 2023). Hence it would be expected that a closer inclusion of the Engagement Groups into the Gs' routines would strengthen their reputation, increase funding, and establish greater accountability of G-representatives. Real-world practices, however, show that close relations bear the danger of undermining the groups' autonomy by allowing for strong interference from host countries. It would also be plausible for non-democratic states to simply not hold or acknowledge the Engagement

Groups, as organisations with more authoritarian states are generally more closed to civil society engagement than those with democratic member states (Uhlin 2016). However, it is within non-democratic states such as Russia and Saudi Arabia where Engagement Group processes have shown their strengths.

In an exploratory study, the interplay and interdependence between autonomy and institutionalisation will be analysed, focusing on the consequences and motivations of changing relations between the Engagement Groups and the heterogeneous member states. The analysis is based on documents published by the Engagement Groups,[3] virtual participation in C20 and C7 working groups and summits from 2020–2022, in-person participation at the C20 summit in 2022, as well as expert interviews with G20, C7, and C20 representatives. To further substantiate the research with regard to the perception of the Engagement Groups by the G7/8 and G20, a content analysis of G-communiqués was conducted. These communiqués (sometimes also called chair's summary or leaders' declaration) constitute the Gs' main, tangible output and present a summary of the recent presidency. The length of the communiqués varies, with a maximum of circa 40 pages. The analysis includes annual communiqués from the G7/G8 from 2000–2022 and G20 from 2008–2022 (a total of 41 documents). The content analysis was used to identify any statements relating to the Engagement Groups in particular and to quantify when and how often the individual groups were mentioned and to analyse references regarding specific policy work or collaborations.

4.1 Tracing G-engagement group practices

Emerging within an informal environment, the Engagement Groups also operate via a rotating leadership system, establish working groups, and hold annual summits. Taking the C20 as an example, this means that every year, a different CSO takes over the lead. Forming a troika, similar to G7 and G20, the leaders of the past and future presidency are also involved, which is supposed to ensure a minimum of organisational learning and cohesion. The Engagement Group leadership, consisting of a chair, secretariat, and international steering committee, is then responsible for forming the operational units, the various working groups. These tend to mirror those of the respective G in an effort to create workable interfaces while also aiming to react to current issues such as the COVID-19 pandemic in 2020 or Russia's reinvigorated attack on Ukraine in 2022.[4] They are led by experts in the respective field; a person belonging to

[3] Many relevant documents are provided by the Toronto Research Groups on the G7/G8 and G20: http://www.g20.utoronto.ca/ & http://www.g7.utoronto.ca/.

[4] In 2022, the C20, for example implemented the following working groups: Vaccines Access & Health; Environmental, Climate Justice, & Energy Transition;

an organisation with significant experience in the topic and in global advocacy (interview C20 presidency member, 04 March 2022). Working groups hold a varying number of meetings throughout the year to develop policy recommendations. Their recommendations are then collected by the Engagement Group's leadership and compiled into an annual communiqué. The communiqué is handed over to a (preferably high-ranking) G-representative at the annual Engagement Group summit, which is mostly a networking and publicity event. The overall goal of the communiqué is thus not only its content but also its function as a publicity instrument. Importantly, the Engagement Group summits are not connected to the G7 and G20 leaders' summits, but tend to happen weeks or even months in advance. An exception to this is the Business Engagement Group, which is often deliberately held just prior to the leaders' summit so as to facilitate the participation of political representatives (Koch 2016).

Interestingly, the C7 for a long time operated in a less formalised fashion than the C20. This is also reflected in the G7 and G8 communiqués, as there is actually no reference to any Engagement Group until 2017. Up until 2022, there was only minimal governmental support from the G7/8 and minimal international coordination on the side of the CSOs who are organising the C7. The German G7 presidency in 2022 marked a turning point as two CSOs were officially mandated to lead the C7, which, for example, meant they received funding through the German Agency for International Cooperation GmbH (GIZ) on behalf of the German Federal Ministry for Economic Cooperation and Development (interview C7 presidency member, 10 August 2022; VENRO 2022a). For the first time, the C7 also formed an international steering committee. Before, leadership positions had been mostly restricted to national representatives, and participation was limited to CSOs from G7 member countries. Reportedly, around 500 NGO representatives from 'more than' 40 countries participated in the C7 process in 2022 (interview C7 presidency member, 10 August; 2022 (VENRO 2022b). The civil society team in Japan in 2023 is mostly copying this process, indicating its consolidation. The CSO leading the process in Japan was, however, not officially mandated, showing that there are different treatments and varying levels of integration even within the more homogeneous G7. It is likely that the overall democratic landscape in the G7 has caused the lack of formalisation to begin with. It is plausible that the organising CSOs did not deem it necessary to become further organised, simply because they were already operating within established structures. Another

---

Gender Equality & Disability; Taxation & Sustainable Financing; Education, Digitalization, & Civic Space; Sustainable Development Goals & Humanitarian; Anti-Corruption (source on file with author).

possibility is that, since the G20 Engagement Groups were established later, they simply started out in a more organised fashion.

This analysis shows that the C7 has become more inclusive over time, as it opened up to more regionally diverse participants. The C20 was open to CSOs from beyond the G20 membership from the beginning, but it still does not regularly reach global representativeness – the rotating presidency, however, at least facilitates regionally diverse participation (Coni-Zimmer, Deitelhoff and Schumann, 2023). Nevertheless, there is room for almost all Engagement Groups to become even more inclusive. There were voices calling for the C20 to become more inclusive of conservative voices that are often under-represented in civil society processes (interview with a C20 committee member, 24 February 2022). The Women Engagement Group (W20) is also is aware that they need to foster participation of 'black women, young women, women of indigenous backgrounds, and women from developing countries' (Women20 Germany, 2017). Regarding the Youth 20 (Y20) Engagement Group, there is criticism that they only enable participation of a 'tiny elite of young people' (interview with a C20 presidency member, 4 March 2022).

The business and labour groups (B20 and L20), on the other hand, are typically in the hands of existing networks and associations, through which they can certainly claim representativeness of their members, even though their composition is less diverse than, for example that of the C20 (Hajnal 2019; Bertelsmann Stiftung 2018). At the same time, they achieve a higher degree of formalisation and more consistent funding, which has allowed the B20 and T20 to be 'a bit more aware of the process' and enabled them to be 'more timely in their inputs' (interview with G20 representatives, 22 November 2021). The C20, on the other hand, was said to lack this kind of knowledge and structure, resulting in their policy recommendations being published very late in the G-calendar, making it almost impossible for G20 officials to react to or implement these recommendations (interview with G20 representatives, 22 November 2021). The informal structure of the Engagement Groups thus impacts knowledge internalisation and resources, and consequently capacities and impact, and also replicates existing power asymmetries.

The relatively high – and increasing – number of Engagement Groups is perceived as ambiguous. On the one hand, it can be argued that a higher number of groups increases their representativeness and thus the respective G's inclusiveness. On the other hand, it can become problematic as the groups' plurality necessarily leads to competition over resources provided by the Gs in form of not only financial support but also attention paid by G-representatives, who have 'to absorb the many hundreds of recommendations the various engagement groups' (Kirton and Warren 2021) and will eventually have to compromise (interview with C20 Committee Member, 10 August 2021).

4.2 Varying relations: between support and interference

In addition to the varying degrees of formalisation, varying degrees of institutionalisation into the G-process make the Engagement Groups vulnerable not only to a lack of support but also to potential interference and control by presiding states. Given the rotating presidencies within the G-system, relations between the presiding country and the Engagement Groups have to be newly negotiated every year. Theoretically, a country could decide not to include or recognise certain Engagement Groups at all, but their routinisation and popularity make this unlikely (Coni-Zimmer, Deitelhoff and Schumann 2023). While it could be assumed that a closer relationship and formalisation of relations could strengthen the Engagement Group process and its impact, research shows that governments also use a closer relationship, or a higher degree of institutionalisation to interfere with the process.

Varying degrees of support become apparent, for example when looking at financial support provided by the host country. For instance, the Australian government granted $250,000 to the C20 (Koch 2016). During the Argentinian presidency in 2017, the civil society process was not funded very well, sidelining the C20 and especially the participation of international organisations (Bertelsmann Stiftung 2018). The Turkish presidency delayed the recognition of the C20, and the People's Republic of China had initially not planned to include the C20 at all, ending up with an engagement process that largely only included national organisations (Koch 2016). The provision of sufficient financial resources proved especially important during the COVID-19 pandemic in 2020, when G20 president Saudi Arabia had the capacity to set up the first fully virtual C20 process and summit. The digitalisation showed to make the process more inclusive, enabling affordable attendance for a larger group of participants (interview with C20 working group member, 26 July 2021).

The diversity of relations established between the presiding countries and the Engagement Groups becomes further visible when analysing the symbolic potential of the attendance of G20 representatives at Engagement Group summits, which varies across presidencies and across groups. As there are no headquarters, personal exchange and engagement cannot be simply facilitated through physical proximity, as it works for the WTO or the OECD. The first C8 Summit during the Russian presidency in 2006 was attended by President Vladimir Putin, who reportedly aimed to broadcast the image of an open and inclusive Russian presidency, while at the same time using the C8 process to monitor civil society engagement (interviews with C20 Presidency Member, 04 March 2022; C20 Committee Member, 10 August 2021). In Germany in 2017, the C20 communiqué was handed to Chancellor Angela Merkel, and in Argentina in 2018, it was handed to President Mauricio Macri. In Japan in 2019, Prime Minister Abe only attended a smaller side-meeting and not the

C20 Summit itself (interview with C20 Committee Member, 10 August 2021). Neither in Italy, Indonesia, nor India was the C20 Summit attended by the respective head of state, leaving C20 members disappointed (interview with C20 presidency member, 04 March 2022).

Moreover, not all of the Engagement Groups receive the same attention from G-representatives. Direct engagement with G20 representatives, for example, is noticeably easier for the B20 than for the C20. The B20 had 'far better access to [G20] deliberations and decision-making processes than civil society and trade unions' (Martens 2017; interview with C20 Presidency Member, 04 March 2022). This is apparent in the regular attendance of B-Summits by high-ranking officials, including state leaders, as well as in the consistent number of references to the B-Groups in both Gs' communiqués, which refer to the B-Groups a total of 17 times. These references, used as a proxy for demonstrated interest and engagement, were significantly lower for the remaining Engagement Groups: W7/W20 and L7/L20 were referenced nine times, Y-Groups were mentioned seven times, T-Groups and C-Groups six times, S-Groups four times, and SAI20 and P20 both once. The number of references is not only scarce but their content is also mostly superficial. More than half of them (34) are simply notes of general appreciation without highlighting particular areas or issues of collaboration. Hence, I disagree with Luckhurst's assessment that the 'G20 leaders' declarations have praised the role of engagement forums' (2019: 7). Instead, I find the references to indicate virtue signaling instead of in-depth exchange and interest. Hajnal concludes that 'civil society's influence would be greatly enhanced if the G20 accorded CSOs the same status that it has bestowed on the business sector' (Hajnal 2019). The close ties between G and B representatives are seen as questionable, especially by civil society actors who accuse the Gs to promote neo-liberal globalisation while disregarding development and human rights. In this respect, it should also be noted that the quality and quantity of direct interactions between the G20 and the different Engagement Groups are not published in any way and are difficult to trace.

5 CONCLUSION

Participative outreach processes with the objective to enable non-state actor inclusion in intergovernmental organisations have been implemented by many (economic) institutions as an explicit legitimation strategy. Even though the institutions do prioritise the advancement of these dialogue fora, and practitioners and researchers criticise their potential to control or silence criticism, the format remains popular (Coni-Zimmer, Deitelhoff and Schumann 2023). It is even more puzzling that the idea of entertaining and organising such fora also proliferated within the informal G7 and G20. Despite a lack of dedicated departments or staff for outreach and operating within changing conditions of a rotating presidency, both Gs developed a whole network of various non-state actor Engagement Groups.

Even though it became clear that increased inclusiveness of civil society is not a priority of the two Gs, the analysis has shown that the Engagement Groups were able to achieve a permanent and prominent role within the G-system, enabling inclusiveness for a broad set of external stakeholders. An important finding of this chapter is how the rotating presidencies influence the Engagement Group processes in different ways. Relations and resources have to be negotiated with the presiding country every year, which means that governments can support or disadvantage different groups. At the same time, the alternating locations of the G-summits also mean that each year their focus shifts to different regions and thus different issues. The study shows that practices of the G-Engagement Group are primarily influenced by the two factors of their degree of formalisation and the institutionalisation into the respective G-process, which can be influenced by the presiding country's form of government.

Formalisation mostly impacts a group's capacities for organisational learning, cohesion, and impact. More diverse civil society groups have greater difficulties achieving strong and timely impact because they require more internal organisational effort while also having fewer (financial) resources than, for example, the Business Engagement Groups. Additionally, Business Engagement Groups profit from much higher interest and more intensive direct engagement with G-representatives, which in turn further disadvantages other Engagement Groups in the competition for attention.

Institutionalisation of the outreach processes has been shown to be highly important but also double-edged. A higher degree of both formalisation and institutionalisation of the C7 in Germany has meant increasing support and liability, whereas a close relation can also result in more interference or the sidelining of unwanted participants. It was a higher degree of autonomy, and decisively not closer institutionalisation, that allowed the C20 to negotiate their role under the Saudi Arabian presidency. The annual negotiations with the different G-presidencies have strengthened the Engagement Groups to become almost independent actors, whose standing within the annual G-calendar has been highly routinised. This also means that the Engagement Groups have a marketing value for countries to promote their openness. Overall, it seems that organising formal engagement processes under conditions of informality has helped global civil society to successfully connect and build a strong network surrounding a prominent, influential global platform that is a successful way of ensuring enhanced inclusiveness of both the G7 and G20.

ACKNOWLEDGEMENTS

The author is grateful to the German Research Foundation for funding the research project 'Legitimacy policy through dialogue forums? Global economic institutions and their critics', in the context of which this chapter was written.

REFERENCES

Abbott, K.W., D. Levi-Faur and D. Snidal (2017), 'Theorizing Regulatory Intermediaries', *The ANNALS of the American Academy of Political and Social Science*, Vol. 670, No. 1, pp. 14–35.

Aust, A. (1986), 'The Theory and Practice of Informal International Instruments', *International and Comparative Law Quarterly*, Vol. 35, No. 4, pp. 787–812.

BBC (7 July 2017), *G20 in Hamburg. Who are the Protesters?*, BBC.

Bendiek, A. and J. Neyer (2016), *Nichts für Demokraten. Die G20 zeigt, welche Probleme durch informelles Regieren entstehen,* https://internationalepolitik.de/system/files/article_pdfs/ip_06-2016_bendiek_neyer.pdf, accessed 29 June 2020.

Benson, R. and M. Zürn (2019), 'Untapped Potential. How the G20 Can Strengthen Global Governance', *South African Journal of International Affairs*, Vol. 26, No. 4, pp. 549–562.

Bertelsmann Stiftung (2018), *Die G20: 9 Fakten und Hintergründe. Die G20 wird zwanzig. Zeit für eine Bilanz des Multilateralismus,* EINWURF Factsheet, No. 6.

Coni-Zimmer, M., N. Deitelhoff and D. Schumann (2023), 'The Path of Least Resistance. Why International Institutions Maintain Dialogue Forums', *International Affairs*, Vol. 99, No. 3, pp. 941–961.

Conzelmann, T. (2012), 'Informal Governance in International Relations', in T. Christiansen and C. Neuhold (eds), *International Handbook on Informal Governance,* Edward Elgar Publishing, 2019.

Cooper, A.F. (2010), 'The G20 as an Improvised Crisis Committee and/or a Contested "Steering" Committee for the World', *International Affairs*, Vol. 86, No. 3, pp. 741–757.

Cooper, A.F. (2019), 'The G20 is Dead as a Crisis or Steering Committee: Long Live the G20 as Hybrid Focal Point', *South African Journal of International Affairs*, Vol. 26, No. 4, pp. 505–520.

Cooper, A.F. and A. Antkiewicz (2010), 'G20 for Global Governance. Lessons from G8 Outreach', *Studia Diplomatica*, Vol. 63, No. 2, pp. 91–103, https://www.jstor.org/stable/44838597.

Cooper, A.F. and R. Thakur (2013), *The Group of Twenty (G20),* Global Institutions, Routledge, New York

Cooper, A.F. and V. Pouliot (2015), 'How Much is Global Governance Changing? The G20 as International Practice', *Cooperation and Conflict*, Vol. 50, No. 3, pp. 334–350, https://www.jstor.org/stable/45084293.

Daase, C. (2009), 'Die Informalisierung internationaler Politik. Beobachtungen zum Stand der internationalen Organisationen', in K. Dingwerth, D. Kerwer and A. Nölke (eds), *Die Organisierte Welt. Internationale Beziehungen und Organisationsforschung,* Nomos Verlagsgesellschaft mbH & Co. KG, Baden-Baden, pp. 290–308.

Daase, C. (2016), 'Institutionalisierte Informalität', in M. Albert, N. Deitelhoff and G. Hellmann (eds), *Ordnung und Regieren in der Weltgesellschaft,* Springer VS, Wiesbaden, pp. 309–326.

Dobusch, L. and S. Quack (2009), 'Internationale und nichtstaatliche Organisationen im Wettbewerb um Regulierung. Schauplatz Urheberrecht', in K. Dingwerth, D. Kerwer and A. Nölke (eds), *Die Organisierte Welt. Internationale Beziehungen und Organisationsforschung,* Nomos Verlagsgesellschaft mbH & Co. KG, Baden-Baden, pp. 235–262.

Downie, C. (2022), 'How do Informal International Organizations Govern? The G20 and Orchestration', *International Affairs*, Vol. 98, No. 3, pp. 953–972.

Fioretos, O. (2019), 'Minilateralism and Informality in International Monetary Cooperation', *Review of International Political Economy*, Vol. 26, No. 6, pp. 1136–1159.

G20 Brazil (22 January 2024), *African Union in the G20. A Geopolitical and Economic Leap for the Continent,* https://www.g20.org/en/news/african-union-in-the-g20-a-geopolitical-and-economic-leap-for-the-continent, accessed 30 January 2024.

Greven, M.T. (2005), 'The Informalization of Transnational Governance. A Threat to Democratic Governance', in E. Grande & L. W. Louis (Eds), C*omplex Sovereignt. Reconstituting Political Authority in the Twenty-first Century*, University of Toronto Press, pp. 261–284.

Gstöhl, S. (2012), 'Informal Governance and the G8', in T. Christiansen and C. Neuhold (eds), *International Handbook on Informal Governance,* Edward Elgar Publishing, Cheltenham, 255–275.

Hack, R. (2019), *Dialog im Reaktionsrepertoire von WTO und G7/G8. Die Einrichtung von deliberativen Dialogforen in Reaktion auf Protest,* Studien des Leibniz-Instituts Hessische Stiftung Friedens- und Konfliktforschung, Springer VS.

Hajnal, P.I. (1999), *The G7/G8 System. Evolution, Role and Documentation*, Ashgate Publishing Company, Aldershot.

Hajnal, P.I. (2000), *Partners or Adversaries? The G7/G8 Encounters Civil Society,* G8 Scholarly Publications and Papers, www.g7.utoronto.ca/scholar/hajnal20000720/, accessed 1 August 2022.

Hajnal, P.I. (2018), 'Civil Society Encounters the G7/G8', in P.I. Hajnal (ed.), *Civil Society in the Information Age,* Routledge, New York.

Hajnal, P.I. (2019), *The G20. Evolution, Interrelations, Documentation*, 2nd edn, Routledge, New York.

Hilbrich, S. and J. Schwab (2018), *Towards a more accountable G20? Accountability mechanisms of the G20 and the new challenges posed to them by the 2030 agenda,* https://www.die-gdi.de/uploads/media/DP__13.2018.pdf (accessed 11 September 2024).

Kirton, J. and B. Warren (2021), 'Engagement group recommendations realized in the G20 Summits', *Global Solutions Journal,* No. 6, pp. 29–37, https://www.global-solutions-initiative.org/wp-content/uploads/2021/01/210114_GS_journal_6.pdf.

Koch, M. (2016), 'Connecting G20 Summitry with Citizenry', *Shanghai International Forum,* www.g20.utoronto.ca/biblio/koch-engagement.html.

Koch, M. (2019), *China's B20 and T20 Leadership in the G20,* www.g20.utoronto.ca/biblio/koch-china-b20-t20-leadership.html.

Lenz, T. and F. Söderbaum (2023), 'The Origins of Legitimation Strategies in International Organizations. Agents, Audiences and Environments', *International Affairs*, Vol. 99, No. 3, pp. 899–920.

Luckhurst, J. (2016), *G20 Since the Global Crisis*, Palgrave Macmillan US, New York.

Luckhurst, J. (2019), 'Governance Networks Shaping the G20 Through Inclusivity Practices', *South African Journal of International Affairs*, Vol. 26, No. 4, pp. 1–277.

Martens, J. (2017), *Corporate influence on G20. The case of the B20 and transnational business networks*, Heinrich-Böll-Stiftung, Berlin, Germany.

Morin, J.-F. et al. (2019), 'How Informality Can Address Emerging Issues. Making the Most of the G7', *Global Policy*, Vol. 10, No. 2, pp. 267–273.

OECD (2021), *Compendium of International Organisations' Practices. Working Towards more Effective International Instruments*, OECD Publishing, Paris.

Pauwelyn, J. (2012), 'Informal International Lawmaking. Framing the Concept and Research Question', in J. Pauwelyn, R.A. Wessel and J. Wouters (eds), *Informal International Lawmaking,* Oxford University Press, Oxford, pp. 13–34.

Reh, C. (2014), 'Is Informal Politics Undemocratic? Trilogues, Early Agreements and the Selection Model of Representation', *Journal of European Public Policy*, Vol. 21, No. 6, pp. 822–841.

Reuters (5 July 2017), *German Police Disperse G20 Protest with Water Cannon Before Summit*, Reuters.

Rinke, B. and U. Schneckener (2013), 'Informalisierung der Weltpolitik? Globales Regieren durch Clubs', in T. Debiel et al. (eds)*, Globale Trends 2013. Frieden-Entwicklung-Umwelt,* Fischer Taschenbuch Verlag, Frankfurt am Main, pp. 27–42.

Roger, C.B. (2020), *The Origins of Informality. Why the Legal Foundations of Global Governance are Shifting, and Why it Matters,* Oxford scholarship online Political Science, Oxford University Press, New York.

Schnabel, A. and J.A. Scholte (2003), *Civil Society and Global Finance*, Routledge, New York.

Slaughter, S. (2013), 'The Prospects of Deliberative Global Governance in the G20. Legitimacy, Accountability, and Public Contestation', *Review of International Studies*, Vol. 39, No. 1, pp. 71–90.

Slaughter, S. (2015), 'Building G20 Outreach. The Role of Transnational Policy Networks in Sustaining Effective and Legitimate Summitry', *Global Summitry*, Vol. 1, No. 2, pp. 171–186.

Slaughter, S. (2019), 'Interpreting Civil Society Engagement with the G20: the Qualified Inclusion of the 2014 Civil 20 Process', *Globalizations*, Vol. 16, No. 1, pp. 36–49.

Slaughter, S. (2021), 'Global Informalism and the G20', *Journal of International Relations and Development*, Vol. 24, No. 3, pp. 533–554.

Tallberg, J. et al. (2013), *The Opening Up of International Organizations. Transnational Access in Global Governance*, Cambridge University Press, Cambridge.

Uhlin, A. (2016), *Civil Society and Regional Governance. The Asian Development Bank and the Association of Southeast Asian Nations*, Lexington Books, Lanham.

Vabulas, F. and D. Snidal (2013), 'Organization without Delegation. Informal Intergovernmental Organizations (IIGOs) and the Spectrum of Intergovernmental Arrangements', *The Review of International Organizations*, Vol. 8, No. 2, pp. 193–220.

VENRO (2022a), *FAQ zu Civil 7. Allgemeine Fragen zum zivilgesellschaftlichen Begleitprozess zur deutschen G7-Präsidentschaft,* https://venro.org/themen/civil-7/faq-zu-civil-7, accessed 11 August 2022.

VENRO (2022b), V*ENRO und das Forum Umwelt und Entwicklung koordinieren den zivilgesellschaftlichen Begleitprozess zur deutschen G7-Präsidentschaft*, https://web.archive.org/web/20230207134911/https://venro.org/themen/civil-7, accessed 09 February 2025.

Viola, L.A. (2015), 'Orchestration by Design. The G20 in International Financial Regulation', in K.W. Abbott et al. (eds), *International Organizations as Orchestrators,* Cambridge University Press, Cambridge, pp. 88–113.

Vollmer, H. (1996), 'Die Institutionalisierung lernender Organisationen. Vom Neoinstitutionalismus zur wissenssoziologischen Aufarbeitung der Organisationsforschung', *Soziale Welt*, Vol. 47, No. 3, pp. 315–343, https://www.jstor.org/stable/40878158.

Westerwinter, O., K.W. Abbott and T. Biersteker (2021), 'Informal Governance in World Politics', *The Review of International Organizations*, Vol. 16, No. 1, pp. 1–27.

Women20 Germany (2017), *Project Handbook,* https://www.w20-germany.org/files/fileadmin/user_upload/documents/w20_projecthandbook-final-web.pdf (accessed 11 September 2024) .

Wouters, J. and S. van Kerckhoven (2011), 'The OECD and the G20. An Ever Closer Relationship?', *George Washington International Law Review*, Vol. 43, pp. 345–374.

10. Digital public consultations: lessons from the European Union

Kseniia Soloveva, Keith Prushankin, Hasan Akintug, Florence Felsheim, Carolina Gerli, Nathalie Koubayova, Cyprian Liske, Claudia Negri Ribalta and Jan Karol Farfal

1 INTRODUCTION

Public consultations have been defined as 'seeking the opinions of interested and affected groups', to be 'developed in an open and transparent fashion, with appropriate and well publicised procedures for effective and timely inputs from interested national and foreign parties' (OECD 2022a: 1). Public consultations represent a dialogue between citizens and governments (OECD 2001). Digital rule-making aims at increasing transparency and empowers citizens to exercise their democratic rights (Adams and Prins, 2017). Public consultations are similarly known to international governance, which focuses on engaging various groups through institutional dialogue (Zingales and Radu, 2017). For example, the OECD states: 'We believe that engaging with civil society helps improve our policy recommendations and our impact on society' (OECD n.d.), while the World Bank describes that 'ongoing dialogue between the World Bank Group and stakeholders – government, civil society, media, academia, and the private sector – is a critical aspect of our work' (World Bank n.d.).

The majority of international organisations ('IOs') choose to involve specific stakeholders. Some organisations, however, allow citizens to participate directly in their policy-making activities (e.g., the World Bank; OECD). Although supranational and international organisations are keen to engage in digital consultations, citizens generally find it hard to get involved compared to national or local levels, irrespective of educational background or place of residence (Hierlemann et al, 2022). This is due to flaws in current e-participation mechanisms. The critique of these mechanisms can be condensed into three categories. First, it reproduces societal inequality, from the absence of equal participation opportunities in online consultations. Second, rules regarding conduct and results of participation exercises are frequently unclear (Adams and Prins 2017). As a result, the process is perceived as excessively time consuming (Gibson et al. 2012). Third, the legitimacy and transparency of the process are overshadowed by factors such as the participation of lobbyist groups and the 'fear that consultations can be tokenistic exercises in which governments ask citizens for their views to legitimise already determined policy decisions' (Gibson et al. 2012, p. 174). These categories contradict the notion of inclusive policy-making, which should be 'transparent, evidence-driven, accessible and responsive to as wide a range of citizens as possible' (OECD 2013, p. 146).

This contribution discusses the aforementioned categories in the context of the 'Have Your Say!' Platform (hereafter, 'HYS' or 'the Platform'). The development of the Platform was announced in May 2015 with the explicit aim of allowing stakeholders to 'participate fully' in the European Commission's ('EC' or 'Commission') work (COM 2015). The basis of this decision is Article 11 of the Treaty on the European Union ('TEU') (2012), which stipulates that the Commission has a duty to conduct broad consultations with interested parties to ensure that the European Union ('EU') action is coherent and transparent. All EU legislators must conduct public consultations during the legislative process, beginning with a consultation strategy by the relevant Directorate-General (with exceptions granted to politically sensitive and urgent issues) (COM 2019). The Secretariat-General of the EC coordinates the launch of all public internet-based consultations on the Platform (EC 2021a).

The EU is a frontrunner when it comes to the use of public consultations, with stakeholder engagement in such consultations being well above the OECD average (OECD 2021a). However, despite these efforts, experiences with the Platform reveal certain challenges in achieving its goals of increasing public participation and inclusive rule-making. In this regard, we follow Smith and Dalakiouridou who define participation as 'inputs to policy and decision-making for political or public policy purposes, within formal systems but also through informal systems where these can have a real impact at any stage of the policy lifecycle' (2009, p. 2). While it is understandable that citizens might be unable to participate on the same footing as professional organisations and businesses in policy-making, an increase in participation should be attempted through raising awareness, simplifying the process, and developing incentives for participation. In the twenty-first century, this implies 'align[ing] the technological affordance with the nature of the specific democratic process involved and the needs of the citizens whose participation is sought' (Adams and Prins 2017, p. 10–11). The Platform itself defines its function as a place where '[c]itizens and businesses can share their views on new EU policies and existing laws' in any of the 24 official languages of the EU (EC, n.d. a). Although the goals are clear, their achievement is impeded.

This chapter discusses HYS from the perspective of three key components for inclusive public participation: accessibility, outreach, and transparency. It combines multiple qualitative data collection methods, such as online participant observation, interviews, and document review. This triangulation of methods provides a synergistic and comprehensive view (Yin 2014; Harrison et al. 2017) of the Platform. Online participant observation provided the primary data on the functioning of the EU online public consultations. In December 2022, the authors participated in one of the consultations on the platform to gather visual and textual data and identify the main challenges (see section 2.3). Conducting interviews with stakeholders involved in digital democracy facilitated collecting information on the functioning of HYS, the process of its creation, associated challenges, and testing tentative recommendations. Between June and August 2023, the authors conducted 11 semi-structured interviews with representatives of the Commission and other relevant stakeholders (e.g., IT providers of digital platforms for citizen participation). The document review involved the collection of secondary data on the broader topic of participatory democracy and public governance. The review was primarily based on regulations, policy documents, reports, press releases, and academic literature. The OECD Guidelines for Citizen Participation Processes (2022b), the Recommendation of the Council on Regulatory Policy and Governance (OECD 2012), and the Compendium of International Organisations' Practices (OECD 2021b), *inter alia*, constitute a solid foundation.

This chapter aims to analyse the Platform and elucidate suggestions for its improvement. The lessons learnt can be extrapolated to other digital tools designed by IOs to ensure the increasing involvement of citizens in the participatory processes. Thus, section 2 of this contribution addresses the existing structure of the Platform, its legal basis, and Feedback Rules. Section 3 provides an overview of specific problems that HYS encounters. Section 4 proposes some solutions, and section 5 provides the conclusions.

2 THE PLATFORM: OVERVIEW

The EU has often faced criticism for being distant from its citizens over its perceived 'democratic deficit' (Moravcsik 2002; Follesdal and Hix 2006; Müller 2016), a shortcoming that even the EU itself acknowledges (EU n.d. a). In response, the EU has attempted to increase its visibility in the lives of its citizens. This has produced the so-called 'Better Regulation Agenda' of 2015 by the Juncker Commission, and this remains the active framework in which HYS functions.

The first consultations and feedback opportunities for selected delegated and implementing acts on the Platform were launched in June 2016, and it is being continuously improved by introducing adjustments. In June 2022, the Commission announced its intention to transform the existing public consultations website into a one-stop-shop for online citizens' engagement (EC 2022a). The new portal will open with an umbrella page leading to three participatory tools: the Platform, the European Citizens' Initiative, and the new multilingual digital platform for citizens' engagement inspired by the Conference on the Future of Europe.

The launch of the new umbrella page was planned for September 2023. However, as of 29 February 2024, this has not yet been implemented. Regardless, no major changes are expected for the HYS part of the new platform. In order to understand the basis and the functioning of the Platform, this section addresses its legal basis and the feedback rules, which are the only guidelines available. In addition, this section maps the process as experienced by users, including the authors.

2.1 The legal basis for the functioning of the platform

Pursuant to Article 11 of the TEU (2012), EU institutions must give citizens and other interested parties the possibility to 'make known and publicly exchange their views in all areas of Union action'. Paragraph 3 of that Article specifically makes the Commission responsible for organising public consultations on EU matters of concern for stakeholders. HYS is the primary tool for EU citizens to participate in that process. Currently, there is no binding EU regulation on public consultations. However, the design of such consultations is covered by a series of internal and interinstitutional documents. The most important are the Interinstitutional Agreement between the European Parliament, the Council of the EU, and the Commission on Better Law-Making (2016) (Interinstitutional Agreement), and the revised Better Regulation Agenda (EC 2021c) ('the Agenda').

The Interinstitutional Agreement does not directly refer to any specific online platforms for public consultations. However, it stipulates general guidelines on the EU consultations' procedure. Pursuant to Paragraph 19 of the Interinstitutional Agreement (2016), the EC should conduct public consultations 'in an open and transparent way, ensuring that the modalities and time-limits of those public consultations allow for the widest possible participation'. It also places focus on inviting end-users and small and medium-sized enterprises to online consultations. As to the analysis of submitted feedback, the Interinstitutional Agreement requires the results to be made public and be communicated to the co-legislators; however, it does not provide any further guidelines on how the EC should proceed with the input and whether it must further keep participants in the loop. When compared to the other parts of the Interinstitutional Agreement, the provisions on public consultations are scarce and vague.

Relying on the findings of the Report of the European Court of Auditors (2019) and the stocktaking of better regulation (COM 2019), the Better Regulation Agenda proposed several commitments from the Commission. First, the EC admitted that there is a need to boost awareness among EU citizens as to the possibility of using the Platform, as well as to more closely engage the academic community (EC 2021c). Second, the EC proposed consolidating the consultation process to present a one consultation per one initiative system (EC 2021c, p. 4) – this has already been implemented on the Platform. Most importantly, the Agenda acknowledged a lack of response to citizens' feedback as one of the main defects of EU public consultations. The EC obliged itself to 'publish a summary report on each public consultation within eight weeks of its closure' (EC 2021c, p. 6).

The Better Regulation Toolbox ('the Toolbox'), published by the Commission in November 2021 as a companion to the Better Regulation Guidelines (the Guidelines), dedicates a chapter to 'stakeholder consultations', outlining their strategy, activities, and outcomes evaluation. Both documents were issued in their revised form to further clarify the commitments under the Agenda and designated HYS as the online platform for publishing calls for evidence and public consultation questionnaires, to which stakeholders can contribute (EC 2021a). As of 2022, the Commission systematically informed stakeholders in advance about the envisaged consultation procedures, published a timeline of the initiatives, and sent emails about the opening of consultations (OECD 2022c). As to the results of consultations, the Guidelines expect that '[b]eyond the factual summary, stakeholders should receive adequate and thorough feedback through a synopsis report, prepared at the end of the consultation activities' (EC 2021a). The format of such a report is more closely set out in the Toolbox (EC 2021b). Nevertheless, neither document provides more intricate rules on the manner in which the EU institutions should further act upon the received feedback.

The Agenda constitutes a policy document of the EC and as such is not based on any of the EC constitutional treaties. The Interinstitutional Agreement was issued under Article 295 of the Treaty on the Functioning of the European Union (TFEU) (2012) as the joint rules of procedure between the concerned EU institutions. Although Article 295 allows for a binding nature of such an Interinstitutional Agreement, it cannot be effectively sanctioned by a third party and is not externally binding (Bunea 2020).

Neither communications nor interinstitutional agreements constitute any of the formal sources of binding secondary EU law under Article 288 of the TFEU. As a result, in most cases, citizens would not be able to file a complaint with the Court of Justice of the European Union in the event of perceived non-compliance (under Article 263 of the TFEU). Consequently, while the current legal framework for public consultations in the EU is flexible and leaves the EC with the initiative to organise an effective system, the absence of binding requirements adopted in the legislative procedure prevents EU citizens from enforcing such requirements in cases of alleged non-compliance.

2.2 Feedback rules

The Feedback Rules (EC n.d. b) provide guidelines to citizens on how to participate on the Platform. These rules refer to the following categories: unsuitable feedback, deadlines, the transparency register, and data and privacy (as per EU Regulation 2018/1725, 2018).

First, the Feedback Rules list types of content in feedback that are considered 'unsuitable', such as abusive, obscene, vulgar, or xenophobic comments, spam, duplicate content, and off-topic comments. Unsuitable feedback is then reported by other users and is eventually removed from the Platform. However, neither guidelines on how to provide appropriate feedback are outlined, nor are details given regarding the assessment of feedback.

Second, according to the Feedback Rules, organisations are advised to register in the EU Transparency Register before submitting their contributions. Ideally, the Register helps keep track of interest groups' interactions with EU institutions. However, registration is not mandatory and remains optional for organisations participating in consultations.

Hence, as addressed in section 2.1, the Guidelines and the Toolbox contain rules on the minimum duration and conduct of the consultation procedures; however, they do not provide easily accessible information on how (and when) the feedback will be processed after the consultation period closes. Moreover, neither the Feedback Rules nor the Guidelines specify *how* the feedback should be provided. The scattered nature of explanatory information may discourage citizens from using the Platform.

2.3 HYS: mapping the consultation process

Following the identification of the legal regime and guidelines for the functioning of the Platform, this section describes the process of participation in the public consultations on HYS. It should be noted that the initiatives submitted on the Platform are divided into three stages: (1) preparation, to inform participants that a public consultation will open for a specific initiative; (2) call for evidence, which describes the problem to be tackled and the objectives, explains why the EU action is needed, outlines policy options, and describes the main features of the consultation strategy; and (3) final adoption of the act by the Commission. The call for evidence is the actual participatory phase during which participants can express their opinions in two ways: by sending feedback through an open-ended field during the opening of the 'feedback period', and by filling in questionnaires (through EU Survey – the Commission's official survey management tool) during the opening of the 'public consultation'. When this chapter refers to public consultations, it encompasses both stages of citizen engagement (i.e., feedback period and public consultations via questionnaires).

The search among the initiatives opened for consultation on HYS can be carried out with the application of multiple filters (e.g., by keywords or topic, stage of consultations, feedback status, etc.). By selecting an initiative, a factsheet opens showing a summary of the initiative, its supporting materials, and information about consultation stages. Participants of the public consultations must register or, if already registered, authenticate via the Platform. Registration/authentication mainly takes place through the standard EU login system (i.e., e-mail and password), which is a single point for user authentication to a wide range of Commission information systems, or social media (i.e., Facebook). Despite being compulsory, this step does not preclude anonymous participation in consultations. Both feedback and questionnaires also require participants to provide compulsory information about their profile during the submission (e.g., whether they are participating in their private capacity as EU citizens or on behalf of an organisation), language of submission, attachments, and privacy statement. Once feedback or the answers to a questionnaire are submitted, participants automatically receive a notification of successful submission on the portal and via e-mail. After the feedback is published on the Platform, participants retain the option to unpublish it as long as the 'feedback period' remains open.

To gain first-hand experience of the process, the authors participated in the call for evidence phase for the 'European Disability Card' public consultation in their capacity as citizens in December 2022. This phase of the consultation was open for approximately six weeks. While the Platform requires various information about the sender who acts on behalf of an organisation, in our case, neither demographic questions were asked nor was the authenticity of the information we provided (e.g., country of origin) verified.

Submitting the feedback text is limited to 4,000 characters and is relatively straightforward. Once published, the feedback becomes instantly visible on the corresponding consultation's webpage, and the participants receive the acknowledgement via HYS and e-mail. The confirmation of the submission is the first and the last piece of communication provided by the Commission. The authors received no information about either the closing of the call for evidence or the opening of the next phase of consultation. Moreover, reminders are communicated only in case of subscription to changes to the initiative –not a default setting even after the active submission. This experience served as a valuable insight into the process, and it revealed certain challenges. These will be addressed in the next section.

3 HYS: CHALLENGES

With Europe's Digital Decade policy programme, the Commission made clear that engaging EU citizens in the digital public sphere is of utmost importance. Namely, in the digital target for 2030, the EC states that digital rights and principles should be solidaristic and inclusive and that 'technology should unite, not divide, people. Everyone should have access to the internet, to digital skills, to digital public services and fair working conditions' (EC n.d. c).

While this appears positive, closer scrutiny demonstrates that the willingness to make a participatory online tool for everyone is insufficient. The crux of the matter often lies in poorly designed user interfaces and a lack of functionality in the public consultation websites that make them unattractive and difficult to use. This part of the contribution will introduce the concerns associated with the functioning of the Platform.

First, we discuss the challenges related to accessibility concerning the technological flaws preventing citizens from meaningful participation. Accessibility usually focuses on people with disabilities and their requirements and tends to have a technical focus rather than on user experience or visual design (WAI 2010). Second, we address transparency, typically understood to be 'the quality of being done in an open way without secrets' (Cambridge Dictionary, n.d.). It is considered to be one of the keywords in the context of effective and legitimate policy-making and is crucial for democratic accountability (Erkkilä 2020). In the context of the Platform, transparency encompasses the following elements: openness to the outside world by producing understandable and credible initiatives; publicly available processes; and an explanation of the 'reasons for disagreeing with alternative views' (EC 2021b). Finally, we touch upon the challenges related to outreach. The term 'outreach' is commonplace in the policy-making sphere; however, it is rare to encounter clear definitions. According to the Commission, outreach entails 'ensur[ing] adequate awareness-raising and publicity, and adapt[ing] communication channels to the needs of all target audiences' (EC 2021a). This definition correlates with the goal of the EC to 'ensure wide participation throughout the policy cycle' (EC 2021b).

3.1 Accessibility challenges

In creating platforms for online consultations, conciseness and practicality should be considered. The platforms should be easily accessible, designed in a user-friendly way that easily and quickly provides information both on their functioning and on their content. In other words, when designing a website, it is important to bear in mind user characteristics, such as perceived usefulness or ease of use, to ensure that users will accept and engage with the technology (Davis, 1989).

There are multiple definitions of accessibility. For example, Petrie et al. (2015) propose a working definition, which states that 'all people, particularly disabled and older people, can use websites in a range of contexts of use, including mainstream and assistive technologies; to achieve this, websites need to be designed and developed to support usability across these contexts'. Thus, accessibility, in this context, would be creating a website for all, focusing on the requirements for people with disabilities (Harper and Yesilada 2008; WAI 2005).

Ideally, the platform should comply with the EU regulations concerning accessibility requirements. The European Union, in Directive 2016/2102 (2016) on accessibility of websites and mobile applications of public sector bodies, indicated in Article 4 that 'public sector bodies [shall] take the necessary measures to make their websites and mobile applications more accessible by making them perceivable, operable, understandable and robust'. Accessibility is not just a checklist (Sloan et al. 2006). It depends on the context and different stakeholders, which requires testing and evaluating the accessibility features with the users (Abou-Zahra 2008; WAI 2022) – in this case, citizens.

Accessibility, therefore, imposes both functional requirements on how the code should work and non-functional requirements on the design and user interaction ('UI') (WAI 2010), including perceivable information, operating interface and navigation, and robust content (WAI 2019). If properly handled, accessibility requirements can be included from the early stages of the web development lifecycle, which makes the final product 'accessible from design' (Abou-Zahra 2008; Sloan et al. 2006). Aside from the fact that accessible design enables the participation of groups of people that could be excluded otherwise, accessibility brings other benefits, namely: improved user experience (UX), increased usability, better search engine optimisation, increased reach, and compliance with regulations and laws (Aizpurua et al. 2016; WAI 2010; Moreno and Martinez 2013; Sloan et al. 2006).

The case study of HYS revealed several insufficiencies concerning accessibility. First, there is no explanation of the consultation process provided in simple language. The landing page[1] of the Platform contains a 'See how it works' section with a video discussing consultations in general. However,

[1] 'Have Your Say!' Landing Page, https://ec.europa.eu/info/law/better-regulation/have-your-say_en.

there is no clear explanation of the concrete steps that participants must take to participate. Second, the search for initiatives is complex, containing filters that are not always intelligible, and no legend is provided. For example, there is no explanation of the differences between 'Type of act' and 'Document category'. Upon further scrutiny, the former appears to refer to the type of act proposed for consultations (e.g., legislative proposal). The latter supposedly indicates the type of documents provided by the Commission to support the initiatives (e.g., staff working document). Moreover, in the field 'Category', participants can also select 'Evaluation' among other filters, which refers to the evaluation of different laws and programmes, and is based on different types of acts: evaluations or reports. The repetitiveness of the language used on the Platform, alongside the absence of clear guidance, incorrectly presupposes in-depth knowledge of the consultation process.

Third, the feedback from participants is published only in the language of its submission and is not translated into English. Similarly, other documents accompanying the initiative, such as impact assessment reports, are frequently available in English only, although their summaries may be translated into all official languages.[2] In contrast, the Calls for Evidence are usually translated into all official languages, although it is not always the case.[3] Although the Commission has indicated that translation into other languages would require efforts beyond what is possible, it has accepted that this is a challenge (ECA 2019). Moreover, the Calls for Evidence tend to use rather complex language, which might render them incomprehensible. The Special Report 14/2019 (ECA 2019) found that users consider questionnaires and surveys from the platform lengthy, unclear, and occasionally containing technical jargon. This perception contradicts the accessibility principles of understandable and perceivable information. Therefore, it should not be surprising that it is mostly interest groups, lobbyists, specialists, and organisations rather than 'regular' EU and non-EU citizens who mostly provide input (Hierlemann et al. 2022).

Furthermore, people with disabilities should be able to enjoy the same right of participation in democratic processes. However, when they attempt to use software or hardware and are confronted with a variety of technical issues, they are likely to stop trying and develop an aversion to technology (Vicente

2 See, e.g., 'Banking Union: Review of the Bank Crisis-Management & Deposit-Insurance Framework' Consultations, https://ec.europa.eu/info/law/better-regulation/have-your-say/initiatives/13812-Banking-Union-Review-of-the-bank-crisis-management-deposit-insurance-framework-SRMR-review-_en.

3 See, e.g., 'Protecting the Euro Against Counterfeiting – the Pericles IV Programme (Midterm Evaluation)' Consultations, https://ec.europa.eu/info/law/better-regulation/have-your-say/initiatives/13729-Protecting-the-euro-against-counterfeiting-the-Pericles-IV-programme-midterm-evaluation-_en.

and López 2010). The interface of both feedback and questionnaires on HYS does not offer any accessibility options for disabled participants (e.g., adaptable font, keyboard navigation assistance) – thus, implicitly excluding people with disabilities from the online consultation process. According to the Accessibility Statement (EC 2022b) published in December 2023, the Commission's content located on their main domain[4] is only partially compliant with the standards set by the European Telecommunications Standard Institute (ETSI 2021) and Web Content Accessibility Guidelines (WCAG 2018). While the former establishes harmonised accessibility requirements for all information and communication technologies' products and services (e.g., hardware, software, web), the latter defines a single shared standard for web content accessibility that meets the needs of individuals, organisations, and governments internationally (e.g., text, image, sound). The Accessibility Statement shows certain limitations, such as videos that lack captions and are not accessible through keyboards; interactive maps that are not accessible to people with vision impairment; and infographics, maps, and charts that do not have enough text alternatives for people with vision impairment. It further indicates that several of these issues are intended to be fixed throughout 2024. The Platform, however, is located on a subdomain, to which the Accessibility Statement does not apply (EC 2022b). No separate accessibility statement is made publicly available on the Platform. Taken together, these factors render the Platform lacking in accessible functionality and user-responsiveness.

3.2 Transparency challenges

The Platform reveals several transparency concerns related to responsibility, public knowledge, participants' identity, and the ultimate use of the feedback. First, as described above (*supra,* sections 2.2 and 2.3), the Commission does not provide clear guidelines on how to submit appropriate feedback on the Platform, and no follow-up is communicated to participants after submission.

Second, the initiatives' factsheets do not contain information about the contact person for the initiative. Only when submitting questionnaires can participants view this information. While the EC, as the EU organ with the right of initiative, clearly communicates that the Platform falls under its responsibility, the fact that the Secretariat-General in particular is responsible for developing the 'better regulation' policy in the Commission can only be deduced from the Guidelines (EC 2021a). Each Directorate-General is responsible for its initiatives, and the website on which the Platform itself is located is managed by the Unit of the Secretariat-General in charge of digital

---

4 See https://commission.europa.eu.

solutions and process efficiency – information not communicated anywhere on HYS. While indication of the owner would increase overall transparency, this is not currently observed.

Third, there are two main limitations of HYS with regard to timing: a lack of clear guidelines on how the timing is defined and a lack of reasons for postponing public consultations. According to the Toolbox (EC 2021b), the timing of a Call for Evidence differs depending on whether they are or will be open for 'public consultation'. If 'public consultation' is not carried out, the call for evidence is open for feedback for four weeks. In contrast, if a call for evidence is open for feedback and 'public consultation' simultaneously, the overall duration of participation in the initiative via feedback and questionnaires is twelve weeks. In case 'public consultation' is not yet ready when the call for evidence is launched, it can be opened later, provided that the twelve-week 'public consultation' period is preserved. In practice, however, the timing does not always correspond to the Guidelines and Toolbox indications. For example, the 'European Disability Card' Call for Evidence that the authors participated in was opened for a period of slightly over six weeks. However, in the consultation strategy laid out in the Call for Evidence for Impact Assessment, the feedback was supposed to be open for four weeks, followed by 'public consultations' for 12 weeks at a later stage (HYS 2022). The reason for the extension remains unknown.

Furthermore, public consultations in planning that are announced on the website are frequently postponed for reasons known only to the Commission. An example of such consultations is the proposal for a Regulation on 'Taking Car Rentals into Other EU Countries'.[5] According to the roadmap published on the Platform, the feedback period is simply indicated as 'upcoming', while the 'public consultation' (questionnaire) was planned for the third quarter of 2022. By the second quarter of 2023, the Commission expected the adoption of the regulation. In fact, the collection of feedback took place between July and September 2024, with no further actions announced afterwards. It is understandable that abiding by the expected timeline may not always be feasible. However, not informing citizens about the delays and their reasons is detrimental to transparency.

Fourth, by allowing registration and authentication with users' social media accounts, the Commission takes the risk of not knowing the real identity of the participants. Due to the increasing number of bots (i.e., software agents that communicate autonomously on social media), this might exacerbate the risk of

---

5 'Taking Car Rentals into Other EU Countries – Rules' Consultations, https://ec.europa.eu/info/law/better-regulation/have-your-say/initiatives/13461-Taking-car-rentals-into-other-EU-countries-rules_en.

misuse of the Platform. The misinformation on climate change generated by malicious Twitter bots is a good example of misuse (Chen et al. 2021). Using social media for authentication carries certain security risks. If the social media platform's authentication details are compromised, the user might also get compromised on the Platform (AEDP 2020). Furthermore, social media companies may keep track of the accounts linked to HYS, which may create conflict regarding privacy (AEDP 2020).

Fifth, checks on the appropriateness of the content of feedback are carried out only manually after its publication on the platform. As a result, inappropriate feedback is visible to the public until it is either reported by users or removed by the Commission itself. Content moderation on the platform is fragmented: it is conducted by each Directorate-General with respect of only the consultations that fall under their responsibility.

Sixth, the fields for public consultations are structured in an excessively complex manner: while an open-ended field for feedback leaves room for ambiguity and elusiveness, the structure of questionnaires can be too limiting and time-consuming. Besides, the platform provides the possibility to attach files to both feedback and questionnaires, a double-edged sword. Some categories of participants, especially experts on the topic (e.g., NGOs and businesses), submit their whole feedback as attachments, thus making it impossible for other participants to familiarise themselves easily without downloading frequently extensive submissions. These attachments also run the risk of containing malware.

Seventh, the Platform lacks a centralised area for data visualisation and consultation. Data on the outcomes and statistics of public consultations are shown on each initiative's webpage. This means that users cannot browse aggregated data across various consultations. Furthermore, the data from public consultations is not displayed by the official portal for EU Open Data,[6] on which more than 1.5 million European public sector datasets (e.g., on agriculture, health, energy) are accumulated daily.

Finally, a potential pitfall of inclusionary practices such as public consultations is the disproportionate resources that interest organisations have in comparison to citizens. Academic research indicates that both draughting and public consultations are actively utilised by interest groups during the legislative process (Joosen 2020). Furthermore, interest groups usually focus on the initial draughting phase of the policy-making process and only show interest in public consultations with the intention of changing the draft rules, indicating that many groups only view public consultations as an alternative to their lack of influence in the drafting stage (Joosen 2020).

---

6 See https://data.europa.eu/en.

Participation in online public consultations is integral to interest groups' digital lobbying strategy. Digital lobbying, defined as using digital tools for public affairs (Zanetto 2019; Carro and Di Mario 2022), is gaining momentum with technology's increasing role in governance. However, interest groups' influence on policy-making raises concerns. Online consultations during crucial phases like agenda-setting and policy formulation attract lobbyists (Quittkat and Kotzian 2011). On HYS, representatives need only formal registration, with no requirement for an EU Transparency Register listing (Năstase and Muurmans 2020). Providing detailed feedback helps lobbyists appear reliable, increasing chances for involvement in exclusive consultation formats such as workshops (Quittkat and Kotzian 2011). Regulation on lobbying remains fragmented, with few formal standards beyond initiatives like the 2006 Green Paper on the European Transparency Initiative and lobby transparency rules in the EU Parliament's 2019 Rules of Procedure (Commission of the European Communities 2006; EP 2019).

In sum, HYS shows a lack of clarity that is disadvantageous for citizens and may allow the potential misuse of public consultations by interest groups. Indeed, through public consultations, such actors might exercise undue influence on EU policy-making. In addition, the absence of detailed information about the responsible unit, unclear timing, and the ultimate use of the received feedback question the transparency of the Platform. Together, these factors undermine accountability, perpetuating the gap between EU policy-making and public participation: the very issue the Platform's creators intended to rectify.

3.3 Outreach challenges

The specific nature of online consultation tools implies the use of technology in order to achieve the desired goal of attracting more participants to democratic rule-making. Nevertheless, the extent to which such technology is used is impacted by the digital divide caused by income and education (Pérez-Morote et al. 2020). In creating inclusive platforms for online consultations, attention should be paid, *inter alia*, to the economic status of potential participants, gender, and age.

Online consultation platforms rarely address the specific needs of economically disadvantaged individuals. The need for their representation in democratic processes is particularly important as they typically represent the vulnerable members of society. Hence, the platform should be easily accessible, designed in a user-friendly way, allowing easy and quick access to information about both on functioning and content. While this may not address long-term structural inhibitors to technological access, it would constitute stopgap measures while working on longer-term solutions.

While gender equality has been a point of focus within the world of policy-making in previous decades, significant hurdles remain in the participation of women in digital public consultations. Although accounting for around half of the global population, women are still in many ways a disadvantaged demographic group, including in the online world. For example, in 2021, men were more than twice as likely to participate in online consultations or vote on civic/political matters than women (EIGE 2022). There are several reasons for this persisting imbalance. The first hurdle is statistical. The European Institute of Gender Equality's (EIGE) statistics database on women's satisfaction with the use of digital public consultation websites (including the ease of finding information and the usefulness of available information) only has data for the year 2013. Without up-to-date information on self-assessed accessibility to different platforms and necessary information, gender-based issues cannot be satisfactorily addressed. HYS does not collect information about the gender of participants and, consequently, does not provide any statistics.

The second main hurdle is the lack of information concerning gender-specific impacts of the policies submitted to digital consultations. As EIGE indicates, 'gender mainstreaming requires both integrating a gender perspective into the content of different policies and addressing the issue of representation of women and men in the given policy area' (EIGE n.d.). Indeed, women are often impacted differently by policies than men in their lives (UN Women 2015), therefore it is imperative to stress these differences in the e-consultations themselves. It is unclear whether the Commission carries out a gender-specific impact assessment, and there is nothing on the Platform that would lead to a positive conclusion.

Finally, another significant hurdle is the lack of time. Digital public consultation platforms need to take into account the unfortunately still-persisting imbalance in the amount of free time women have, especially working mothers and women in non-standard or low-paid jobs. According to European Working Conditions Survey data, it is estimated that the burden of unpaid household-related care work is greater for women in low-paying professions than for women in stable and/or higher-paying jobs. This is compounded by childcare: partnered women with children have twice as many daily unpaid care responsibilities as partnered women without children (ECWS 2015). The combined weight of household workload and childcare, added to the professional workload, severely restricts the time, interest, and motivation necessary for participation in e-consultations.

The age gap is the second significant element in public consultations that often remains neglected. For example, in participatory tools that are available in the EU, the average age of citizens varies greatly: in the European Parliament's elections, EU nationals over 55 are most engaged, while those under 40 are far less engaged (Hierlemann et al. 2022). In contrast, the European Citizens'

Initiative (EU n.d. b) has an over-representation of those between 21 and 30, while older people ranging from 71 to 80 are underrepresented (Hierlemann et al. 2022). The distribution is far from equal, and the situation will likely not be different for public consultations.

A reason for this may be the choice of online and offline formats for the conducted activities, the latter being chosen more by senior members of society. Given rising life expectancy, declining birth rates, and lack of generational substitution, especially in developed countries, the issue of senior digital inclusion is becoming a pertinent consideration in the development of social policies and is anticipated to become more prominent over time (Ciesielska et al. 2022). It results from a variety of factors, including apprehension over technology, diminished manual and mental abilities, socioeconomic status, and a disconnect between the needs of the elderly and the technological environment.

The relationship of young people to digital consultations is equally complex. While young people tend to trust digital public consultation tools less than older citizens (Alzahrani et al. 2018; OECD 2022d, p. 52), those with higher education and residing in densely populated areas are more likely to utilise e-government tools (Botrić and Božić 2021). No guidelines are expressed on the participation of underage citizens. Provided that on HYS the registration/authentication takes place through EU login or social media, minors of any age can participate in consultations, but it is not clear whether the Commission takes this into account for the purposes of data protection and data privacy.

In sum, HYS offers targeted engagement and a limited reach. The former stems from the fact that the Platform, and the overall process, is more accessible to experts rather than the public. The latter is due to the absence of efforts to encourage certain categories of people to take part in consultations. Although, on a national level, 19 EU Member States attempt to promote the involvement of stakeholders in the Commission's public consultations (OECD 2022c, p. 67), the practices vary, and the effectiveness of these outreach efforts remains subject to the limitations outlined above.

4 IMPROVING THE PUBLIC CONSULTATIONS PROCESS: RECOMMENDATIONS

This section introduces possible recommendations to the challenges identified above regarding the Platform, namely (a) accessibility, (b) transparency, and (c) outreach. The proposed recommendations are not exhaustive; however, they strive to address the principal issues that digital public consultations endure. These recommendations are in line with the principles and standards envisaged in the OECD Recommendation of the Council on Regulatory Policy and Governance (2012), such as the principle of open government (Principle 2) and the principles of stakeholder engagement outlined in the OECD Compendium of International Organisations' Practices (OECD 2021b).

4.1 Accessibility recommendations

Some of the identified accessibility concerns have straightforward solutions. For example, the application of unclear filters on the HYS website can be overcome with the introduction of a simple legend. Similarly, the complex and technical language could be simplified to address average citizens. The introduction of a chatbot will assist citizens in navigating across the website and through policy initiatives. There are pre-existing open-source tools[7] that can serve as a basis for the development of an assistant for HYS. The challenges of language accessibility and accessibility for people with disabilities deserve more elaboration.

4.1.1 The use of EU languages on the platform

Given the multilingual nature of the EU, translation into multiple languages should be approached thoroughly. There are several ways to improve language accessibility. First, the Platform should make use of machine translation. In cases where the content is not accessible in every language, the Commission recommends using eTranslation, the Commission's machine translation service (EC n.d. d). Despite the recommendation to use this tool, currently the feedback provided by the respondents and the supporting documents do not get translated and there is no option to use machine translation. Second, with the advent of big new language models, some artificial intelligence ('AI') tools might be helpful to support the task of translating information and documentation. The Commission makes limited use of ePoetry – its internal system that allows the connection and translation of parts of information that are published on the Platform. As a downside, AI tools carry various risks, such as bias in the language. Therefore, the recommended usage of AI should also come with a framework and guidelines to mitigate risks of bias, discrimination, and unfairness. Finally, another solution to improve language accessibility is to present content in a combination of formats: textual, visual, or audio. It could make the content easier to process and avoid cognitive overload (Mayer and Moreno 2003). By providing a portfolio of a webpage's layout, language accessibility can be significantly increased.

[7] See, e.g., https://github.com/CitizensFoundation/active-citizen/tree/master/models.

4.1.2 Access for people with disabilities

There are relatively simple tools which, once included, can substantially increase web friendliness for people with disabilities and the public in general. For instance, a harmonised European standard for digital accessibility (ETSI 2021) covers in detail the requirements for information and communications technology products and services, while a checklist from the Web Accessibility Initiative (WAI 2013) addresses the most basic point that a website should be accessible.

One of the tools that should not be overlooked is an accessibility toolbar that enables access to the content for those visually or hearing impaired. Such a toolbar includes functions such as increasing or decreasing text size, grayscale, high or negative contrast, or readable fonts, to name a few. Easy-to-read summaries of European regulations may be a convenient solution for intellectually disabled citizens. Guidelines on how to make information understandable are available on the Inclusion Europe website (Inclusion Europe n.d.). In fact, the Commission issued an easy-to-read report (Publications Office of the European Union 2022) on public consultations on the Web Accessibility Directive. Despite the existence of these solutions, the Platform does not make use of them.

Additionally, the Platform should prepare and publish an accessibility statement indicating the remaining challenges and the course of action to eliminate them. The European Accessibility Act, the main framework in the EU, and the Directive 2016/2102 complementing this Act, require every website and app to have a separate accessibility statement, a feedback mechanism, and regular monitoring of public sector websites of the Member states (EU 2016). In the EU, the case of Finland is worth mentioning as an example of best practices regarding accessibility. The 'otakantaa/dinåsikt.fi' platform[8] has a subsection showing the 'accessibility stamp' granted to the platform by the Finnish Association of the Visually Impaired. The stamp was granted on 16 November 2016 following a review by an external company, Ixonos, in December 2015. Ixonos made 16 observations with varying degrees of severity, of which six were published on the platform's website. Additionally, the external review by Ixonos was provided via a link on the same page. The accessibility statement is also available on the platform's website, describing the level of accessibility of the portal as 'partially meet[ing] accessibility requirements' and openly stating the non-accessible parts of the platform. Similarly, the Commission's general domain's Accessibility Statement (2022d) is prepared based on a review of a representative sample of web pages by

---

[8] See https://www.otakantaa.fi/sv/tietoa-palvelusta/18/.

the International Association of Accessibility Professionals – a division of the Global Initiative for Inclusive ICTs (G3ict) housed in Atlanta, Georgia.[9]

4.2 Transparency recommendations

The lack of clarity within the EU public consultation process could be addressed by introducing comprehensive guidelines. The World Bank Consultation Guidelines may serve as an example (World Bank 2019), comprised of one document, it is easily accessible to citizens. They explicitly provide for the duration of consultations, consultation principles (i.e., openness, access to information, accountability, transparency, visibility, accessibility), and detail the key components of well-conducted consultations, such as the design of consultations according to the parties directly affected by the proposed consultation, accessible lists of consultation participants, and appropriate ways to publicise consultations through a notification period of four weeks.

Moreover, it is advisable to improve the platform by adding a dedicated field (e.g., 'reasons for postponement/delay') on the initiatives' factsheets, which should be filled in when consultations are delayed or postponed. The Commission may discretionarily decide on the level of disclosure to participants when outlining the reasons for postponement. However, the more detailed and accurate the reasons are, the more transparent the public consultation process becomes.

The lack of the unit responsible for consultations should be addressed by making it visible on the website. A good example of a public consultation platform that explicitly shows the responsible unit for each public consultation is the Italian 'ParteciPa'.[10] Having the digital platform display the public organisation or the organisational unit that initially promoted the participatory initiative positively impacts the overall accountability of participatory tools. Moreover, the key participants (e.g., the managers of the website, generally responsible divisions of the Commission) should be detailed in the aforementioned comprehensive guideline and indicated on the Platform.

To overcome the lack of aggregated statistics, HYS should be equipped with a centralised dedicated dashboard to allow users to visualise and consult open data about public consultations. The dashboard should be designed and developed in line with the principles of transparency, integrity, accountability, and stakeholder participation developed in the OECD Recommendations on Open Government (2017). The dashboard should contain infographics and include statistics in a simple and user-friendly manner. Users should be able to

---

9 See https://www.accessibilityassociation.org/s/.

10 https://partecipa.gov.it/.

apply multiple filters (e.g., by topic, feedback status) to visualise general trends and results both during and after consultations. There are existing examples that can be considered a starting point for the creation of the dashboard. For example, the dashboard developed by CitizenLab[11] allows collecting relevant metrics, accumulating insights, and producing reports. Introducing the dashboard on the platform will not only contribute to transparency but also allow the identification of areas for improvement (e.g., under-represented categories that require additional outreach efforts). Moreover, the dashboard can be integrated with the EU Open Data portal, thus facilitating access to it.

The open-ended fields, in conjunction with the ability to attach files of unlimited size, should be adjusted. From a security perspective, files attached and uploaded to the platform must be scanned for vulnerabilities. For example, there is significant evidence of malicious PDF files, which are files that exploit the vulnerabilities of PDF readers (Nissim et al. 2015). The Commission makes use of the virus-scanning service provided by the Directorate-General for Informatics. However, without publicly available information about the service, it is not possible to determine whether the implemented measures are sufficient. Considering that citizens cannot easily familiarise themselves with the content without downloading each attachment, and the fact that no translation is available, we suggest either eliminating the option to submit files or ensuring that proper processes and technical measures are in place.

Due regard should also be given to content moderation, given the potentially harmful nature of comments. The usage of automated tools (such as AI) could increase the efficiency of the moderation process (Gillespie 2020). As the technology is improving, AI-based tools can support humans in the process of content moderation. However, the drawbacks of using AI-based tools need to be carefully assessed and defined. There is a record of the inability of AI to distinguish hate speech from offensive language or sarcasm, biases, lack of understanding of cultural context, errors with marginalised groups, accountability in moderation, and false positives, among other (Gillespie 2020; Gröndhal et al. 2018; Gorwa et al. 2020; Davidson et al. 2017). Similarly, malicious actors may try to fool automated models by inserting typos, adding white spaces (or removing them), appending words, or using words to the limit of their meaning in a specific context to avoid detection (Gröndhal et al. 2018; Gillespie 2020).

Finally, there are several approaches to prevent bots' presence, including (but not limited to) CAPTCHA, IP rate limits, ID verification, 2FA authentication, spam detection tools, time patterns, log analysis, user agents, and specialised software (García et al. 2014). New tools using machine learning might also

---

11 See https://www.citizenlab.co/en-gb/platform-online-engagement-toolbox.

be interesting (Orabi et al. 2020). It should be noted, however, that these approaches may not always be effective against advanced persistent threats or sophisticated attacks.

4.3 Outreach recommendations

Human-centred design elements may help attract wider audiences and ensure a balanced representation of stakeholders. Family, partners, communities, and policymakers who may shape a user's knowledge or motivation to interact should be taken into account. Besides, certain behavioural factors, such as motivation, elements of simplicity, and individual triggers, may lead to the desired behaviour (Fogg 2009), in our case, participating in public consultations. Recalling that participation is limited and there is no evident attempt to broaden inclusion across ages, genders, and economic groups, the problem of participation in digital public consultations must be addressed from multiple angles.

Regarding economic disadvantages, much of the literature recommends long-term structural solutions, omitting discussion of specific solutions for quick implementation (Quershi 2019). These include, for example, the provision of free Wi-Fi access, subsidised laptops, and internet cafés offering digital skills training (Maceviciute and Wilson 2018). Indeed, the effectiveness of individuals' self-efficacy in using digital public consultation applications can be significantly increased as a result of digital public consultation training. Through these measures, the digital divide may be narrowed, citizens' potential may be enhanced, and developing societies may encourage more equitable use of public services (Chohan and Hu 2022). Additionally, targeted communication in locations where disadvantaged groups of citizens live, may be consideredto inform them about where and how to access consultation and to encourage participation.

Similar to economically disadvantaged groups, gender diversity concerns should be addressed. First, systematically on a general level, and second, deduced from up-to-date information on self-assessed accessibility to different platforms. The accessibility of online consultation platforms needs to maximise user-friendliness, provide succinct explanations of individual policies, and privilege a fast-voting process. In addition, the inclusion of female developers would be beneficial for gender equality. The imbalances of design created by male-only developer teams (Burnett et al. 2016; Rowan and Dehlinger 2012; Nunes et al. 2023), represents a long-standing issue (Keuchler et al. 2012; Hsu 2012). Ensuring gender diversity at the developers' level would assist in rectifying the existing imbalances. Finally, including gender-responsiveness – that is, a consideration of how gender relates to specific policy content – in e-platforms is another solution for improvement. A precise summary of the ways in which each policy may affect women (possibly accounting for other factors such as age, race, disability, etc.) would prove particularly useful.

These suggestions are, however, separate from the concrete recommendations to improve the Platform and are therefore beyond the scope of our work. In contrast, the recommendations to improve the age group's representation require further examination.

4.3.1 Age

Considering the potential issues of diverse age groups is a major step for HYS and other online consultation platforms towards reaching their intended purpose: the expansion of citizen political participation. Currently, the Commission is engaging with the Committee of the Regions to give greater visibility to the Platform in the Member States. However, additional efforts should be introduced to get various age groups on board. The age of participants should not constitute a hindrance to their participation in the decision-making processes of the EU. Engagement and access for all citizens in democratic processes are at the core of digital rights and principles the Commission aims to accomplish with the Digital Decade policy programme. Thus, a digital action plan to assist elderly EU residents in acquiring better digital competencies should be established, which would be in line with Europe's Digital Decade targets for 2030 (EC n.d. c). Moreover, the older population can generally benefit from training programmes designed to increase their information and communication technology skills by overcoming their fears and scepticism about modern technology (Botrić and Božić 2021). In the EU context, Europe Direct, a network of EU contact centres with bases in all EU member states, might therefore mediate the role of a place where citizens could engage with the EU digitally. Currently, there are organisations whose projects, co-funded by the EU, are focused on social inclusion of the elderly through the gaining of ICT education, for example, ICT4Elders (n.d.), PROADAS (n.d.), and Ageing in the Digital Age (n.d.) to name a few. Most of these projects enhance the digital literacy of seniors through training programmes or digital assistance.

With regard to the younger population, nearly all citizens aged 16–24 and 25–34 (97.6% and 96.4%, respectively) use the internet (Eurostat 2023). Although youth are more mobile, this does not necessarily mean that they are aware of the digital public consultation services offered. The recommendations of current users may help to increase the adoption of digital public consultation services. The perceived usefulness of digital public consultation services affects one's decision to recommend them (Mensah 2020). For example, a considerable amount of money is being spent on youth participation activities as a part of the Erasmus+ 2021–2027 programme. One of the core goals the ongoing Erasmus+ programme seeks to accomplish is to make participation in democratic life in Europe at the local, regional, national, and European levels easier for young people (Erasmus n.d.). Wider publicity of citizens' participation tools among EU nationals aged 16–34, complemented with actions and knowledge earned from Erasmus+ projects, might help better target a younger audience.

The introduction of a mobile application for the Platform will also benefit youth engagement. As noted by Vohland et al. (2021), '[a]s smartphones and their user interfaces have become mainstream technology, people are able to interact more intuitively with their installed apps'. Digital democratic processes gradually discover the benefits of using mobile applications. For example, in 2018, the UN-Habitat, in partnership with Colab, launched a platform for Brazilian citizens to provide feedback on their cities' living conditions (UN-Habitat 2018). The partnership also provided the possibility for citizens to use a mobile application, which could be downloaded from both the App Store and Google Play.

The use of mobile applications requires a solid framework. An illustrative example is the Flashpoll application, which allowed citizens to provide feedback on urban development issues. A study showed that although the use of mobile applications increases participation, other outreach techniques, such as raising awareness, motivating people to participate, and addressing privacy concerns, should be applied to attain wider use of mobile applications (LSE 2015).

Moreover, we propose explicitly introducing a minimum age of 16 for participation in digital public consultations. Reducing the minimum age to use the system to 16 is in line with the minimum voting age in European Parliament elections in Austria, Malta, and Belgium (EU 2022). Similarly, the European Citizens' Initiative also allows the participation of 16-year-olds from Austria, Estonia, Germany, and Malta (EU, n.d. c). Introducing the minimum age would help to align the rules for participation on European deliberative democracy platforms. Recalling that any age limit is completely absent from the platform's regulations and layout, this proposal is in line with the idea of increasing the involvement of young adults in EU decision-making while introducing a reasonable age limit.

However, this also brings with it the consideration of introducing a secure age verification system on the Platform. This is to avoid potential abuse involving minors in this process by other minors or adults with malicious intent. Online age verification systems for underaged users of the Platform might include, but are not limited to, digital ID, credit card, or verification by a specific app (Negreiro 2023). The European Declaration on Digital Rights and Principles for the Digital Decade proposed by the Commission includes improved age verification techniques for adolescents online (EC 2022c), and the EC is currently working on an EU code of conduct on age-appropriate design (EC n.d. e). To compare with international practices, the United Kingdom already has an age-appropriate design code in force (ICO n.d.). The UK's Children's Code includes 15 standards that online services must follow. These measures compel domestic and foreign companies that process the personal data of UK children to verify the age of visitors to their website, app users, or game players (ICO n.d.)

5 CONCLUSION

HYS remains one of the most ambitious consultation platforms promoting a communication line between citizens and their governments. It constitutes a foundation of Europe's Digital Decade, promoting digital governance. With a growing propensity for digital rule-making, it is envisaged to address criticisms of the Platform to foster further improvement. HYS poses several challenges, which this contribution has sought to identify. Most importantly, the challenges to accessibility, outreach, and transparency hinder the Platform's overall effectiveness as a means of encouraging public participation.

Although our recommendations are designed for HYS, ideally, they should become a point of reference for other public consultation platforms as well. Specifically, digital platforms holding public consultations could improve their inclusiveness by implementing accessibility recommendations such as machine translation and an accessibility bar. For example, consultations held on the main OECD website[12] are only offered in English, suffer from the use of excessively technical language, and provide limited assistance to citizens with impairments. Additionally, in line with the recommendations made for the Platform for outreach practices, existing and future digital public consultation platforms would benefit from having the content and layout compounded in a concise and easy-to-understand manner to attract a wider array of citizens of all genders and ages, including economically disadvantaged groups. Finally, platforms other than HYS similarly encounter transparency challenges. For example, in the World Bank Consultations[13] the feedback gathered from interested parties is not always visible to the public, even though, according to the World Bank Consultations Guideline (World Bank 2019), a summary of the consultation should be published on the dedicated consultation website. Following the recommendations for HYS, feedback should be available in real time to bolster transparency. In instances when the content should remain confidential, a summary should be made available.

In sum, there are many challenges that can be identified and improved through a meticulous process. Amid ever-progressing digitalisation, the need

---

12 https://www.oecd.org/about/civil-society/

13 See https://consultations.worldbank.org/.

for effective platforms promoting public participation in decision-making processes becomes even more pressing. The first step for all digital public consultation platforms would be to prioritise accessibility, outreach, and transparency considerations, which are the cornerstones of effective digital rule-making.

ACKNOWLEDGEMENTS

The authors would like to thank the Europaeum for their support of this project, which was conducted while the authors were part of the Europaeum Scholars Programme in 2022 and 2023.

REFERENCES

Abou-Zahra, S. (2008), "Web Accessibility Evaluation", in: Harper, S. and Y. Yesilada (eds) *Web Accessibility. Human-Computer Interaction Series*, Springer, London, https://doi.org/10.1007/978-1-84800-050-6_7.

Adams, M. and C. Prins (2017), "Digitalization through the Lens of Law and Democracy", in Prins, C. et al., *Digital Democracy in a Globalized World*, Edward Elgar Publishing Limited, Cheltenham, https://doi.org/10.4337/9781785363962.

AEDP (Agencia Española De Protección de Datos (2020), Privacy Risks When Logging in Other Applications with Social Media Accounts, https://www.aepd.es/en/prensa-y-comunicacion/blog/privacy-risks-logging-in-applications-with-social-media-accounts.

Ageing in the Digital Age (n.d.), http://digitalageing.eu.

Aizpurua, A., S. Harper and M. Vigo (2016), "Exploring the Relationship between Web Accessibility and User Experience", *International Journal of Human-Computer Studies*, Vol. 91, pp. 13–23, https://doi.org/10.1016/j.ijhcs.2016.03.008.

Alzahrani, L., W. Al-Karaghouli and V. Weerakkody (2018), "Investigating the Impact of Citizens' Trust toward the Successful Adoption of E-government: A Multigroup Analysis of Gender, Age, and Internet Experience", *Information Systems Management*, Vol. 35/2, pp. 124–146, https://doi.org/10.1080/10580530.2018.1440730.

Botrić, V., and L. Božić (2021), "The Digital Divide and E-government in European Economies", *Ekonomska Istraživanja*, Vol. 34/1, pp. 2935–2955, https://doi.org/10.1080/1331677X.2020.1863828.

Bunea, A. (2020), "Understanding the European Commission's Use of Politicisation in the Negotiation of Interinstitutional Agreements: the Role of Consultations and Issue Framing", *Journal of European Public Policy*, Vol. 27/3, pp. 439–459, https://doi.org/10.1080/13501763.2020.1712461.

Burnett, M. et.al. (2016), "GenderMag: A Method for Evaluating Software's Gender Inclusiveness," *Interacting with Computers*, Vol. 28/6, pp. 760–787, https://doi.org/10.1093/iwc/iwv046.

Cambridge Dictionary (n.d.), Transparency, https://dictionary.cambridge.org/dictionary/english/transparency.

Carro, M., and C. Di Mario (2022), "Digital Lobbying" in *The Palgrave Encyclopedia of Interest Groups, Lobbying and Public Affairs*, Springer International Publishing, https://doi.org/10.1007/978-3-030-44556–0.

Chen, C.F. et al. (2021), "Social Bots' Role in Climate Change Discussion on Twitter: Measuring Standpoints, Topics, and Interaction Strategies", *Advances in Climate Change Research*, Vol. 12/6, pp. 913–923, https://doi.org/10.1016/j.accre.2021.09.011.

Chohan, S.R. and G. Hu (2022), "Strengthening Digital Inclusion through E-government: Cohesive ICT Training Programs to Intensify Digital Competency", *Information Technology for Development*, Vol. 28/1, pp. 16–38, https://doi.org/10.1080/02681102.2020.1841713.

Ciesielska, M., N. Rizun and J. Chabik (2022), "Assessment of E-government Inclusion Policies toward Seniors: a Framework and Case Study", *Telecommunications Policy*, Vol. 46/7, 102316, https://doi.org/10.1016/j.telpol.2022.102316.

COM (European Commission) (2019), Better Regulation: Taking Stock and Sustaining Our Commitment, Communication from the Commission to the European Parliament, the Council, the European and Social Committee and the Committee of the Regions, COM/2019/178.

COM (European Commission) (2015), Better Regulation for Better Results – An EU Agenda, Communication from the Commission to the European Parliament, the Council, and the Committee of the Regions, COM/2015/0215.

Commission of the European Communities (2006), Green Paper, European Transparency Initiative, https://eur-lex.europa.eu/EN/legal-content/summary/green-paper-on-the-european-transparency-initiative.html.

Davidson, T. et. al. (2017), "Automated Hate Speech Detection and the Problem of Offensive Language", *Proceedings of the international AAAI conference on web and social media*, Vol. 11/1, pp. 512–515, https://doi.org/10.48550/arXiv.1703.04009.

Davis, F.D. (1989), "Perceived Usefulness, Perceived Ease of Use, and User Acceptance of Information Technology", *MIS Quarterly*, Vol. 13/3, pp. 319–340, https://doi.org/10.2307/249008.

EU (European Union) (2016), Directive 2016/2102 of the European Parliament and of the Council , *On the Accessibility of the Websites and Mobile Applications of Public Sector Bodies*, Official Journal of the European Union, L 327/1.

EC (European Commission) (2022a), Remarks by Vice-President Maroš Šefčovič at the press conference on the Communication on the Conference on the Future of Europe, https://ec.europa.eu/commission/presscorner/detail/en/SPEECH_22_3839.

EC (European Commission) (2022b), Accessibility Statement, https://commission.europa.eu/accessibility-statement_en.

EC (European Commission) (2022c), European Declaration on Digital Rights and Principles for the Digital Decade, COM(2022) 28.

EC (European Commission) (2021a), Better Regulation Guidelines, Commission Staff Working Document, SWD(2021) 305, https://commission.europa.eu/system/files/2021-11/swd2021_305_en.pdf.

EC (European Commission) (2021b), Better Regulation Toolbox, https://commission.europa.eu/system/files/2023-02/br_toolbox-nov_2021_en.pdf.

EC (European Commission) (2021c), Better Regulation: Joining Forces to Make Better Laws, Communication from the Commission to the European Parliament, the Council, and the Committee of the Regions, COM(2021) 219.

EC (European Commission) (n.d. a), Have Your Say, https://ec.europa.eu/info/law/better-regulation/have-your-say_en.

EC (European Commission) (n.d. b), Providing Suitable Feedback, Rules for Feedback and Suggestions, https://ec.europa.eu/info/law/better-regulation/rules-feedback-and-suggestions_en.

EC (European Commission) (n.d. c), Europe's Digital Decade: Digital Targets for 2030, https://commission.europa.eu/strategy-and-policy/priorities-2019-2024/europe-fit-digital-age/europes-digital-decade-digital-targets-2030_en.

EC (European Commission) (n.d. d), eTranslation, https://commission.europa.eu/resources-partners/machine-translation-public-administrations-etranslation_en.

EC (European Commission (n.d. e), Special Group on the EU Code of Conduct on Age-Appropriate Design, https://digital-strategy.ec.europa.eu/en/policies/group-age-appropriate-design.

ECA (European Court of Auditors) (2019), "Special Report No 14/2019 – "Have Your Say!": Commission's Public Consultations Engage Citizens, but Fall Short of Outreach Activities", Official Journal of the European Union, 2019/C 314/05.

ECWS (European Working Conditions Survey) (2015), Sixth European Working Conditions Survey, https://www.eurofound.europa.eu/surveys/european-working-conditions-surveys/sixth-european-working-conditions-survey-2015.

EIGE (European Institute for Gender Equality) (2022), Indicator: Individuals Using the Internet for Taking Part in Online Consultations or Voting, Gender Statistics Database, https://eige.europa.eu/gender-statistics/dgs/indicator/ta_resdig_dig_egov__tin00129_comp.

EIGE (European Institute for Gender Equality) (n.d.), What is Gender Mainstreaming?, https://eige.europa.eu/gender-mainstreaming/what-is-gender-mainstreaming.

EP (European Parliament) (2019), EU Parliament Rules of Procedure, https://www.europarl.europa.eu/doceo/document/RULES-9-2019-07-02_EN.pdf.

Erasmus (n.d.), Priorities of the Erasmus+ Programme, https://erasmus-plus.ec.europa.eu/programme-guide/part-a/priorities-of-the-erasmus-programme.

Erkkilä, T. (2020), "Transparency in Public Administration", *Oxford Research Encyclopedia of Politics*, https://oxfordre.com/politics/view/10.1093/acrefore/9780190228637.001.0001/acrefore-9780190228637-e-1404.

EU (European Union) (2022), At What Age Should One Be Able to Vote in Elections?, European Youth Portal, https://youth.europa.eu/get-involved/democratic-participation/what-age-should-one-be-able-vote-elections_en.

EU (European Union) (2022), At What Age Should One Be Able to Vote in Elections?, European Youth Portal, https://youth.europa.eu/get-involved/democratic-participation/what-age-should-one-be-able-vote-elections_en.

EU (European Union) (n.d. a), Democratic Deficit, https://eur-lex.europa.eu/EN/legal-content/glossary/democratic-deficit.html.

EU (European Union) (n.d. b), European Citizens' Initiative, https://europa.eu/citizens-initiative/_en.

EU (European Union) (n.d. c), European Citizens' Initiative, Data Requirements, https://europa.eu/citizens-initiative/how-it-works/implementation-national-level/data-requirements_en.

Eurostat (2023), Individuals – Internet Use, https://ec.europa.eu/eurostat/databrowser/view/ISOC_CI_IFP_IU__custom_4690665/default/table?lang=en.

Fogg, B.J. (2009), "A Behaviour Model for Persuasive Design", *Proceedings of the 4th International Conference on Persuasive Technology*, Vol. 40, https://doi.org/10.1145/1541948.1541999.

Follesdal, A. and S. Hix (2006), "Why There is a Democratic Deficit in the EU: A Response to Majone and Moravcsik", *Journal of Common Market Studies*, Vol. 44/3, pp. 533–562, https://doi.org/10.1111/j.1468–5965.2006.00650.x.

García, S. et al. (2014), "An Empirical Comparison of Botnet Detection Methods", *Computers & Security*, Vol. 45, pp. 100–123.

Gibson, R. et al. (eds) (2012), "Democratic Consultation and the E-Citizen", in *Connecting Demoracy: Online Consultation and the Flow of Political Communication*, MIT Press, Cambridge, MA, USA.

Gillespie, T. (2020), "Content Moderation, AI, and the Question of Scale", *Big Data & Society*, Vol. 7/2, https://doi.org/10.1177/20539517209432.

Gorwa, R. et al. (2020), "Algorithmic Content Moderation: Technical and Political Challenges in the Automation of Platform Governance", *Big Data & Society*, Vol. 7/1, https://doi.org/10.1177/2053951719897945.

Gröndahl, T. et al. (2018), "All You Need Is 'Love' Evading Hate Speech Detection", Proceedings of the 11th ACM workshop on artificial intelligence and security, pp. 2–12, https://doi.org/10.48550/arXiv.1808.09115.

Harper, S. and Y. Yesilada (2008), "Web Accessibility and Guidelines", in: Harper, S. and Y. Yesilada (eds) *Web Accessibility*. Human-Computer Interaction Series, Springer, London, https://doi.org/10.1007/978-1-84800-050-6_6.

Harrison, H. et al. (2017), "Case Study Research: Foundations and Methodological Orientations", *Forum Qualitative Sozialforschung Forum: Qualitative Social Research*, Vol. 18/1, Art. 19, https://doi.org/10.17169/fqs-18.1.2655.

Hierlemann, D. et al. (2022), *Under Construction: Citizen Participation in the European Union*, Beltz Verlag, Weinheim, Germany.

Hsu, C.C. (2012), "Comparison of Gender Differences in Young People's Blog Interface Preferences and Designs", *Displays*, Vol. 33/3, pp. 119–128, https://doi.org/10.1016/j.displa.2012.04.001.

HYS ("Have Your Say!") (2022), Call for Evidence for an Impact Assessment, https://ec.europa.eu/info/law/better-regulation/have-your-say/initiatives/13517-European-disability-card_en.

ICO (Information Commissioner's Office) (n.d.), Introduction to the Age-Appropriate Design Code, https://ico.org.uk/for-organisations/guide-to-data-protection/ico-codes-of-practice/age-appropriate-design-code/.

ICT4Elders (n.d.), https://www.ict4elders.eu/.

Inclusion Europe (n.d.), Easy-to-Read, https://www.inclusion-europe.eu/easy-to-read/.

EU (European Union) (2016) Interinstitutional Agreement of 13 April 2016 between the European Parliament, the Council of the European Union and the European Commission on Better Law-Making), Official Journal of the European Union, L 123/1.

Joosen R. (2020), "The Tip of the Iceberg – Interest Group Behaviour in Rule Drafting and Consultations during EU Agency Rulemaking", *Journal of European Public Policy*, Vol. 27/11, pp. 1677–1697, https://doi.org/10.1080/13501763.2020.1817131.

Keuchler, V. et. al. (2012), "Gender Differences in Early Free and Open Source Software Joining Process", IFIP Conference on Open Source Systems, Springer, pp. 78–93.

LSE (London School of Economics) (2015), "Smartphone Apps for Public Engagement: The Value of Combining Online, Offline and Mobile Strategies", Blog Post, https://blogs.lse.ac.uk/impactofsocialsciences/2015/08/19/smartphone-apps-for-public-engagement/.

Maceviciute, E. and T.D. Wilson (2018), "Digital Means for Reducing Inequality: A Literature Review", *Informing Science: The International Journal of an Emerging Transdiscipline*, Vol. 21, pp. 269–287, https://doi.org/10.28945/4117.

Mayer, R. E., and R. Moreno (2003), "Nine Ways to Reduce Cognitive Load in Multimedia Learning", *Educational Psychologist*, Vol. 38/1, pp. 43–52, https://doi.org/10.1207/s15326985ep3801_6.

Mensah, I.K. (2020), "Impact of Government Capacity and E-government Performance on the Adoption of E-government Services", *International Journal of Public Administration*, Vol. 43/4, pp. 303–311, https://doi.org/10.1080/01900692.2019.162805.

Moravcsik, A. (2002), "In Defense of the Democratic Deficit: Reassessing Legitimacy in the European Union", *Journal of Common Market Studies*, Vol. 40/4, pp. 603–624, https://doi.org/10.1111/1468–5965.00390.

Moreno, L. and P. Martinez (2013), "Overlapping Factors in Search Engine Optimization and Web Accessibility", *Online Information Review*, Vol. 37/4, pp. 564–580, https://doi.org/10.1108/OIR-04-2012–0063.

Müller, J.-W (2016), "The EU's Democratic Deficit and the Public Sphere", *Current History*, Vol. 115, Issue 779, pp. 83–88, https://doi.org/10.1525/curh.2016.115.779.83.

Năstase, A., and C. Muurmans (2020), "Regulating Lobbying Activities in the European Union: a Voluntary Club Perspective", *Regulation & Governance*, Vol. 14/2, pp. 238–255, https://doi.org/10.1111/rego.12200.

Negreiro, M. (2023), Online Age Verification Methods for Children, European Parliamentary Research Service, https://www.europarl.europa.eu/RegData/etudes/ATAG/2023/739350/EPRS_ATA(2023)739350_EN.pdf.

Nissim, N. et al. (2015), "Detection of Malicious PDF Files and Directions for Enhancements: a State-of-the-art Survey", *Computers & Security*, Vol. 48, pp. 246–266, https://doi.org/10.1016/j.cose.2014.10.014.

Nunes, I. et. al. (2023), "GIRE: Gender-Inclusive Requirements Engineering", *Data & Knowledge Engineering*, Vol. 143, pp. 102–108, https://doi.org/10.1016/j.datak.2022.102108.

OECD (2022a), Background Document on Public Consultation, https://www.oecd.org/mena/governance/36785341.pdf.

OECD (2022b), OECD Guidelines for Citizen Participation Processes, OECD Public Governance Reviews, OECD Publishing, Paris, https://doi.org/10.1787/f765caf6-en.

OECD (2022c), Better Regulation Practices across the European Union 2022, OECD Publishing, Paris, https://doi.org/10.1787/6e4b095d-en.

OECD (2022d), Building Trust to Reinforce Democracy: Main Findings from the 2021 OECD Survey on Drivers of Trust in Public Institutions, Building Trust in Public Institutions, OECD Publishing, Paris, https://doi.org/10.1787/b407f99c-en.

OECD (2021a), OECD Regulatory Policy Outlook 2021, OECD Publishing, Paris, https://doi.org/10.1787/38b0fdb1-en.

OECD (2021b), Compendium of International Organisations' Practices: Working Towards More Effective International Instruments, OECD Publishing, Paris, https://doi.org/10.1787/846a5fa0-en.

OECD (2017), Recommendation of the Council on Open Government, https://legalinstruments.oecd.org/en/instruments/OECD-LEGAL-0438#_ga=2.37822115.1251313301.1554450220–751648841.1537891795.

OECD (2013), "Inclusive Policy Making", in *Government at a Glance 2013*, OECD Publishing, Paris, https://doi.org/10.1787/gov_glance-2013-51-en.

OECD (2012), Recommendation of the Council on Regulatory Policy and Governance, OECD Publishing, Paris, http://dx.doi.org/10.1787/9789264209022-en.

OECD (2001), "Citizens as Partners: Information, Consultations and Public Participation in Policy-Making", OECD, Paris.

OECD (n.d.), OECD Civil Society, https://www.oecd.org/about/civil-society/.

Orabi, M. et al. (2020), "Detection of Bots in Social Media: a Systematic Review", *Information Processing & Management*, Vol. 57/4, 102250, https://doi.org/10.1016/j.ipm.2020.102250.

Pérez-Morote, R., C. Pontones-Rosa and M. Núñez-Chicharro (2020), "The Effects of E-government Evaluation, Trust and the Digital Divide in the Levels of E-government Use in European Countries", *Technological Forecasting & Social Change*, Vol. 154, 119973 https://doi.org/10.1016/j.techfore.2020.119973.

Petrie, H., Savva, A. and Power, C. (2015), "Towards a Unified Definition of Web Accessibility", in Proceedings of the 12th International Web for All Conference, pp. 1–13, https://doi.org/10.1145/2745555.2746653.

ProADAS (n.d.), ProADAS, https://proadas.eu.

Quershi, Z. (2019), "Inequality in Digital Era", in *Work in the Age of Data*, BBVA, Madrid, https://www.brookings.edu/wp-content/uploads/2020/02/BBVA-OpenMind-Zia-Qureshi-Inequality-in-the-digital-era.pdf.

Quittkat, C. and P. Kotzian (2011), "Lobbying via Consultation – Territorial and Functional Interests in the Commission's Consultation Regime", *Journal of European Integration*, Vol. 33/4, pp. 401–418, https://doi.org/10.1080/07036337.2011.582280.

Rowan, M. and J. Dehlinger (2012), "Observed Gender Differences in Privacy Concerns and Behaviors of Mobile Device End Users", *Procedia*, Vol. 37, pp. 340–347, https://doi.org/10.1016/j.procs.2014.08.050.

Sloan, D. et al. (2006), "Contextual Web Accessibilty – Maximizing the Benefit of Accessibility Guidelines", W4A: Proceedings of the 2006 international cross-disciplinary workshop on Web accessibility (W4A), pp. 121–131, https://doi.org/10.1145/1133219.1133242.

Smith, S. and E. Dalakiouridou (2009), "Contextualising Public (e)Participation in the Governance of the European Union", *European Journal of ePractice*, Vol. 7, pp. 4–14. https://interoperable-europe.ec.europa.eu/sites/default/files/document/2014-06/ePractice%20Journal-Vol.7-March%202009.pdf

TEU (Treaty on the European Union) (2012), "Consolidated Version of the Treaty on European Union", Official Journal of the European Union, 2012/C 326/01.

TFEU (Treaty on the Functioning of the European Union) (2012), "Consolidated Version of the Treaty on the Functioning of the European Union", Official Journal of the European Union, 2012/C 326/01.

UN-Habitat (2018), UN-Habitat and Colab Launch a Mobile App for Open Public Consultation on Living Conditions in Brazilian Cities, https://unhabitat.org/un-habitat-and-colab-launch-a-mobile-app-for-open-public-consultation-on-living-conditions-in-brazilian-cities.

UN Women (2015), Progress of the World's Women 2015–2016. Transforming Economies, Realizing Rights, https://progress.unwomen.org/en/2015/pdf/UNW_progressreport.pdf.

Vicente, M.R. and A.J. López (2010), "A Multidimensional Analysis of the Disability Digital Divide: Some Evidence for Internet Use", *The Information Society*, Vol. 26/1, pp. 48–64, https://doi.org/10.1080/01615440903423245.

Vohland, K. et al. (2021), *The Science of Citizen Science*, Springer, https://doi.org/10.1007/978-3-030-58278–4.
WAI (2022), Evaluating Web Accessibility Overview, Web Accessibility Initiative, https://www.w3.org/WAI/test-evaluate/.
WAI (2019), Accessibility Principles, Web Accessibility Initiative, https://www.w3.org/WAI/fundamentals/accessibility-principles/.
WAI (2013), Easy Checks – A First Review of Web Accessibility, Web Accessibility Initiative, https://www.w3.org/WAI/test-evaluate/preliminary/.
WAI (2010), Accessibility, Usability, and Inclusion, Web Accessibility Initiative, updated March 2010, https://www.w3.org/WAI/fundamentals/accessibility-usability-inclusion/.
WAI (2005), Introduction to Web Accessibility, Web Accessibility Initiative, updated 31 March 2022, https://www.w3.org/WAI/fundamentals/accessibility-intro/.
WCAG (2018), Web Content Accessibility Guidelines (WCAG) 2.1, W3C Recommendation, https://www.w3.org/TR/WCAG21/, updated 21 September 2023.
World Bank (2019), Consultation Guidelines, https://thedocs.worldbank.org/en/doc/248301574182372360-0290022019/original/WorldBankconsultationsguidelines.pdf.
World Bank (n.d.), Consultations, https://consultations.worldbank.org.
Yin, R. (2014), *Case Study Research: Design and Methods*, 5th edn, Sage Publications: Applied Social Research Methods Series, Vol. 5.
Zanetto, P. (2019), Digital Lobbying: Una Metodologia, Management & Lobbying, https://www.cattaneozanetto.it/ml/wp-content/uploads/sites/2/2019/01/Digital_lobbying_una_metodologia.pdf.
Zingales, N. and R. Radu (2017), "In Search of the Holy Grail: a Principled Approach to Multistakeholder Governance in Internet Policy-Making", in Prins, C., Cuijpers, C., Lindseth, P.L., Rosina, M., *Digital Democracy in a Globalized World*, Edward Elgar Publishing Limited, heltenham, https://doi.org/10.4337/9781785363962.

11. Inclusive rule-making by international organisations: lessons learned and persisting challenges

Rita Guerreiro Teixeira, Marianna Karttunen, Axel Marx and Jan Wouters

1 INTRODUCTION

The need for international organisations (IOs) to open up and be more inclusive has been considered an important way to increase their democratic legitimacy and effectiveness in terms of international rule-making. As a consequence, many IOs have started to develop agenda-setting and decision-making frameworks and procedures that are more representative and inclusive of the different interests and stakeholders with whom they engage.

The different contributions to this edited volume have sought to identify general trends in the development of IO decision-making processes, reveal innovative practices through which these processes are becoming more inclusive, critically assess persisting challenges, and draw out lessons for IOs seeking to revise and improve their engagement practices.

In the introductory chapter, we noted that the inclusion of stakeholders in international rule-making can play a key role in increasing their awareness and improving their understanding of new rules and standards. It may lead to decisions that have broader acceptance because they were developed during deliberative processes involving actors with various preferences and permits enriching the quality of decision-making with the information and knowledge that such stakeholders hold. In addition, inclusiveness contributes to improving legitimacy and fostering trust in IOs, contributes to their accountability, and enhances the effectiveness of rule-making and rule-implementation by bringing in specific knowledge, expertise, and operational capacity.

Simultaneously, several challenges persist in improving the inclusiveness of rule-making practices of IOs. The contributions to this volume identified key challenges, which can be grouped into three main categories.

1. Identification and selection of relevant stakeholders: Potential stakeholders and other actors are numerous in each issue area in global governance. The literature on global governance regimes, complexes, and architectures identifies many public, private, and public-private stakeholders. Participation in, for example, a Conference of the Parties (COP) to the UN Framework Convention on Climate Change (UNFCCC) exemplifies the many thousands of relevant stakeholders related to climate change. Additionally, open consultation processes on new regulatory initiatives often show the sheer number of stakeholders involved in an issue area. How to select and identify relevant stakeholders in agenda-setting and decision-making procedures is both crucial and difficult. Moreover, ensuring that stakeholders with clear private interests do not dominate stakeholder involvement and use stakeholder participation processes for lobbying purposes remains a clear challenge.
2. Effective participation. Once the relevant stakeholders are identified and selected, organising their effective participation can take many forms. Different IOs devise different instruments to engage with stakeholders in different phases of the regulatory process and grant them different degrees of input and participation. This volume identified and discussed several of these instruments. A central challenge for all of them is to design procedures that provide genuine opportunities for stakeholders to participate in a context where member states of IOs remain the main actors with final decision-making power – and often veto power. In other words, IOs need to design instruments that go beyond window-dressing but also respect the limits of their autonomous decision-making powers.
3. Unequal power and resources among stakeholders. Once IOs have selected stakeholders and set out to engage with them in participatory processes, the degree to which such stakeholders are able to contribute can vary significantly. This is influenced by both the incentives and interests that each stakeholder has in contributing to the process and their available resources. Civil society organisations, marginalised groups, stakeholders from the Global South, and citizens often have fewer resources available for participating in stakeholder initiatives, even when their interests are at stake. How to overcome this hurdle is a third main challenge that has been explored in this volume.

This concluding chapter summarises the volume's main contributions on these three challenges and seeks to advance how they can be addressed by IOs, providing novel insights and policy recommendations.

2 IDENTIFICATION AND SELECTION OF RELEVANT STAKEHOLDERS

Transparency of institutional processes and the adoption of a clear and intentional engagement strategy with stakeholders are key elements in determining the success of IOs' efforts at improving their inclusiveness, while also providing clarity to member states and other interested parties on who is having a say in their rule-making initiatives. As the chapter by Femi Amao, Michèle Olivier, and Konstantinos D. Magliveras (chapter 4) demonstrates, the absence of these elements can lead to situations where external stakeholders, who do not have a real stake in the decisions that an IO makes nor feel the effects of the rules it adopts, manage to unduly set the agenda and influence decision-making.

Accordingly, an important question that IOs must address when setting out to broaden their stakeholder engagement base is who should be allowed to participate. Recently, the participation of for-profit stakeholders has been central to the debate in many IOs due to the risk of corporate capture of decision-making processes by those actors, for the pursuance of their economic interests. Simultaneously, there is a recognition that these actors can contribute key resources to IO rule-making and implementation (namely expertise, capital, and political influence), and are more likely to comply with resulting rules when they participated in the process for their adoption (chapter 5 in this volume, section 1). This is particularly relevant in fields such as climate change and energy, where the achievement of governance goals is closely linked to compliance by private actors (chapter 6 in this volume, section 2.1).

Any IO strategy on engagement with for-profit stakeholders must first account for the fact that singling out these actors is often not an easy task. For-profit interests may be represented by individual business entities, trade and industry associations, but also by NGOs, academics, and think tanks – with the private sector sometimes financing, participating in decision-making, or otherwise influencing these entities – and even by member state delegations. Melissa J. Durkee (chapter 5) argues that, because of the sometimes invisible links between for-profit actors and other groups, approaches that attempt to isolate and separate participation of for-profit actors are not likely to prove durable over time. Not only do these approaches impose a formidable burden on institutional gatekeepers who must identify for-profit entities (as the operation of the World Health Organization Framework of Engagement with Non-State Actors illustrates), but they may also have the unintended effect of making rule-making processes less transparent, as for-profit influences might be driven underground if a strict distinction is imposed. Durkee's chapter also highlighted the limitations of stakeholder involvement processes that are based on representing different 'types' of stakeholders (companies, NGOs, foundations, and others) in the rule-making process, since the boundaries between these ideal 'types' are blurred and can easily be circumvented. In situations where private actors have a strong interest in the rule-making activities of an IO, they can easily find access via stakeholder participation in parallel to other lobbying activities.

Kaho Yu, Xinchuchu Gao, and Xuechen Chen (chapter 6) suggest that IOs can overcome some of the challenges of improving engagement with the private sector by (i) establishing clear incentives for compliance and engagement (such as improved market access, brand reputation, or consumer trust) and consequences for non-compliance; (ii) fostering open and efficient communication channels that can improve transparency; and (iii) reducing the complexity of standards across the areas they regulate.[1] Through these practices, IOs can enhance their cooperation with the private sector by demonstrating that there are clear benefits of engagement with IOs in terms of enhancing market access, risk assessment and mitigation, expertise in crisis management, and opportunities for knowledge sharing, while simultaneously giving an opportunity to private actors to better understand and act upon standards with foresight. These authors further suggest that IOs may gain from institutionalising their engagement with private companies, in particular by creating membership networks that are specifically tailored for these actors, providing opportunities for them to participate in rule-making and training initiatives, and leading to sustained progress in climate mitigation efforts (chapter 6, section 3).

An additional question to be considered in relation to stakeholder determination is whether participation will be open to all stakeholders that seek it or whether IOs will set a limit on the number of participants. The thousands of observers that participate in COP meetings illustrate the trade-off between inclusiveness and opportunities for effective participation that IOs often face when opening their decision-making processes to the presence of a broad set of stakeholders. As noted by Emma Bertipaglia and Hayley Walker (chapter 3), observers have complained that simply attending COP-UNFCCC meetings is not enough, that meaningful engagement opportunities are finite (including speaking slots, side event slots, registration quota, meeting space, and access to negotiation meeting rooms) and become insufficient as the scale of participation increases. Stakeholders feel that they do not have opportunities to inform and influence decision-making, convey concerns, and contribute positively to the process with their expertise, and that whatever contributions they manage to make do not result in real impact and influence.

---

[1] In their contribution, the authors are concerned with the number and complexity of sustainability standards established by IOs, which establish a multitude of metrics and frameworks that make it difficult for companies to adjust their business models – chapter 6 in this volume, section 4.

These difficulties point to the need for reconsidering modes of engagement with stakeholders, particularly in scenarios where the potential pool of interested actors is extensive, in order to ensure the effectiveness of participation. Durkee's chapter puts forward two governance models for IO engagement with stakeholders that are more likely to succeed in this scenario: a roundtable model, including only a small set of actors through an invitation or application and selection process, that allows stakeholders to offer more extensive input; or a public comment model, that allows participation by all interested parties but that, drawing from domestic models of notice-and-comment procedure of lobbying laws, keeps participation at an arms-length level of engagement to minimise the potential for undue influences (chapter 5 in this volume, section 5).

3 EFFECTIVE PARTICIPATION

Participation can take different forms, ranging from granting an official status to stakeholders which enables them to provide regular inputs, to establishing advisory groups or expert committees, stakeholder consultations on proposed instruments, opportunities for commentary from the general public, or inviting them to participate in the dissemination, implementation, monitoring, and evaluation of instruments. A central challenge to improving the inclusiveness of IO rule-making processes is designing modes of participation that, in the particular context of each IO, provide effective opportunities for stakeholders to present and argue for their interests and influence decision-making.

The different approaches, strategies, and policies that IOs have adopted for improving their stakeholder engagement are analysed in the chapters in this volume, drawing various conclusions as to what models might be more successful in particular contexts. Antonio Marcacci (chapter 7) analyses the International Organization of Securities Commissions' (IOSCO) inclusiveness practices as an example of successful collaboration between public regulators and private actors in transnational standard-setting. Under the framework of the 2005 Consultation Policy and Procedure, IOSCO systemically pursues public consultations to collect private actors' input and obtain specific information and knowledge that allows it to gain a better understanding of the highly technical issues that it is called upon to regulate (chapter 7, section 3). With each consultation, IOSCO provides background information alongside the reasons why it seeks the opinion of the public and, when applicable, specific questions on which it seeks input. The final consultation reports explain how public comments were addressed or disclose the reasons why these were not addressed. Transparency is ensured by the publication of consultation reports and all comments received (subject to anonymity). Consultations are furthermore complemented by additional activities aimed at collecting feedback from the private sector, such as roundtable and fact-finding exercises. Through these mechanisms, IOSCO stakeholders – particularly private-sector actors – have been able to influence the contours of the policy propositions coming from regulatory authorities and even propose alternative solutions. Simultaneously, IOSCO is able to develop more effective global standards and more accurately evaluate their implementation by industry.

Ensuring effective participation is often more challenging in the case of civil society actors and the general public, as the chapters of Bertipaglia and Walker, María Rodríguez Alcazar, Diane Schuman, and Kseniia Soloveva et al. illustrate. On the one hand, these actors are often at a disadvantage in terms of the resources and knowledge required to participate when compared with private actors – an imbalance that IOs must take into account and seek to compensate, as discussed in the next section. On the other hand, they are often more dispersed, more difficult to identify and reach, and it is not always clear what interests each actor represents. As Durkee noted (chapter 5), often civil society actors such as NGOs and academic institutions serve as channels for pushing the interests of private corporations.

Rodríguez Alcázar (chapter 8) demonstrates that the participation of citizens in IO decision-making processes has been possible in regional organisations at least since the 1950s, with a clear trend emerging in the 1990s. Mechanisms for citizen participation range from the election of representatives to IO parliamentary organs, public access to meetings and deliberations, the organisation of referendums, consultations, and the opportunity to present petitions, to engagement at group level through non-governmental stakeholders. They have been met with different levels of success in practice. A recent attempt to provide opportunities for direct citizen participation in rule-making processes within the European Union through an online platform for public consultations has had limited success so far. Soloveva et al. (chapter 10) point out various shortcomings of the 'Have Your Say!' platform. Various technical flaws and the lack of user-friendly information and interface make participation cumbersome, unattractive, and limit accessibility for people with disabilities. Furthermore, lack of transparency concerning the rules and timeline of public consultations as well as on the use of inputs provided and the identity of participants negatively affect legitimacy and public trust in the process. Lack of awareness-raising and publicity means that only a limited part of the targeted audiences is effectively reached and participates.

Finally, contributions to this volume have shown that, when it comes to opportunities for effective participation, quantity does not equal quality. In fact, a multiplication of opportunities for engagement can be detrimental to effective engagement, particularly for those with the least resources and capacity to manage the additional workload. This is illustrated by the low rate of take-up that characterises engagement opportunities offered within the UNFCCC, outside of the COPs (chapter 3 in this volume, section 8). The multiplication of engagement opportunities throughout the year remains largely under-utilised as stakeholders have to prioritise where to invest their limited capacity and resources, and generally choose to prioritise participation in COP meetings for their higher profile and media attention. However, these are not necessarily the most effective means for stakeholders to influence decision-making, particularly because opportunities for effective participation are very limited in those meetings – a finding that also points to the need for improving communication and awareness-raising by the Secretariat towards non-state actors.

Accordingly, Bertipaglia and Walker suggest that IOs should consider focusing their resources on tailoring a smaller quantity of engagement efforts to the specific needs of different groups of stakeholders and avoid multiplying processes, initiatives, and other calls for engagement – particularly while resources remain unequally distributed among stakeholders.

4 UNEQUAL POWER AND RESOURCES AMONG STAKEHOLDERS AND CIVIL SOCIETY PARTICIPATION

Bertipaglia and Walker's experiences in the UNFCCC review process to strengthen observer engagement highlight that an important dimension of achieving participation and representation is ensuring that participants share a common level of capacity to engage, both in terms of financial and human resources to participate and knowledge and understanding of opportunities for participation. They identified a 'capacity-building paradox', whereby under-resourced groups of stakeholders (namely, Indigenous peoples, youth, and developing country stakeholders) lack the capacity to benefit from the opportunities that are made available to them (chapter 3, section 7).

The study of IOSCO's public consultation conducted by Marcacci equally noted that, while these IO's public consultations have been very successful in collecting the views of private sector associations, large financial institutions, clearing houses, self-regulatory organisations, and trading venues like stock exchanges, they have far more rarely reached civil society representatives (chapter 7, section 4).

The unequal power and resources of different stakeholders are perhaps even more consequential in the context of informal governance and participation in informal intergovernmental institutions such as the G7 and G20. Schumann (chapter 9) looked at the Engagement Groups and the role that they have come to play in the G-system. These are self-organised and fairly informal groups, where different sets of stakeholders meet and discuss policy recommendations, and which have assumed prominent roles in influencing the agenda of the G-meetings. These Engagement Groups depend on acceptance and support by the rotating G-presidency to have access to negotiations. This dependence is particularly acute in the case of civil society groups, which depend on the financial and institutional support received from G-presidencies to conduct their activities. Accordingly, while it is remarkable that these groups have become influential actors with a voice and even secured their existence when meetings were hosted by non-democratic host countries such as Saudi Arabia, they are also much more vulnerable to interference and attempts to control them and silence criticism, as well as to being misused as marketing tools by certain states to promote a positive image of their engagement with civil society that does not materialise in practice.

Overcoming inequalities of power and resources among stakeholders is not an easy task, but it is nonetheless fundamental to ensure that stakeholder participation in IOs is representative of all relevant interests. Soloveva et al. showed that providing open opportunities to an ample circle of stakeholders to participate is not enough to guarantee representation by all groups and can, in fact, reproduce existing inequalities under the guise of inclusive participation. Their analysis of the EU online platform for public consultations reveals that it is business and interest groups that overwhelmingly make use of this resource (chapter 10, section 3.2). Improving citizen participation requires stipulating clear objectives, addressing accessibility issues, improving the transparency of consultation processes, and raising awareness of the importance of participating. This includes everything from improving access to computers and the internet, to simplifying the language used in consultations, overcoming language barriers, and developing targeted communication and capacity-building initiatives directed at disadvantaged groups of citizens to encourage participation.

An additional challenge is that often IO Secretariats have less than optimal resources to engage with all stakeholders on an individual level, addressing their individual needs (chapter 3 in this volume, section 7). As an alternative, Bertipaglia and Walker propose grouping participants in consultation processes according to their level of experience and resources, allowing for tailored delivery of modes of engagement that take into account the relative capacities of each group. Additionally, processes that aim to be inclusive of typically under-represented stakeholders could include a prior round of capacity-building, whereby participants would acquire a baseline level of understanding of the functioning of the IO and the process in question and what is expected of them (and what outcomes they can, in turn, expect).

Finally, increasing the participation of new, more diverse actors might require convincing them of the benefits of participation. Yu, Gao, and Chen have pointed out the importance of IOs reaching out to small and medium enterprises, in addition to multinational corporations, in the energy sector. These smaller entities are less resourceful actors but have an important impact on the global climate agenda when considered collectively. Here, clear and targeted communication by IOs is key. The authors suggest that, in order to encourage participation and engagement by these smaller actors, it is essential for IOs to better communicate the business relevance of their activities and the advantages for companies of aligning their profit-driven objectives with sustainable practices (chapter 6, section 3.1).

5 IMPROVING INCLUSIVENESS: TAKING ACTION

The momentum is high to increase the inclusiveness of IOs, and the various contributions to this volume underline just how important this is for international rule-making. A recent OECD citizen survey on 'trust in government' highlights that IOs are trusted by citizens more than national and regional governments, parliaments, and political parties. However, they are trusted by less than half of the respondents (OECD, 2024). The same survey underscores how important inclusive decision-making is to gain public trust. More than two-thirds of those who feel they have a say in government actions trust the national government. As levers for government action in a global context, IOs also have work to do to reinforce trust and enhance the legitimacy of their actions.

This volume showed how IOs can gain, and are gaining, from being more inclusive. The IOs with the most far-reaching stakeholder engagement efforts have more positive perceptions in news media than IOs with less inclusive processes (chapter 2 in this volume). IOs, such as the African Union, that have made significant reforms to empower stakeholders to participate more actively in their rule-making, have also progressively increased their global relevance and legitimacy (chapter 4 in this volume). IOs regulating private behaviour and proactively collecting private actors' inputs throughout the rule-making process can enhance the effectiveness of their standards and gather better evidence to evaluate their implementation (chapter 7 in this volume).

However, there is no doubt that global governance remains nebulous for most citizens and stakeholders and that many challenges remain to inclusive international rule-making. This volume seeks to shed light on areas where there is progress and on the most persistent challenges that require specific attention.

The IO Partnership for Effective International Rulemaking has developed ambitious principles for strengthening stakeholder engagement practices to improve the inclusiveness of international rule-making (OECD, 2021; chapter 1 in this volume). In particular, it noted that it is crucial for IOs to adopt a strategic and comprehensive approach to stakeholder engagement, ensuring that actions are deliberate and transparent. IOs are encouraged to refine their identification and outreach processes, meticulously map stakeholders based on type, mandate, function, expertise, interest, and responsibilities, and establish clear criteria for selection to enhance inclusiveness. Establishing transparent and robust procedures, aligned with organisational strategies and leveraging digital tools, can facilitate global participation efficiently. Moreover, timing consultations to align with key moments of rule-making processes and allowing adequate response time is important for meaningful engagement. Finally, clear and effective communication throughout the consultation process is essential for fostering a productive two-way dialogue, ultimately contributing to more transparent and accountable international rulemaking. This volume underlined how much IOs can grow their relevance and impact by pursuing these principles and, more broadly, by opening their rule-making processes.

BIBLIOGRAPHY

OECD (2024) *OECD Survey on Drivers of Trust in Public Institutions – 2024 Results: Building Trust in a Complex Policy Environment*, OECD Publishing, Paris, https://doi.org/10.1787/9a20554b-en.

OECD (2021) *Compendium of International Organisations' Practices: Working Towards More Effective International Instruments*, OECD Publishing, Paris, https://doi.org/10.1787/846a5fa0-en.

Index